YORKSHIRE BARONETS

UNIVERSITY OF HULL PUBLICATIONS

YORKSHIRE BARONETS

1640–1760

Families, Estates, and Fortunes

PETER ROEBUCK

Published for the UNIVERSITY OF HULL by the
OXFORD UNIVERSITY PRESS
1980

Oxford University Press, Walton Street, Oxford OX2 6DP

OXFORD   LONDON   GLASGOW
NEW YORK   TORONTO   MELBOURNE   WELLINGTON
KUALA LUMPUR   SINGAPORE   JAKARTA   HONG KONG   TOKYO
DELHI   BOMBAY   CALCUTTA   MADRAS   KARACHI
NAIROBI   DAR ES SALAAM   CAPE TOWN

Published in the United States by
Oxford University Press, New York

British Library Cataloguing in Publication Data

Roebuck, Peter
    Yorkshire Baronets, 1640–1760
    1. Yorkshire, Eng. – Nobility – History
    I. Title
    II. University of Hull
    929.7'2   CS424   79–42915

ISBN 0–19–713439–4

Set, printed and bound in Great Britain by
Fakenham Press Limited, Fakenham, Norfolk

FOR
My
Parents

PREFACE

THIS book seeks to contribute to the long-standing and still very active debate over the role of the larger landowners in the English economy during the seventeenth and eighteenth centuries. Although a great deal has been written on this subject in the past forty years, relatively few case-studies of individual landed families have appeared. In addition we know rather more about the largest, aristocratic landowners than we do about those of lesser wealth and social status. With these considerations in mind, the core of the book is devoted to a detailed examination of four Yorkshire landowning families, members of whom were raised to the baronetage at some point between the foundation of the order in 1611 and the end of the eighteenth century. An attempt is made in the remainder of the work to set their history within the context of that of the other eighty-nine families who made up the rest of the county's baronetage in the period down to 1800. The aim is to establish their priorities, policies, and circumstances and thereby to throw fresh light on the characteristics of landowners and landowning in general, and their significance in this period. However, until such time as the number of regional and case-studies is substantially increased it will remain difficult to formulate adequate conclusions as to the nature of the relationship between landownership and economic growth. It is hoped that, by providing a reminder of the wealth of primary sources available in provincial repositories, this book will stimulate further research on this and other, related topics.

While in no way involving them in responsibility for what I have written, I take great pleasure in acknowledging my debt to the many individuals who have helped me in the course of my work. I would like first of all to thank all those who gave me access to the manuscript material on which the greater part of the book is based. I am particularly indebted in this regard to Lord Hotham, the representatives of the Whitley-Beaumont family, the Duke of Norfolk, and Earl Fitzwilliam and the Trustees of the Wentworth Woodhouse Settled Estates. The late Professor R. Davis introduced me to the study of economic history and suggested the topic of the thesis out of which the book has grown. As the supervisor of that thesis, Dr H. A. Lloyd could not have been more generous in his efforts on my behalf. Dr A. Harris guided my earliest searches among Yorkshire estate records; Mr J. A. Williams and Fr W. V. Smith gave me much help with regard to the problems of recusancy; and Professors J. P. Kenyon and W. V. Wallace have frequently given me the benefit of their encouragement, assistance, and advice.

A number of people were kind enough to send useful replies to my queries: the late Mr K. A. McMahon, Professor P. L. Payne, Mr G. C. F. Forster, Dr A. Forster, Dr D. G. Hey, Dr P. G. Holiday, Mr D. Byford, and Mrs M. C. Keogh; and I am grateful to the following for making their theses available to me: Dr J. T. Cliffe, Dr W. R. Emerson, Dr P. G. Holiday, Mr A. M. Mimardière, and Mr S. C. Newton. I received generous financial assistance from the Twenty-Seven Foundation and the New University of Ulster; the University also granted me the sabbatical leave during which the bulk of the work was completed. I would like to thank a friend and former colleague, Dr S. G. F. Spackman, now of the University of St. Andrews, for valuable comments on an early draft of the first five chapters; Mrs R. Rainey, who typed a difficult manuscript with exemplary patience and skill; Mr D. Waite, who made the maps; and Mr B. Henry, Miss S. Wimbush, Dr R. B. Wragg and Mr S. T. Dibnah, who gave me invaluable help with the illustrations. Dr P. A. Larkin, Secretary to the University of Hull Publications Committee, and his assistant, Miss M. Elliott, offered me every assistance during the final stages of my work. I am also, of course, heavily indebted to a host of librarians, archivists, and their subordinates who have provided me with services over many years: but of none of them is this more true than Mr N. Higson, Archivist of the Brynmor Jones Library, University of Hull, who on innumerable occasions has gone out of his way to help me.

My best thanks are reserved for my wife, Fiona, who has sustained and encouraged me from start to finish, persistently created circumstances in which work could go on, and done so much more besides.

Portstewart, Co. Londonderry
May, 1978.

CONTENTS

LIST OF PLATES

(between pages 174 and 175)

The reproduction quality of some of the illustrations is less satisfactory than the author and publisher would wish. This is due to the lack of better original material.

LIST OF TABLES

ABBREVIATIONS

Ag. Hist Rev.	*Agricultural History Review*
Bag. Coll.	Bagshawe Collection: Central Library, Sheffield
BAX	Baxter Collection: Central Library, Sheffield
BDR	Registry of Deeds, Beverley
BFM	Bacon Frank MSS: Central Library, Sheffield
BL	British Library
BR	Bright Papers: Central Library, Sheffield
CB	G. E. Cockayne (ed.), *The Complete Baronetage 1611–1800*
CCAM	*Calendar of the Committee for the Advance of Money*
CCC	*Calendar of the Committee for Compounding*
Clay, *Dugdale*	J. W. Clay (ed.), *Dugdale's Visitation of Yorkshire, with Additions*
CM	Crewe Muniments: Central Library, Sheffield
CP	V. Gibbs, H. A. Doubleday, *et al* (eds.), *The Complete Peerage*
CRS	Catholic Record Society: *Publications*
CSPD	*Calendar of State Papers Domestic*
CTB	*Calendar of Treasury Books*
CTBP	*Calendar of Treasury Books and Papers*
CTP	*Calendar of Treasury Papers*
CWAA	Cumberland and Westmorland Antiquarian and Archaeological Society: *Transactions*
DAR	Darley of Aldby MSS: North Yorkshire Record Office, Northallerton
DD	Miscellaneous Deeds and Documents: Yorkshire Archaeological Society Library, Leeds
DDBC	Beverley Borough MSS: Humberside Record Office, Beverley
DDBM	Macdonald of Sleat MSS: Humberside Record Office, Beverley

DDDA	Darley of Aldby MSS: North Yorkshire Record Office, Northallerton
DDEV	Constable of Everingham MSS: University of Hull
DDGE	Gee (Watt) of Bishop Burton MSS: University of Hull
DDGR	Grimston of Grimston Garth and Kilnwick MSS: Humberside Record Office, Beverley
DDHA	Langdale of Holme on Spalding Moor (Harford Collection) MSS: University of Hull
DDHO	Hotham of South Dalton MSS: University of Hull
DDSY	Sykes of Sledmere MSS: University of Hull
DNB	*Dictionary of National Biography*
DX	Miscellaneous MSS: University of Hull
Econ. Hist. Rev.	*Economic History Review*
Foster	J. Foster, *Pedigrees of the County Families of Yorkshire*
HMC	Historical Manuscripts Commission: *Reports*
JHC	*Journals of the House of Commons*
MS	Miscellaneous MSS: Yorkshire Archaeological Society Library, Leeds
PRO	Public Record Office
R	2nd Marquis of Rockingham Papers, Wentworth Woodhouse Collection: Central Library, Sheffield
RCHM	Royal Commission on Historical Monuments: *Publications*
THAS	Hunter Archaeological Society: *Transactions*
TN	Temple Newsam MSS: Sheepscar Library, Leeds
TRHS	Royal Historical Society: *Transactions*
WB	Whitley-Beaumont MSS: Kirklees Metropolitan Library, Huddersfield
WW	Miscellaneous Deeds and Documents: Wentworth Woodhouse Hall

WWM	Wentworth Woodhouse Collection: Central Library, Sheffield
YAJ	*Yorkshire Archaeological Journal*
YASRS	Yorkshire Archaeological Society: *Record Series*
YATJ	*Yorkshire Archaeological and Topographical Journal*

Note: Before the change of calendar all dates given are in old style, except that I treat the year as beginning on 1 January. The spelling and punctuation in all quotations has been modernized.

I

INTRODUCTION

I. THE HISTORIOGRAPHICAL BACKGROUND

The writing of the history of landownership was initiated by landowners themselves. The dissolution of the monasteries in the early sixteenth century – the largest permanent transfer of ownership since the Norman Conquest – produced spectacular growth in the size and wealth of the landed classes, who trebled in numbers at a time when total population scarcely doubled. Simultaneously the gentlemen became an English institution, and the definition of ideals of gentility something of a popular pastime among the upper classes. Among the chief characteristics of a gentlemen was the ability 'to live idly and without manual labour'.[1] Wealth and leisure, together with superior education and a natural interest in genealogy and the descent of landed property, encouraged landowners to become practitioners of local history. Many early works were written by gentlemen for gentlemen; most were primarily concerned with the property, pedigrees, and exploits of the landed élite. By the mid seventeenth century numerous such works were being published. In Kent, for example, 'nearly every family in the county community had its own writer' by 1660.[2] While this was clearly exceptional, everywhere efforts were sustained by a rising enthusiasm for genealogy and topography, and by a readership which steadily increased. As substantial landowners achieved a national predominance which was not seriously challenged for over two centuries, authors became more varied and ambitious in their endeavours. Family, parish, and county history were all pioneered in the late seventeenth century; soon they were as prolific as they were popular. But even if by 1800 only seven counties awaited a chronicler, the heyday of antiquarianism had yet to come. As writers landowners gave way to the professional classes, whose members formed the backbone of the learned societies which sprang up from the later decades of the eighteenth century. Most family histories appeared in the century after 1830, while the leisurely construction of parish histories continued almost to the present day. Despite the steady increase in the number of authors, their major preoccupations – the landed classes and the institutions through which their influence was conveyed – remained essentially the same. 'The dead hand of the squire still guided, until recently, the hand of the living antiquary.'[3]

The majority of these writers were enthusiastic amateurs with a strong subjective interest in their work. The quality of their material and techniques varied enormously. Neither the questions they asked nor the answers they provided withstand for long the scrutiny of modern historians. Collectively they were guilty of every historiographical vice from misinterpretation and bias to sheer fabrication. Yet their work continues to form the basis of sound scholarship. It often furnishes valuable evidence, either because authors used material now unavailable, or because the very flavour of their writing is indicative of historical change. Moreover, they provided numerous case-studies which modern historians have yet to supersede, and editions of primary sources on which scholars continue to rely.

During the nineteenth century, as the hegemony of the landed classes was challenged, a new type of literature appeared. Again, few of the authors were, or attempted to be, disinterested. Divided into two camps, those who sought to justify the established structure and functions of land-ownership, and those who urged reform, they were mainly concerned with contemporary developments, though many of them engaged in extensive historical research. In particular, they examined the evolution of the legal and constitutional position of the landed élite, and their past contribution to economic development. Hitherto both issues had been virtually ignored. The ferocity of their public debate inevitably coloured the popular histories that followed. Lord Ernle was the self-appointed champion of agricultural landlords, while the Hammonds regarded the landed establishment as a formidable bulwark to mass emancipation. Yet many aspects of land-ownership which now exercise historians were first scrutinized during the polemics of the late Victorian era.[4]

The following period witnessed the rapid demise of the

landed élite. The monastic dissolution was paralleled during the two decades after 1914, when no less than a quarter of England changed hands. Assailed on all sides, many great estates and town houses, together with the life associated with them, disappeared. With landed society largely a thing of the past it became possible to study its evolution and evaluate its achievements more soberly. Two other factors facilitated this development. In 1925 the Law of Property Act initiated a flow of family and estate records into local repositories, with archives thereafter acquiring massive quantities of primary source material; while at the same time the study of economic and social history became fully professionalized.[5]

In recent decades our understanding of the causes, nature, and effects of changing patterns of ownership has been widened and deepened. Numerous scholars have studied the landed gentry of the century before 1640. Besides illuminating varied aspects of the history of the upper classes, their work has finally resulted in a comprehensive analysis of the causation of the mid seventeenth-century revolution.[6] Moreover, the revolution's impact on landowners has been reappraised. It is now clear that property turnover during the Interregnum was much less than originally supposed. Many Royalists were able to re-purchase their forfeited estates, albeit at the cost of burdening their property with debt; while the majority of the other penalties imposed by Parliament were relatively insubstantial and frequently evaded. Those forced to alienate property had usually contracted debts before the war; similarly, later difficulties can sometimes be attributed to the debts incurred in the aftermath of the hostilities.[7] However, the turmoil of the 1640s and 1650s had a creative as well as a destructive aspect. Under the pressure of events there were developed the means – strict settlements, 'returns', and cheaper, more secure mortgages – whereby many of the more substantial landowning families subsequently consolidated and improved their position. There was also significant growth in the number of scrivenors, attorneys, and other 'agents' who specialized in providing and co-ordinating professional services of this kind for landowners in need of them.[8]

The core of the period with which this book is concerned was the subject of an introductory essay in 1939.[9] Based on the records of landed families in Northamptonshire and Bedford-shire, this identified a drift of property in those counties after 1690 in favour of the aristocracy and the substantial squire-archy, and at the expense of the smaller squires, freeholders, and leaseholders. This occurred, it was argued, because the aforementioned developments relating to mortgages and settlements had made the substantial owners more secure. Moreover, although their income continued to consist mainly of rents, new investment opportunities, particularly the National Debt, enabled them to increase the proportion of their income derived from non-agricultural sources. Consequently they withstood slow rent movement and heavy taxation, expanded and consolidated their estates, and spent more on comfort and ostentation. The wealthiest families gradually acquired most of the property, and therefore most influence and control, in the areas where they lived. Their prosperity reflected the diffi-culties of smaller owners who, with stable incomes and rising expenditure, were frequently forced to sell land. As larger estates were consolidated owners improved them by enclosure and by converting leases for lives into leases for terms of years. This in turn adversely affected small freeholders and lease-holders. These developments, it was alleged, produced a major change in the disposition of English landed property.

Considerable stress was placed on the increased use of strict settlements in the post-Restoration era. Previously families had executed a variety of forms of settlement, none of which had ensured either that property settled on an eldest son at marriage descended intact to his eldest son, or that younger children of either generation were adequately provided for. However, in the mid seventeenth century the invention of the legal device whereby trustees named in a settlement preserved 'contingent reminders' enabled a landowner to settle an estate for life on his eldest son at the latter's marriage, and to entail the property on that son's prospective eldest son and heir. The life-tenant could not enlarge his interest. Nor could he undermine the provisions made for his sisters and younger brothers. Indeed, at marriage he himself had to specify what future provision would be made for his own younger children. The general adoption of this strict form of settlement maintained the size of existing estates. Moreover, in so doing it improved the chances of landowners marrying well. Financial considerations outweighed all others in marriage negotiations and, as the marriage market became better organized and more competitive, marriage and associated inheritance assumed greater importance in the growth of estates. For, it was argued, while portions were usually spent in purchasing additional property, they were raised not by land sales but in the mortgage market. Thereby the landed élite raised itself 'by its own bootstraps'.[10] Indeed, because land could not be sold or given away and provisions were usually, therefore, in the form of lump sums, and because strict settlements increased the value of land as security for loans, the mortgage market expanded and interest rates fell. The latter were further depressed by the growth of government borrowing. Eventually landowners' ability to remain indebted for long periods at falling rates of interest greatly reduced turnover in the land market. Mercantile wealth was diverted into alternative avenues of investment, and new purchasers were increasingly drawn from among those most successful in the government service or the legal profession. Especially after 1760 when rapidly rising rents reduced the pressure to sell, the heavy demand for land could not be satisfied. Property sales became 'the product of deliberate decision' rather than 'the result of sudden emergencies', and many investors turned instead to the money market.[11]

Of course, as land prices rose pure finance became relatively more profitable, even though interest rates fell. Nevertheless, various non-economic factors kept the demand for land at a high level. Large-scale landownership was a major source of political power, which in turn provided widespread patronage. It was also socially prestigious, enabling individuals and families to benefit from the high degree of social mobility which England enjoyed compared to her Continental neighbours. In fact in England there was often little distinction between aristocratic and other substantial landowners. Both played a crucial role in the economy and, under a constitutional monarchy, were dominant in politics and society. The permanence of landed society was a vital factor in the stability of society as a whole, which contrasted sharply with 'the preceding turbulence of the seventeenth century and the subsequent tensions of the age of reform'.[12]

Initially the development and management of the larger estates received rather less attention than the changing pattern of ownership. Several of the economic functions of landowners were examined: their role as potential promoters of agrarian change; the size and possible uses of their capital resources; the scope of the derived effects of some of their investments; their attitude towards the exploitation of mineral resources; and their behaviour as the largest consumers within the domestic economy. The conclusion was that, although English landowners played a distinctly more active economic role than their Continental counterparts, they were more interested in the possession of a well-run, well-tenanted estate than in the active promotion of agricultural and other economic improvements. Consolidation of property and the gradual creation of a substantial tenantry who enjoyed security of tenure prompted and facilitated improvements, but on the whole the more substantial proprietors enjoyed rather than developed their property. Some landowners, particularly those who transferred wealth from business, public service or the professions, acted in a genuinely entrepreneurial capacity. The economic behaviour of the majority, however, was characterized by consumption, not production.[13]

Until recently the bulk of research was concentrated on the period after 1700 for which most primary evidence was available, estate accounts and correspondence being the richest sources. The contribution of the stewards or agents who drew up these accounts, and to or from whom most estate correspondence was directed, has been examined in depth. Efficient management, particularly of the estates of absentee owners, was heavily dependent on such correspondence; and, although many gentry owners continued personally to manage their property down to the mid eighteenth century, the majority appointed one or more stewards to oversee their affairs long before then. Landed estates were immensely complex economic entities which, in addition to various branches of agriculture, not infrequently embraced a variety of industrial, transport and urban developments. The exalted social position of landowners made the management of their purely domestic concerns an onerous task, while many stewards also played an important part in the political and other public activities of their employers. Stewards had to be hardy individuals, capable of dealing in a broad range of business with people from all social classes, whilst at the same time supervising the work of a host of other full- and part-time employees. During this period they became increasingly necessary to the smooth functioning of the larger estates, not least because of the difficulties associated with the sluggish growth of rental incomes in the century after 1660.[14] Another major problem with which they had to contend was the increase in land taxation, which was 'heavier under Queen Anne than ever again until the twentieth century'.[15] Country attorneys, many of whom later joined the ranks of estate agents or effectively acted in both capacities, also made a significant contribution to the management of landowners' affairs. The demand for their services, which were largely, though not exclusively, legal and financial, was stimulated by the complicated processes of land sale and recovery in the mid seventeenth century. Thereafter the widespread resort by landowners to stricter forms of settlement and, as they became safer and cheaper, to mortgages provided attorneys with plenty of work. In their capacity as financial undertakers and advisers, as well as experts in the running of institutions such as manorial courts, they gradually assumed 'a pivotal position in local affairs', meeting the requirements of a wide cross-section of contemporary provincial society, but none more so than those of the landed gentry.[16] A further development of considerable importance was the establishment in London of private banks which specifically catered for the needs of the larger proprietors.[17] By the early eighteenth century, therefore, landowners had access to a far greater range of professional services than had been available two or three generations earlier.

The situation in regard to agricultural prices, rarely particularly favourable between 1660 and 1750, deteriorated during the last quarter of the period.[18] Many tenants were unable to pay their rents, and some reduced the acreage of their holdings or gave up farming. Once land had become untenanted owners often experienced difficulty in re-letting it. They were obliged to withstand large running totals of overdue rents and to write off some arrears altogether; and attempted to relieve distress by reducing rents, meeting taxes where these had previously been paid by tenants, and by making additional sums available for repairs and improvements. The severity of the depression varied from one region to another, as did the nature of landlord responses to it. Indeed, the variety of experience and behaviour during these years warns against generalizing too easily about the evolution of management techniques. There was considerable scope for adaptation in the face of changing circumstances and on the whole landlords or their agents acted quickly, though in different ways and to varying degrees, in support of their tenantry.[19] Nor over the longer period should the effect on agriculture of the developing pattern of ownership be exaggerated. The growth of large estates did not shatter the landlord–tenant relationship, which remained flexible enough to promote good husbandry. In particular England continued to be a country of small farms. Though estate consolidation was accompanied by some increase in farm size, the decline of the small farmer and the part played in this by enclosure have both, it has been suggested, been overestimated. Many factors made for stability in the countryside and down into the nineteenth century small farms were characteristic of English agriculture.[20]

For many years the striking feature of the modern historiography of this subject was the breadth of its consensus. By and large scholars accepted conventional wisdom as it accumulated and then proceeded to add to it by opening up fresh lines of inquiry. It was noted that the structure of ownership in certain areas, for example Devon and Kent, differed from the general pattern; and that some groups of landowners, for example Catholic families in the north-east, declined during this period.[21] Only recently was the original explanation of the rise of the large estate questioned: in an article which maintained that the nature of the relationship between marriage and inheritance and the growth of estates during this period had been oversimplified and misunderstood.[22] The situation, it was argued, was far from straightforward. Wives who expected to inherit property did not always do so; where they did, it was often only for one generation. Demographic factors upset the most intricate plans, producing unexpected gains for some families and dashing the hopes of others. None of these considerations applied to portions, which became vested in the groom's family at marriage. However, doubt was cast on the view that by using portions to buy land, and raising them on mortgages, the larger landowners were expanding some estates without contracting others. For, though interest rates fell, yields on capital invested in land fell even further. According to the original hypothesis, therefore, debt charges would eventually have exceeded receipts from new property, thereby forcing sales. In reality, it was suggested, some land was sold to raise portions, which were used both to discharge debts and to raise other portions. On the whole the more substantial landowners neither gained nor lost from this interchange of capital between families. As in other periods, the direct effects of marriage and inheritance worked impartially for all groups in landed society. Nevertheless, both factors were involved in the rise of great estates as a result of failures of male heirs and consequent female or indirect inheritance. In the latter circumstances strict settlements were often circumvented; and in any case the amount of property ungoverned by such settlements was not insubstantial. In either instance land was alienable. As it usually came to females burdened with debt, and because of the disparity between interest rates and returns on investment in land, it was often sold. Such sales were particularly significant, firstly because, owing to demographic trends, there were more of them during this period, and secondly because they were most frequently of land belonging to lesser gentry and freeholders. It was by snapping up these properties that more substantial owners expanded their estates over several generations.

Since the appearance of this article the debate has been extended to other fronts. A study of land prices in the century and a half after 1650 has suggested that rates of purchase did not rise continuously throughout the eighteenth century, as they would have done had the supply of property for sale steadily diminished. Less property came on to the market then than in the aftermath of the civil wars, but there was no serious shortage of property for sale. Indeed, fluctuations in prices were largely determined by the level of demand for landed property, government stock constituting a major alternative area of investment activity.[23] Moreover, a study of the land market in eighteenth-century Lincolnshire has failed to identify a concentration of property in the hands of the great magnates. Gentry families and estates continued to rise and fall, and new estates were acquired by 'lawyers, merchants, clergy, speculators, and officials besides existing proprietors of land in a medley fully as rich as in the expansive era of "Tawney's century"'.[24] The pattern of landownership in Cumbria was also of a rather different kind from that originally suggested for Northamptonshire and Bedfordshire. There peerage interest was generally lacking. The major beneficiaries of sales of land by the lesser gentry and yeomanry were the more substantial gentry, particulary the Lowthers, and several new families who derived their income from trade and the law. Moreover, there was no single, major reason for the emergence of this pattern. The use of marriage settlements and mortgages was of limited importance; the proceeds of government office were of even less significance. Nor did the land tax exert a particularly adverse influence: owing to the prevalence of customary tenants, few landlords were directly responsible for paying the tax, while in any case Cumbria was a notoriously lowly-rated area. Finally, rent movement was less sluggish there than elsewhere, and those landowners who found it impossible to live within their incomes were from all social levels.[25]

Furthermore, in the past decade or so agrarian historians have traced the origins of many of the significant changes in agriculture back to the seventeenth century and even earlier. Debate continues as to when, and to what extent, these changes transformed the economic performance of the farming industry; and as to which group of participants played the most important role in this process.[26] According to one school of thought, however, the Restoration represents a recognizable turning-point in English agrarian history, not least because it was from then onwards that substantial landowners became progressively more interested in adopting improved methods of maximizing estate incomes. It was not just that they were much less aloof from economic affairs than Continental landowners. Henceforward, spurred on by a swing in the ratio of cereal to livestock prices which was favourable to livestock production, they played a 'catalytic role as innovators'. Above all they had a marked influence on levels of agricultural investment by diverting capital from other spheres of economic activity, providing premises and occasionally stock and other items, making rent abatements and tolerating arrears, and by generally aiming for long-term increases in their landed incomes. Even their conspicuous personal expenditure played a part by providing landowners with a strong incentive to estate improvement.[27]

These and other views on the broad pattern of developments have in the main been derived, not from the comprehensive study of individual landowners and their estates, but rather from more general surveys of larger bodies of evidence. Indeed, when research first emerged from the learned journals less than two decades ago 'no full account of the economy of any one large estate' had 'yet been published'.[28] Each of the two most notable case-studies to appear since then has served to qualify earlier generalizations. Thus, the achievements, such as they were, of the Cokes of Holkham were firmly based on a fortuitous minority in the early eighteenth century, when guardians discharged heavy debts and inaugurated the system of management which in large measure governed the estate for over a century. Despite this, the accounts of succeeding incumbents were often in substantial deficit, with sizeable sums having to be raised through borrowing and sales of outlying properties, as well as from extra-agricultural sources such as a Crown lease of Dungeness lighthouse. Moreover, the family encouraged popular exaggeration of their contribution to the improvement of farming on their estate. Building, collecting, and politics competed with agriculture for scarce resources, agricultural progress was slow and distinctly unrevolutionary, and alternative avenues of investment were neglected.[29] In the case of the Duke of Newcastle an utter failure to manage private and estate affairs led eventually to the disintegration of his huge estate, despite the fact that he earned salaries of over £5,000 a year for over forty years. Political expenses were partly responsible for his gross indebtedness but much more important were absenteeism, sheer neglect, and a permanent inability to control expenditure. Repeated resolves to retrench were interspersed with more drastic measures: trusts for the payment of debts were established and in 1741 a settlement barring the entail on his estates allowed the sale of two-thirds of his property. Old debts were thereby reduced but so too was income, while new debts were constantly created. After the Duke's death in 1768 much of the rest of his property and effects was sold to satisfy creditors.[30]

If these and other case-studies have emphasized the influence of personal attitudes and behaviour on the fortunes of landowning families, other, more general works have had the like effect. A comparative study of patterns of inheritance and settlement among the greater landowners in Europe has underlined the difference between the projected and the actual consequences of entail and primogeniture. These practices were traditionally defended on the grounds that they kept large estates intact and thus preserved social and political stability. Yet, it is argued, pursued over several generations such a system almost invariably created financial difficulties owing to the number of dependants who had to be provided for out of a family's estate. Throughout Europe many great families went into demographic decline from the later seventeenth century as marriages were delayed or avoided in pursuit of solvency. English landowners were economically more successful because of the relative ease with which, when necessary, they could break entails and alienate property. Moreover, in England the post-1650 fall in agricultural profits was less severe than in many other countries, while in addition non-agricultural sources of income were both more numerous and more accessible. In the face of financial difficulties, therefore, the range of options available to English landowners was wider than elsewhere: a great deal depended on the policies and capabilities of individual landowners.[31] This line of interpretation is supported by the most recent general work, which analyses changes in the type of family to be found among the English upper classes between 1500 and 1800. The dominant type until the later sixteenth century was the 'open lineage family': this was characterized by its permeability by outside interests, its members sense of loyalty to ancestors and to living kin, and by its insistence that the interests of the group outweighed the wishes of the individual. From 1600, however, this family type was rapidly replaced by the 'restricted patriarchal nuclear family', which neglected loyalties to lineage, kin, patron, and local community in favour of more universalistic loyalties to the nation state and its head, and to a particular sect or Church. In this type 'boundary awareness' became more exclusively confined to the nuclear family and was more immune to other, external influences. Then, from the post-Restoration period, a third type, 'the closed domesticated nuclear family', gradually became predominant. With the waning of religious fervour, the quickening pace of economic development, the relaxation of social tensions, and the political stability which followed the establishment of a limited monarchical state in 1688, there was less need for the old familial authoritarianism. Henceforward upper class families were increasingly characterized by 'affective individualism'. They were organized around the principle of personal autonomy, gave recognition to the rights of self-expression and personal freedom, and were bound together by emotional ties rather than by those of lineage or authority.[32]

Thus, while it has been guided by, and has drawn inspiration from, the large body of earlier research, the work of the past decade has cast considerable doubt, not just on the previously accepted view as to the major trends in English landownership during the late seventeenth and eighteenth centuries, but also on the reasons originally adduced for the development of those trends. The manner in which the larger estates were managed and developed during this period also remains a matter of debate. And finally, the emphasis placed on the role, for good or ill, of individual proprietors has steadily increased. Acknowledgement that many large estates were expanded and consolidated no longer implies that, with few exceptions, substantial owners enjoyed rising prosperity after the Restoration. Scholars are now more aware of the number of those who encountered difficulties as well as of the reasons for their lack of success. Demographic failure, a threat to all families at all times, increased among the upper classes during this period.[33] Although there were regional variations, the century after 1660 was one of comparative agricultural depression when rents, and with them landed incomes, remained remarkably stable for long periods.[34] Despite opportunities for income diversification, many landed families remained heavily dependent on rent rolls which were slow to grow and which, in periods of particular difficulty for farmers, fell or were reduced. Strict settlements were neither universally applied nor immutable. At times direct taxation was onerous, while the costs of a lengthy lawsuit might be crippling. The expenditure of certain families, for example

Catholics, was heavier, and their sources of income fewer, than those of most of their contemporaries. Credit facilities were not extended indefinitely, especially if a debtor's behaviour departed too far from conventional norms. Without doubt landed families, especially those with the largest estates, did enjoy numerous and substantial advantages, but the overall effect of such advantages has perhaps been exaggerated. Before the late eighteenth-century rise in agricultural profits, family success was no easy achievement; still less was it inevitable.

The difficulties facing historians of landownership in this and other periods have long been recognized. 'The proper unit of study is the individual family; it must be seen from the inside; and the most fruitful path in this field is the detailed study of particular cases, based upon the family documents, where these are available.'[35] In following this injunction, however, historians are inexorably drawn to the most prolific archives, which exacerbates an already inherent bias in the evidence available to them. For, far from being a random sample in any statistical sense, surviving records are merely a selection, 'heavily weighted on the side of those families which were rising in the world, and those which were already so rich that total dispersion and dismemberment of their estates were unlikely'.[36] Although the problems which arise from this situation cannot be completely overcome, their effect can be mitigated by the study of large groups of families from one geographical area, one band of the social strata, or from both. For a fresh consensus as to the broad pattern of developments and the reasons for it to emerge, we need 'more detailed studies both of families and, in particular, of regions and counties'.[37]

With these considerations in mind, the purpose of this book is firstly, to provide detailed case-studies of four Yorkshire landed families during a crucial part of this early modern period; and secondly, to place their history within the context of that of a larger group of families from the same region. The aims are to examine their policies, priorities, and circumstances, both economic and social; to identify whether, and why, the size of their estates altered during the period in question; and thirdly, to assess their contribution to the development of the area in which, for the most part, they operated. The subjects of the case-studies were chosen simply because the records relating to the four families concerned, besides being voluminous, were relatively evenly spread throughout the period. The criteria adopted in selecting the larger group had, ideally, to take account of wealth and social position without simultaneously resulting in the automatic choice of the most successful, or the inevitable rejection of those who failed. They had also to provide a sizeable number of families from a relatively uniform, though not narrowly confined, geographical area. The group comprises the ninety-three families, or branches of families, who were described as 'of Yorkshire' when they were raised to the baronetage at some point between 1611 and 1800. (See Appendix 1.) The use of the baronetage is not altogether ideal, for both the number and the causation of nominations to the order were subject to marked fluctuations. The latter, however, are themselves revealing. In addition, besides meeting the above requirements, this method of selection ensured the availability of basic information relating to each family. The group is coherent and manageable, yet of sufficient size to lend credibility to general conclusions drawn from its history.

Particular attention is devoted to the decades 1640–1760. These embrace the plateau of agricultural prices which followed the price rise of the sixteenth and early seventeenth centuries, and preceded the dramatic economic developments of the industrial revolution. They also encompass the gamut of social and political changes which occurred between the Civil War and the accession of George III. It will often be necessary to take a wider view of the subject, if only because some baronetcies were created after 1760, while others were created or became extinct before 1640. In such cases either the previous or the subsequent history of the families concerned is included within the scope of this work where appropriate. Finally, no attempt has been made to examine all the evidence relating to each of the ninety-three families. Rather the detailed history of the four families has been placed within the context of the main features of the experience of the entire group. Published sources, both primary and secondary, provide a general framework within which the case-studies, based on very full collections of family and estate records, are set. This plan stems from a dual conviction: that the study of individual families

over long periods is a fruitful approach to this subject, but that
their history must be viewed in a wider, and preferably regional, setting.

2. THE GROWTH OF THE YORKSHIRE BARONETAGE

The origin of the baronetage lies in the Crown's use, and
abuse, of the honours system in the early seventeenth century.
Elizabeth I had been sparing with honours of all kinds. James I
went to the opposite extreme, especially in granting knight-
hoods. In 1603, when support for his succession was in doubt,
he dubbed no less than sixty knights from Yorkshire alone. The
inevitable result of this flurry of creations was a sharp reduction
in the distinction formerly associated with them. Soon there
was a need to fill the wide gap which developed between the
mere knight and the peer of the realm. The government was
also searching for new sources of revenue. The baronetage,
instituted in 1611, was designed to meet both requirements and
various conditions were intended to ensure that it did so. The
number of baronets was never to exceed 200. The honour was to
be granted only to men whose estates were worth £1,000 a year,
and whose paternal grandparents had possessed coats of arms.
Unlike knighthood, baronetcies were to be hereditary. In
addition to incidental expenses, each nominee was to pay
£1,095 into the Exchequer. Besides raising revenue this final
undertaking further guaranteed a candidate's worthiness, and
thereby the new order's strategic position in the hierarchy of
honour.[38]

For a brief period the scheme operated satisfactorily. There
was intense competition for the honour among leading Yorkshire gentry, seven of whom were nominated in 1611. All but
one had previously been knighted and members of five of their
families were later raised to the peerage. Sir George Savile of
Thornhill, Sir William Constable of Flamborough, Sir Francis
Wortley, and Sir Marmaduke Wyvill all belonged to old-
established dynasties. The remainder were of lesser vintage but
equally eligible. Sir Henry Belasyse owned the largest estate in
the North Riding, while William Wentworth's property in
south Yorkshire was worth nearly £4,000 a year. By contrast the
landed income of Sir Henry Savile of Methley was only just

sufficient to qualify for the honour and his fear of neighbours' unfavourable reaction to his baronetcy, 'our births being equal' but 'my state inferior', indicates that initially criteria for nomination were carefully scrutinized.[39]

In these circumstances competition soon turned first to jealousy and then to rancour. Allegations of corruption in the administration of the scheme together with arguments over matters of precedence greatly reduced the demand for nominations. When the government undercut the list price many offers of nomination were refused for fear that such honours would not gain public recognition. No further Yorkshire baronets were created for seven years. Under financial pressure the authorities considered raising both the number and the price of baronetcies, but rejected these alternatives as unrealistic. Instead the other undertakings were progressively disregarded, causing further falls in the market price. The establishment of separate orders for Ireland and Scotland, in 1618 and 1625 respectively, encouraged this trend. When Charles I ignored the restriction on the number of English baronetcies, their price plummeted to around £200 – only slightly above the official price of nomination to the other orders. Before long he began making grants free of charge and most of the Yorkshiremen honoured during his reign paid nothing for their awards.[40]

Despite these developments, many of those nominated from 1618 were rich and influential gentlemen. Sir Matthew Boynton paid £1,100 in cash for his baronetcy, though this was later refunded. Edward Osborne and Sir John Hotham were among the wealthiest squires in the county. Henry Griffith, Sir Thomas Gower, and Sir William Bamburgh, all substantial landowners, had held, or were holding, important local offices on the receipt of their baronetcies. Two nominees to the Scottish order, Henry Slingsby of Scriven and the recusant John Gascoigne, were also men of substance. Gascoigne was the only Catholic in the country to pay for nomination under Charles I, while Slingsby was a rich M.P. who had previously married the eldest daughter of Viscount Fauconberg.[41] The credentials of others were more questionable, particularly as pure favouritism appeared to have dictated the royal choice. Thomas Vavasour of Hazlewood, Sir David Foulis, and William Chaloner were courtiers, of whom the last two had earlier received substantial grants of Crown property. William Pennyman of Marske was nominated in 1628 following the death of his father, who, though illegitimate, had held high judicial office in London.[42] Whether, or how much, most of these men paid for their awards is uncertain, but all of them could have afforded the official price. Others undoubtedly could not have done so. Anthony Slingsby of Scriven (Henry's cousin) owned little if any property. When nominated he was a professional soldier in the Low Countries. Part of the estate of Sir Richard Beaumont, whose gross annual rental was £1,200, had been freely obtained from the Crown. He was heavily indebted and reputedly sold his property in Huddersfield to finance his inveterate gambling. Philibert Vernatti, who settled in the East Riding, was a Dutch entrepreneur involved in the drainage of Hatfield Level. Though temporarily saved by royal intervention, his affairs eventually terminated disastrously. Arthur Pilkington was also in financial difficulties, being imprisoned for debt both before and after his nomination.[43]

Inevitably the Crown's stewardship of the honours system met with mounting criticism. Consequently there were few awards in the 1630s. Caution was disregarded, however, prior to the Civil War, when honours were widely dispersed in an attempt to win or sustain political support. Even so, in Yorkshire most of the baronets created in 1641 later sided with Parliament. Sir William Strickland was an avid committee man and subsequently a Cromwellian peer. Along with Sir William Constable of Flamborough and the brothers of Sir Thomas Chaloner, Thomas Mauleverer was a fanatical Parliamentarian and a future regicide. Sir Hugh Cholmely fought for Parliament until confronted by the Queen at his home in Whitby. While Richard Sprignell's allegiance is unknown, Francis Armitage's loyalty to the Crown was never in doubt. Only John Goodrick switched to the royal cause following his award.[44] The eleven Yorkshiremen honoured in 1642 included several future Royalists, for the King was then favouring known supporters or sympathizers. However, William St. Quintin fought for Parliament; John Reresby and William Ingleby vacillated before siding with Charles; and Edward Payler and Christopher Dawnay died soon after obtaining their titles. Moreover, only fifteen of the twenty-five families who received baronetcies before 1641 supported the King; five backed Parliament, and five were either extinct, of divided allegiance, or with heirs too young to be involved in hostilities.[45] But the Crown needed financial as well as political support. Cholmely, Goodrick, Dawnay, Ingleby, Bland, and Constable of Everingham were all wealthy and long-established landed families. Others, like Kaye and Armitage, inherited property acquired through commercial activity in the sixteenth century. Matthew Valkenberg had been a member of the Dutch East India Company before joining Vernatti on Hatfield Level. The Sprignells remained London merchants, Richard possessing merely a lease of property in Copmanthorpe. Naturally the few grants made after war broke out went to active Royalists. Also of Copmanthorpe, William Vavasour, an able commander though an insubstantial landowner, died in service with the Swedish army after being banished in 1645. The much wealthier Richard Forster acted as Treasurer to the Queen Dowager and Charles II during their exile, and was created baronet at St. Germain-en-Laye.[46]

By the mid seventeenth century, therefore, Yorkshire baronets were not characterized by political uniformity; their economic circumstances were similarly varied. Primarily this was because the original criteria governing nominations were frequently ignored in favour of other considerations, which likewise altered from time to time. None the less, however small a part this played in their nomination, the majority were established members of the gentry. This qualification was frequently absent after the Restoration when the baronetage became even less exclusive than before.

Charles II came under considerable pressure to reward those who had suffered in supporting the royal cause. Although there were such individuals among the twenty-seven Yorkshire baronets created between 1660 and 1665, there were many more to whom the King was personally attached or indebted, or whose support he wished to maintain in the uncertain political situation which prevailed. Nineteen nominees were Royalists. Yet only ten had been punished for their allegiance, and of these only three had to contend with acute financial difficulties as a result. Because the Lawsons and the Tancreds were Catholics as well as Royalists, their estates had been sold. Both contrived to regain their property, but only by burdening their estates with debt. James Pennyman of Ormesby escaped sequestration but he and his father were heavily fined. Having spent much raising troops for the King, he was forced to sell property before being able to satisfy the Parliamentary authorities. Two other nominees experienced moderate financial difficulty. Despite his large fine, Godfrey Copley's estate remained intact, while speedy composition and the existence of entails on his property enabled Thomas Wentworth of Bretton to sustain a fine and heavy plundering without selling property.[47] Five other Royalists had been penalized, though only comparatively lightly. Sir William Robinson of Newby and Richard Graham were fined, and William Rokeby sequestered; Graham also sustained billeting and free quarter. All three quickly regained prosperity. Sir Robert Hildyard, a royal favourite, was fined £610, a paltry sum for someone of his wealth. Before distinguished military service – he was knighted on the battlefield for slaying the Scottish champion in a duel – he had been Gentleman of the Privy Chamber to Charles I. Besides giving him a baronetcy, Charles II reappointed him to this position. George Cooke claimed to have lost up to £15,000 by his allegiance. Though this was an exaggeration, his father, after repeated attempts at evasion, had been forced to compound on three separate occasions. Yet, when pressed, he had raised more than £1,000 in three days. As his land purchases during the Interregnum indicate, he was exceedingly wealthy, and extended credit to numerous impecunious Royalists.[48] Thus, few of the Royalists granted baronetcies after the Restoration were in financial distress.

A surprisingly large number had completely avoided involvement with the Parliamentary authorities. Demographic factors had occasionally proved helpful. The father of John Savile of Copley died in 1644 when the latter was only four years old. Christopher Wandesford, earlier one of Strafford's chief henchmen in Ireland, died on the eve of war. His son, George, opted for neutrality but, after refusing to swear allegiance to Parliament or subscribe to the Solemn League and Covenant, was sequestered. This was rescinded on petition and the family escaped a fine. The Catholic Stapletons of Carlton were even more fortunate. The nominal head of the family, Richard, was a lunatic; but for this their large estates would almost certainly have been confiscated and sold. In fact they were the only unmolested recusant gentry in Yorkshire. The Stapletons of Myton also escaped punishment, despite being related to leading Cavaliers and involved in saving the forfeited Slingsby estates. William Cayley probably owed his immunity to his wife, the daughter of the Parliamentarian Sir William St. Quintin; and able to concentrate on personal affairs, he expanded his estate during the Interregnum. Mark Milbanke, George Winn, and Hugh Smithson, left alone by Parliament, were granted baronetcies in return for the financial assistance they had pro-·vided for the royal family in exile. Among the first nominations in 1660 was Solomon Swale, who proposed the restoration in Parliament. Though his allegiance was undoubted and three of his brothers served in the royal forces, he too had been untroubled by the Parliamentary authorities.[49]

The baronets created in the immediate post-Restoration period also included individuals of a quite different hue. George Marwood was a prominent Calvinist. Following dismissal from the peace commission for disloyalty in 1642, his house had been sacked by a Royalist mob, and his wife denounced as a 'Puritan whore'. Sheriff of Yorkshire in 1651–2 and M.P. in 1659 and 1660–1, his support of the Restoration was welcomed and rewarded. John Bright provides another such example. From a strong Puritan background, he emerged in the 1640s as a Parliamentary commander and administrator. His executive influence enabled him to increase his wealth in the aftermath of war, and by 1660 he was living on the Badsworth estate previously owned by the Royalist, Thomas Dolman. Although Bright had resigned his commission following the King's execution, he had helped Lambert to crush Sir George Booth's Presbyterian-Royalist rebellion in 1659. His support of the Restoration, rewarded with a baronetcy, smacks of political opportunism. Charles II also coveted the local influence and support of William Frankland and John Tempest. The former's father, still alive in 1660, had fought for Parliament, while Tempest, a zealous Puritan, had served on Parliamentary committees and been M.P. for Yorkshire in 1654. Both John Jackson and John Legard had been too young to be involved in hostilities. Jackson apparently owed his award to his marriage to the granddaughter of Sir George Booth (empowered by Charles II to make two nominations for baronetcies). Legard, a collateral branch of whose family had supported Parliament, was an influential East Riding M.P. by 1660, and helped to secure York for Charles II. Sir John Lewis had also remained politically uninvolved in the 1640s. He had developed commercial interests on the Continent where he became acquainted with the exiled king. Shortly before the Restoration and his grant of a baronetcy, he was knighted at the Hague.[50]

The circumstances of Francis Burdett highlight another aspect of this batch of honours. Leaving £1,600 in debts and an estate worth £800 a year, Burdett's father had died in 1644 without having made arrangements for the guardianship of his heir, then only two years old. Thereafter the duties of guardian were assumed by Robert Rockley, the minor's great-uncle, and then by Rockley's son. The difficult situation facing the latter, together with Burdett's extravagance, precipitated lawsuits which eventually ruined them both. Burdett was not alone among those honoured in the period 1660–5 in being on the verge of economic decline. The Jacksons, who had become major West Riding landowners following success as lawyers in the sixteenth century, never overcame the fiscal problems which beset them in the 1630s. Sir John left a heavily encumbered estate to the second baronet, whose recklessness hastened the disintegration of their property. Solomon Swale had inherited property worth merely £140 a year. A generous guardian, lucrative marriage, and success at the bar increased his means, enabling him to purchase the ancestral home, Swale Hall. However, despite grants and interest-free loans totalling £4,000 from Charles II, his prosperity was short-lived. He became embroiled in fruitless attempts to mine lead in Swaledale and by 1700 the family was bankrupt. Clearly, the Crown was not unwilling to grant baronetcies to men of insubstantial means. Before the Civil War the estate of the Saviles of Copley was worth less than £200 a year; by 1651 William Rokeby's property earned only £580 annually.[51]

Moreover, less importance was now attached to established gentility. Both the Marwoods and the Brights were among the

newer county families. John Bright's father, the son of a yeoman farmer, was only granted arms in 1642. Hugh Smithson,
son of a husbandman, received his arms in the same year as he
was made a baronet. This situation was partly due to the
devaluation of the currency of the baronetage by the early
Stuarts, to the extent that during the Interregnum one Royalist
suggested that baronetcies 'hath been a greater cause of
debasing nobility and undervaluing gentry, and hath generally
given more offence and scandal to all degrees than any
dignity that ever was devised'.[52] The proliferation of grants
by Charles II, who, like his predecessor, usually remitted
official fees, did nothing to dispel, and much to confirm, this
feeling.

While demand for the honour from established gentry
declined, it rose among the wealthy commercial classes, who
sought landed property and titles in order to acquire the influence and prestige which their pedigrees could not provide. The
capacity to fulfil these aims following achievement in non-
agricultural sectors of the economy had always been considerable. The Legards and the Robinsons of Newby, both nominated in 1660, were neither the first nor the last to reach the
baronetage via commercial success during Elizabeth's reign.
After the Restoration access to the higher ranks of the gentry
was more readily attainable. This stemmed partly from the
opportunities for aggrandisement available during the Interregnum. Brian Cooke, father of George, was a leading merchant and local government official in Doncaster; he purchased
Wheatley – the family seat – in the 1650s. Mark Milbanke, who
declined a baronetcy in favour of his son, pursued a similar
career in Newcastle upon Tyne before establishing himself at
Halnaby in the North Riding. Both George Winn and his
brother Rowland, whose grandfather had been draper to
Elizabeth I, were merchants and aldermen in London prior to
collaborating in the purchase of Nostell Priory in 1654. In
1638 Hugh Smithson had invested the profits of his London
haberdashery in purchasing Stanwick. Sir John Lewis
made his fortune in trade with India and Persia, and continued in commerce after buying Ledston and acquiring a
baronetcy.[53]

While awards were relatively few and far between in the

period 1665–1800, these trends persisted. Although a majority of nominations went to families with commercial backgrounds, the fortunes of others had often been exceedingly mixed. William Chaytor, whose father had married into property, came from a minor gentry family in Durham. His own inheritance of the Croft estate, following the death of the heir of his second cousin, increased his substance, though the only office which he acquired, in 1689, was the colonelcy of the Richmondshire militia. By then he was heavily indebted and had a large family. Forced to make provision for the payment of debts and maintenance by private act in 1695, he spent his last seventeen years in the Fleet prison for debt. Walter Hawksworth on the other hand was fairly wealthy. However, his grandfather's extensive litigation and stormy marriage had earned the family a public notoriety which for long deprived them of office and honour. After the death of his father, who repaired enough damage to become a J.P. and Deputy Lieutenant, Walter strove to do better still. He met and married within twenty-four hours the daughter of a Lincolnshire baronet, and shortly afterwards was himself nominated for an award. The Calverleys, friends and neighbours of the Hawksworths, were also driven by a desire to exorcize the past. After a sensational court case in 1605 Walter Calverley's great-grandfather had been executed for murdering two of his sons and attempting to stab his wife. Wardship subseqently reduced the family's circumstances and, following panic sales during the Interregnum, net income from their estate fell below £100 a year. Thereafter rackrenting, wise mortgaging, and a successful marriage brought steady recovery. This was furthered by Walter's own marriage in 1707 to the heiress of the north-eastern magnate, Sir William Blackett, and sealed with a baronetcy in 1711. John Wentworth also benefited from marriage and inheritance. From the minor Brodsworth branch of the family, he unexpectedly succeeded his cousin Thomas of North Elmsall, whose estate was reputed to have been worth £3,000 a year. This won him the daughter of Sir James Lowther, the future 1st Viscount Lonsdale, whom he soon joined in the baronetage. Roger Beckwith was even more energetic in the marriage market, though he achieved much less. From a minor gentry family who experienced considerable financial difficulties in the early seventeenth century, he failed to obtain office even at the provincial level, and committed suicide in 1700.[54]

In contrast to these somewhat chequered careers the history of families with commercial origins, both before and after accession to the baronetage, was one of relentlessly increasing wealth and solidity. This was partly because all members of these families who were of age tended to go into business and were thereby able to assist one another, whereas a landowner's sons were usually less productive and more widely distributed in their careers. Collaborative effort is evident in the case of the Winns and their acquisition of Nostell. It is even more apparent with the two Yorkshire branches of the Lowther family. Both were descended from younger sons of the wealthy and landed Cumberland Lowthers; both conducted highly successful business ventures; and both reached the baronetage after establishing estates and public careers in the north. Together with his nephew, Robert Lowther, a London draper, purchased Marske and Oughborough in 1649–50. Subsequently, having bought out his relative, he continued in business, living on additional property at Walthamstow. Though generations of younger sons remained in commerce, his heir, Anthony, gradually withdrew to develop Marske after marrying the daughter of Admiral Sir William Penn, and became M.P. for Appleby. His heir, William, married the heiress of a large estate at Holker, was created baronet, and represented Lancaster at Westminster. After moving to Holker Sir William left Marske to his brother, John, who had previously 'improved his fortune considerably' as a merchant in Danzig.[55] William Lowther, of the other branch of the family, established a business in Leeds, married a local merchant's daughter, but made his fortune while exiled in Holland in the 1640s. On returning to Yorkshire he and his brother bought several properties in the Leeds area. Having contributed to the royal purse during the Interregnum, he was knighted in 1662 and appointed a Customs Commissioner. He became active in Leeds politics, M.P. for Pontefract, and High Sheriff. His heir followed him in these positions, married a landowner's daughter, and became Deputy Lieutenant of the West Riding. The next heir married a peer's daughter, was appointed a Gentleman of the Royal Bedchamber, and created baronet in 1715. By that time the family had acquired several estates in the vicinity of Leeds. Except for Swillington, which became the main seat, these were let to successive brothers and younger sons once they had completed their active careers, most of which were in commerce.[56]

As national economic activity quickened, the wealth of some newcomers to the baronetage became massive and varied. When William Milner was granted arms in 1710 his family had already provided Leeds with three generations of merchants and city fathers. Besides being the largest entrepreneur in the local cloth market, he was the principal promoter of the Aire and Calder Navigation scheme. For 'many years' he 'returned £70–80,000 and upwards a year in the way of business'.[57] Though he purchased three estates near Leeds, Milner continued to live in the town and to run his affairs personally until his death in 1740. Long before then, in 1717, his son was created baronet. Unlike his father who was educated locally, served an apprenticeship, and married a businessman's daughter, the first baronet went to Eton, Cambridge, and the Middle Temple and married the daughter of the Archbishop of York. He was M.P. for York 1722–34 and on his father's death settled permanently at Nunappleton, leaving the family business to a cousin. The Ibbetsons were also well-established in the Leeds cloth trade and influential in local politics. Though his father had purchased the manors of Denton and Askwith, the first baronet, in contrast to Sir William Milner, was an active businessman with an estimated annual turnover of £25,000. Indeed, only after his award, in 1748, was he elected to the Corporation and appointed Mayor. He was later involved in coalmining, turnpike schemes, land tax remittance, and the Aire and Calder Navigation, as well as having more conventional investments in the funds. He also improved the Denton estate and served as High Sheriff. The variety of his activities persuaded him to convert the family business into a partnership but he never relinquished his own interest.[58]

Two other families operated in Hull. Originally from Cumberland yeoman stock, the Sykes had long been merchants in Leeds before the brothers William and Daniel settled at Hull in the mid seventeenth century. Daniel's son, Richard, married the heiress of a local businessman, thereby acquiring the Sledmere estate for his family. Both he and his heir and namesake, however, continued in business as leading importers of iron and iron-ore from Germany and Sweden. They were also concerned in whaling and among the promoters of the Hull Dock Company. The younger Richard Sykes died without issue and was succeeded by his brother, the Revd Mark, who was created baronet in 1783, and under whom the estate and merchant house parted company. Business inclinations remained, however, for the second baronet was co-founder of a bank which financed agricultural development in the East Riding. The commercial pedigree of the Etheringtons was shorter and less distinguished. Both the first baronet and his father sailed as master-mariners before entering business on their own account. They established themselves in local politics and purchased land in the East Riding and the Isle of Axholme. Created baronet in 1775, Sir Henry eventually became something of a father-figure in the merchant community. He commuted to Hull from his country house at Ferriby, and is reputed to have sat in the attic of his town house with a telescope watching for the safe arrival of his ships.[59]

First noticeable after the Restoration, this tendency for wealth to become more important than pedigree in the allocation of baronetcies was furthered by the revolution of 1688. The political outlook and influence of nominees assumed paramount importance. Because political success was rarely achieved without substantial private means, newcomers to the order were, almost without exception, extremely wealthy. Purely personal factors continued to operate but inevitably reflected the public attitudes of the ruling oligarchy. For after the revolution the initiative in the management of the honours system passed from the Crown to its ministers, forming one strand in an immensely wide and tangled web of patronage.[60] Thus, it was the political power of the Milners and the Etheringtons in Leeds and Hull respectively which was honoured, not their wealth, though the two were inextricably intertwined. Sir William Lowther of Marske was nominated when seeking to capitalize on the political influence of his relatives in the north-west. Subsequently he and his son represented Lancaster at Westminster for forty-three years. Besides his standing in Leeds Sir William Lowther of Swillington was the major burgage holder in Pontefract. First returned there as M.P. in 1715, the year of his baronetcy, he voted regularly with the administration thereafter and controlled the constituency for the rest of his life. Through the influence of his future father-in-law the Earl of Carlisle, Sir Thomas Robinson of Rokeby was elected M.P. for Morpeth in 1727. He regularly supported the government, was created baronet in 1731, and later obtained various offices both at home and abroad. Some politicians, like Charles Turner M.P. for York 1768–83, clung obstinately to their independence. The descendant of a London woollen manufacturer who bought a North Riding estate, Turner had extensive property and influence both there and on Teesside. A Whig, though self-confessedly an 'old-fashioned' one, he eventually accepted a baronetcy from Rockingham who had constantly solicited his support but only occasionally received it. Sir Charles explained that his acceptance was 'to commemorate the era of a virtuous Minister and Administration . . . and not from any impulse of personal vanity or desire of title'.[61] Few contemporaries could have voiced such sentiments; still fewer would have believed them.

As the political situation grew less fluid the price of baronetcies rose. Their cost was usually expressed in terms of the quality of personal connections or the eminence of public service. Sir John Silvester-Smith, descended from the London blacksmith who made the chain across the Thames in the 1660s, owed his award to his mother-in-law, the sister of the Archbishop of Canterbury. Sir Henry Ibbetson's baronetcy recognized his efforts as High Sheriff to counteract the Jacobite rebellion of 1745. The Sykes' award was first offered to Christopher (justly famous for his reclamation of the Wolds) who successfully petitioned to alter the grant in his father's favour.[62] Three of the families honoured for professional and public services had previously lost or neglected their status as landed gentry. For them the wheel of fortune came full circle. The Wombwells, after expanding their estate during Elizabeth's reign, had to alienate much of it owing to their extravagance and unsuccessful litigation. Later heirs established legal practices in Leeds, while Roger Wombwell (1708–40) was a Barnsley grocer. His eldest son, George, joined a commercial partnership in London, became a Director and ultimately Chairman of the East India Company, and M.P. for Huntingdon. Amassing his wealth from government victualling contracts, he was a staunch Parliamentary supporter of the administration and devoted a large part of his profits to re-purchasing the Wombwell estate. In 1778, after subscribing £40,000 to a government loan, he was created baronet. Though they purchased the manor of Monk Bretton in 1610, the Wood family held insufficient property to remain among the leisured class. After dabbling in iron manufacture they too established a law practice – in Barnsley. The four sons of attorney Francis Wood (1696–1775) went into the Church, the East India Company, the Navy, and the Army respectively. Having made his fortune in Canton, the second son, Francis, returned to England and married an East Riding heiress. His baronetcy in 1784 was granted with appropriate remainders to commemorate the brilliant naval career of his younger brother, Charles, who had died of battle wounds in the East Indies two years earlier. Finally, the Coghills who in the early seventeenth century were minor gentry of Coghill Hall near Knaresborough. After the Restoration and without relinquishing his Yorkshire property John Coghill pursued a legal career in Ireland, becoming a Master in Chancery there. His son turned to politics and, after holding a variety of offices, was appointed Chancellor of the Irish Exchequer. His sole heiress left her property to a cousin, John Cramer, provided he assumed the name of Coghill, which he did. Though Irish M.P. for Belturbet for many years, Cramer-Coghill reintroduced the family to Coghill Hall before his death in 1790, having been created baronet of the English order in 1778.[54]

Thus by the end of the eighteenth century most baronetcies

TABLE I

The Yorkshire Baronetage: Creations, 1611–1800

1611–20	13	1681–90	3	1741–50	1
1621–30	8	1691–1700	2	1751–60	–
1631–40	4	1701–10	–	1761–70	–
1641–50	19	1711–20	3	1771–80	3
1651–60	12	1721–30	–	1781–90	5
1661–70	15	1731–40	1	1791–1800	1
1671–80	3				

Source: *CB*.

were obtained through connection with those who had patronage at their disposal or, more directly, by conspicuous success
in one of the several branches of the public service; whereas
when the order was founded in 1611 baronetcies had been
designed to be granted as of right, according to precisely
defined criteria which had more to do with breeding, wealth,
and private station than with public position or performance. In
the intervening period the factors governing nominations
altered continually with a majority of creations being determined by frankly political considerations, which likewise
changed dramatically from time to time. One consequence of
these developments was the marked fluctuation in the numbers
of baronets created over the decades. Following an initial flurry
of creations under James I, many baronetcies were granted by
Charles I in an attempt to confirm, win, or reward support
during the months preceding or succeeding the outbreak of the
Civil War. Charles II was even more lavish, using grants of
baronetcy as one means of consolidating his position in the
years following his restoration. However, relatively few
baronetcies were created from the later seventeenth century.
The oft-repeated claim, that numerous politically motivated
grants would devalue the honours system and lead to a fall in
the demand for honours, had long proved correct; though only
latterly, under George III, was this argument advanced by the
Crown as a justification for a general restriction of creations of
title.

A further consequence of the manner in which the order was
manipulated was that an exceedingly varied selection of
individuals and families was admitted to it. As a group they
came from many types of background, pursued a host of
economic activities, and adopted a whole spectrum of attitudes
towards their role in public life. A significant proportion of
them were not long-established members of the gentry and
some were economically insubstantial by any criterion. Subsequent to their admittance to the order, as is already apparent,
not all of them met with success; while for various reasons the
existence of a number of baronetcies was distinctly transitory.
On the other hand twelve of the families concerned were sufficiently wealthy and influential to gain access to the peerage, and
many more were throughout this period and beyond among the

landed élite. The evidence of the sheer variety of individuals and families who acceded to the baronetage runs counter to the suggestion, fostered by genealogists and antiquarians and scarcely qualified by later writers, that in studying English history of the seventeenth and eighteenth centuries titles can be used as a convenient means of identifying particular levels of the economic and social strata. In reality, at least in Yorkshire, the order of baronets was characterized by a wide-ranging and growing diversity.

Whether this was true of other areas and other titles must remain a matter for speculation, though the evidence presented here would suggest that it was, at least below the level of the peerage. It is important for present purposes, however, to stress that the pattern of this group's fortunes as outlined below was not predetermined by the manner in which the group was chosen, as would undoubtedly have been the case had record survival, almost invariably a reflection of success, been the chief criterion. Examination of the fortunes of the baronetage may be relied upon to reveal a broadly representative, rather than a predictably uniform, picture of life as experienced in the middling and upper echelons of landed society during this period.

3. LANDED INCOME AND THE ECONOMIC ENVIRONMENT

Clearly not all these families were primarily dependent on income from land. Nevertheless, on admittance to the baronetage the majority owned substantial real estate. Landed incomes consisted mainly of rents, agricultural involvement though large being essentially indirect. Policies were influenced by various factors, not least by national economic trends. Together with extensive sales of Crown and monastic property, the price rise of the century before 1640 boosted both the size and the wealth of the landed gentry. After the dislocation of the war years and a brief boom in the early 1660s the rise in agricultural prices halted. Thereafter a trend of stable and fluctuating prices was only broken decisively in the late 1740s by bad harvests and outbreaks of cattle plague. The subsequent rise in population produced substantial increases in prices which, with some breaks, persisted into the nineteenth century. Thus, much of the period from the mid seventeenth century to the mid

eighteenth century was one of comparative agricultural depression. The main effect of this depression on landowners was
the sluggish growth of income from rents. Arrears became
much more common; and rent improvement proved difficult
and at times impossible. To the individual landowner, however, regional conditions were as important as national trends.
In some respects prospects in the North were perhaps more
favourable than elsewhere. The area was more attuned to pas-
toral or mixed farming than to arable, and the price of meat was
consistently more buoyant than that of cereals. Compared with
some parts of the country a greater proportion of land had yet to
be worked effectively or, indeed, at all. There was untapped
potential for the more extensive, non-arable types of production. In addition remoteness and relative underdevelopment
had allowed old-established practices to remain fairly widespread and this provided opportunities for raising incomes by
increasing efficiency. Moreover, local commercial and industrial development tended to reduce restraints on agriculture,
providing new sources of demand for food and raw materials,
and additional avenues of investment and entrepreneurship.
None of this is to suggest that northern agriculture escaped
the depression. There was widespread hardship in the late
1660s, the 1680s, and in the second quarter of the eighteenth
century.[64] As the case-studies below illustrate, existing
rents remained stable for long periods and were occasionally
reduced.

The degree to which incomes were affected by trends in
prices depended not only on the nature and extent of agricultural involvement, but also on the size and position of estates.
Few were as compact as the Boyntons' property, whose land all
lay in the north of the East Riding between their seat at Barmston and that only a couple of miles away at Burton Agnes,
which they inherited in 1654. Most holdings, though not
necessarily comprising a greater acreage, were scattered over a
wider area. Many families owned estates outside Yorkshire;
some in several counties both north and south of the Trent.
John van de Bempdé, grandfather of the first baronet Sir
Richard, had estates in Yorkshire, Buckinghamshire, Kent,
Middlesex, Lincolnshire, 'and elsewhere'. Despite his sale of an
estate in Lancashire in 1721, Thomas Belasyse still had five

'chief seats' to fall back on: Newburgh Priory and Allerton Castle in Yorkshire, Sutton in Cheshire, St. Thomas in Staffordshire, and a property in Hanover Square, London.[65] The economic conditions governing such widely dispersed estates varied enormously. More significantly, the wealth derived from them was so great as to render their owners immune from all but the worst disasters. Besides huge estates, John Savile of Methley left his successor personal estate worth £14,267 in 1659; this included more than £10,500 in ready money. Fifty years earlier the future Earl of Strafford had been provided with property worth over £4,000 a year. Along with several other families the Wentworths acquired property in Ireland. Situated in the least developed part of the British Isles in the seventeenth century, these estates greatly increased in value thereafter. By the 1790s those of the Dawnays of Cowick, Viscounts Downe were worth £7,000 a year, while as early as 1748 Rockingham was drawing £8,000 annually from his Irish estate. The Wandesfords of Kirklington, Viscounts Castlecomer lived permanently in Ireland from the 1690s, so valuable had their property there become. The Osbornes of Kiveton, Dukes of Leeds also acquired vast estates and a peerage; exceptionally, their property was almost entirely confined to Yorkshire.[66] Most families owned much smaller estates and were correspondingly less secure. By the mid seventeenth century some already had alternative sources of income; others diversified at a later stage. However, in more than one sense, the middle years of the seventeenth century were a watershed for all but the richest owners. During two decades of revolutionary change self-confidence often gave way to a pervading sense of unease. The trend in agricultural prices after the Restoration sharpened this incentive to careful management.

Earlier, partly because agricultural prices had led inflation, northern landowners had generally kept landed incomes ahead of expenditure: by converting copyhold into leasehold, replacing entry fines with economic rents, consolidating strips in open-fields, enclosing both there and on common land, and by themselves engaging in farming.[67] In later decades many of these processes continued. Indeed, in the mid seventeenth century endeavours frequently remained hamstrung by the shortsighted policies of previous generations. In 1644 Sir

George Savile of Thornhill inherited an estate of more than 50,000 acres which, because his great-grandfather had preferred entry fines to economic rents, produced an annual rental of only £7,000. On smaller estates this type of situation was more problematical especially where fines were associated with leases for lives; such leases terminated intermittently and often only after lengthy periods. In 1641 Sir Richard Hawksworth, whose estate was then worth £1,127 a year, believed that 'if all leases were expired . . . . my estate is worth per annum £1,400 or better'. His annual rental rose to only £1,276 during the following decade. Circumstances forced some owners to pursue conflicting objectives. Short of capital, Sir John Reresby levied entry fines in the 1660s, though by satisfying his immediate needs he automatically exacerbated long-term problems. Recusant gentry, under threat from the authorities and more in need of additional income than most, sometimes preferred to maintain their paternalistic position in an inefficient manorial system. Labour services, food rents, and the like were more common on their estates. Local influence and control were thereby prolonged, but literally at a price.[68] Certain alternatives were no longer as viable as they had been. Fluctuating prices not only stabilized rents but made direct farming less profitable. Always relatively limited in scope, it had nevertheless been 'a valuable weapon in the Price Revolution'.[69] After 1660 demesne farms diminished in size and estate correspondence bristled with warnings against keeping land 'in hand'. Nor could income be as readily increased by estate expansion as previously. Though agricultural profits declined, social and political factors gradually boosted land prices; the purely economic return on capital invested in this way fell proportionately. Other possibilities, such as enclosure and changes in land utilization, were costly, managerially difficult, and above all liable to provoke legal retaliation. Distrust of lawyers, which was endemic, was exceeded only by the demand for their services. In the prevailing economic circumstances, however, few landowners were deterred by threats. Moreover, as agriculture became more oriented towards animal husbandry, enclosure was more frequently achieved by agreement, purchase, or on request. Much land was under-utilized, many families owning property in what were, agriculturally, frontier areas. As late as the 1730s, for example, the steward of an estate on the flat, fertile land between the Wolds and the Derwent was instructed to 'contrive . . . a farm or two in the remotest parts of the lordship'.[70] Elsewhere, on the Wolds, in Holderness, and among the uplands of north and west Yorkshire, the scope for permanently increasing income by such means was greater. However, agricultural improvement was by nature a slow process, and before the mid eighteenth century rise in prices was only rarely achieved on an impressive scale.

Against these difficulties have to be set those legal changes of the early to mid seventeenth century – the emergence of strict settlements and the recognition of the equity of mortgage redemption – which made landownership more secure. Moreover, the abolition of wardship in 1646 reduced outgoings, increased control over property, and enabled the beneficial aspects of minorities to operate. None of these developments, however, positively raised landed incomes, whereas from the 1690s net income was reduced by government taxation. Although the long-term effects of the land tax have been exaggerated, it posed severe problems in the years immediately following its introduction; and where tenants were required to pay the tax the scope for rent improvement was further reduced. Many more landowners began to employ full-time, salaried stewards (previously engaged only by the owners of the largest estates) whose primary task to begin with was the collection of rents and arrears. The advent of the land tax boosted their numbers and, almost incidentally, led to the growth of skills and experience upon which successful management later came to depend. For rentiers the road to success throughout this period lay via increased efficiency. Most were well-placed to reap the profits which accrued later in the eighteenth century. Before then their capacity to increase profits from purely agricultural activities was limited.

Though the virtues of income diversification were obvious, not all landowners were either willing or able to adapt their affairs to the degree that the situation required. Much property offered little beyond its farming potential. Even timber resources, in heavy demand for fuel and construction work, were scarce on the Wolds, the north Yorkshire moors, and parts of the Pennines. Those who acquired estate and title through commercial activity were usually anxious to break with the past, albeit at the cost of narrowing their economic base. Where property contained mineral deposits a formidable array of problems sometimes discouraged exploitation. Equipment was expensive, labour and management skills scarce, and marketing costs high. Returns on investment were comparatively slow and largely unpredictable, with ultimate success frequently depending as much on luck as on judgement. By contrast, moneylending was much safer. Nevertheless, following recent legal changes and against a background of falling interest rates, circumstances in this area moved gradually in favour of borrowers. Finally, although public finance developed rapidly during this period, it provided secure rather than lucrative returns. Yet a majority of those families who produced heirs were economically successful over the period as a whole. For some this was because they were exceedingly wealthy at the outset. Others already possessed a broadly based, if relatively insubstantial, economy. Another consideration, however, was that in the longer term the nature and location of many estates provided opportunities for increasing non-agricultural incomes.

Farmland adjacent to urban areas yielded higher than average rents. Sir Henry Slingsby, for example, owned arable on the outskirts of Knaresborough which he let for 18s an acre in 1640. Urban property was even more profitable. By contemporary standards Yorkshire had a high proportion of urban and suburban areas, most of which grew during this period. Always the nub of the machinery of local government, York also became a leading social centre in the early eighteenth century, as to a lesser extent did Harrogate, Scarborough, Knaresborough, and Ripon. Moreover, as commercial and industrial development gathered momentum during the early eighteenth century the West Riding towns of Leeds, Halifax, Bradford, Huddersfield, and Sheffield encroached more rapidly on the surrounding countryside, while the port of Hull gradually responded to the needs of the entire area east of the Pennines. As has already been demonstrated, families involved in commerce often exploited their wealth and local influence to obtain property in the leading commercial centres. Many older-established families already owned urban property or subsequently acquired it through purchase or inheritance – the

Robinsons of Newby in York, the Hildyards in Hull, the Pennymans of Ormesby in Beverley, and the Ramsdens in Huddersfield, to name but a few.[71]

Such property consisted not only of valuable residential and commercial premises, but also in many instances of industrial plant and machinery. Before they purchased the Badsworth estate in the 1650s most of the Bright family's property was situated in the Sheffield area. Besides agricultural land it comprised houses, shops, collieries, smithies, cutlers' wheels and wheels for scythe-grinding, and a brickyard. Throughout this period the Ramsdens tightened their grip on the centre of Huddersfield, half of which they had secured cheaply from the Crown in 1599. They acquired forges, collieries, and fulling mills, engaged in extensive enclosure and housebuilding, and in 1671 obtained royal permission to organize a market in the town. In 1766 they built the first Cloth Hall, extending this by a storey in 1780. The diversity of the property which their neighbours, the Beaumonts of Whitley, owned nearby can be gauged from an analysis of the occupational distribution of their tenantry. Of 133 tenants whose occupations are known, only thirty-eight described themselves as farmers, yeomen, or husbandmen. There were fifty-nine clothiers, six shoemakers, four blacksmiths, three carpenters, three linen-websters, two wallers, two tanners, two tailors, two alehouse keepers, a labourer, a skinner, a cordwainer, a glover, a butcher, a mason, and a collier, besides several millers and gentlemen. In the vicinity of Leeds urban and suburban property changed hands more frequently and at higher prices than overall national trends would suggest. This pattern of activity was perhaps true elsewhere in Yorkshire and not merely associated with the commercial classes. The Calverleys, for instance, accelerated out of their difficulties by selling land inherited in Cumberland and purchasing, among other property, several fulling mills near Bradford. Other owners were under similar pressure to extend their operations in and into such areas to escape the consequences of insecure and falling profits in the countryside.[72]

For some the need to diversify encouraged the exploitation of mineral and other resources. In the case of timber increased demand provided additional stimulus. South Yorkshire owners found themselves in a particularly favourable position. There much land was heavily wooded, while local demand, especially from ironmasters, was continuous and high. The Wortleys had enormous stands of timber on Wharncliffe Chase and around Pilley; the Rockinghams had more than 1,000 acres of woodland on their Wentworth Woodhouse estate alone. Compared with other forms of economic activity there were fewer seasonal or other limitations on exploitation. Moreover, because the purchaser usually shouldered all the trouble and expense of felling, costs were reduced to a minimum. Profits were correspondingly heavy, demand being so great that payments were frequently made long in advance of cutting. Sir John Reresby had no difficulty in obtaining pre-payment of £7 an acre for his timber. In the same period the Saviles of Thornhill were earning some £250 a year from wood sales, and had reserves whose capital value was estimated at £10,000. Nevertheless, by the mid seventeenth century management often remained rudimentary. Income from this source might be large – £15,000 to the Duke of Leeds in a single year – but was also sporadic. The result was the increasing employment of timber bailiffs who, besides maintaining existing resources and phasing exploitation, engaged in systematic re-afforestation. In 1723 a scheme for a twenty-year felling cycle was inaugurated on the Rockingham estates; by the mid eighteenth century the Smithsons of Stanwick were planting more than 12,000 trees annually on a single property. Only a minority of owners could boast operations of this size and complexity. Several, indeed, owned no timber worth speaking of. For those who did, however, policies were implemented where virtually none had existed before.[73]

The extractive industries required much heavier capital investment, while profits were far more elusive. Yet there was a quickening of interest in such activity: during this period operations included coal, lead, iron, and copper mining, alum production, and quarrying. Those looking for land to buy were attracted to property containing minerals. When the Lowthers bought Swillington and Great Preston in 1655 they noted that 'there is in it rich coal mines and lime quarries which is of good value there'. Walter Calverley passed a similar comment after purchasing leave to enclose common land at Idle: 'I think it may

be of advantage in time, for a great part of the wastes are coal.'
Many pits were sunk on waste but even where seams ran under
farmland mining might be given priority. In 1718 Viscount
Castlecomer's agent reported that tenants at Hipswell were
'mighty uneasy at their parting with their old farms and entering on their new ones'. Plans to mine lead and copper had
necessitated this reorganization.[74] The most crucial decision
facing owners concerned the precise nature of their involvement. Some, like the Kayes at Woodsome, went no further than
producing coal for personal domestic purposes. The majority,
while allowing large-scale development, preferred to lease
mining rights. This usually involved them in the provision of
some fixed capital; besides rent they in turn were often allotted
a percentage of the commodity produced. Where, as in much of
south Yorkshire, resources were varied exploitation might be
integrated. In 1658 Sir Edward Wortley granted a nine-year
lease to a London merchant, providing the latter with ore-
mining rights, the use of two forges, and an annual allowance of
1,800 cords of logwood from his timber stands in return for a
rent of £510 a year.[75] Though potentially more profitable,
direct involvement was riskier, not least because increased production meant wider marketing at a time when bulk transport
was tortuously slow and exceedingly costly. It was partly for
this reason that the Brights terminated their extensive lead
production in the 1640s.[76] Nevertheless, West Riding owners
were comparatively favourably situated. Few estates there were
entirely devoid of exploitable resources of some kind, while the
structure of the local economy encouraged their development.
Nor was enterprise lacking elsewhere. Sir Solomon Swale failed
miserably attempting to mine lead in Swaledale (one of the most
sparsely populated and inaccessible of regions), but in the 1660s
the Cholmelys' share in the alum works which they established
at Whitby yielded £2,500 a year, while later the Turners were
heavily engaged in mining lead in the North Riding and on
Teesside. Some of the largest and most successful concerns
were outside Yorkshire. The Wandesfords mined lead and
copper in the West Riding but after moving to their Irish estate
mined coal and iron, and were involved in iron and textile
manufacturing too. Three other families promoted huge collieries on Tyneside. Sidney Wortley-Montagu used his wife's

fortune to acquire leases of church lands in Northumberland and Durham on favourable terms and by the end of Anne's reign was one of the greatest coal owners of his day. Though neither as successful nor as closely involved, the Milbankes drew a major part of their income from mining leases; while Sir Walter Calverley's inheritance of the Blackett estate included some of the biggest coalmines in the country. By the mid eighteenth century his family were also drawing £5,000 a year from lead mines in the same vicinity.[77] If not unknown, spectacular success was unrepresentative. On the other hand a growing commitment to these alternatives to more traditional forms of ownership was evident.

In marketing their products some families became involved in shipping and commerce. A few owned craft which operated on the river networks and coastal routes, transporting provisions and other necessities for themselves and neighbours. Occasionally part shares in vessels of greater tonnage were purchased. Normally, however, titled gentry did not venture into these avenues of economic activity, where convention was at its strongest and grew perhaps more rigid as the substantive differences between landed gentlemen and merchants faded. One might outlive commercial origins, marry a merchant's daughter, encourage brothers and younger sons in trade, and even dabble speculatively on the fringes thereof; but not, acceptably, proceed much further. With few and explicable exceptions – Lewis, Etherington, Ibbetson, and some Tyneside coal-owners – this unwritten law was respected, if only because in most instances personal aspirations were synonymous with social requirements. Attitudes towards transport development were somewhat, though not entirely, dissimilar. Land-ownership provoked a natural interest which was, however, often matched by a disinclination to risk capital where experience had yet to tread. Several families were connected with turnpikes, dock companies, and the Don, Derwent, and Aire and Calder navigation schemes, but apart from Milner, Ibbetson, and Etherington financial involvement was slight. Though personal interests were safeguarded, public functions discharged, and token gestures made, participation rarely went further than this. More worthy of attention but quite unrewarding were churches, hospitals, and a variety of other public works. Private benevolence was generally deemed more appropriate to dynastic endeavour than public subscription.[78]

Pure finance, in contrast, was one sphere where gentry of all descriptions were deeply engaged. This stemmed inevitably from their position among the largest producers and consumers of capital, though their role was increasingly shared with the commercial classes and, not least, with the government. Recognition of the equity of mortgage redemption – the mortgagor's right to retain his security as long as interest was forthcoming – made large-scale, long-term borrowing safer and, by lowering interest rates, easier. Moreover, the peculiar circumstances of the Interregnum produced permanent expansion and growing sophistication in the money market. Interest rates, which were then around 6 per cent, fell by a further 2 per cent during the following century. Short-term credit facilities also multiplied. Landowners exchanged capital not only with each other but increasingly with farmers, merchants, industrialists, and bankers. Together with the emergence of specialized services both in the provinces and in the capital these developments boosted borrowing capacity and with it the security of landed economies. Though equally secure, lending became progressively less remunerative. In one important respect, however, it was often preferred to other forms of investment. From the mid seventeenth century mortgagees had fewer opportunities of benefiting from foreclosures. None the less, channelling loans to impecunious neighbours often resulted in debts being discharged by sale of property to the creditor. This could never be guaranteed and, even if successful, might be a lengthy process. But rising land prices and a prevailing desire to consolidate estates made it a common policy. Public finance would appear to have been only slightly less popular with the more substantial landowners in Yorkshire. Visits to London became progressively more frequent after the Restoration and in the early eighteenth century many families engaged the services of agents or bankers in the capital, who actively encouraged investment in the 'funds'. The speculative fever of the period 1690–1720 had a considerable impact; and thereafter the National Debt and the stock market constituted important avenues of investment for surplus capital. A growing sophistication in financial matters made the majority of substantial landowners more resourceful, and the circumstances in which their economies operated much more flexible.[79]

Many of these economies gradually became more diverse partly because fresh opportunities existed, but also because the prevailing economic situation prompted new departures. While owners in south and west Yorkshire enjoyed what one of them described as a 'goodly heritage in a plentiful country' their advantages should not be exaggerated.[80] Estates there, though generally of more varied potential, tended to be smaller than those elsewhere: on acceding to the baronetage the main estates of no less than forty-eight of these ninety-three families were in the West Riding. Moreover, the benefits accruing from the more vibrant economy of that region were shared. Their effect on agriculture in the East and North Ridings, as urban and suburban populations looked further afield for sustenance, is especially evident. By the end of the 1680s animal husbandry constituted the backbone of Yorkshire farming almost irrespective of region. Touring some years later Defoe remarked on the degree to which North Riding farmers specialized for markets further south; while during the first four decades of the eighteenth century sheep flocks doubled in size on the East Riding Wolds, where the Legards and later the Sykes achieved renown as landlords. The estates of the Winns and the Smithsons were noted for cattle production and Sir Marmaduke Wyvill became known as 'a great man for sheep'.[81] By 1760 those families who had survived were ready to take advantage of rising prices precisely because earlier, if less spectacular, opportunities had not been neglected.

4. POLITICS, SOCIETY, AND EXPENDITURE

Because effective government in England depended on the support and energy of the landed élite, landed wealth and high politics were for long intertwined. Only during this period, however, did the more substantial landowners acquire a virtual monopoly of political influence. The Civil War and Interregnum fundamentally altered their aspirations. Thereafter, having witnessed the reality of revolution, they sought to preserve, indeed to incorporate themselves within, a new establishment. Success in this endeavour profoundly influenced the development of their economies and way of life.

Though initially mollified by the benevolence of James I, leading Yorkshire gentry were involved both locally and nationally in the events which progressively divided King and Parliament during the early seventeenth century. They were led by two rivals, Sir John Savile of Howley and Sir Thomas Wentworth of Wentworth Woodhouse. Rooted in personal animosity, their struggle for power centred increasingly on broad political issues: Savile identified himself with the Court and Wentworth with the Country party. Until 1628 most leading gentry sided with Wentworth. However, following the assassination of Savile's patron, the Duke of Buckingham, Wentworth, always a believer in strong central government, established a position at Court and became a major promoter of government policy. While some of his associates, notably Christopher Wandesford, Sir William Pennyman of Marske, and Sir Edward Osborne, followed in Wentworth's footsteps, most leading gentry remained in opposition; several ultimately fell foul of authority.[82]

The Chaloner brothers had already been alienated by the Crown's refusal to pay arrears of an annuity granted to their father on his surrender of a patent for alum manufacture. Along with Wentworth himself, Sir John Hotham and Sir William Constable of Flamborough had been imprisoned in 1627 for non-payment of forced loans. Sir William, Thomas Mauleverer, and William Ingleby were summoned before the Privy Council three years later for not complying with the scheme for knighthood composition. Sir David Foulis's criticisms of the establishment were punished in 1633. On failing to account for sums previously due to him as royal cofferer, he was fined £8,000 and confined to the Fleet prison for seven years. Others were dealt with summarily though not as severely. Henry Belasyse was imprisoned in 1631 for publicly insulting Wentworth, while in 1632 Sir Thomas Gower was confined for defying the Council of the North. In 1635 Brian Stapleton of Myton was dismissed from the peace commission for failing to pay a muster master's fee. After refusing to disclose the content of their recent speeches in Parliament, Sir John Hotham and Henry Belasyse were committed to the Fleet in 1640, and Sir Hugh Cholmely and Sir William Savile of Thornhill forbidden to leave London. Disaffection stemmed not only from arbitrary government, particularly in regard to taxation, but also from unpopular policies in religious matters. North Riding gentry were incensed by Wentworth's efficient levying of recusancy fines. At the other extreme Sir William Constable of Flamborough and Sir Matthew Boynton were sufficiently disenchanted with their lot as Puritans to consider emigrating to New England. They chose Holland instead and by 1640 were domiciled in Arnhem.[83]

With the outbreak of civil war direct involvement in public affairs increased dramatically. Although several of those who had previously clashed with authority sided with Parliament, the bulk of the wealthier Yorkshire gentry were Royalists. Most of them were subsequently penalized by Parliament, though to widely varying degrees. Not one Royalist family from this group suffered irreparable damage, while only a handful permanently lost or alienated real estate, or became very heavily indebted through paying fines or repurchasing property. Yet the impact of developments in the short-term was considerable. In various ways events reduced families' control over their private concerns and, not infrequently, removed it altogether, albeit only temporarily. Yorkshire saw much of the fighting and the consequent destruction and dislocation of life, property, and affairs were substantial. The contemporary situation of seventeen of these families is not recorded. A further twelve were either already extinct or with heirs too young to be involved. Of the rest a high proportion, thirty-four, took up arms – twenty-seven for the Crown and seven for Parliament. Many others, too old to fight, declared unequivocally for one side or the other. The consequences included the death by execution or while fighting of seven heads of families or prospective heirs, and the serious injury of at least three others. A further nine individuals were imprisoned for varying periods, during which one of them died. As many again were either banished or went into voluntary exile abroad. Numerous families were separated by force of circumstances and obliged to spend months and, in some cases, years away from their homes and estates. Their property meanwhile was subject to plunder, free quarter, and other damaging features of the conflict. Finally, though often reduced or circumvented, the exactions of Parliament deprived many of significant amounts of capital over a comparatively short period of time.[84]

The variety and cumulative effect of events can only be adequately appreciated by scrutiny of individual case-histories. Sir John Goodrick, originally sympathetic to Parliament, switched allegiance on receiving a baronetcy in 1641, though an uncle and two cousins fought against the Crown. Sir John served as a captain under the Earl of Newcastle and was seriously wounded in the attack on Bradford in December 1642. Taken prisoner shortly afterwards, he was confined in Manchester and then in the Tower, during which time his young wife died. He escaped in 1645 but was quickly recaptured, finally being released in March 1646 and fined a total of £1,650. Despite assistance from Parliamentarian relatives, he had to sell some land to raise this money and as Hunsingore Hall had been destroyed in the fighting he travelled abroad until 1650. Only after a second marriage in 1653 did he re-establish himself and his family. The case of the Wandesfords is perhaps more pertinent for they did not fight and emerged at the Restoration with their estates intact. Christopher Wandesford died in 1640 while on government service in Ireland, where his widow remained until the outbreak of the Irish rebellion in 1641. The family then sailed to Chester where they lived until after the unsuccessful siege of the city in July 1643. Only after a further period with in-laws at Snape Castle did they return home to Kirklington. Their first dispute with Parliament concerned the right of presentation to the rectory there. Then, on refusing to subscribe to the Solemn League and Covenant or swear allegiance to Parliament, George Wandesford, Christopher's heir, was forced to flee in disguise to the Dales, and the rest of the family to move to additional property at Hipswell. Kirklington was sequestered and granted to a relative who was also a substantial family creditor. The sequestration was rescinded in 1654, by which time no rent had been received from the Irish estate at Castlecomer for thirteen years. Indeed, several years passed before that property became at all remunerative.[85] The experience of neither the Goodricks nor the Wandesfords is representative: and the sheer variety of individual circumstances makes generalization difficult; but, if the long-term consequences of composition, sequestration, and forfeiture have in the past been overestimated, contemporary disruption has, in contrast, been neglected.

Such disruption heightened apprehension as to the aims and motives of the victors. In retrospect it is clear that in punishing Royalists Parliament was more concerned to clear its growing burden of debt than with any desire to cripple its opponents. At the time, however, developments appeared in a quite different light. Even where a particular Royalist's situation remained virtually undisturbed, the course of public events placed him under a threat which only gradually diminished in the years before 1660. Sir John Hotham, initially among the most active Parliamentarians, altered his allegiance through fear of anarchy. In 1643 he believed that 'the necessitous people . . . will presently rise in mighty numbers, and . . . will set up for themselves to the utter ruin of all the nobility and gentry'.[86] Fifteen years later, when addressing the mob from his scaffold, Sir Henry Slingsby voiced the feelings of many of his fellow landowners: 'time was when we were the head and you the feet, but now you are the head and we the feet'.[87] Neither comment was realistic, but they help to explain the enthusiasm and, above all, the relief which greeted the Restoration. As before 1642 some families, such as the Brights and the Marwoods, exploited the opportunities provided by changing political circumstances. Others, previously neutral or of altered allegiance, emerged in the less turbulent 1650s. For the majority, however, in the words of Sir John Reresby, 'there was little means of improvement'. On returning to Thribergh from his studies at Cambridge and Gray's Inn in 1653, he found 'the nobility and gentlemen of the best rank and estates living retired in the country to avoid the jealousies of the then suspicious government of every act or word that could be construed in favour of the royal family'. Unable to bear this atmosphere, he went abroad, being careful whenever he met exiled members of the English Court to use an assumed name to avoid possible adverse consequences at home.[88]

At the Restoration the primary aim of the landed élite was to re-establish the way of life to which they felt entitled. Consequently, though the Crown, lords, and bishops returned, the various institutions which had coerced the gentry prior to 1642 were not restored. The Courts of Star Chamber, High Commission, and Wards and Liveries remained defunct, as did the Councils of the North and of Wales; and the Privy Council's control over local government was greatly reduced. Leading landowners reinforced their earlier position in the provinces and at Westminster by freeing their localities from more distant and powerful influences. In Yorkshire the boroughs were rapidly brought under their control, while all the successful candidates in the county constituency in the period 1660 to 1760 were from either peerage or baronetage families. Charles II had the Triennial Bill repealed by stealth in 1664 but from 1688 it became impossible to govern without Parliament. In the meantime the gentry were forced to stomach many unpopular policies. Significantly, however, the failure of James II was due, not so much to his policies, as to the way in which he attempted to carry them out. The systematic purging of men of proven wealth and substance from all levels of government was fundamentally intolerable. On the other hand the supremacy of the landed élite after 1688 did not of itself produce political stability. But, while the in-fighting of the period 1689–1720 was more intense than ever before, it was conducted on lines broadly acceptable since the Restoration. The result was oligarchical government through the medium of a substantially landed Parliament. Conducted by the few, the system gained the increasing, if occasionally grudging, acceptance of the many.[89]

Acceptance was won not only by constitutional and policy changes, but also by growth in the executive which brought many more landowners into active participation in government. The frustrations and hardships of the Interregnum generated a massive demand for favour and place in the immediate post-Restoration period. However, the number of creations of baronetcies and the pattern of their distribution indicate Charles II's need to compromise between reward and retribution. Sir Philip Constable of Everingham's relative and steward was grateful for 'good regards from the King by the title of "honest Shirburne"', but many other Royalists were grievously disappointed.[90] 'Finding that nothing came from Court, and that attendance there was chargeable', they 'betook' themselves 'to the country' in the mid 1660s.[91] Yet legislative changes, foreign policy developments, and a growing awareness of government needs gradually boosted the number of posts available to the influential and ambitious. The armed, civil, and diplomatic services were all expanded. By the end of Charles II's reign far more individuals had experienced involvement in public affairs other than at a purely local level than had been the case under his father.

Sir Thomas Belasyse, 2nd Viscount Fauconberg, was appointed Ambassador to Venice, Turin, and Florence in 1669, and Sir Henry Goodrick Envoy Extraordinary to Spain in 1678. Less substantial but welcome opportunities took the Coghills semi-permanently to Ireland and Sir Hugh Cholmely to Tangiers, where he supervised construction of a mole. John Wytham of Goldsborough was raised to the baronetage while serving as Deputy Governor of Barbados. At home Sir Robert Hildyard and Sir Richard Mauleverer became Gentlemen of the Royal Bedchamber. Mauleverer and Sir Henry Goodrick also acquired posts in the army and in tax administration. Sir William Lowther of Swillington became Commissioner of the Customs and Steward of the royal barony of Kendal.[92] Contemporaries, notably Pepys, leave us in no doubt that unofficial earnings were often greater than actual salaries. Consequently, the highest placed executives amassed great wealth. At the Treasury Sir Thomas Osborne, Earl of Danby, obtained enough capital to expand his estate considerably and rebuild Kiveton Hall. Sir George Savile of Thornhill, also ennobled as Marquis of Halifax and occupied successively as Trade Commissioner, Lord Privy Seal, Lord President of the Council, and Chancellor to James II's Queen Consort, was able to build a magnificent town-house in St. James's Square.[93] Such success eased competitive pressures at a lower level of society and acted as a spur to those operating there, where ambitions were pursued no less avidly as Reresby's diary illustrates. Improvident predecessors had left Sir John with little room for financial manoeuvre coupled with an eye for opportunity. His failure to secure a potentially lucrative patent on a steel manufacturing process and, despite considerable effort, a profit of more than £300 from the high shrievalty in 1666–7 led him to avoid the trouble and expense of the peace commission and the risks of a place in the excise farm. In 1678, however, he obtained the governorship of Bridlington Castle at an annual salary of £200.

Although the imprisonment of his patron, the Earl of Danby, 'confirmed me in the opinion that a middle estate was ever the best', his aspirations were moderated rather than entirely deterred. Successful parliamentary elections at Aldborough and York were costly, but on becoming Governor of York at more than £500 a year in 1682 Sir John made a substantial net improvement to his finances.[94]

Amidst the upheavals of James II's reign the expanded executive structure was in danger of disintegration. Following the accession of William III it not only survived but underwent further and spectacular development. Though earlier growth factors continued to operate, this was primarily due to a fundamental realignment of foreign policy which created a huge demand for additional forces, and a rapid expansion of the service and revenue-raising departments of government. 'Offices were created in abundance; next to none, except at Court, were abolished.'[95] Indeed, according to one historian, the modern civil service owes its origin not to the nineteenth-century bureaucratic expansion but to the creation of the government machinery needed to combat France from 1689.[96] Many landowners seized the opportunity which public service gave them of diversifying their incomes. The value of the profits of success in the fight for place has perhaps been underestimated in analyses of upper class economies in the eighteenth century.

Those Yorkshiremen who played a key role in establishing William III were quickly rewarded. The Marquis of Halifax, who with his customary ease had changed sides at the last, crucial moment, was appointed Lord Privy Seal. The Earl of Danby, originally the chief promoter of the marriage between William and Mary, and a signatory of the petition to the former, became Lord President of the Council, Marquis of Carmarthen, and finally Duke of Leeds. His son, Peregrine, was appointed Colonel of the City of London Dragoons, and of the 1st Regiment of Marines. At sea Peregrine progressed from Captain to Rear-Admiral within three years. Sir Henry Goodrick, who had helped Danby to secure York for William, held the post of Lieutenant-General of the Ordnance 1689–1702 and joined the Privy Council. In the new political environment certain families achieved major public office for the first time.

Sir Godfrey Copley became Commissioner of Public Accounts and Controller of the Army Accounts. Sir William St. Quintin was successively Commissioner of Customs, Commissioner of the Irish Revenue, Lord of the Treasury, Commissioner of the Alienation Office, and Vice-Treasurer, Receiver-General, and Paymaster of Ireland. Sir Thomas Robinson of Rokeby combined a variety of official and unofficial activities. Besides practising as an architect, he served briefly in the army, was Commissioner of the Excise 1735–42, and Governor of Barbados 1742–7.[97]

Like the majority of their most successful contemporaries, all these men enjoyed long careers in Parliament. Moreover, political influence not infrequently enabled one generation to build on the achievement of its predecessor. Although the Hothams were among the most influential families in the county before 1688, their public activities had been confined to local government and backbench criticism in Parliament. Sir Charles Hotham, who succeeded in 1691 and represented Scarborough or Beverley at Westminster from 1695 till his death in 1723, obtained several important army commissions during his career and spent long periods in Scotland, Spain and Portugal. Besides having equally successful military and parliamentary careers, his successor was Groom of the Royal Bedchamber 1727–38 and George II's Special Plenipotentiary in Berlin in 1730–1. Official salaries eventually exceeded the income from his estate.[98] After representing Malton, the county of Yorkshire, and Old Sarum in Parliament between 1689 and 1720 Sir William Strickland's loyalty to the Whig party was rewarded with the post of Commissary-General of the Musters. His son, who in the period 1708–35 sat for Malton, Carlisle, and Scarborough, was successively Commissioner of the Revenue, Lord of the Treasury, Treasurer of the Queen's Household, Privy Councillor, and Secretary of State for War. The second and third baronets Frankland, whose combined parliamentary careers stretched from 1685 to 1747, held perhaps the greatest variety of posts between them. Sir Thomas began as Commissioner of the Exchequer in 1689, was Joint Postmaster-General 1690–1715, and then Commissioner of Customs 1715–18. His successor was appointed Clerk of the Deliveries in the Tower 1714–15, Secretary to the Muster Master General and Clerk of

Deliveries in the Ordnance 1718–22, Commissioner of the Irish Revenue 1724–8, of the Board of Trade 1728–30, and Lord of the Admiralty 1730–41.[99]

Although cumulative success on such a scale was exceptional, these examples indicate only in part the breadth of new opportunities. Major posts in London constituted merely the apex of rapidly expanding government services both there and in the provinces. Before joining the Excise Commission Sir Marmaduke Wyvill served in a lowlier capacity in the Salt Duties Office. Richard Beaumont's unsuccessful efforts to gain a post following the Tory landslide election victory of 1710 centred on that department, the Customs Commission, and the Stamp Office 'which is £300 or £400' a year.[100] Besides his other rewards Sir Henry Goodrick was appointed Treasurer for the collection and disbursement of all taxes in Yorkshire in 1689. The impoverished Sir Bradwardine Jackson was glad to be involved in collecting land taxes in Yorkshire during Anne's reign. Later the Wyvills, Milners, and Ibbetsons all earned substantial sums in local tax administration. On the other hand the Hothams and Sir Thomas Robinson of Rokeby were not alone in being required to travel widely in their official capacities. Posts in the various branches of the Irish executive did not necessarily require residence in Ireland, although as Postmaster-General of Ireland from 1736 to 1754, Sir Marmaduke Wyvill visited the country at regular intervals. Service in the army or navy, which in several families became traditional even for prospective heirs, took many individuals overseas for lengthy periods. A more select group were semipermanently domiciled abroad as members of the diplomatic corps – for example, Edward Wortley-Montagu for three years in Constantinople, Sir John Goodrick for nine years in Stockholm, and Thomas Robinson of Newby for a total of twenty-five years in Paris and Vienna.[101]

A further important aspect of these developments was the increased scope which they provided for those sons who were not prospective heirs. Their lot, which had long been a matter of public controversy, was eased considerably.[102] Sir William Lowther of Swillington, for example, had seven sons who attained their majority. Two inherited property, one became a lawyer, another went into commerce, while no less than three joined the army. Although younger sons of those families who enjoyed most political influence, like the Lowthers, Gowers, and Watson-Wentworths, generally obtained the richest pickings, the situation of the rest was far from bleak. In the 1740s Sir John Ramsden, an independent Whig, had one brother in the Secretary of State's Office, another in the Wine Licence Office, and a third serving as Lieutenant-Governor of Carlisle and Equerry to the King. Occasionally even handicapped sons could be catered for. Because his second son, Hungerford, was born without a right hand, Sir John Bland thought him unsuited to a legal or ecclesiastical career. Instead Sir John bequeathed £2,500, stipulating that it be used to purchase for Hungerford the reversion of a patent place for life. Nor were women completely excluded. Sir John Goodrick's granddaughter, Adeliza, earned £400 a year as seamstress to George III.[103]

From 1688 onwards members of at least half of these families were involved in paid public service of one kind or another. Of the rest, many were extinct, lacked male heirs, were ineligible for office on religious grounds, or were too impoverished to obtain positions of responsibility and prestige. In other words those families who, though eligible and otherwise able, provided no public servants during this period were in a clear minority. Consequently, for many income from non-agricultural sources rose at a time when increased earnings from land were hard to achieve. For some the accretion of additional income was modest. In other instances, however, particularly where several members or generations of families were concerned, income from public sources was considerable, and occasionally dramatic, in its effect. As contemporaries were quick to acknowledge, unofficial earnings continued in many cases to outstrip salaries. When threatened with a second impeachment in 1695 for accepting a *douceur* of 5,000 guineas from the East India Company, the Duke of Leeds stated publicly that 'to receive bribes was a custom characteristic of the age since he had been in public life'.[104] There is little indication thereafter that this and allied conventions fell into disuse.

Other consequences associated with these developments were no less significant. Trips to London and the south had been infrequent during Elizabeth's reign. In the early seventeenth century education at the Inns of Court and attendance at Court and in Parliament had encouraged in some landowners a taste for the metropolis which later they more frequently indulged. Concerned at the implications of their behaviour, the government issued proclamations exhorting gentry to return to their localities. The Civil War and Interregnum shattered this slowly changing routine. Widely dispersed by the events of the 1640s, many landowners were marooned on their estates during the following decade. After the Restoration the increasing centralization of political, legal, financial, and administrative institutions in the capital required many gentry to travel there more frequently. Developments after 1688 greatly accelerated this process. Leading gentry adopted a more peripatetic life style, and became less closely associated with the everyday management of their property and the affairs of the area where it was situated. Between 1689 and 1715 elections to the House of Commons were more numerous and hotly contested than ever before or since. Many politicians acquired town-houses in London or provincial boroughs, spending less of each year on their estates. Though political activity waned after 1715, this pattern of behaviour persisted. The sudden expansion of job opportunities in the public sector took many more landowners to London or abroad on public business. It became increasingly difficult to arrange purely private concerns without visiting the capital. This is reflected in the growing involvement of land-owners in fields of investment such as the National Debt, and in the proliferation of private banks in the West End which speci-fically catered for their needs. It was facilitated by gradual improvements in transport. In the 1690s even a middling squire like Walter Calverley had to go to London on business two or three times a year. However, after a brief ride from Esholt to Ferrybridge on the Great North road, he was able to take the London coach, which in good weather took only four days from there.[105]

Social developments also drew landowners away from their estates. Catholics had been educated abroad for generations. But from the end of the seventeenth century 'the grand tour which followed university became almost *de rigueur*' for the eldest sons of wealthy families, whereas previously it had been an optional extra for the few.[106] This same period saw the rise of

the London season as a social phenomenon of substantial proportions, while other centres such as Bath and Newmarket
began annually to attract large numbers of the aristocracy and
gentry. There was, in fact, 'a transformation of behaviour in
polite society' which involved a change in character as well as
tone.[107] Rustic pursuits were neglected in favour of frequent
journeys about the country and to the capital and such
behaviour soon became essential to acceptance in high society.
Whenever a family was in residence the country house remained
at the centre of social life, but for the first time during this
period it had to face considerable competition. The gentlemen's
seats of Georgian England, behind their palings and shrubberies, were not as rooted in local soil as their predecessors had
been.[108]

TABLE 2

Wives of Heads of 93 Families 1600–1800:
Place of Residence Before Marriage

	Yorkshire	Outside Yorkshire		Yorkshire	Outside Yorkshire
1600–20	12	9	1701–20	10	13
1621–40	15	10	1721–40	12	14
1641–60	10	18	1741–60	11	15
1661–80	10	13	1761–80	12	22
1681–1700	10	13	1781–1800	4	20

NOTE In many instances, particularly during the early part of the period,
relevant information is unavailable.

Sources: *CB*; *CP*; Clay, *Dugdale*; J. Foster; supplemented where necessary with material from local and family histories listed in the
bibliography.

If the rise in the incidence of absentee landlordism is to be
seen in its proper perspective, it must be remembered that a
degree of absenteeism was inherent in the prevailing system of
landownership. Most substantial landowners, not just those
with the largest estates, owned property in more than one
locality. Many estates were exceedingly scattered and, though
estate expansion did involve consolidation, it could also lead to
segmentation. Thus, even when resident at home, many

owners were necessarily absent from a considerable proportion of their property. Amongst the additional factors which exacerbated this situation changing marriage patterns were not the least important. Increasingly the marriage market became national rather than local in scope as far as the more substantial gentry were concerned.[109] More and more wealthier landowners tended to look beyond their own locality when choosing a wife, partly because increased physical mobility enabled them to do so, but also because financial considerations gradually came to outweigh other factors governing their choice. Consequently, property inherited by marriage was often at a considerable distance from that they already possessed. The result, particularly noticeable from the 1690s onwards, was the engagement of an ever-widening range of estate employees, led by the steward or agent, whose activities for much of the year were directed by correspondence.

Inevitably the wealthier gentry retreated from the humdrum responsibilities of local government. The diaries of Reresby and Calverley indicate that even less substantial men resented the time and money consumed by service on the peace commission; the high shrievalty was a post to be avoided if possible.[110] Those who spent much, if not most, of their time outside the county made way for others, many of them relative newcomers to the gentry such as the Milners and Ibbetsons, whose local economic concerns were paramount, and to whom the declining prestige and influence attaching to local government remained attractive. Magnates like Sir George Savile of Thornhill and Lord Rockingham might serve as Governor and High Steward of Hull respectively, but these were 'honorary posts to which they were nominated by the Bench as a mark of esteem'.[111] By temperament certain individuals preferred to operate at the local level. Not surprisingly Sir Digby Legard of Ganton, who devoted most of his career to the improvement of his estate, was also active in the municipal affairs of nearby Scarborough. The first two baronets Pennyman of Ormesby attended quarter sessions at Thirsk, some thirty miles from home, on a combined total of 106 occasions. Although they obviously enjoyed the proceedings, such close involvement in local affairs was usually dictated by economic interests or by the need to maintain political support. Not infrequently, as with the St. Quintins in

Hull or the Milbankes in Newcastle, these two considerations coincided.[112] In the absence of either, landowners were often unwilling to undertake unpaid and onerous public duties in the provinces.

All these trends reflect the increasingly cosmopolitan behaviour of the wealthier gentry. It would be wrong to infer, however, that physical mobility was quite uncharacteristic of them before this period, or that they were in every respect more closely associated with the county then than they were later. A significant proportion moved in and out of Yorkshire for different reasons from those already mentioned. The Chaloners and Grahams were younger branches of families whose main properties lay in Buckinghamshire and Cumberland respectively. The Sykes and the Lowthers of Marske and Swillington, all of whom purchased land with commercial profits, also originated in Cumberland. The Forsters and the Foulis family travelled south from Scotland with James I. The Dutch Vernattis and Valkenbergs tried their luck in England under Charles I; neither was domiciled in Yorkshire by 1650. The Milbankes and van den Bempdé-Johnstones both had major interests elsewhere but purchased attractive seats in the county. There was mobility in the opposite direction too. When the Saviles' house at Thornhill was destroyed in 1644 they moved permanently to Rufford in Nottinghamshire. The Coghill and Wandesford families moved to Ireland, one in pursuit of public office, the other to an economically more viable property. Some not only increased their wealth and expanded their estates by marriage, but left their former property, judging it to be less convenient or less suited to their altered status. The Calverleys moved to Northumberland, the Gowers to Staffordshire, and the Hewetts to Huntingdonshire and then to Bedfordshire. *In extremis*, Sir Marmaduke Beckwith made a fresh start in Virginia, and Sir Charles Burdett in Florida.[113]

Barred from politics and office-holding, and hence from much of the accompanying social life, Catholics were the one sub-group within the baronetage who for long retained a separate and distinctive identity. Following heavy fines during Charles I's personal rule, the estates of the entire hard core of the county's recusant gentry, with the single exception of the Stapletons of Carlton, were sequestered and in several cases sold by Parliament. Yet the devices adopted for coping with this situation were remarkably successful; comparatively little property was permanently lost. After the Restoration, though often burdened with debts, Catholics were either unmolested or well able to defend themselves. This period of relative prosperity was abruptly halted by the Popish Plot episode. Members of the Gascoigne, Stapleton, Tempest, Vavasour, and Hungate families were tried, albeit unsuccessfully, for treason; while others who escaped this charge, like Sir Philip Constable of Everingham, were imprisoned under the penal laws. For a brief period under James II Catholics enjoyed opportunities from which they had previously been excluded. From 1688, however, their position deteriorated and did not alter radically for several decades. The penal laws were strengthened and, for the first time, incorporated clauses stipulating double taxation. The expansion of public employment at all levels increased Catholics' sense of deprivation; the change of dynasty and the miserable failure of the '15, their frustration. Though powerful in their immediate localities, they yearned for the wider opportunities enjoyed by so many of their contemporaries. While not totally excluded from high society, they were by no means readily accepted.[114]

Of the fourteen families who were Catholics in the mid seventeenth century, the Forsters and the Saviles of Copley were completely extinct a century later. After the Restoration the Swales, who had previously conformed, reverted to marginal Catholicism, while the Tempests, hitherto strict Puritans, became Catholics under the second baronet. In several other instances, however, economic pressures and a desire for social acceptance led inexorably towards religious conformity. Sir Hugh Smithson conformed at the turn of the century and was followed in 1706 by Sir Philip Hungate. Thereafter both the Wyvill and the Belasyse families achieved marked success in public life after renouncing their Catholicism. Sir John Lawson conformed in mid-century. Occasionally those who persevered sought refuge abroad from almost monastic seclusion at home. Sir Marmaduke Constable of Everingham spent most of his last sixteen years on the Continent; successive heads of the Gascoigne family lived semi-permanently in France until the eighth baronet, Sir Thomas, conformed in 1780. By the closing decades of the century, therefore, only a handful of substantial Catholic landowning families remained, sustained by a closely-knit group of friends and relatives, by pride in their heritage, and, not least, by a markedly improved situation for exclusively landed economies.[115]

A trend towards conformity was evident in many areas other than religion. Simultaneously, as the élite's way of life became more expansive, the cost of adhering to acceptable standards rose. In education, for example, domestic tutors and provincial schools were gradually superseded by institutions such as Westminster School and Eton. Though universities and, more particularly, the Inns of Court grew less popular, almost every established family provided prospective heirs with a grand tour in the eighteenth century. Especially if their fathers remained in control of family affairs, they frequently spent five or more years moving leisurely from one European capital to another. Their itineraries normally included the Low Countries, France, Italy, and some of the German principalities, but it was not uncommon for them to reach Greece or Russia. Always accompanied by a tutor and sometimes by younger brothers, they might easily spend several thousand pounds in rounding off their education. At home, life in the popular social centres became steadily more expensive. Before the Civil War contempories remarked on basic differences between the cost of staying on the estate and of spending time elsewhere. According to Sir Henry Slingsby, 'curiosity in the art of cookery I do not much value, nor have we much use for it in our country housekeeping'.[116] If one wanted to acquire anything out of the ordinary, one had usually to go south. The household books of Sir Miles Stapleton reveal that he often travelled to London after the Restoration for clothes, jewellery, and the like. What was convenient for some, however, became habitual in others. In rebuking his son Sir Thomas Gascoigne prescribed a quiet life in the North as the infallible remedy for his extravagance. Sir Thomas Robinson of Rokeby 'gave balls to all the men and women in power and in fashion, and ruined himself'.[117] In the new world of high society which flourished in the eighteenth century he was not alone in accepting the more frequent invitations to excess. Provincial life gradually lost its immunity from metropolitan fashion. Nowhere was this more true than in regard to architecture, which was perhaps the single most expensive Georgian taste. The post-medieval rebuilding, which had been so prominent a feature of the Tudor and early Stuart periods elsewhere, was delayed in many parts of the north until the eighteenth century.[118] In Yorkshire lavish architectural display was further encouraged by Lord Burlington, the arch-Palladian, who designed the Assembly Rooms at York and had a country seat at Londesborough. His protégés, Flitcroft and Campbell, were active long before the county produced its own major architect, John Carr.

Of the major avenues to fame and fortune, politics and marriage in particular could be enormously expensive. Forced to spend £350 in 1685 in being elected M.P. for York, Sir John Reresby consoled himself with the thought that 'it cost them more that lost it'.[119] Costs in this sphere, as in so many others, spiralled after 1688. Both prospective candidates and sitting M.P.s had to spend much more time, effort, and money in bolstering their support. Both in private and in public the electoral tactics of the eighteenth century were notoriously unscrupulous. The Tory Sir Miles Stapleton, elected M.P. for the county after the fiercest contest of the period in 1734, spent so much then and subsequently in sustaining his position that he approached the government in 1750 for a place to ease him 'from the trouble and expense of Parliament'.[120] He soon left the Commons to become a Customs Commissioner. In accepting an invitation to stand for the city of York in 1734 Sir John Kaye was adamantly unwilling to buy success. This 'did not at all please, for the great love they have for Sir John was for the money they were in hopes he would spend amongst them'.[121] Being unopposed, he was safely returned on his own terms. Property markets in borough constituencies were unusually active as families vied with one another in purchasing burgage tenements. Thereby, for example, the Lowthers of Swillington gained control of Pontefract, though in 1740 Sir William Lowther could only solve his financial difficulties satisfactorily by selling his holdings there for £9,400. Nominees to such seats from outside a family paid a fee similar to the £2,000 which Sir Robert Hildyard disbursed for Great Bedwyn in 1754.[122]

This group provides plentiful reminders that marriage could

transform a family's fortunes. Indeed, 'no better example of the forging of a great estate through careful marriage' could be found than in the history of the Gowers of Stittenham.[123] However, the length and intricacy of contemporary marriage negotiations indicate that participants realized that future developments were largely beyond their control. Heirs and heiresses were made and unmade by demographic factors and it was beyond the wit of the most capable solicitors to cater for the full range of possibilities. Sir Hugh Smithson did not realize the scale of his achievement in marrying a peer's daughter in 1740, though doubtless he felt that he had done well for himself. His wife became her family's sole heiress when her brother died in 1744, and by special remainder Sir Hugh succeeded as Earl of Northumberland at his father-in-law's death in 1750, being created Earl Percy and Duke of Northumberland in 1766. Armed with a peerage and the wealth which accompanied it, his subsequent rise to high office was predictable. Nevertheless, because marriage, like life itself, was a lottery, spectacular successes were matched by equally dramatic failures. If a prospective heiress died before producing children, her inheritance normally remained within her own family, though her portion had changed hands irretrievably and no jointure was payable. On the other hand if a husband died young and childless, not only was his widow's inheritance frequently diverted from his family, but successive jointure payments soon overtook the value of her money portion. The third Duke of Leeds was outlived by his widow for sixty-three years; at £3,000 a year her jointure eventually totalled £190,000. Therefore, the consequences of marriage in one generation often placed succeeding generations under pressure to marry well. A string of marriageable daughters in a family was preferable to one or two well-jointured widows and coincidence of the two was apt to pose severe problems. Potentially most dangerous was the situation in which the judgement of an elderly widower and family head was affected by the charms of a much younger woman. In 1743 Sir Thomas Frankland took Sarah Moseley as his second wife. She was very pretty and at eighteen some forty years younger than her husband. At his death in 1747 all his property passed absolutely to Sarah by his last will. His family upset this in court, but under an earlier will Sarah inherited his property for life. During the next thirty-six years she accumulated a fortune of £35,000, all of which she settled away from the Frank-lands.[124] At this level of society, and with land values rising, marriage stakes were high.

All these developments took place long before rents, the permanent and major component of most incomes, resumed an upward trend. Consequently, expenditure exhibited a much greater propensity to rise than did income. As far as landed economies are concerned this would appear to have been the hallmark of the decades from the mid seventeenth to the mid eighteenth centuries; the characteristic, above all others, which gives the period economic unity. Income diversification, greatly improved credit facilities, and, in periods such as minorities, some substantial reductions in previous outgoings, were key factors where prosperity was increased. Nevertheless the major responsibility for the performance of individual economies remained in the hands of each generation. Not infrequently the eccentricity, extravagance, or sheer inability of a single individual was sufficient to tip a delicate economic balance decisively against a family's interest. At times even capable men were overtaken by developments which were quite beyond their control. It was precisely the same with success: chance and personality so often underlay it.

THE HOTHAMS OF SCORBOROUGH AND SOUTH DALTON

FACTORS such as those of chance and personality pose serious problems for the historian if only because firm evidence relating to their influence tends to be highly elusive. In studying landed families in the early modern period it is sometimes difficult to establish the pattern of events, and frequently impossible to proceed further than this. In the vast majority of cases character analysis in any depth is out of the question. Only where diaries or extensive series of correspondence survive can one begin to assess the influence of particular personalities. For every Sir John Reresby or Sir Walter Calverley there are dozens of other contemporary landowners who are unrecognizable as individuals. Only comparatively rarely in this area, therefore, can one reconstruct the past in sufficient detail to be able to make confident judgements in regard to both circumstance and behaviour. And yet when the sources provide opportunities for making such judgements, as they do in the case of the four families whose history we shall now consider, the actions of a single individual during, perhaps, a very short period of time can sometimes be seen to have had a profound effect over many subsequent generations.

The history of the Hotham family provides a classic example of this. The key to an understanding of their fortunes during this period lies in an appreciation of the sharp decline in their income from 1645, following the deaths of the first baronet, Sir John Hotham, and of his eldest son, John. Having originally backed Parliament in the Civil War, the two men had developed contacts with supporters of the Crown in 1643. Unlike most of those who shifted their allegiance during the war, who acted purely out of self-interest, their strategy represented a brave, honourable, but distinctly naïve attempt to identify the middle ground and bring the warring sides together. In the event it was doomed to failure and earned them the opprobrium of both parties to the conflict. Their property was sequestered by Parliament and after a lengthy period of imprisonment they were executed. Shortly before his death Sir John disposed substantial portions of his estate away from the main branch of his family in an attempt, apparently, to circumvent the full effects of the sequestration. This not only proved unnecessary – the sequestration was lifted soon after his execution – but, as a result of his action, the income from the family's estate did not again reach the level enjoyed in the 1630s until the late eighteenth century. It would be difficult to find another family which had to live for so long with the private consequences of its experiences during the Civil War.

In the post-Restoration era the family's affairs continued to be influenced by their involvement in national politics. The second baronet, grandson of the first and another Sir John, was an active parliamentarian and a leading exclusionist. His outspoken opposition to James II, and the consequent threat to his personal liberty, forced him into exile in 1684. When, four years later, his entire estate was confiscated by the Crown the family was confronted, albeit briefly, with the prospect of economic extinction. Sir John's accompaniment of William III on the invasion which precipitated the revolution of 1688 brought him political rehabilitation and enabled his successors to obtain the public positions to which he and his forebears had long aspired. Thereby they also obtained sources of income other than land which, together with the benefits of a long minority, allowed the family to live in a fashion which could not otherwise have been sustained. For, despite reversions of property, considerable investment in new land, the rise in rents over the period, and much stricter settlements than those effected prior to 1645, the gross annual rental of the Hotham estates rose to only £2,850 by 1768. This was £150 less than in 1640; for most of the intervening period the rental was well below this sum.

I.   RUIN AND RE-EMERGENCE 1640–80

The Hothams were one of the oldest and most influential landed families in Yorkshire. The village of Hotham near North Cave was their original holding but from the mid thirteenth century they lived at Scorborough, a few miles north of Beverley. Their history between the eleventh and seventeenth centuries was undistinguished, but beginning with the first baronet the family produced a series of noteworthy public servants in nearly every walk of life and subsequently became one of the largest landowners in the East Riding, indeed in the whole of Yorkshire. According to Clarendon, Sir John Hotham, the first baronet, 'was master of a noble fortune in land, and rich in money'; Strafford thought him 'as considerable a person as any other gentleman in the north of England'.[1] Knighted in 1617 and created baronet in 1622, Sir John later served under Count Mansfeld in the Thirty Years War. He was M.P. for Beverley in the five parliaments of Charles I's reign, High Sheriff of Yorkshire in 1634–5, and then, at a salary of £5 per day, Governor of Hull. He had come into the family estate in 1605: by 1640 there was property at Filingdales in the North Riding, at Wilton and Ampleforth in the Vale of Pickering, and in Holderness, but the core of his holding lay in the area south of Driffield and north of Beverley. Sir John's wealth was increased, and his estate expanded, by the portions which accrued from no less than five marriages: from £2,000 at his succession the family's gross annual rental rose to £3,000 by 1640. His personal estate, which included interests in the East India Company and other trading concerns as well as large amounts of cash, was estimated to be worth around £10,000. On the eve of the Civil War his was clearly one of the largest fortunes in Yorkshire.[2]

Although on entering Parliament he had quickly joined the anti-court faction, Sir John was not closely associated with any political grouping during the 1630s. However, following the preferment of a professional soldier, Captain Legge, as Governor of Hull in 1639, he repeatedly clashed with the government. On refusing to pay ship-money he was dismissed from all his commissions and briefly imprisoned. After his release he was active in organizing petitions against abuses on behalf of other Yorkshire gentry. Early in the Civil War Sir John secured Hull for Parliament, refused entry to Charles I and his forces, and was publicly declared a traitor. He nevertheless remained uncertain in his allegiance and wished to bring the war to a quick conclusion. To this end he negotiated secretly with the Royalists Digby and Newcastle, while his eldest son, John – a General in the Parliamentary army, contacted the

Queen and other Royalists. In 1643 both men were arrested by Parliament, charged with treason, and their real and personal estates sequestered. After a long, controversial trial, and despite Sir John's plea that one of them be spared so that his 'whole family might not be cut off root and branch', they were executed on consecutive days in January 1645.[3]

The succession then passed to General Hotham's only son, John, who was a minor.[4] Family affairs were in chaos, primarily because of the sequestrations and executions, but also owing to Sir John's earlier attempts to mitigate the effects of sequestration. His five marriages had produced seventeen children, at least twelve of whom were alive in 1640, and during the previous decade he had begun to make future provision for this large family, settling property, money, or both on each of five sons, and a jointure on his fifth wife, Sarah. Though most of the property concerned in these transactions was settled in trust after his death to the use of his eldest son, and his male heirs in succession, at no point did Sir John attempt to settle the whole of his estate on his prospective heir. Indeed, after his arrest he made further dispositions which, besides dealing with property as yet undisposed, revoked parts of previous settlements. Sir

TABLE 3
Particulars of Sir J. Hotham's Estate, 1645

Land Owned by Sir John	Annual Value £
Scorborough & Lockington	560
Hutton Cranswick	300
Wilton & Pickering	342
Risam	300
Filingdales	320
	1822
Leases	
Howsham	700
Beswick & Allerston	130
	830
Total Annual Value	2652

Source: DDHO/20/7.

John then diverted most of his property to his younger children, hoping thereby to create grounds on which sequestration, and perhaps also wardship,[5] might in large measure be evaded. Consequently, the annual value of the property still vested in him immediately before his execution was £2,652, whereas at his death his successor was left with a mere £690 a year. The Parliamentary authorities soon placed Sir John's grandson under the wardship of Sir John Wray for an annual fee from the estate of £680. Ironically, however, sequestration was completely lifted and wardship abolished shortly after Sir John's final dispositions had taken effect. Utilization of his personal estate by his heir was out of the question for it had been settled on daughters for their portions. Any further improvement in the difficult situation inherited by young John Hotham depended chiefly on the reversion of some of the real estate carefully, but as it turned out unnecessarily, diverted from him during his grandfather's captivity.[6]

The effective head of the family until 1653 when the second baronet came of age was Durand Hotham, the minor's uncle, who was a lawyer and author as well as something of an authority on local agriculture.[7] He arranged a highly successful marriage for his charge in 1650 to Elizabeth, eldest daughter of Sapcote, Viscount Beaumont of Swords. The bride's portion comprised both money and land though unfortunately details of neither are available. However, the post-nuptial settlement, executed in 1653, indicates that by then the manors of Weighton and Risam had reverted to the main branch of the family; so too had Hutton Cranswick following the death of General Hotham's widow. Sir John conveyed his entire real estate to trustees. Scorborough and Lockington were for the use of his wife as a jointure, with a remainder to a male heir of the marriage and his male heirs; the rest of the property was for his own use for life with a remainder as before. Significantly, the strictness of this settlement contrasted sharply with the wide-ranging nature of those executed in the previous decade.[8]

Neither Sir John nor Durand Hotham experienced difficulty in securing public office during the Interregnum. Durand served regularly as a magistrate and commissioner and, in 1653, was nominated to a committee of the Council of State, while a few months later Sir John was recommended for the post of

Paymaster to the Commissioners for the Sick and Wounded. In 1658 Sir John was elected M.P. for Beverley and became the senior of the borough's two representatives at Westminster from 1660. After the Restoration he was also appointed Custos Rotulorum of the East Riding.[9] Like his grandfather before him he was a frequent and severe critic of many aspects of government policy. Consequently, while the authorities respected his local standing, they did not trust him. In August 1663 along with others 'of eminence' in the East Riding he was committed to York prison on suspicion of plotting a rebellion. Nothing could be proved against him, however, and he was soon released and permitted to resume his duties.[10] In view of this and subsequent events Sir John was none too popular, even locally. Several of his relatives and friends served under him as magistrates and as a group they held distinctly nonconformist views in matters of religion. Whilst intimating, for example, that 'presentments against sectaries, [such] as anabaptists, quakers and the like . . . would not be received', they proceeded against Catholics 'as well in places exempt as not exempt', and in so doing went a good deal further than government policy intended.[11] Nor was Sir John's relationship with his constituents always cordial. Although he preserved a family interest in Beverley which persisted, with important results for both, until beyond the middle of the eighteenth century, he made enemies there from the time of a dispute over a new charter in 1662.[12] The sequel to a colourful episode in 1669 indicates the strength of local feeling against Sir John which, apart from its purely personal aspect, may have owed something to lingering memories of the family's role in the Civil War. Whilst riding alone near York he was attacked by Edward Phillips, a notorious highwayman, who attempted to rob Sir John but was pulled to the ground by his intended victim and kept there until help arrived. On being convicted of a felony Phillips begged the Crown for a reprieve in a petition which was supported by 'the chief nobility and persons of quality' in the county, who argued that as the attack was only an 'attempt' the assailant should be treated with compassion. No doubt to Sir John's consternation, Phillips was granted a full pardon in November 1669.[13] Nevertheless, Sir John gained his most powerful opponents at Westminster where, as a prominent exclusionist, he frequently intervened in debates and eventually came to be regarded with deep suspicion by the chief supporters of the Crown.[14]

In the midst of a busy public life Sir John had little time for private concerns but avoided neglect at home by persuading Durand Hotham, who in 1645 had inherited the property at Filingdales in the North Riding, to continue to reside in east Yorkshire, granting him a lease of land at Lockington where Durand lived for many years. Sufficient capital had been accumulated by the late 1650s to expand the estate by purchase. In 1659 Sir John bought two small farms in Rotsey for an unknown sum, and in 1660 Sir Thomas Williamson was paid £2,070 for property in Cranswick. There are other signs of growing prosperity. In 1663 the manor of Wilton, which had passed to the daughters of the first baronet in 1645 when it had been worth £322 a year, reverted to the main branch of the family. Moreover, within a month of his daughter Elizabeth's marriage in 1664 to William Gee, Sir John was able to pay over her entire portion of £1,500. The comments of at least one contemporary are also indicative of progress. In 1663 the Earl of Winchelsea wrote a worried letter from abroad to Sir Heneage Finch. The Earl had quarrelled with two of the tenants on his Yorkshire estate and expected them to spread harmful propaganda concerning its poor condition and the size of his rents. Should he subsequently feel obliged to sell the property cheaply to neighbouring landlords, he suspected that Sir John Hotham would be eager to take advantage of his difficulties. These seem to have been overcome, but in 1667 he was considering whether or not to join Sir John in enclosing parts of Cranswick.[15]

Yet another property reverted to the main branch of the family during the 1670s: this was the land in Filingdales, worth £30 a year in 1645, which the first baronet had settled on his fourth son, William. Furthermore, by January 1678 Sir John was able to lend his prospective heir £900. Shortly after the latter's marriage a month later the whole of his bride's money portion was immediately lent at interest to various neighbours. Without doubt, however, the most successful investment of these years was the purchase in 1680 of the manor and lands of South Dalton. These had once formed the country seat of the abbot of St. Mary's, Beverley, but since the dissolution had been held by the Aislabies of Bridlington, who sold them for £1,600. It was an impressive property, lying close to the Hotham estate: besides the manor house, it comprised 180 acres of land, the advowson of the local church, cottages, a windmill, and some timber.[16] The annual rental amounted to £95, but the value of the property to the family was later enormously increased in a way impossible to foresee at the time of its purchase. For after the destruction of the Scorborough house by fire in 1705, and the fifth baronet's dislike for its successor in Beverley, South Dalton was developed as the family's country seat, which it remains. Although no rentals or accounts are extant for the period 1645–1709, by 1680 the family's gross annual rental would appear to have been in the region of £1,900. As yet the estate constituted their sole source of income, but the rise of some £1,200 in the rental since Sir John's succession had proved more than sufficient for their needs.

2. DECADE OF DIFFICULTIES 1680–91

This satisfactory situation was disturbed by political developments which wrecked Sir John's public career and drove him into exile in 1684. Apprehension at Charles II's pro-French and pro-Catholic sympathies exploded hysterically in 1678 in the Popish Plot episode, which led in turn to the Exclusion crisis. The Commons severely criticized Charles's policies and four Parliaments were called and dissolved in quick succession. Repeatedly frustrated, the government punished its opponents with increasing severity until many of them, fearing for their safety, fled abroad. The earliest move against Sir John came in November 1680 when, together with Durand Hotham and William Gee, he was excluded from the East Riding peace commission. A group of his constituents disagreed with his political views and during 1681 he became involved in a dispute with Beverley Corporation concerning re-imbursement for his services at Westminster.[17] During 1682–3 the government tried to increase its support in cities and boroughs with a view to modifying their charters so as to secure sympathetic juries and electorates. As a result of these moves Sir John was the subject of anonymous letters sent to Lords Sunderland and Dartmouth and Secretary Jenkins in 1683. These alleged that he and a

certain Alderman Grey had not only engaged in 'factious dis-
courses against the government' but had won over the local
trades and companies 'by providing them with regular feasts of
venison'. Moreover, the informers maintained that Sir John
had amassed a store of arms and equipment at Scorborough
which had escaped detection because 'out of courtesy' the
deputy-lieutenants had not included his house in a recent
general search.[18] The failure of the Rye House Plot in 1683 led
to the arrest and trial of many leading Whigs. The number who
chose exile increased, and Sir John joined them in the summer
of 1684. He spent most of the next four years in Holland,
eventually taking up arms against the French. Responsibility
for the conduct of family affairs devolved upon his wife, Lady
Elizabeth, who was able to turn to Durand Hotham for advice.
Sir John's previous absences in London had led him as early as
1678 to delegate to her by power of attorney authority to conduct the negotiations prior to their eldest son's marriage.[19]

The arrangement of this marriage to Katherine, one of the
heiresses of John Heron of Beverley, proved problematical.
Like the second baronet, Heron had been active in local politics
and had accumulated property close to the Hotham estate; but,
in remarking of her son's ardour that it had 'been so long fatal to
his quiet and prejudicial to his fortune', Lady Elizabeth indicated that she at least felt that John Hotham could have done
better for himself. Maintaining that she herself 'had not the care
to provide for burying my husband before I had him', she was
particularly critical of the mercenary attitude adopted by both
the girl and her mother, though she was finally forced to admit
that it was 'neither consistent with honour nor religion that
there should now be a breach'.[20] Katherine's portion consisted
of £2,000 in cash and £1,000 in goods; she was also entitled to
part of her father's real estate which, it was decided, was to be
settled on her husband and his male heirs once Katherine came
of age. In return she was provided with a jointure of £100 for
each £1,000 of her portion. The clause in the 1653 settlement
which had provided Lady Elizabeth with a jointure from Scorborough and Lockington was revoked, while by the current
marriage settlement of 14 January 1680 the whole estate, except
the property in Hutton Cranswick purchased in 1660, was
conveyed to trustees for the use of John Hotham for life after his

father's death, then to the use of the successive male heirs of his marriage. Katherine's jointure was provided from land in Lockington and Winthorpe, while Lady Elizabeth was to receive an annuity of £500 in lieu of her jointure. Later, by his will of April 1682, Sir John bequeathed the property in Hutton Cranswick purchased in 1660, and that at South Dalton purchased in 1680 after the execution of the above settlement, to Lady Elizabeth, instructing her to provide for their younger son, Robert, from the same. In 1685, as stipulated earlier, Katherine Hotham's landed portion was settled on trustees to her husband's use for life, then to herself for life, then to the use of their heirs by each other, and finally in default of such to the use of John Hotham's right heirs.[21]

By this time support for James II's accession had dashed hopes of Sir John's early return. Indeed, the Crown's arbitrary actions raised fears for the safety of the property of his opponents. Also Sir John's younger son, Robert, had died. These events necessitated a further re-disposition. In the light of his son's death and to provide more effectively for his wife's maintenance, Sir John supplemented his will of 1682 with a deed of March 1687. The property mentioned in his will was conveyed to trustees, who were charged firstly with the payment of £300 a year to Lady Elizabeth for her personal use, secondly with the payment of £900 in cash and £230 in annuities to various people after Sir John's death, and thirdly with the payment of his debts and funeral expenses. The fears which lay behind this move were seen to have been justified when the family estates were seized by the Crown and a grant of them made out to Lord Langdale, a leading East Riding Catholic and neighbour of the Hothams, in 1688. Meanwhile, John and Katherine Hotham's childless marriage had failed and some time before April 1687 the couple had separated. John then transferred the reversion in fee to all the property included in his marriage settlement to his parents. He himself had not given up hope of a reconciliation, though his parents undoubtedly thought it unlikely.[22]

Family affairs, therefore, were in turmoil during the last months of James II's reign. Although Sir John's will and the deed of March 1687 reflect a continuation of the financial and economic progress of previous decades, the subsequent grant to Lord Langdale was the most serious development that the family had ever had to face. However, in December 1688, before the grant had taken effect, the second baronet landed at Brixham with William of Orange, James II went into exile, and many of his marks of favour, including the grant to Langdale, were revoked. The swing of the political pendulum had suddenly boosted Sir John's influence at the highest level. Years of opposition, arid in terms of favour and recognition, were over and he had every reason to regard his appointment as Colonel and Governor of Hull, and the offers of a parliamentary candidacy from both Hull and Beverley, as signs of still greater things to come. Yet, almost before he had time to savour his prospects, he died – ironically of a chill contracted during his tumultuous return to Scorborough.[23]

John Hotham succeeded as third baronet. By now his health was poor and he soon went into a sharp decline. He replaced his father as M.P. for Beverley and attended the House of Commons for a few months, but then abandoned his seat, allowing William Gee to succeed him at Westminster. He also neglected his private affairs, squandered money, and became heavily indebted, particularly to his mother.[24] This errant behaviour stemmed not just from the breakdown of his marriage, but from the proceedings which his wife initiated in the Consistory Court at York in 1691, in which she sought either a divorce or a nullity of the marriage on the grounds of her husband's 'frigidity'. Her petition was unsuccessful, though the brief of the lawyers for the defence, which is the only detailed record which survives, indicates that the proceedings were sensational. While it was admitted that Sir John had suffered some 'deficiency in appearance' in recent years, his wife's claim that, owing to his impotence, the marriage had never been consummated was vigorously disputed. Sir John himself swore that he had 'carnally known his wife often, and one night no less than four times'; others deposed that on one occasion Katherine had intimated that she thought she was pregnant. Her participation, it was argued, in the execution of the deed of 1685, whereby her landed inheritance was settled on her husband and his male heirs, was a sure indication that she was then satisfied with her marriage. According to the defence, it was her subsequent dalliance with Sir Suester Payton, a 'spark out of the south', which constituted the real reason for her decision to institute the proceedings. Finally, Sir John 'did expose himself to the view of those who will make oath that to all appearance there was not then the least of that deficiency his Lady charges him with'.[25]

Nevertheless, despite the failure of his wife's petition, Sir John fled to Holland in April 1691. Allegedly, the case had resulted in his being hounded by creditors: he acknowledged that his own behaviour had contributed to his indebtedness, but cited as additional factors the failing of tenants, public taxes, and, not least, his wife's extravagance. Before his departure Dame Elizabeth, who was then £500 in arrears with her rent charge, obtained a judgement against him in the Court of Common Pleas. A few months later Sir John owed her a total of £3,000. He made his mother his legal attorney, empowering her to receive all his rents and profits, and to appoint one of her own servants to administer the family property. He died in Holland in August 1691, having survived his father for less than three years. After his death further debts amounting to more than £750 came to light, his funeral cost £200, and his only financial assets at death were £128 in rent arrears.[26]

During this difficult period the recently widowed Dame Elizabeth exhibited considerable resourcefulness. After failing to curb Sir John's extravagance by other means, she did not hesitate to take him to court or to press him into granting her the power of attorney. Moreover, besides being aware of her son's poor health and of the likelihood of his failing to produce an heir, Dame Elizabeth had in fact inherited Hutton Cranswick and South Dalton by the second baronet's will, and by the deed of April 1687 was seized of the reversion to the rest of the family property in the event of the third baronet dying childless. She had accordingly begun to plan for the future as soon as her husband had died. She offered the succession, should the third baronet die childless, to her nephew, Charles Hotham, who would also succeed to the title; she also offered him her niece and his cousin, Brigid Gee, in marriage. As Dame Elizabeth's aim was the 'support and preservation of the family and name of Hotham', Charles's dual acceptance was no doubt a source of profound satisfaction to her, coming as it did during the last months of the third baronet's disastrous career. By Charles and Brigid Hotham's marriage settlement the whole estate, except for South Dalton and Hutton Cranswick, was settled on trustees to the use of Charles for life, then to the use of the successive male heirs of his marriage. Later the excepted properties were similarly disposed by Dame Elizabeth's will. Because Sir John died intestate a legal dispute followed with his widow concerning the administration of his goods and chattels; Dame Elizabeth won on the grounds that she was the principal creditor of the deceased. By the time of her death in 1697 she had completed the repayment of all her son's debts.[27]

The period 1680–91 was clearly one of misfortune and deep uncertainty. Having inherited a penchant for political conflict, the second baronet, like his predecessors, had to face the consequences. Once the acute economic difficulties which he also inherited had receded his private affairs were marked by solid achievements, but subsequently these were somewhat qualified by the irresponsible behaviour of his successor. By 1691 the estate was in urgent need of managerial attention, debts were outstanding, and family morale was low. Nevertheless, the events of this decade, however disturbing, did little fundamental damage to the family's economy. The prime source of the prosperity carefully garnered before 1680 – the estate – remained intact. Charles Hotham inherited not only a sizeable property and basically sound economic circumstances, but also the power and influence in the East Riding which again attached to the head of the Hotham family. His opportunities were clear-cut.

3. TILT AT SUCCESS 1691–1723

Following a brilliant but stormy career during the Interregnum, Sir Charles Hotham's father (the third son of the first baronet) had been ejected from the rectory of Wigan in 1662 because of his nonconformity. Elected a Fellow of the Royal Society in 1667, he emigrated to Bermuda in order to be able to practise his ministry. Charles, his eldest son, returned to England for schooling at Sedburgh, later gained an M.A. and a Fellowship of St. John's College, Cambridge, and by 1690 was regarded as one of the leading classical scholars of his day. He had planned to follow his father into the ministry and was ordained deacon, but changed his mind on receiving Dame Elizabeth's offers. According to her brother, 'besides the justice you do the family ... all persons living most highly commend your choice in this gentleman'.[28]

There was some delay before the fourth baronet assumed control. Four months after Sir John's death the house at Scorborough was empty, and most of the hay in the fields there was rotten. However, the situation which Sir Charles inherited was soon improved by the reversion of Durand Hotham's property at Filingdales, which had been worth £290 a year in 1645. Notwithstanding this addition, which only occurred because all Durand's eleven children died young, Sir Charles's income persistently proved insufficient for his needs. Although the situation never got out of hand, over the course of his career he became steadily more indebted. Besides numerous, small, short-term loans on bonds, there was a series of mortgages – for £300 in 1692, £1,200 in 1698, and £6,600 in 1720. In his will Sir Charles exhorted his successor to repay his debts 'with all convenient speed'.[29] The fifth baronet was obliged to use his bride's portion in repaying the largest mortgage, while remaining debts were responsible for regular and sizeable expenditure in the years after Sir Charles's death.

There were several reasons for the growth of his indebtedness. Jointure payments from the estate to the widows of the second and third baronets amounted to £1,020 yearly until 1698, and £520 yearly thereafter; the first sum comprised approximately half the gross annual rental. Resources were further depleted in 1697 when Dame Elizabeth bequeathed more than £1,000 in legacies and, perhaps more significantly, £200 in life annuities.[30] Moreover, on his succession Sir Charles became involved in a legal dispute which lasted for six years. Later, in 1705, the Hall at Scorborough was completely destroyed by fire. Sir Charles not only financed suitable temporary accommodation but also built at considerable expense a new house in Beverley which was not completed until 1723, the year of his death. Furthermore, despite these difficulties, he was determined to live in a fashion and at a level which he considered befitted himself and his family. Between 1710 and 1712, for example, he sent his eldest son on a tour of Holland, Germany, Italy, and Switzerland; he himself pursued a varied career as landlord, public administrator, M.P., and army officer. His activities, which involved him in lengthy absences from his estate in places as far removed as Spain and Scotland, did not permit retrenchment. Rather they necessitated more expenditure than he could prudently afford when so many other demands were being made on his resources. He also appears to have received less from his military service than was his due. Finally, a second marriage, which promised to increase his means substantially, quickly ended in separation. And yet in 1723 the family's position in society was considerably greater than it had been in 1692. Their support of the revolution had much to do with this, but in addition Sir Charles's vigorous public career more than compensated for the loss of prestige in the years before his succession. Moreover, during his grand tour Sir Charles's eldest son and heir had struck up a friendship with the future George II which later resulted in the transformation of the family's financial circumstances. In the long-term, therefore, Sir Charles's refusal to allow indebtedness to curtail the family's life-style proved extremely beneficial.

By the turn of the century Sir Charles was serving regularly as Deputy Lieutenant or Justice of the Peace for the East or North Ridings, or for both. However, though sworn in as a burgess of the borough in 1695, he had difficulty initially in winning the family's traditionally safe parliamentary seat at Beverley. Only after three defeats there and two periods as M.P. for Scarborough was he elected at Beverley in July 1702, but he then held the seat until his death.[31] If voters were not bribed, they were at least 'entertained'. In 1721, for instance, the Mayoress was asked 'to manage' a 'treat' on Sir Charles's behalf. Such feasts were normally provided either before or after an election, but Sir Charles gave an additional one on the occasion of George I's coronation. After retaining his seat at the Tory landslide election in 1710 Sir Charles bestowed the advowson of Hollym on Beverley Corporation. His constituents were not above demanding extra favours. In 1708 Beverley Corporation decided that a new cross was needed in Saturday Market-place. The committee set up to organize its erection sent the two M.P.s a progress report in 1714, asking them 'to order the moneys down that the workmen may be paid and the receivers re-imbursed'. Twice in succeeding years Sir Charles was asked to pay for work on the cross, and a bill for £35 was sent to him. The M.P.s were also expected to provide money for poor relief. Towards the end of his life Sir Charles became something of a father figure in local politics, intervening with the Archbishop of York on one occasion to settle a contentious dispute over the misapplication of the revenues of Beverley minister. He was appointed Borough Recorder in 1714, and shortly before his death was made a freeman for his services to Beverley.[32] Those services, however, boosted his expenditure. Sir Charles used his local influence to some advantage, leasing land from the Corporation on favourable terms and being granted special facilities for building. But the new house which political considerations persuaded him to erect in the borough proved costly, indeed wasteful, both to himself and to his successors.

From 1705 Sir Charles's military career consumed much of his time and energy. He raised a corps of infantry in Yorkshire and was appointed its Colonel. Subsequently he served in Spain and Portugal, and was promoted Brigadier-General in 1710. In 1713 his regiment was disbanded, but he raised a new one in July 1715 and was again appointed Colonel. Following the Jacobite rebellion he marched to the relief of Newcastle, pursued the rebels over the Scottish border, and during his stay in Scotland was once again promoted Brigadier-General. In 1717 Sir Charles refused to join his regiment in Ireland and resigned his commission. Later he was appointed Colonel of a regiment of dragoons which was disbanded in November 1718. In 1719 he was given the colonelcy of the 36th Foot and transferred to the King's Foot in 1720. Finally, he gained a colonelcy in the Royal Dragoons which he retained until his death in 1723. At times Sir Charles's military service cut him off completely from family affairs. Engagement in the Peninsular War prevented his returning home during his first wife's last illness. Consequently, his otherwise excellent relationship with his father-in-law deteriorated to the point of curtness. As Sir Charles relied on Mr Gee for the smooth running of the estate during his absence, this was unfortunate. For long periods this reliance was total for both Sir Charles's sons joined the army at an early age and were likewise unavailable. Significantly, Sir Charles's army service began shortly after the fire at Scorborough. Deprived of his home, already in debt, and with the prospect of rising expenditure, he looked to the army as an additional source of income as well as an alternative way of life.[33]

He was certainly preoccupied with the financial aspects of his service. In 1706 Treasurer Godolphin charged Sir Charles and other colonels with neglecting instructions concerning the provision of clothing for their men, and with using the money allocated for clothing for their own purposes. The men had complained of poor quality uniforms and the Treasury, fearing that clothiers would raise their prices, threatened to break the commission of anyone guilty of similar offences in the future. Payments were to be made only on the receipt of special certificates and regimental agents were to submit regular accounts of how public money was spent. It is not surprising that officers indulged in malpractices for the danger of personal financial loss during the course of their duties was high. They normally honoured clothing contracts by transferring to the clothier deductions from men's future pay. However, if a regiment was suddenly disbanded, as happened to Sir Charles on two occasions, a clothier had to be paid for an entire contract. The only relief for loss lay via a petition to the Treasury or the Crown, but legitimate claims sometimes took years to pass through the proper channels. Profiteering, then, was often an attempt to insure against the possibility of future loss.[34]

Claims submitted by Sir Charles and his officers were subject to lengthy delays. Having lost horses and baggage at the siege of Alicante in 1710 and spent three years in Spain without receiving the customary allowance for mules, they petitioned for relief from the extraordinary expenditure which had been forced upon them. Moreover, on their return they had met the cost of bringing their regiment back to full strength following heavy losses. By 1715 this petition had not been answered and on being referred by the Treasury to Lord Carnarvon was subject to further delay. A second petition concerned the disbandment of Sir Charles's regiment in 1712, officially arranged for 24 August at Berwick. As the men were stationed in two groups at Perth and Stirling, they did not complete the march to Berwick until 30 August and 1 September respectively. While the Treasury issued pay up to and including 24 August, the men had to be paid up to the actual time of disbandment. Sir Charles and his officers claimed the extra sum; they were reimbursed, but only after a delay of five and a half years. Unlike men in the ranks, officers often had to wait for years for their pay. Only fragmentary details of the amounts due to the Hothams have survived, but other evidence indicates that, even if they were paid their due, they had to wait a very long time before receiving it. In 1713 commissions were appointed to examine the difficulties preventing the clearing of pay accounts; in the case of Sir Charles's regiment delay was due to the absence of muster rolls for the period April to August 1709. As late as 1717 Sir Charles was petitioning for arrears of pay due between December 1711 and August 1712. Eventually an act was drafted providing for the payment of 4 per cent annuities to those concerned, but this was not passed until February 1722. In the meantime Sir Charles had suggested that 'exigiencies' might force him to sell his commission.[35]

Sir Charles's public career was pursued against a background of mounting domestic problems. Above all, a rise in his income in no way paralleled the contemporary growth of his expenditure. By 1709 his gross annual rental amounted to £2,111. Jointures reduced this sum by £1,020 until 1697, and by £520 thereafter. Even after Dame Elizabeth's death, therefore, he received under £1,600 a year from his rental. At no time was he able to add to his property, and thereby to his major source of income, by purchase. Moreover, although during this entire period the Hothams did not sell much farm produce, there was a home farm at Scorborough until 1705; but the fire and Sir Charles's subsequent, prolonged absences from the East Riding led him to reduce this modest enterprise to insignificant proportions. In addition entry fines and customary services had both been made redundant, except on the remote property at Filingdales. The leasing structure of his estates, however, permitted frequent readjustments of rents: long leases were granted very rarely, most tenants obtaining leases, or more commonly tenancy agreements, for periods of only three years, two years, or even one year. Comparison of the rental figures available for the period before 1645 with those of the early eighteenth century is exceedingly difficult because of complications arising out of the first baronet's final settlements, though the evidence suggests that overall increases in rents during the intervening period were of very modest proportions. What is certain is that the fourth baronet effected a rise in his rental of around 18 per cent in the period after the fire at Scorborough. Excluding jointure property, rents due amounted to £1,591 in 1709, whereas in 1726–7 the rents received by Sir Charles's successor from the same property totalled £1,884. Nor was this rise primarily due to the letting of previously untenanted land, for several parts of his estate were involved in frequent reassessments of rent levels. It would be wrong to assume from this, however, that Sir Charles was a harsh landlord, though clearly he was an impecunious one. Tenancy agreements contained only general clauses dealing with the repair and maintenance of property, and tenants were usually allowed all the timber required for such tasks. Moreover, Sir Charles adopted a flexible policy in regard to the payment of taxes, requiring tenants of outlying properties to pay all parliamentary taxes, but paying part or occasionally all the parliamentary taxes levied on the property in the vicinity of Scorborough. Local dues were normally the responsibility of the tenants, though in 1711 he paid half those levied at Filingdales despite the fact that according to their agreements the tenants there were liable for all of them.[36]

Some years after the death of his first wife in 1707 Sir Charles married Dame Mildred, widow of Sir Ovedale Corbett and youngest daughter of the Earl of Salisbury. As her jointure lands in Montgomeryshire were worth £836 a year, the marriage promised to solve his financial difficulties. The marriage settlement provided Dame Mildred with £200 of this sum for her personal use, the remainder constituting a welcome addition to Sir Charles's resources. However, after the birth of a son who died young, the couple separated, and subsequent arrangements were much less favourable to Sir Charles. After paying his wife £100 and returning her linen, plate, coach, and horses, he was allowed £200 annually. The marriage brought a permanent increase in his income which was, however, quite insufficient for his needs.[37]

Like that of many of his contemporaries, Sir Charles's expenditure was increased by the cost of defending his interests in the courts. The dispute concerned the reversion to lands which the third baronet's wife had settled on Sir John after she

came of age and before they separated. According to the settlement, this property passed to Sir John's 'right heirs' after his
death, his marriage having been childless. Besides Sir Charles
these heirs included the deceased's two sisters. The dispute
arose from the fact that the second sister died before the settlement was executed; it came to a head when her eldest son tried
to sell that part of the reversion which he claimed, and lasted
until 1697. Reversion to half of the property was then awarded
to Sir Charles; the second half was shared by the other two
parties. However, Sir John's widow retained the entire
property, together with her jointure from the Hotham estates,
until her death in 1728.[38]

There is no doubt, however, that the major reason for Sir
Charles's indebtedness was the fire at Scorborough in 1705 and
his subsequent decision to build a new house in Beverley. The
family found temporary accommodation in a number of places.
Until Brigid's death in 1707 they lived with the Gees at Bishop
Burton; they then leased a house from the Gees and went to
considerable expense in renovating it; later they lived for a
while in Hull and also rented a house in London. Acquisition of
property on which to build in Beverley began in 1713 when they
obtained a lease from a relative; and leases of further property
were acquired from Beverley Corporation in 1714. In 1716 the
Corporation permitted Sir Charles to make bricks on the Westwoods and building commenced in the following year. In 1719
two houses with orchards and gardens and three parcels of
adjacent land were purchased, while in August of that year Sir
Charles was allowed to extend the courtyard of his house into
the adjoining street, provided he widened the street on the other
side. By the time the house was completed in 1723 Sir Charles
had acquired a substantial urban property surrounding the
building, which was among the earliest neo-palladian town
houses in the country. No expense was spared in its erection.
The building itself, designed by Colin Campbell – one of the
most distinguished architects of his generation, cost £7,000; the
sum total spent on furniture and fittings is unknown, though
the grand staircase and chimney-pieces alone cost over
£1,000.[39]

This lack of caution characterized Sir Charles's general hand-
ling of family affairs. Besides the cost of two jointures, his aunt's

will, the lawsuit, and of his new house, he sent his eldest son on a grand tour and gave his second son enough money to establish him in a merchant house in Amsterdam. He also provided his eldest daughter with a portion of £2,500 on her marriage to Sir Thomas Style. At the time of Sir Charles's death both his younger daughters had yet to receive their portions: each was granted £2,000 by his will, a considerable addition to the debts which his successor had to discharge. Many of these debts could have been avoided had Sir Charles been willing to lower his standard of living. Though for long he failed even to contemplate this, he eventually showed concern at expenditure which earlier he would either not have noticed or have ignored. For example, in 1721, shortly after taking out his last and largest mortgage, he asked William Gee to arrange for some gravel pits to be dug on the estate. Gee accordingly hired labourers, at a shilling per day. When Sir Charles protested at the size of this wage, Gee bluntly told him that pits could not be dug for less at that time of year. It was also at this time that Sir Charles considered selling his army commission, exhibiting a failing man's concern for the consequences of his extravagance. Apart from the portions for his younger daughters, which were unavoidable, the provisions of his will were meagre: £6 to each of his servants, £20 to the poor of Beverley, and mourning to the Mayor, Aldermen, and Capital Burgesses of the borough.[40]

Nevertheless, Sir Charles's somewhat carefree policies proved to be entirely justified for they provided his successor with a platform from which to launch his own career. The family's increased social standing enabled the fifth baronet to marry a peer's daughter with a portion of £6,000. His friendship with George II led to his appointment to the royal household in 1727, and later to successive military promotions. Lucrative official salaries as well as less formal perquisites were thereby added to the income from the estates. As a result the family's financial circumstances improved dramatically. Debts were repaid, their life-style was further embellished, and for the first time for nearly half a century substantial purchases of real estate were made. Thus, if the fourth baronet's non-essential expenditure was calculated, it was wise; if impulsive, it proved highly fortuitous.

4. ACHIEVEMENT AND REWARD 1723–38

The fifth baronet, another Sir Charles, was thirty years old at his succession. He was already mature and experienced, having travelled widely since 1712, first on grand tour and then with the army. In 1720 he had been granted a lieutenant-colonelcy in the 7th Dragoon Guards. Although a military career was then 'what of all others suits the most with my inclinations', he was 'little solicitous of coming at regiment any other way than by succeeding' his father in one. Nevertheless, he found the years prior to his father's death frustrating, suffering the 'mortification of seeing every day people not superior in birth or fortune, and with no better pretensions, get above me only because they have a vote'. Lacking 'philosophy to bear with' this, he determined to obtain a 'vote', and suggested that his father stand down in his favour at the 1722 election. However, a strong body of opposition prompted the fourth baronet to stay on. A further suggestion that his father surrender his commission to him was also unavailing.[41]

Sir Charles was sure that the opposition defeated by his father at the 1722 election, whose candidate was a Mr Ellerker Bradshaw, would revive. Yet he was safely elected to replace his father in 1723. He hoped to prevent 'an interest we have preserved' in Beverley 'near a century' from being defeated, and to maintain both that and his fortune 'in good condition'.[42] While he experienced little difficulty in maintaining and improving the latter, he found the preservation of the family's political power base more troublesome. Anticipating stiff opposition at the 1727 election, he made great efforts to bolster his support. In 1725 he paid for the transport of a borough freeman from a London hospital to Beverley. He treated the Corporation in 1725 and again in 1726, and just before the election attempted to collect a long-standing debt on its behalf. He also piloted a bill for the improvement of Beverley Beck through Parliament before the dissolution. Despite careful canvassing, Sir Charles was defeated by Bradshaw, but only by means of gross corruption. Hoping to get the result annulled, he immediately petitioned the Parliamentary Committee of Privileges and Elections, obtained access to the Corporation's files, and leave to have relevant documents brought to London by the Town

Clerk, who was summoned to attend the committee. In February 1729 Bradshaw was unseated and replaced by Sir Charles. Although this episode resulted in the passing of yet another statute against bribery, Sir Charles devoted a considerable amount of money to the election campaign of 1734 when his opponents were Charles Pelham and, inevitably, Bradshaw. After canvassing the electorate he provided the freeman with a treat which cost £70. He spent a further £250 during the election and gave each freeman 2s. 6d. A contemporary forecast that 'our elections in Yorkshire will be the same as last, except Bradshaw in the room of Hotham', but he was mistaken.[43] Pelham was defeated and Bradshaw joined Sir Charles at Westminster. In the next two years Sir Charles spent a total of £158 on maintaining his support in Beverley. From 1736 he paid £10 annually towards the salary of the new master of the local grammar school. As another election approached both he and Bradshaw entertained the Corporation at their homes. Later Bradshaw withdrew and Sir Charles was safely elected for what proved to be his final term at Westminster.[44]

A major reason for the local opposition to Sir Charles was that his career at Court was much more important to him than representation of his constituents in Parliament. On George II's accession he was appointed Groom of the Royal Bedchamber, a post which he held until his death. In 1730 the King sent him to Berlin as Special Plenipotentiary to conduct negotiations for a double marriage alliance between the British and Prussian royal families. King Frederick's volatile behaviour brought the negotiations to an abrupt and abortive end but Sir Charles was warmly praised for his demeanour throughout.[45] To add to his annual Court salary of £400, he made a profit of £1,400 from this trip. He also received personal gifts from the King: gilt plate on the christening of two of his children and, in 1730, a grant of exemption from the land tax. Influence and success at Court furthered his military career. In 1732 he was promoted to a colonelcy in the 18th Royal Irish regiment, and three years later became commander of the 1st Troop of Horse Grenadier Guards, of which the King was inordinately and neurotically proud. As a result of these developments Sir Charles's combined salaries trebled. By 1736 they totalled £2,247 a year, which was more than each of his three predecessors had derived from the family estates. Sir Charles's career also brought him considerable power and prestige. In an age when success was heavily dependent on patronage he was frequently solicited for place and favour. His acquisition of a town-house in Stratton Street, Piccadilly symbolized the wealth and influence which his career brought him. At last the family had reached the highest level of society.[46]

Total annual income rose from £2,200 in 1724 to nearly £4,700 in 1736. A rise in estate income of some £800 a year in the decade 1727–37 contributed to this, and resulted from the death of the third baronet's widow in 1728 and from the rentals of the properties which Sir Charles purchased. Despite the short terms of the majority of leases and agreements, almost all existing rents remained static throughout this period. While estate income consisted almost entirely of rent receipts, there were a few miscellaneous sales. There was a ready local market for wood in the form of firkin staves, and for wild duck from the family's decoy at Scorborough. A few sheep, cattle, and oxen were sold at local fairs, and in 1732–3 produce worth £104 was purchased by people living near South Dalton. The latter reflects Sir Charles's decision when in the provinces to live there rather than in Beverley. Direct income from the home farm was generally minimal and declined towards the end of the period. However, as Sir Charles spent more and more time at South Dalton in the 1730s, indirect income from this source probably rose more than proportionately. From 1723 to 1736 a total of £555 was earned in dividends and interest on stocks and shares. This comparatively modest sum was accumulated in small amounts and at irregular intervals, but it represented further successful efforts to broaden the base of the family's economy. Though Sir Charles's accounts do not embrace the last two years of his life, they indicate that his annual income more than doubled in the short space of thirteen years. The expenditure which this increase permitted altered his family's economic position and prospects.[47]

The accounts were in deficit during six of the seven years prior to 1730 and in 1724 and 1725 the sums involved were substantial. During these early years Sir Charles discharged his father's debts, raised portions for two of his sisters, and financed both the acquisition of a town-house and the transfer

TABLE 4
Sir Charles Hotham's General Accounts, 1723–36

Income	Estate			Office			Stocks etc.			Total			Balance		
	£	s.	d.	£	s.	d.	£	s.	d.	£	s.	d.	£	s.	d.
1723	1863.	3.	3	400.	0.	0	150.	0.	0	2413.	3.	3	− 14.	19.	7
1724	1834.	6.	7	400.	0.	0	50.	0.	0	2284.	6.	7	−1005.	14.	6
1725	1733.	19.	9	400.	0.	0				2133.	19.	9	− 232.	5.	6
1726	1738.	16.	8	400.	0.	0	75.	0.	0	2213.	16.	8	− 8.	13.	4
1727	1849.	5.	6	510.	0.	0				2359.	5.	6	− 99.	1.	4
1728	2301.	11.	11	800.	0.	0				3101.	11.	11	+ 256.	15.	11
1729	2418.	17.	4	800.	0.	0				3218.	17.	4	− 42.	7.	6
1730	2490.	18.	0	2939.	19.	6				5430.	17.	6	+1650.	5.	10
1731	2485.	19.	5	800.	0.	0	80.	0.	0	3365.	19.	5	+ 606.	13.	11
1732	2466.	0.	0	1775.	0.	0	40.	0.	0	4281.	0.	0	+1055.	7.	11
1733	2398.	14.	10	1680.	0.	0	150.	0.	0	4228.	14.	10	+ 913.	16.	5
1734	2463.	4.	9	1665.	0.	0	30.	0.	0	4158.	4.	9	+ 730.	0.	4
1735	2334.	16.	4	2183.	6.	1				4518.	2.	5	+1651.	18.	4
1736	2359.	12.	11	2247.	0.	0	80.	0.	0	4686.	12.	11	+1579.	7.	7

TABLE 4
Continued

Outgoings	To Others £ s. d.	Plate, Books, Furniture £ s. d.	Beverley & S. Dalton £ s. d.	Purchases & Improvements £ s. d.	Self, Family, Travel, etc. £ s. d.	Total £ s. d.
1723	811. 6. 0	292. 1. 8	166. 3. 8	139.10. 3	1019. 1. 3	2428. 2.10
1724	381. 3. 0	823.10. 3	121.11. 9	40. 1. 7	1923.14. 6	3290. 1. 1
1725	232.10. 0	210.13. 7	92.11. 3	51.19.11	1778.10. 6	2366. 5. 3
1726	270. 0. 0	121.11. 0	145.19. 8	84. 1. 0	1600.18. 4	2222.10. 0
1727	305.13. 0	71.19. 6	168.11. 6	17. 4.10	1894.18. 0	2458. 6.10
1728	321. 0. 0	50. 6. 0	394. 7. 2	20. 0. 0	2059. 2.10	2844.16. 0
1729	331. 0. 0	377.13. 6	330. 0.10	29.11. 6	2192.19. 0	3261. 4.10
1730	343. 0. 0	263.16. 0	380. 7.11	26. 1.11	2767. 5.10	3780.11. 8
1731	288. 0. 0	93. 4. 6	131. 3. 9	25. 3. 9	2161.13. 5	2699. 5. 5
1732	284. 0. 0	94. 4. 3	140.14. 3		2706.13. 6	3225.12. 0
1733	225. 0. 0	106. 1. 3	113. 8.11	16. 6. 6	2854. 1. 8	3314.18. 4
1734	225. 0. 0	95.19.10	144.18. 7	277.10.10	2684.15. 1	3428. 4. 4
1735	142. 5. 0	62. 0. 2	151. 7. 6		2510.11. 5	2866. 4. 1
1736	75. 0. 0	76. 4. 6	278.11.11		2676.18.11	3107. 5. 4

Source: DDHO/15/16.

of the family's provincial seat from Beverley to South Dalton. There were also expenses connected with his marriage. Fortunately, jointures did not have to be paid to either of the fourth baronet's wives, though the third baronet's widow received hers for a further five years. The huge deficit of £1,006 in 1724 resulted from Sir Charles's marriage in that year to Lady Gertrude Stanhope, eldest daughter of Philip, Earl of Chesterfield. In return for a cash portion of £6,000 Lady Gertrude was provided with a jointure of £900 together with £200 annually for her personal use during Sir Charles's lifetime. The whole of the Hotham estate was settled on trustees to the use of Sir Charles for life, and then to the use of the eldest son of the marriage and his male heirs in succession. Both financially and socially this match was a family triumph and, not surprisingly, Sir Charles displayed an uncharacteristic extravagance in celebrating it. Although his father-in-law was responsible for most of the cost of the wedding, Sir Charles disbursed £500, and went on to spend a further £724 on furniture for his bride's new home. Expenditure on 'Self and Family' increased by £450 in 1724 and continued to rise steadily thereafter. Lady Gertrude's portion was devoted entirely to the repayment of the fourth baronet's last and largest mortgage. Legacies provided under the latter's will necessitated further heavy expenditure. Sir Charles was forced to mortgage in order to provide his sister, Charlotta, with a portion of £2,000 in 1725 on her marriage to Sir Warton Pennyman. An additional loan of £1,000 was probably devoted to a similar portion for another sister, Philippa, when she married William Gee. The repayment of these and other sums continued until 1735.[48]

Besides considerable expense, Sir Charles's rejection of the Beverley house involved a complete break with his father's policy soon after the property became habitable. However, he considered the building completely unsuitable for his purposes. A London base was all important to his career; he quickly moved books and furniture from Beverley to the house in Piccadilly. He thought it unbecoming for a person of his standing to reside in a busy market town like Beverley, and rapidly developed South Dalton. Furnishings were transferred from Beverley, and work begun on a new dovecot, new stables, and a variety of other buildings. In 1726 an opportunity of adding to the existing property there was seized and a farm purchased for £820. This was the first purchase of agricultural land since the acquisition of South Dalton by the second baronet in 1680. Sir Charles's first items of expenditure on the Beverley house were probably connected with its completion. But as late as May 1729 he was still adding to this urban property, buying a house, three shops, and a small parcel of land. Though the house was no longer needed for family purposes, its eventual sale might be facilitated if appropriate adjacent property was purchased whenever possible. The house was let in 1724 to Rosamund Estoft, whose family were in dire financial difficulties following a lengthy lawsuit against the Moysers, the family into which the third baronet's widow had remarried. In 1727, encouraged by his Court appointment and sensing, perhaps, that Katherine Moyser's jointure would soon revert, Sir Charles purchased more than 100 acres in Lockington from Rosamund for £2,621. On his return from Berlin he bought three parcels of land in Lockington, Goatland, and Wilton in Pickering.[49] During this same period he made only one sale – of a small house in 1729. Though repayments continued for many years, the bulk of his debts had been discharged by 1726. By that time also the expenses involved in establishing himself both publicly and privately had been met. Money for purchases of property was loaned on bonds and gradually repaid in succeeding years. Even so deficits were soon succeeded by large surpluses. In three of the seven years 1730–6 surpluses amounted to considerably more than half Sir Charles's gross annual income at his succession.

The growth of Sir Charles's income was accompanied by an increase in the efficiency with which the estate was managed. He himself had a distinct flair for administration but, unlike his predecessors, he also engaged a full-time steward, William Wight, who was directly responsible to Sir Charles for every aspect of estate management. He collected rents, presided over the manorial courts, supervised repairs and maintenance, checked tenants' husbandry, and managed the home farm. His assistants included two housekeepers, one for South Dalton and another for Beverley, though one gardener served both establishments. There was a tutor for Sir Charles's children and a number of maids. Others were occasionally employed to survey land, timber, or the warren, and each year someone was paid 'for showing us over the moors to Filingdales'. One of the tenants supervised the property there and collected the rents for Wight. The estate created employment for many people in the vicinity and Wight periodically hired local craftsmen and labourers. By delegating major responsibility to this highly competent individual Sir Charles overcame many of the disadvantages which arose from his long absences from South Dalton. The decision to engage him was perhaps prompted by the difficulties which his father had encountered, but never satisfactorily solved.

The estate included several leases of property: one from the Duke of Somerset for an annual rent of £80, another from the Moysers for £38, and others of land in Beverley and Beswick. Sir Charles had to pay the local dues levied on some of this property as well as various taxes and assessments relating to his own. Except for items such as the tithe rent due annually to the Dean and Chapter at York, which stemmed from his ownership of the ex-monastic manor of South Dalton, Sir Charles required his tenants to meet most local dues and assessments, as well as a proportion of the land tax. He paid the rest of the land tax and, of course, all levies on untenanted property. Another matter of great importance to tenants was the extent to which their landlord was willing to maintain their property, not only by undertaking major repairs but also, where necessary, by erecting new buildings. After 1738 the guardians of Sir Charles's successor had a magnificent record in this respect, but it was Sir Charles himself who prompted their highly beneficial activities. Inevitably other matters were given higher priority in earlier years but after 1730 Sir Charles's brick kiln at Lockington was in frequent use. During the last six years of his life he spent more than £700 on the erection of new houses and barns for tenants. No doubt investment of this kind was necessary after enforced neglect under his predecessor. However, Sir Charles instituted a wideranging campaign of repair and rebuilding which was enthusiastically completed after his death. As a result many of the buildings on the estate were new, and the rest in an excellent state of repair, when the sixth baronet came of age in 1755.

There are further indications of the manner in which the large and sustained growth of Sir Charles's income after 1728 was reflected in the pattern of his expenditure. He spent far more on the election of 1734 than on that in 1727. He also gave regular financial assistance to a variety of local causes. There were gifts of money to the poor of Beverley, and annual donations to the Beverley hunt and the race meeting on the Westwoods. He subscribed to three schools, one in York and two in Beverley, subsidized the building of the York Assembly Rooms, and assisted the foundation of a friendly society in Beverley. Furthermore, at a cost of £50 he provided St. Mary's, Beverley with a new pulpit. As befitted a successful man at the height of his career Sir Charles began to live more lavishly following his trip to Berlin. He extended his library and collection of plate, spent £400 on a trip to France and Minorca in 1732, and £200 on a new coach and four on his return. Later he erected a magnificent monument to his father in Beverley Minster. Meanwhile the development of South Dalton continued apace. A great deal of money was devoted to the gardens, including £300 for a new summer house. Sir Charles eventually decided to build a new house there but, having begun to make bricks and lay in timber, his death brought the project to an end.[50] The last recorded annual sum spent on 'Self and Family' was £2,600, more than two and a half times the corresponding figure for 1723. Yet each year from 1730 onwards there was a large surplus of income over expenditure.

Sir Charles was survived by his widow, three daughters, and a son. By his will each daughter was left a portion of £3,330, plus maintenance until she married or came of age. Besides her jointure of £900 a year, Dame Gertrude received a legacy of £500 and, during her life, 1,800 ounces of plate, her jewels and dressing plate, and all Sir Charles's coaches, horses, and furniture. Sir Charles's brother, Beaumont Hotham, was named his executor, and Beaumont, Dame Gertrude, and James Gee were appointed guardians of the sixth baronet, who was still a minor.[51] The subsequent valuation of Sir Charles's personal estate provides additional evidence of his prosperity. He owned £3,750 worth of New South Sea Annuity stock as well as an army clothing assignment which was valued at nearly £3,000. Moreover, he was owed more than £600 on mortgages or bonds. Although the valuation recorded a surplus of £3,648, it greatly underestimated Sir Charles's assets. The value of large amounts

TABLE 5
Sir C. Hotham's Personal Estate, 1738

Credit	£ s. d.
Received of several	770.0. 0
Due for last Michaelmas rents	1050.0. 0
Due for Court Salary	125.0. 0
6 months' dividend on S. Sea stock	75.0. 0
£3,750 S. Sea stock valued @ 110%	4125.0. 0
Clothing Assignment	2823.5.11
Mortgage and 2 Bonds	630.0. 0
Rents due at Ladyday 1738	1300.0. 0
	10,898.5.11

Besides 5,200 ounces of plate, books, furniture etc.

Debit	
Paid & to be paid to Tradesmen etc.	1000.0. 0
Legacies to Servants	250.0. 0
Dame Gertrude: Legacy	500.0. 0
Dame Gertrude: ½ year Fortune & arrears	570.0. 0
Children's maintenance	120.0. 0
Bond for Mrs Glynn's Legacy	4000.0. 0
Due from him on that account	400.0. 0
Promissory note to Dame Gertrude	300.0. 0
Annuity of £8 valued at	110.0. 0
	7250.0. 0

Source: DDHO/71/48.

of goods and chattels was not recorded. Furthermore, more than half of the debit side of the account comprised a bond of £4,000 for Mrs Glynn's legacy. One of his major sources of credit in earlier years, this lady had loaned Sir Charles £4,000 by 1733. However, by a stroke of good fortune, she then bequeathed this debt to Dame Gertrude. Thereby the nature of the debt was transformed and its repayment postponed indefinitely.

During a relatively short career Sir Charles had broadened the base of the family's economy and become a wealthy man. The management of his estate had been reorganized, its acreage substantially increased, the home farm redeveloped, South Dalton turned into an elegant country seat, and the fourth baronet's debts discharged. The fact that much of his success

had come about more by luck than judgement, as a result of his
friendship with George II, had not prevented profits from
being judiciously invested. While some of the ground lost in the
early years of the Civil War had still to be regained, the opportunities which the fifth baronet had so readily grasped guaranteed continuing prosperity.

5.   A MINORITY 1738–55

Sir Charles's first son had died soon after birth. A second son
and heir, Charles, was preceded by three daughters and was
only two years old when his father died. Formal responsibility
for the management of family affairs devolved on the three
guardians, although in practice Dame Gertrude left matters
largely to the two men. After her husband's death she went to
live in Kensington, then in Cavendish Square, and for a while
in Bath. Living in the East Riding, James Gee supervised the
steward's management of the estate. Beaumont Hotham concerned himself with other aspects of the guardianship, such as
the payment of maintenance to his sister-in-law and nieces, and
the investment of surplus capital in the funds. On Gee's death
in 1750 Beaumont assumed total responsibility for the conduct
of family affairs. Before its ruin in the Bubble affair Beaumont
had been a partner in an Amsterdam merchant house. Later he
worked for the British Board of Customs, and by 1738 was
Secretary to the Scottish branch and living in Edinburgh. In
1742 he transferred to the English Customs Commission in
London. Equipped with long-standing experience and exper-
tise, 'he was much consulted by the Ministry on subjects of
finance and trade, of which he had a perfect knowledge united
with an uncommon skill in calculation'.[52]
In common with many of their contemporaries faced with
similar responsibilities, the guardians sought legal sanction for
their actions in the Court of Chancery, which had assumed
control over minors and their guardians following the abolition
of the Court of Wards in the mid seventeenth century. Because
of the minor's interest in its disposition Sir Charles's personal
estate was the first matter to be brought before the court. This
occurred in 1742 as soon as the complex account had been
finalized. Later, during 1751–2, the guardians' administration

Table 6
General Accounts During the Minority, 1738–55

Income	Rent £ s. d.	Others £ s. d.	Total £ s. d.	Balance £ s. d.
1738	2642.12. 6	29.16. 6	2672. 8. 6	+ 35. 8. 0
1739	2655. 6. 6	111.11. 6	2802. 6. 0	+ 46. 8. 5
1740	2651.19. 0	58.18. 0	2757. 5. 3	+ 44.17. 0
1741	2660.19. 6	40. 7. 8	2746. 4.11	+105. 8. 2
1742	2670.10. 0	31. 8. 0	2807. 6. 2	+105. 6. 7
1743	2697. 7. 6	21.10. 6	2824. 4. 7	+105.14. 8
1744	2720.19. 8	57. 0. 6	2883.14.10	+105. 9.11
1745	2725. 1.10	61. 2. 4	2891.14. 1	+103.16. 3
1746	2725.17.10	29. 1. 0	2858.15. 1	+103. 6. 3
1747	2731.17.10	40.13. 2	2875. 7. 3	+104. 8. 1
1748	2742.17.10	35.10. 6	2882.16. 5	+103. 3. 2
1749	2667. 0. 8	32. 7. 0	2802.10.10	+103. 4. 0
1750	2645.19. 9	50. 4. 6	2799. 8. 3	+ 12. 8. 9
1751	2712.13. 7	27. 5. 0	2752. 7. 4	+ 7. 4. 3
1752	2723.19. 4	25. 4. 6	2756. 8. 1	+ 21. 2. 2
1753	2736.18. 6	32. 9. 0	2790. 9. 8	+ 89. 2. 5
1754	2756. 5. 2	27.11. 0	2872.18. 7	+ 74.13. 3
1755	2766. 0. 2	26.11. 0	2867. 4. 5	+ 52.19. 0

TABLE 6
Continued

Outgoings	Outpayments £ s. d.	Beverley House & Incidental £ s. d.	Repairs & Improvements £ s. d.	Payments By Order £ s. d.	Family Payments £ s. d.	Total £ s. d.
1738	294. 4. 4	65.16. 3	223. 2. 5	83. 5. 0	1970.12. 6	2637. 0. 6
1739	296.18. 3	170. 6.10	219.15.10	755.16.10	1313. 0. 0	2755.17. 9
1740	327. 1. 1	77. 0. 7	243. 2. 4	789. 3. 6	1276. 0. 0	2712. 7. 6
1741	376.11. 0	57.14. 0	279.17. 3	650.14. 6	1276. 0. 0	2640.16. 9
1742	358. 5.11	50. 9. 4	237. 4.11	779.19. 5	1276. 0. 0	2701.19. 7
1743	426. 5.10	64.16. 8	168. 4. 6	783. 2.11	1276. 0. 0	2718. 9.11
1744	360. 8. 2	66. 4.11	330. 9. 2	745. 2. 8	1276. 0. 0	2778. 4.11
1745	415.10. 8	67. 0. 9	174. 1.11	855. 4. 6	1276. 0. 0	2787.17.10
1746	356.16. 5	61. 2. 6	227.15. 6	833.14. 5	1276. 0. 0	2755. 8.10
1747	381.15. 6	82. 3. 9	546.13. 5	484. 6. 6	1276. 0. 0	2770.19. 2
1748	358. 5. 4	462.19. 0	158.19. 7	512. 4. 8	1287. 4. 8	2779.13. 3
1749	365.15.10	252.17. 9	90. 5. 1	681. 1. 6	1309. 6. 8	2699. 6.10
1750	331. 4. 6	85.10. 7	627. 8. 5	585.16. 0	1157. 0. 0	2786.19. 6
1751	321.16.11	54. 9. 5	124.11. 3	999.15. 6	1244.10. 0	2745. 3. 1
1752	320. 5. 5	49. 5. 5	117.19. 8	1069.18. 9	1177.16. 8	2735. 5.11
1753	292.16. 9	53. 3. 0	84. 5.10	1074.15. 0	1196. 6. 8	2701. 7. 3
1754	279.17. 3	67.14.11	79.17. 1	1174. 9. 5	1196. 6. 8	2798. 5. 4
1755	283.15. 1	60. 3. 6	48.18.10	1182. 5. 8	1239. 2. 4	2814. 5. 5

NOTE: Income includes previous year's surplus. The first column of outgoings includes rents, the charges of courts and receiving, and taxes.

Sources: DDHO/15/6, 7

of the minor's affairs 'for the time past and to come' came under scrutiny.[53] In each case the minor's 'next friend', Philip, Earl of Chesterfield, appeared as plaintiff, the executor or guardians, as appropriate, as defendants. After examination of witnesses, accounts, and vouchers by the clerks of the court as well as by the respective lawyers, proceedings were referred to one of the Masters in Chancery. He duly submitted a report to the Lord Chancellor who, finally, pronounced himself in agreement with the past actions and future plans of the defendants. The guardians' solicitor had previously warned against the presentation of insufficient evidence: 'it seems to me to be quite necessary to specify . . . to let the court know what it is we really have done'.[54] He was motivated both by the vigilance of the court and by the possibility, despite broad agreement between the two parties, that the sixth baronet might raise objections to the Chancellor's decree once he came of age. Accordingly the defendants fully explained both their general strategy and many of their individual policy decisions. Thus, together with a full series of estate accounts, the records of Chancery provide a detailed picture of family affairs during the minority.[55]

Following the fifth baronet's death income was greatly reduced by the cessation of his huge salaries. For the next eighteen years the family's sole earnings came from the estate and from returns on investments in the funds. Although the latter had previously been small and irregular, further investments were made. As executor Beaumont Hotham reported that profits were 'much above the trusts imposed' on him: after the payment of debts and legacies nearly £3,000 of the fifth baronet's personal estate remained. As instructed by Sir Charles's will, Beaumont devoted this sum to the purchase of additional New South Sea annuities.[56] Total estate income rose, but only slightly. Sales of produce dwindled with the contraction of the home farm at South Dalton; there was little point in maintaining this establishment following Dame Gertrude's decision to live elsewhere. While existing rents remained at their former level, total rent receipts rose as a result of the further expansion of the estate by purchase. However, two factors ensured that the rise in receipts was less than proportionate to this expansion. Following severe outbreaks of cattle plague in Yorkshire during 1748–9 there were large increases in rent arrears: subsequent allowances of rent raised 'incidental' expenditure by over £200 in 1748 and by £150 in 1749. Secondly, especially in those areas worst hit by the plague, there was an increase in the amount of land which was untenanted. Owing to the drop in sales of produce, the rise in total estate income was even smaller than that in rent receipts – less than £100 a year throughout the minority. This in no way compensated for the loss of income from salaries, and the resources at the disposal of the guardians were thousands of pounds less than those previously available. Nevertheless they had no difficulty in keeping within the bounds of this reduced income. Besides essential payments, they made varied and substantial investments. Moreover, the improvement of the position from which their charge was later to launch his career in no way qualified a policy of benevolence towards tenants, or the enjoyment of Dame Gertrude and her family of a suitably comfortable way of life. Annual surpluses were never very large but they were persistent; and consequently income was regularly supplemented by cash in hand.

Outrents exhibited a minimum amount of fluctuation over the years. They included £80 a year for the lease of land from the Duke of Somerset; others were for adjacent closes, a farm in Wilton, and the tithes of Beswick, Lockington, Wilton, Scorborough, and Filingdales. There were also payments of duty to the Dean and Chapter at York, the salary of the Vicar at Hutton Cranswick, and of fee farm rents at Filingdales, Wilton, and Lockington. The total sum fell after 1738 when the family ceased to lease a parcel of land from a Mr Wressle, but rose again in 1743 and 1745 owing to the payment of entry fines to the Duke of Somerset. 'Charges of Courts and Receiving' were most regular, consisting largely of the steward's annual salary of £40. The remainder went towards providing tenants with meat and ale when rents were collected and courts held. Taxes consisted almost entirely of land tax payments, the size of which varied according to government policy; other taxes were minimal and comprised assessments and dues on property which the family could, or chose, not to let. 'Incidental' expenditure was a miscellany but, among other items, included legal expenses. In 1740 the family was involved in a dispute concerning tithes at Eastburn, and in 1748 they spent nearly £190 on another suit.

Investment in the home farm normally appeared under this heading too. Three horses were purchased in 1738, ten oxen and thirty wethers in the following year, but these were the last such entries. Direct farming on any scale was soon abandoned but entries such as the 'mowers and haymakers bill' of 1748 indicate that some use was made of such land as remained untenanted. Most of these items, such as the cost of valuing land for prospective purchase or of hiring someone to count the rabbits in the warren at Eastburn, were truly incidental; perhaps most bizarre was the cost of providing the 'swanner' with a new hat and coat at three-yearly intervals. Bad debts also occurred sporadically: at the Mayday rent collection in 1741, for example, there was 'nothing to be had' from Robert Wilson, 'he being gone'.

In his will Sir Charles had specified that the Beverley house was to be sold 'within fifteen years of my death for £2,000 or upwards'.[57] The money was to be used to purchase land and the guardians lost no time in advertising the sale. However, they were unable to dispose of the property at the stipulated price, and the cost of its upkeep remained a constant item of expenditure throughout the minority. Being urban, the property was liable to a great variety of taxes: land, window, poor, church, and highway taxes as well as fee farm and burgage rents; there were also rents for those parts of the site which were leased. William Taylor was paid £5 annually for looking after the house, and there was always at least one housekeeper to assist him. Each year some repairs, either to the house or the stables, were necessary and labour was hired for cleaning the yard and 'area'. In addition there was the cost of coal, soap, candles, house sand, and, less often, of items such as headed paper and 'for a man to fetch J.M. to open locks and get at writings'. Sometimes the housekeeper hired other women to help her; they needed brooms, charcoal, and materials 'for cleaning locks etc.'. Others were responsible for sweeping chimneys or simply 'mending a spade and a shovel'. Although annual maintenance costs were fairly constant and never large, cumulatively they constituted a drain on resources. It is impossible to calculate the full cost to the family of the fire at Scorborough, but the capital investment and recurrent expenditure in Beverley which followed it represented almost total loss. The furniture and fittings were publicly auctioned by the sixth baronet in 1758; a decade later his successor managed to dispose of the shell for a token sum, whereupon the building was pulled down 'for the value of the materials'.[58] In sombre contrast to other aspects of family affairs, the entire venture was an elaborate and costly blunder.

The column in the accounts entitled 'Repairs and Improvements' was not exclusive. The fine for renewal of a lease at Beswick was entered here at seven-yearly intervals. Moreover, although the major sums of money spent on the purchase of land were listed under 'Payments by Order', a number of smaller purchases appeared here instead. The figures include £50 spent on a moiety of the tithes at Battleburn in 1739, £75 on a similar purchase at Eastburn in 1746, and the £900 disbursed between 1747 and 1749 on the purchase of farms at South Dalton.[59] Furthermore, certain items under this heading had little connection with the estate. After Sir Charles's death alterations were made to the family vault in South Dalton church, and in 1746 a new roof was erected over the chancel of the church at Hutton Cranswick. However, following the lead given by Sir Charles, the rest of this money was devoted to the wholesale improvement of conditions on the estate. Some of this expenditure, including that on the repair of a brick kiln and the decoy, and on the erection of a malt kiln, a tithe barn, and a brick and tile barn, directly benefited the family. Some benefited both landlord and tenant: for example, a windmill was repaired and a new watering pond constructed. Most of it, however, was of direct benefit to the tenantry. The accounts record at least forty-four separate instances of new construction on their behalf. Projects included the erection of a new house and stable at Wilton in 1738, a new garden wall at Beverley in 1740, a new mill at Filingdales in 1744, and a new cottage at Cranswick in 1750. Of a total expenditure between 1738 and 1755 of just over £4,000, nearly £1,500 was spent in this way. A further £1,500 was devoted to the repair of old buildings as distinct from the erection of new ones. The original construction bills vividly illustrate the manner in which the resources of the neighbourhood were tapped. Local carpenters, glaziers, masons, bricklayers, locksmiths, and blacksmiths secured plenty of employment. Some materials, particularly bricks, were supplied from the estate but lime, tiles, and timber had to be purchased in quantity. Haulage costs were heavy; and, if materials came from Hull or Hedon, private hauliers were contracted. However, tenants were paid for providing transport over shorter distances: thus, during the erection of his stable at Fitling in 1739 Thomas Collinson earned £5. 7s. 2d. by bringing sand and bricks from places nearby. The programme of improvement was completed towards the end of the minority.[60] Tenants were also assisted by allowances during the cattle plague and, above all, by the continuing absence of increases in rents. Following the completion of individual building or repair projects, even new tenants held property at old rents, and continued to do so. Given the lack of rent increases between 1723 and 1738 this was remarkable, and represented true benevolence during what were difficult years for the farmer.[61]

'Payments by Order', which fluctuated markedly, are unfortunately most difficult to interpret. The purpose of a small proportion is certain. They included the wages of the gardener and the housekeeper at South Dalton, and the payment of £100 Association money in 1744 in connection with the threatened Jacobite rebellion. Otherwise this category consisted of bulk payments, in 1739–40 to William Mould, and thereafter to Bartholomew Burton. The latter was a London merchant, but a separate account of his with the guardians gives no clue as to how this money was spent.[62] However, since during this period the family was based in London, Mould and Burton almost certainly acted as bankers. The latter was responsible for the purchase and management of annuity holdings, for which he was paid a commission. Moreover, he probably serviced the guardians' major purchases of property. In 1743 Dorothy Shafto, the daughter of a London merchant, was paid £1,450 for a 'very pretty compact farm' which lay near Hotham property at Wilton. She sold owing to difficulty in redeeming a mortgage. Wight surveyed the farm, and then informed Beaumont Hotham via James Gee that there was scope for enclosure and that an early increase in rent was possible. In 1749 the guardians paid £750 to two widows and two spinsters for the manor of Barghe, seventy acres in Beswick, two plots of common in Wilfholme, and a cottage in Aike.[63] Together with the £1,025 spent on the other purchases mentioned above, these acquisitions produced an even greater expansion of the estate than that achieved by the fifth baronet.

'Family Payments' comprised, firstly, Dame Gertrude's annual jointure of £900. There was also the cost of children's maintenance for which £400 was set aside each year. Moreover, till the age of fourteen each daughter was allowed 3 per cent a year on her prospective portion, and 4 per cent a year between fourteen and marriage. Added to these sums was the cost of a few months' recuperative holiday in the country for one of the daughters. The minor's maintenance also came under this heading until 1750 when he left Westminster School. For some years thereafter he went on an extensive Continental tour which took him to France, Switzerland, Italy, Russia, Denmark, Sweden, Prussia, and most of the German principalities. Chancery allowed £800 a year for this tour and most of the cost came under 'Payments by Order', no doubt because Burton was responsible for exchange arrangements. This category also included the expenses connected with the sickly Melusina's visit to a number of European spas in 1750. However, the decrease in 'Family Payments' after the transfer of the costs of Charles's tour was only a small one. This was because Dame Gertrude and her daughters led a much more active life as the latter grew up after 1750, spending as much time in Bath and other resorts as in London.[64]

The guardians undoubtedly carried out their responsibilities meticulously and with great effectiveness during these years. None of the sums settled on the various members of the family fell into arrears, and extraordinary expenditure on their behalf was forthcoming whenever necessary. Charles Hotham was sent to one of the best schools and given a splendid grand tour. Dame Gertrude and the other children continued to enjoy the standard of living to which they had grown accustomed and, far from being neglected, the estate benefited from considerable investment. It was substantially and judiciously expanded, the improvements initiated by the fifth baronet were completed, and in the three aspects of their situation most important to them – their accommodation, their stock, and their rents – the tenants were treated generously. Finally, the administration of the family's finances was put on a sounder footing by the employment of Mould and Burton, while holdings in the funds were substantially increased. It is difficult to fault the conduct of affairs during the minority. The Beverley house remained unsold, but not for want of effort. Also, in 1755 both the marriage portions of Dame Gertrude's surviving daughters and her own legacy from Mrs Glynn remained to be paid. However, the former had not become due and the latter was not in demand. An expanding and prosperous estate, together with sizeable annuity holdings, was more than sufficient to meet both needs if and when they arose. During the minority non-productive or conspicuous expenditure was at a minimum owing to the fact that the cost of maintaining a baronet's position in society did not have to be borne. Consequently substantial investment was possible even though income dropped in 1738 and rose only very slowly thereafter. Although low costs were primarily responsible for the period's achievements, the efforts and abilities of Beaumont Hotham and William Wight were additional causes of success. The family was fortunate to be served by such experienced professionals. The minority witnessed solid and, in regard to estate improvements, impressive progress. It was an entirely beneficial sequel to the public successes of Sir Charles's career.

6. BEYOND 1755

Again, as in 1688, the character and behaviour of the head of the family, in this case the sixth baronet, Sir Charles, militated against further progress; but he also experienced considerable misfortune. He came of age and returned to England in 1755. Servants received 'birthday tokens' and the 'ringers of Beverley' who welcomed him home were given five guineas. An air of expectancy was quickly justified. In 1757 Sir Charles was appointed to the same salaried post at Court which his father had held – Groom of the Bedchamber to the now ageing George II. In the same year he married a wealthy Essex heiress, Clara Anne Clutterbuck. Though it certainly included real estate, the exact value and content of her dowry are unknown; but, as it earned her a jointure of £1,000 a year should she outlive Sir Charles, it was clearly substantial. However, the resulting rise in income lasted for only a very short period: for when Clara died in 1758 Sir Charles disposed of the whole of her dowry, 'which in present and expectation was very considerable', to his sister, Melusina, and his wife's relations. In addition Sir Charles's own health, which had never been good, also began to deteriorate. He attended Court less frequently and resigned his post, and with it his salary, in 1760.[65]

Meanwhile expenditure had risen substantially. With Sir Charles's coming of age personal expenditure, moderate during the minority, increased rapidly. In 1755, for instance, besides payments made on his orders, £840 was forwarded to him for his personal use. In 1757 his two remaining sisters claimed both their own portions and their share of that of their deceased sister, Caroline. Each received £4,167. Although Dame Gertrude did not claim her legacy, she was provided with the interest on it annually. Moreover, until her death in 1775 she continued to draw her annual jointure of £900 from the estate. An annuity of £100 was also paid to Dr Tollot, who had accompanied Sir Charles on his grand tour.[66]

Unfortunately, the years following the minority are not well documented. The long series of estate accounts dating from 1723 ends with that for 1755. However, the next available account, for 1768, indicates that there were no rent improvements in the intervening period. For the thirteen years after 1755 the gross annual rental remained at around £2,800. The absence of estate accounts suggests that Wight resigned his post in 1755, not surprisingly in view of his lengthy service, and was not replaced. Why Sir Charles failed to increase rents which had remained unimproved for more than thirty years, especially when contemporary price rises were everywhere leading to greatly increased farming profits, is a mystery. The answer lies perhaps in his personal inadequacies. On being nominated M.P. for Beverley he declined to serve at Westminster. Then, after spending many solitary months at South Dalton, he made a series of costly visits to foreign resorts in an attempt to improve his health. He drew up plans for a new house at South Dalton on his return from one of these journeys in 1767; but his condition further deteriorated and he died at the German spa of Stavelo in the following year. According to his uncle and successor, the highly capable Beaumont Hotham, Sir Charles had 'had the means and the opportunity which few possessors of the estate can again expect', but nevertheless 'did not avail himself of those advantages, but on the contrary ... left his successor as bare of money as well possible to be from such an estate'.[67]

TABLE 7
Particulars of Sir B. Hotham's Estate, 1768

Gross Annual Rental	£	s.	d.
Scorborough	626.	0.	0
Lockington	472.	0.	0
Cranswick	287.	0.	0
East Rotsey	162.	10.	0
Swaythorpe	160.	0.	0
Fitling	80.	0.	0
South Dalton	138.	10.	0
Beswick	40.	0.	0
Wilton	540.	0.	0
Filingdales	344.	0.	0
	2850.	0.	0

Annual Outpayments			
Lady Gertrude's Jointure	845.	0.	0
Her Interest on £4,833 6s. 8d.	178.	6.	8
Life Annuity to Dr. Tollot	100.	0.	0
To the Steward	42.	0.	0
To late Housekeeper	20.	0.	0
Land Tax (3/– in the £)	117.	6.	0
Allowed for South Dalton	138.	0.	0
Annual Outrents	97.	17.	0
Repairs and Incidentals	86.	10.	0
	1620.	19.	8
Clear Profit	1229.	0.	4

Source: DDHO/70/33.

Thereafter the pendulum of capability and fortune swung once more in the family's favour. Over the years Sir Beaumont had judiciously invested his own earnings of £1,000 a year as a customs commissioner; and consequently in making provision for his younger children was not dependent on the income from his inherited estate. By this time, moreover, the general economic situation was much to the family's advantage. Sir Beaumont calculated that the amount of annual income available to him after essential expenditure was £1,229. In disposing of these resources he gave high priority to the payment of Dame Gertrude's legacy. He also went ahead with the new house at South Dalton which his predecessors had hoped, but failed, to build. To meet its cost he made strenuous efforts to increase his annual income, having the estate surveyed with a view to mining the alum deposits which it was rumoured to contain. While his hopes in this respect were unfulfilled, he was able to make substantial rent increases – the first for nearly fifty years – particularly at Cranswick and Lockington, which were enclosed by act of Parliament in 1769 and 1776 respectively. Thereafter work on the house proceeded more quickly, not least because in 1771 the large estate in the East Riding which Sir Beaumont's wife had inherited passed permanently into the Hothams' possession. The seventh baronet died in that year and was succeeded by his son, Sir Charles. Besides bringing large public salaries to assist with family finances, he continued the process of enclosure and rent improvement, and consolidated the estate by purchasing a huge property at Gardham. Under him South Dalton Hall Garth was completed at a total cost of £30,000. Meanwhile the profits of landownership soared as the demands of a rapidly increasing population raised food prices. By the early years of the nineteenth century the gross annual rental of the Hotham estate, which was then one of the largest in Yorkshire, amounted to more than £15,000.[68]

The dominant feature of the Hothams' history during this period was the execution of the first baronet and his eldest son in 1645, and the financial and economic consequences which flowed from this. Much of the large estate which he possessed was dispersed at his death and, although the bulk of this property later reverted to the main branch of the family, not until the 1770s did they regain the level of wealth as landowners which they had enjoyed before the Civil War. This was merely the greatest of a series of misfortunes. The second baronet was forced into exile and died soon after his return; in the meantime his estate was confiscated. His successor contracted an unsuccessful and childless marriage, neglected family affairs, ran into debt, and finally died of an obscure malaise after wandering alone to Holland. Under the fourth baronet the house at Scorborough was burnt down and a second marriage ended in separation. On joining the army Sir Charles was unavoidably absent from the estate for long periods, and became heavily indebted through building a new house in Beverley which the family never occupied, maintained at considerable expense, and eventually disposed of at a huge loss. The fifth baronet was conspicuously successful in every aspect of his career but died in his prime. Then, after a long minority, he was succeeded by a sick and listless son whose life and career were not as short, but nearly as barren, as his marriage.

Despite these misfortunes the period was one of relatively slow but cumulatively substantial growth in the family's economy. By 1760 they had not regained all the ground lost in the early 1640s but, except for a few years after 1645, had nevertheless enjoyed increasing wealth and prosperity in the intervening period. The estate was consolidated, expanded, and improved; various members of the family made notable contributions to public life; their manner of living gradually became more luxurious; and their influence and prestige steadily increased.

Among the factors which enabled them to progress in the midst of difficulties was the manner in which they approached the task of managing their estate. Quite apart from the adverse and largely chance factors mentioned above, economic recovery was rendered difficult by the extremely sluggish growth in the family's major source of income, rent receipts. Although under the sixth baronet opportunities for rent improvement were lost through sheer neglect, there is no evidence that this was the case earlier. Apart from a short period in the early eighteenth century, stable or falling agricultural prices did not permit rent improvement before 1755. Existing rents remained remarkably stable for most of this period and increases in the rental stemmed largely from reversions and purchases of property. Despite, or perhaps because of this, the Hothams did invest in support of their tenantry. There is little evidence relating to estate management during the late seventeenth century but in the early eighteenth century they paid at least part of the land tax levied on their property, thoroughly refurbished housing, outhousing, and other facilities on tenanted property, and gave assistance to their tenants during the cattle plague. Like many of their contemporaries, the Hothams also engaged both a banker and an estate steward. The former was an important source of advice and contacts; the latter played a key role in the administrative network of family affairs. By managing important aspects of business efficiently both men made substantial contributions to the family's success and left their employers with greater freedom to pursue their public careers. Thus, though rarely particularly enterprising, as landowners the Hothams were careful and constructive; as landlords they were benevolent and compassionate.

Appreciation of their tenants' difficulties was reflected in the family's decision to reduce the scale of their own farming to the point where profits from it were of little consequence. The need for income diversification was met not so much by investment in the funds, which were used as a means of banking profits rather than speculatively; but by the rewards of office-holding, which were eagerly sought after and which, under the fifth baronet, reached substantial proportions. The change of dynasty from Stuart to Hanoverian, and more especially the fifth baronet's friendship with George II, were of profound importance in this connection. After 1738, however, there was a return to the heavy reliance on income from the estate which was characteristic of the family's financial situation for most of this period.

A large proportion of expenditure comprised family payments. Eldest sons were well educated, generous provision was made for younger sons and daughters, and during more than half of this entire period the Hothams devoted very substantial sums to the maintenance of widows. Other expenditure was designed in large measure to sustain or improve the family's social position. This was why political success was avidly pursued and, once obtained, was vigorously defended. The desire for social prestige was also the chief motivating factor behind the Beverley house project, the subsequent maintenance of two establishments – one in London and the other in Yorkshire – and also, for example, the sixth baronet's trips to German rather than English spas. Paradoxically, opulence was regarded as a form of social insurance. Especially in regard to expenditure, therefore, family fortunes were much influenced by the attitudes and behaviour of individuals. Here fate served the Hothams well for, while the most adequate of them were short-lived, the more able were in control for longer periods. The fourth baronet falls easily into neither of these two categories; but the risks which he took were eventually justified. The lengthy minority after 1738 enabled the family to consolidate earlier achievements precisely because non-productive expenditure was then low, a fact which was subsequently thrown into sharp focus during the short but costly career of the sixth baronet.

In the final analysis, however, progress depended on developments more fundamental than any of those previously mentioned. After the disintegration of the estate in 1645 successive heads of the family employed stricter forms of settlement, thereby producing a greater degree of stability than the family had previously enjoyed. None the less, two episodes in the period after 1645 illustrate the uncertainty which continued to prevail, despite the gradual acceptance of the principle of primogeniture, and the development of means whereby it could be legally effected. The sixth baronet, for reasons which remain obscure, deprived his family of a lucrative and additional inheritance by dividing the succession to his wife's estate between her relations and his own sister. Earlier, following the turbulent and unpredictable events of the period 1680–91, Dame Elizabeth Hotham was solely responsible for maintaining the link between the estate and the family and name of Hotham. Following the death of her husband in 1688, far from being under any obligation to settle the estate on Charles Hotham and his male heirs in succession, she was in fact free to dispose of the property in any way she wished. As her brother was quick to recognize in a letter to Dame Elizabeth, the subsequent prosperity of the Hothams depended finally on 'the justice you do the family'.[69]

III

THE BEAUMONTS OF WHITLEY AND LASCELLES HALL

ALTHOUGH, in cases where settlements were overtaken by events, sentiment alone might preserve the link between a family and a particular property, it should not be assumed that landowners were uniformly concerned to settle the whole of their patrimony on a single individual – even where a representative of the direct male line had survived. Few owners were uninterested in expanding their holdings but not all of them were intent on consolidating their property into a single unit. Sir Thomas Beaumont of Whitley Hall in the West Riding, for example, who died more than a decade after the emergence of the full-blown strict settlement in 1657, split his estate between two direct male heirs. The properties were later reunited following the failure of the senior line but this could not have been foreseen when Sir Thomas made his dispositions. Moreover, he arranged the division of his inheritance quite deliberately for reasons which had just as much to do with family loyalty as had Dame Elizabeth Hotham's actions in 1691. Though adjacent to each other, the properties had originally been separate. In addition Sir Thomas himself had been born into the junior branch of the family at Lascelles Hall, and had only inherited Whitley in 1631 following the death of his cousin, Sir Richard Beaumont, who was unmarried and childless. Sir Richard had chosen Thomas Beaumont as his chief beneficiary because he was anxious to maintain the core of his property in the name of Beaumont; but had nevertheless left half his real estate to various other relatives. Thus, partible inheritance was a major characteristic of this family's settlement policy in the seventeenth century.

The wealth of neither branch of the family approached that which the Hothams enjoyed for most of this period. Even when the two branches and properties were reunited in a single individual in the eighteenth century the Beaumonts remained among the less substantial members of the county gentry. In times of adversity they were more dogged, but also more vulnerable, than many of their contemporaries. Of necessity their way of life was comparatively restricted and they wielded little influence beyond the immediate locality of their estate. Unhesitatingly Royalist in the Civil War, and later obdurate Tory backwoodsmen, their endeavours were almost exclusively private and provincial. Though far from unsuccessful, their achievements were generally modest, only briefly remarkable, and never spectacular.

I.   A SUCCESSFUL ROYALIST 1631–68

Like many old-established landed families, the Beaumonts believed themselves to be descended from the Norman invaders. Their earliest known ancestor is William de Bellemonte, who was granted land at Huddersfield in the West Riding in recognition of his service in the third Crusade. He later acquired additional property in Meltham and Crosland, and within a few decades the family became lords of the manor of Whitley. In 1426, following Henry Beaumont's marriage to a local heiress, a collateral branch of the family was established at nearby Lascelles Hall. By 1540 the Whitley Beaumonts owned a compact estate in the area between Huddersfield and Wakefield.[1] The first and only baronet, Richard Beaumont, inherited this property in 1575. At the turn of the century, when he built a new hall at Whitley, his annual income from land amounted to some £1,000. Knighted at Whitehall by James I in 1603, he served briefly as M.P. for Pontefract in 1625. In 1628 Charles I made him free grants of a baronetcy and of tithes adjacent to his estate. Though Sir Richard's local influence was then quite considerable, he was heavily in debt, having long been addicted to cards and cockfighting. Allegedly indebtedness forced him to sell property in Huddersfield; it would also appear to have contributed to the failure of his repeated attempts to marry. One recipient of his advances, Elizabeth Armitage of Kirklees, replied caustically that she had 'received more letters than I ever found content in, so I am resolved to rest'.[2] Nevertheless, when he died unmarried in 1631 Sir Richard's estate was reputedly worth £1,200 a year. Lack of direct heirs led him to divide the estate among various relatives, but property worth around £600 a year went to his cousin, Thomas Beaumont, who had already succeeded to part of the smaller Lascelles Hall property on his marriage in 1629.[3]

Thomas Beaumont's inheritance of 1631 comprised the manors of Whitley, Lepton, Meltham, and South Crosland, property in Little Lepton, and the castle and park at Sandal. As the main beneficiary of his cousin's will Thomas had to discharge most of Sir Richard's debts, which were more substantial than either had anticipated. However, a maximum of £2,200 in debts was a small price for an estate which was larger than, and adjacent to, that of Thomas's own family at Lascelles Hall. Little information exists concerning the years prior to the Civil War. Sir Richard had provided for a trusteeship of up to seven years while his debts were paid, if necessary from estate income. The first signs of more positive activity, involving several property transactions, date from 1638. Thomas then sold the unprofitable and inconveniently situated property at Sandal to neighbouring gentry for £1,100. In 1639 he purchased property near Lascelles Hall and in Kirkheaton for £300 and £205 respectively. Two years later he acquired further land in Kirkheaton for £8, and in 1643 sold premises in Crosland for £50. This rationalization was accompanied by severe rack-renting of his tenants at Whitley. By 1640 his property there was worth £212 a year; unfortunately there is no contemporary indication of the gross annual income of his estate.[4]

Thomas was an ardent Royalist. He served as Major of a Regiment of Foot, then as Garrison-Commander and Deputy-Governor of Sheffield Castle until its capitulation in July 1644. After surrendering upon composition to go and reside at his dwelling, he subsequently fought for the King at Pontefract. His delinquency, therefore, was repeated and indisputable. The original penalty for delinquency was sequestration but from February 1644 Parliament allowed composition to be substituted. The family benefited greatly from this relaxation. In November 1645 Thomas and his wife petitioned that she be allowed to compound for him because he was too ill from wounds to travel to London. This was granted and the County Committee ordered to submit details of his delinquency and estate. These were duly presented in

December, and Thomas took the National Covenant and the Negative Oath. The original permission for composition must have been rescinded for in February 1646 Elizabeth Beaumont again petitioned, on similar grounds, to compound on her husband's behalf. This was allowed in April and a fine fixed at £700. Other penalties included two assessments, the first in 1646 for £500 and another in 1647 for £265. In 1650 a further £200 was demanded because Thomas had signed the Yorkshire 'Engagement'.[5]

TABLE 8

T. Beaumont's Depositions to the Commissioners for Compounding with Delinquents

First Deposition – December 1645

a. *'Before these unnatural wars'*				b. *'At this present'*		
	£	s.	d.		£	s. d.
Whitley Demesne	90.	0.0			60.	0.0
Free Rents		15.5				15.5
Lands	250.	0.0			240.	0.0
Mill	8.	0.0			5.	0.0
Coalmine	15.	0.0			10.	0.0
In Reversion	30.	0.0			20.	0.0
In Expectancy	150.	0.0			100.	0.0
	543.15.5				435.15.5	

Second Deposition – April 1646

'Before these troubles'	£	s.	d.
Free Rents		15.	5
Lands	283.15.	5	
In Reversion	30.	0.	0
In Expectancy	150.	0.	0
	464.10.10		

Source: J. W. Clay (ed.), *Yorkshire Royalist Composition Papers*, I, *YASRS*, XV (1893), pp. 147–9.

In common with other Royalists, he successfully evaded or reduced these impositions. While his wife was compounding in London Thomas was fit enough to travel to York. As she petitioned for three other relatives 'not able to travel on account of sickness', one suspects that they felt, justifiably, that the authorities would deal more leniently with a woman. Both his depositions of estate revenue substantially underestimated his annual income. Curiously, though the second deposition contained merely an estimate for the period 'before these troubles' which was lower than the equivalent estimate in the first deposition, it was accepted. Before paying his fine Thomas submitted a list of what reputedly were annual outpayments from his estate, hoping thereby to have the fine reduced. Once again he was successful, being required to pay only £478 instead of £700. His dealings with the Committee for the Advance of Money were equally devious. In calculating his second assessment the authorities considered two schedules of debts which Thomas submitted within a month; one amounted to £524, the other to £1,000. Though promised a discharge on payment of the assessment, he had not paid by January 1650 whereupon the Committee ordered his sequestration. There is no evidence, however, that he paid or that the order was implemented. The 'Engagement' money was levied in May 1650; yet Thomas had only paid half by November, was negotiating for a refund, denying that he had signed the document, and demanding extra time in which to pay the second instalment should the authorities remain obdurate.[6] Clearly, the family suffered little on account of his delinquency. While their own efforts were partially responsible for this, there were other factors. The speed with which composition on easy terms was obtained was due to Parliament's endeavours to boost revenue by streamlining the process whereby Royalists surrendered. Sequestration for non-payment of the second assessment was probably avoided as a result of the general pardon granted to those not sequestered by December 1651. The family may also have capitalized on friendship with members of parliamentary committees in Yorkshire. Officials were constantly criticized for partiality in their treatment of delinquents. For whatever reason the civil disturbances and the impositions which followed no more than delayed the progress in his private affairs which Thomas had made prior to the war.

Unofficial sources provide a more realistic picture of his current situation. In 1650 he was a liberal contributor towards the erection of the chapel at Meltham. In 1651 he purchased a farm, four houses, and three cottages in Lepton for an unknown sum and, in a separate transaction, four small properties nearby for £200. Significantly, capital expenditure did not lead to large rent improvements. During 1652–4 Thomas renewed many estate leases and made only slight upward changes in rents. The settlement of October 1651 on the marriage of his eldest son, Adam, to Elizabeth Asshton provides perhaps a partial explanation of this, as well as further evidence of prosperity. In return for a portion of £1,500 Elizabeth was provided with a jointure of £200 should she outlive her husband. The entire Whitley estate was vested in trustees for Thomas Beaumont's use for life, then similarly for Adam, and finally for the use of the latter's male heirs in succession. A maximum of £2,000, with annual maintenance of £100 each before marriage, was provided from the same property for the portions of any daughters of the marriage; younger sons were each to receive £30 annuities. A further £2,000 was to be raised from Whitley to augment the portions of Thomas's younger children as directed by his will. Finally, Elizabeth Beaumont having recently died, he reserved the right to raise a jointure of up to £100 for a future wife.[7] In two respects this settlement is most revealing. In relating only to the Whitley estate it provides the first indication that Thomas planned to maintain the separate identity of his two properties. Secondly, the settlement was executed when seven of Thomas's younger children, four sons and three daughters, were still alive. Full details of the portions or annuities provided for them have not survived, but that numerous, additional provisions were planned from Whitley alone while Thomas's immediate family remained so large is indicative of considerable financial confidence.

In the decade before the Restoration estate expansion continued. In 1655 further property near Lascelles Hall, including a mill and kiln, was purchased for £140. In 1656 Thomas's father, Richard Beaumont, died and, if it had not already done so, the remainder of the Lascelles Hall estate then reverted to him. Moreover, in August of that year Thomas took as his second wife Mary, widow of Richard Pilkington, who possessed real and personal estate inherited from both her father and her first husband. In the same year Thomas's daughter, Elizabeth, was provided with a portion of £1,000 on marrying Francis Nevile of Chevet, whose family had purchased Sandal in 1638. The only sale of these years, in 1656, was of a house in

Kirkheaton for £42. Meanwhile, in 1655 Adam Beaumont had died at the early age of twenty-four, leaving a son, Richard, who eventually succeeded Thomas at Whitley, and two daughters. After the payment of debts and funeral expenses Adam's personal estate, the value of which is unknown, was divided into three equal parts: one went to his widow, another to his younger children, and the third to various relatives, including his father. The latter was also left all Adam's rights to the personal estate of his grandfather-in-law, provided he paid Adam's widow 'the sums ... disbursed in the administration of the same'. Before 1660, therefore, the circumstances of the head of the family steadily improved.[8]

At the Restoration Thomas Beaumont was knighted for his previous support of the Royalist cause. Thereafter he served as Justice of the Peace and Deputy-Lieutenant of the West Riding, and was appointed Lieutenant-Colonel of the local trained bands. He took no part, however, in the post-Restoration hunt for more lucrative offices, concentrating on the administration and expansion of his property. In February 1662 he concluded a major purchase for £970 of eleven messuages in Lepton from a Mr Woolley of Riber in Derbyshire, and shortly afterwards bought an adjacent small holding for £12. In 1665–6 for a total of £1,080 he acquired two further properties near Lascelles Hall; many of his additions in this vicinity had previously been alienated by his father when obliged to provide for the five daughters of his second wife's first marriage. Finally, in 1667 Sir Thomas made two other purchases, one in Crigglestone for over £100, the other of lands in Kirkheaton, Lepton, and Dalton for £50. Together these transactions, most of which consolidated existing holdings, represented a substantial addition to the family estates. Expenditure during this decade also included repairs and alterations to Lascelles Hall, and benefactions to the local grammar school at Almondbury.[9]

Sir Thomas's main source of income at this stage as earlier was his rental, which gradually increased as he accumulated property. By his death in 1668 the gross annual rental of both estates probably exceeded £1,000. There is no evidence, however, that he raised rents following the modest increases of the early 1650s. Indeed, in 1668 £750 was owing in rents due and arrears. Some of the latter dated back to 1663, reflecting the difficulties experienced by tenant farmers during these years. These difficulties did not dissuade Sir Thomas himself from engaging in farming. The corn either 'garnered or barned' at his death was worth £165, while there was more in the fields and in mills at Crosland and Lepton. In addition to a 'waynehouse' full of tools and machinery, he held large stocks of manure, and clearly practised mixed farming on a fairly large scale. In 1668, besides horses, 'turkeys, ducks, geese, and other poultry', he had fifty-one sheep, thirteen oxen, eighteen cows, five calves, four heifers, two bulls, and nine pigs. As estate accounts are unavailable for this period it is impossible to calculate Sir Thomas's farm income. However, even if he did not market much produce (and the 'bills' mentioned in his executor's accounts suggest that at least he marketed some) this branch of his activities must have greatly reduced his outgoings. When a household included not only the family, which in this case was large, but also numerous visitors, acquaintances, and servants, such a reduction was often a key factor in the production of an annual surplus. Nor was farming Sir Thomas's only additional source of income. By using covenants in leases to preserve his access to property in order to fell wood or quarry stone, he was able to do more than merely supply his own needs. The same was true of the mills and kilns which he either inherited or purchased. There is sporadic evidence of wood sales; and besides the 'bills' owed to him at his death, he also held stocks of wood and stone 'fit for building' worth £100. Furthermore, much of his estate lay on thick coal seams. Though always inclined to lease mining rights, Sir Thomas required lessees to supply him free of charge with as much coal as he himself required, thereby avoiding all expense on this item. Despite heavy family commitments, his economy produced a surplus of capital for investment. This is clear not only from his purchases and improvements, but also from his operations as a money lender. By 1668 Sir Thomas had purchased one property previously mortgaged to him, had foreclosed on another mortgage, and was owed £1,270 in mortgages, bonds, bills, and miscellaneous debts. This figure, which excludes rents due and arrears, well exceeded his personal debts of £965.[10]

TABLE 9
Accounts at the Death of Sir T. Beaumont, 1668

Credit

	£ s. d.
Inventory	965.12.4
Silver	12. 5.0
Poultry	2. 0.0
Goods in Mills	16. 0.0
Wood & Stone	100. 0.0
Rents Due & Arrears	725.12.9
Tithe Due	20. 0.0
Debt Book	80. 0.0
Mortgage	250. 0.0
Bonds & Bills	939.18.0
	3111. 8.1

Debit

Deduction (Goods kept by Widow)	69.18.9
Due for Principal & Interest	505. 0.0
Funeral Expenses	201. 0.0
Legal Expenses	61. 0.0
Rest	188. 4.0
	1025. 2.9
Surplus	2086. 5.4

Source: WBW/35/5, 7.

In October 1666 Sir Thomas's eldest surviving son, Richard, married Ann Ramsden of Hemsworth. Sir Thomas took this opportunity of disposing of some of the property acquired since 1651, settling the land purchased from Mr Woolley on the couple, and after their deaths on their heirs in succession. In November Sir Thomas sold the land in Lepton purchased for £200 in 1651 to Richard 'for a competent sum'. Then in April 1668 he bequeathed the rest of the property excluded from the 1651 settlement or purchased since then (comprising the Lascelles Hall estate), to Richard and his 'lawfully begotten heirs', subject only to a legacy of £500 to Sir Thomas's widow. Turning to the Whitley estate, besides £9 in life annuities and miscellaneous legacies totalling £40, Sir Thomas left £1,500 to his daughter, Sarah, and £500 to his younger son, William, according to his previously reserved right.[11]

Without doubt the career of Sir Thomas Beaumont, who died in June 1668, was a considerable success. A major factor apparently was the self-imposed restriction of his activities, both public and private, to the area where he lived. He played a vigorous role in the Civil War in Yorkshire, but not elsewhere; and with skill and luck avoided the harshest penalties which might have resulted from his part in the hostilities. After the Restoration he performed such public duties as were expected of him, but had no ambitions beyond them. Instead he raised a large family, arranged worthy marriages for both himself and his children, and steadily increased the scope and profitability of his economy. By 1668 his accounts were in surplus and his general economic situation was healthy. The family's standing had advanced since the days of the carefree Sir Richard, while many of the losses earlier sustained by the collateral branch had been recouped. As had long been his plan, Sir Thomas split his property along lines similar to the division which had existed before 1631. Motivated by the fact that he himself had come from the Lascelles Hall branch, he was also, no doubt, convinced that each part of the estate was capable of maintaining a family of its own.

2. CONTINUED PROSPERITY 1668–1704

Sir Thomas was succeeded at Whitley by his grandson, Richard, the first of three minors to inherit the property during this period. Richard's mother, Elizabeth, acted as guardian until he came of age in 1676. The reduced outgoings of a minority made it easier for her to discharge the heavy settled payments to which the estate had, and was to, become liable. There were, firstly, two jointures, one of £200 to Dame Elizabeth and another of £100 to Sir Thomas's widow. Then there was the £2,000 bequeathed by Sir Thomas. Finally, Adam Beaumont's daughters, who married before the minority ended, both received augmented portions; originally entitled to £750 each, Elizabeth was given £1,000, and Anne £750 plus a further £2,000 later. These payments did not result in financial stringency in other respects. Two feoffments to the uses of the poor of Kirkheaton were executed, while in 1675 building was in progress at Whitley Hall. In 1676 the family's means were boosted by Dame Elizabeth's decision to accept an annuity of

£170 in lieu of her jointure of £200 and, even more so, by Richard's marriage in that year to Frances, daughter of the wealthy Sir William Lowther of Swillington. As Frances was promised a jointure of £350 her portion, which is not recorded, was probably in the region of £3,500. £4,000, together with annual maintenance of £40 each before marriage, was provided for younger children. Dame Elizabeth surrendered her jointure lands to Richard and gave him, with certain exceptions, the furniture and machinery at Whitley. In return Richard guaranteed his mother's annuity and the additional £2,000 for his sister, Anne. Clearly, the rise in the family's fortunes was unimpeded in the years following Sir Thomas's death.[12]

Although no accounts are extant for this period, surviving leases provide much information about the estate. All the lessees lived locally and most farmed on a part-time basis. The occupational distribution of the tenantry was extremely wide and reflected the industrialized nature of the locality. The houses, cottages, smithies, kilns, and mills owned by the family were either leased together with farmland, or were situated in a cluster of buildings upon which a farm was centred. Only the coalmine was let as a separate and purely industrial concern. Some land lay in townfields but most was enclosed in small parcels, a few or more of which leased together constituted a single holding.[13]

Most leases were for periods of twenty-one years, rents being due half-yearly at Ladyday and Michaelmas, or at Mayday and Martinmas. Tenants were forbidden without prior permission to assign their leases to other than their wives or children while, if rent was in arrears, the landlord could declare a lease void. This latter power was rarely invoked for, despite the persistence of arrears, most leases were renewed in the name of the previous tenant or a member of his family. It is more difficult to assess how realistic were the other clauses governing the landlord-tenant relationship. Theoretically much emphasis was placed on the landlord's rights on the one hand, and tenants' duties on the other. The landlord was allowed to hunt or hawk on any property without being liable for the damage which he caused. At all times he had completely free access for purposes of mining coal, felling timber, or quarrying stone. In these cases, however, he was liable for damage, the cost of which was assessed by two impartial witnesses, one for each party to the deed. Tenants' duties were numerous and occasionally included the purchase of coal from the family's mine.[14] Attendance at manorial courts, and obedience to their decisions, were constant obligations. In most cases tenants had to grind their corn at one or other of the landlord's mills, though precise clauses guarded against abuses on the part of the millers. They were allowed to take only the customary allowance from tenants, had to provide candlelight for grinding after the day's work, and were obliged to organize operations on the basis of first come, first served.[15] Tenants were required to pay all taxes levied on their property, whether local or national, civil or ecclesiastical. They had also to provide their landlord with food, labour, and other services. Most of the food, which consisted of poultry or occasionally a sack of grain or oats, was due at Christmas or Easter.[16] Labour was required in the arable with a plough, or with a sickle or cart at harvest time. The Beaumonts also boarded out hounds with their tenants, usually asking them to keep one or two animals per year. Sometimes tenants were given the choice of doing this or, for example, providing a sack of grain.[17] The number and variety of such clauses suggest that the tenantry made a significant contribution to the family's personal needs.

Part of each lease concerned the maintenance of property. Normally a general clause obliged the tenant to hand over the property in as good a condition as he had received it. There then followed specific instructions relating to the preservation of soil fertility. For each day's ploughing during the year tenants had to deposit twelve horseloads of lime or manure on the land. Furthermore, they were forbidden to reap more than three successive crops without manuring proportionately above the usual amount. Each time they returned to tillage this process had to be repeated. Clauses against sowing or ploughing in the year immediately prior to the expiry of a lease only appeared in the eighteenth century.[18] The family rarely allowed heavy timber for repairs, and were sparing with small timber needed for hedging or fencing, much of which was preserved for sale to ironmasters. Finally, and somewhat surprisingly, there was an almost total lack of clauses dealing specifically with sowing and reaping, grazing, hedging and fencing, ditching and draining, or the maintenance of work or household premises.[19]

Although leases are an inadequate substitute for other types of estate record, these documents create the firm impression that the family adopted a conservative approach to estate management. Apart from the clauses governing tax payments, which were uncompromising, there is little indication that their relationship with the tenantry was strictly businesslike. In particular, the complete disregard of certain matters was probably more advantageous to themselves than to the lessees of their property, though the behaviour of both parties was circumscribed by local courts and customs. Indeed, most of the arrangements prescribed in these leases merely confirmed customary procedures which doubtless formed the basis of the region's farming practice. Perhaps this sufficed in areas where estates were compact, tenants insubstantial, and landlords resident and themselves engaged in farming.

Progress continued after Richard Beaumont assumed control of affairs in 1676. The £2,000 due to his sister, Anne, was paid by 1684. Moreover, he made three purchases of property. In 1677 he bought premises and closes for £40 from the administrators of the effects of a Mirfield yeoman. In 1682 a much larger property, a house, barns, and fifteen closes, was purchased from a tanner who lived in Kirkheaton; the price, which must have been substantial, is unfortunately not recorded. Finally, in 1688 Richard bought a messuage and land in the fields at Kirkheaton for £48 10s. 0d. Another indication of prosperity was his commission of a York architect in 1680 to design a new hall at Whitley, even though the plan was not acted upon when delivered. At no stage was it necessary to sell property to finance either these developments or the payments due on earlier settlements. In fact there was sufficient surplus capital for at least one sizeable loan. In 1677 James Jefferson, a Leeds yeoman, mortgaged his property in Great Woodhouse to Beaumont for £560, the sum being repaid with interest three years later. The absence of accounts makes it impossible to define the various sources of income and their relative importance. However, there would appear to have been none other than the portion, the rental, the proceeds of wood and other such sales, interest from loans, and profit from the home farm.

The rental no doubt grew in relation to other items as the estate expanded, while financial resources increased overall as the property was freed from settlement debts. Not only had the £2,000 due to his sister been paid by 1684, but jointure commitments had decreased following the death of Dame Mary Beaumont in 1682.[20]

Richard Beaumont devoted his career to running his estate. There is no evidence that he aspired to local or national office, though he no doubt performed the voluntary tasks expected of a gentleman of his standing. James II appointed him to the Privy Council along with eighty-four other Yorkshire squires, but this was of no practical significance. The scope of his public activities is well represented by the fact that 'Squire Beaumont's' horse came second in the county race at Kiplingcoats in 1676, and that a relative asked for one of Richard's fine hounds as a Christmas present in 1688. Of course he speculated about national politics notably in a gossipy wine order to a York merchant in the same year, but fundamentally his life and interests centred on his family, friends, and estate.[21] When Richard died in 1692 the Whitley estate was free of debt, and had been steadily expanded without thereby having become essentially less compact. By his will he left the entire estate 'if neither of my sons have issue' to his wife for life, and then to Richard Beaumont junior of Lascelles Hall and his heirs. Of the £4,000 reserved for younger children, Richard bequeathed £3,000 to his younger son, Thomas, as his portion. But this was never paid as all his children died young, except the eldest son and heir – another Richard. He inherited the Whitley estate, while Dame Frances enjoyed a jointure of £350; if Dame Elizabeth Beaumont was still alive, which is doubtful, her annuity of £170 continued to be paid. In succeeding years these were the only financial burdens on what was by now a sizeable landed property.[22]

Once again the succession passed to a minor, Richard Beaumont being only fourteen years old at his father's death. Although Dame Frances Beaumont, Richard's guardian, purchased property and lent on mortgage, there is no further information concerning family affairs before 1699. However, there are several indications from the period 1699–1704 that the rise in the family's prosperity continued unabated. In June 1699

Richard contracted a highly successful marriage to Katherine, daughter and sole heiress of Thomas Stringer of Sharleston near Wakefield. At her father's death Katherine had succeeded to his entire estate, which comprised ten manors in Yorkshire, Lancashire, Westmorland, Cambridgeshire, and Huntingdonshire, and subsequently her guardians had purchased additional property on her behalf. On the marriage the whole estate was vested in trustees to the use of Richard and Katherine for life, then to the use of their lawfully begotten heirs. The Whitley estate, still subject to Dame Frances's jointure, was settled to Richard's use for life, then to the use of his male heirs and their heirs in succession. In default of male heirs the estate was to devolve on daughters and their heirs in succession. On further default the estate became vested in Richard's right heir who, in accordance with the will of 1692, was Richard Beaumont junior of Lascelles Hall. Katherine was provided with a jointure of £600, and of £900 should she fail to have children by the marriage. A maximum of £4,000 was set aside for younger sons, with up to £7,000 for daughters.[23] This marriage promised to transform the family's circumstances. Progress from local to national importance in landowning circles, and all that that implied, seemed virtually assured.

Not surprisingly, the Whitley property was improved and further expanded after the marriage. In 1699 Richard commissioned an architect to plan a garden house. Later he made numerous alterations and additions to the Hall, erecting a new and magnificent north front. At least two purchases were made. In 1702 a farm, house, and three closes in Flockton were bought for £560, and in 1703 two farms, one in Whitley and the other in Kirkheaton, were purchased for £300. It was estimated later that in 1704 the Whitley estate was worth £1,350 a year, not counting wood, coal, and stone.[24] Mainly because of purchases, the property had more than doubled in value since Thomas Beaumont's succession in 1631. Yet it was small in comparison with the Stringer estate. Future prospects could not have been more promising.

None of this promise, however, was fulfilled. Family fortunes took a dramatic turn for the worse when Richard Beaumont died childless in 1704. Consequently, Katherine's inheritance passed from her husband's family. The Whitley estate was inherited by Richard Beaumont junior of Lascelles Hall whose own family, meanwhile, had encountered substantial and prolonged difficulties. As a result of the deceased's will a long and costly legal dispute ensued between Dame Frances Beaumont, Katherine Beaumont, and Richard Beaumont junior. Following a verdict which was utterly disadvantageous to him, Richard had to provide Katherine, who soon became Countess of Westmorland on marrying Thomas Fane, with huge sums of money whilst being denied entry to the Whitley estate. The price of defeat was a burden of debt which bedevilled the Beaumonts for nearly forty years.

3. DECADES OF DISPUTE 1704–23

Richard Beaumont of Whitley died in June 1704. His father had previously arranged, should Richard produce no heirs, for the Whitley estate to pass to Dame Frances Beaumont for life before reverting to Richard Beaumont junior of Lascelles Hall. In his own will Richard made that reversion conditional on the payment of 'all such legacies and sums of money' as he bequeathed.[25] Then, despite the fact that future net income from Whitley was totally committed either by jointure or annuity, he imposed additional fiscal burdens on the property. These comprised a further annuity of £40 and legacies totalling £7,100. Among the latter was a legacy of £6,000 to his widow, although she was already provided with an annuity of £900 from her husband's death. Furthermore, Richard gave Katherine his entire personal estate and appointed her his sole executrix. Thus a situation arose in which three individuals, the two widows and Richard Beaumont junior, all had large and conflicting interests in Whitley. Rumours that Katherine had unduly influenced her husband during the drafting of his will encouraged Richard to precipitate a long, costly, and acrimonious dispute.[26]

Although the prospect of the reversion transformed the future outlook of Richard's career, he had no reason to welcome the dispute for his family was beset by numerous difficulties, having endured a surfeit of legal involvement since Sir Thomas Beaumont's death. There had, firstly, been a dispute with Dame Mary Beaumont, Sir Thomas's widow. Once a wealthy woman, she had received a jointure of only £100 under the terms of the 1651 settlement. Bitterly disappointed by the provisions of her husband's will, particularly the sole executorship of her stepson, Richard, she took the matter to court and created confusion by secreting Sir Thomas's papers before, eventually, settling privately. In 1671 Richard Beaumont had been accused in a petition to the King of the simonaical use of his right of patronage to Kirkheaton parish church. Finally coming to nought, the affair nevertheless contained all the ingredients of a major local scandal. Richard himself went to law in 1674 in an attempt to foreclose on a mortgage inherited under his father's will. The result of the dispute, which was ultimately settled out of court, is unrecorded. Far more serious was Richard's unsuccessful involvement in the collection of the hearth tax in Lancashire and Lincolnshire. Having along with several colleagues given security for payment of large sums to the national tax farmers, he failed to collect the stipulated amount. Consequently, during the two decades prior to 1700 he was ejected from part of his estate while the tax farmers, their heirs or assignees were reimbursed from its revenue. In 1694 the family had also been involved in a tithe dispute. Not surprisingly, in the face of this morass of problems, they had been forced to borrow heavily and in 1684, having otherwise failed to repay one mortgage, had sold property worth more than £1,000. Thereafter both Richard Beaumont and his son pursued military careers in an effort to augment their depleted incomes; by 1702 they owed a total of £1,050 between them. Richard junior married Susannah Horton of Barkisland in 1700, receiving her portion only after yet another lawsuit. Moreover, the background to his suit with Dames Frances and Katherine was one of continuing difficulty. He was troubled not only by his in-laws but also, ironically, by the inability of his own debtors to repay him. The last vestiges of the hearth taxes suit dragged on, complicating the settling of the Lascelles Hall estate, an urgent matter once the health of Richard senior began to fail in 1705. Significantly, in a settlement agreed between father and son the entail on the Lascelles Hall estate was barred, thus allowing Richard junior to sell the property if the lawsuit failed to improve his financial prospects.[27]

The legal battle over his nephew's will was Richard junior's chief preoccupation during these years.[28] He had two aims: to reduce the fiscal demands on the Whitley estate to a minimum; and to secure as long a period as possible in which to discharge them. By 1707 he had succeeded in getting the payment of the legacy deferred until Dame Frances died and the Whitley estate reverted to him. He next tried to persuade Chancery that, because payments from Whitley more than equalled the estate's value, the legacy had been granted in lieu of Dame Katherine's annuity, not in addition to it. Richard also complained of Katherine's behaviour following her husband's death. While remaining at Whitley, he alleged, she had felled timber, failed to collect rents, destroyed deer in the park, and left the house and gardens 'in a very ruinious condition'. He also maintained that, despite having inherited her husband's personal estate, she had converted several items belonging to the freehold to her own use, and secreted the testator's deeds and documents. Richard finally accused Katherine of refusing his offer of security for payment of her legacy, and of insisting on having the estate to herself and her heirs for ever.

In reply Katherine stressed that suitable security for payment of her legacy had not been provided within twelve months of her husband's death and that, therefore, the estate ought to pass to her. Not only had her husband intended 'of his free good will and pleasure' to grant her both the annuity and the legacy, but he would have granted her the whole estate had she not persuaded him otherwise. She accused her opponent of 'pretending' that the estate was charged with more than it was worth, pointed out that revenue from miscellaneous sales had not been included in valuations, and proclaimed herself sufficiently sure of its true worth to want to buy the property and discharge the payments personally. She was willing to accept such security for payment of her legacy as was offered, but demanded interest on it from the date of her husband's death. She acknowledged remaining at Whitley for three months after his decease, but maintained that this was not unreasonable and, in any case, was justifiable because her annuity was in arrears. She agreed to account for what she had taken from Whitley but denied felling timber, appropriating parts of the freehold, or damaging the house and park. Finally, she argued that certain lands jointly purchased with her husband were hers and, needless to say, claimed both the annuity and the legacy. Dame

Frances also replied to Richard's petition, reiterating that by her husband's will the Whitley estate was hers for life owing to her son's childless marriage. She also claimed various properties purchased during her widowhood, demanding that these be not subject to the annuity. She too accused Katherine of misconduct, and suggested that she had 'gained' those clauses in the will of 1704 which were most favourable to her. Finally, though to avoid trouble she had not yet done so, Dame Frances reserved the right to enter the Whitley estate at any time.

Chancery delivered its decision in November 1707, reversing previous decrees in one important respect and, in so doing, dealing a sharp blow to Richard Beaumont's fortunes. As expected, the court resolved that Katherine should enjoy both the annuity and the legacy, accepting the best security offered for payment of the latter and receiving interest on it at 5 per cent. The court also decreed that the legacy was payable from the death of Katherine's husband and not, as previously decided, when Richard entered into Whitley at Dame Frances's death. Thus, unless his lawyers gained further time, Richard faced the prospect of having to raise both the legacy and accumulated interest within the six months allotted by the court. An assurance that further time would be allowed on application did not obviate the fact that he would eventually be forced to raise the money much earlier than hitherto anticipated and without the resources of the Whitley estate at his disposal. However, although Dame Frances was confirmed as life-tenant of Whitley, Richard was allowed to include the estate in the security with which he provided Katherine. On the other hand he was only to be permitted to enter Whitley at Dame Frances's death if the entire legacy account had been cleared. Katherine was ordered to schedule the profits which she had received from the estate over and above her annuity; these were granted to Dame Frances. The latter also received the purchases made during her widowhood which, however, were declared subject to the annuity. Finally, while Richard gained access to papers previously secreted by Katherine, costs were awarded against him.

Richard's lawyers hoped that the Earl of Westmorland, who had assumed control of Katherine's affairs, would not press for early payment of the legacy. However, the Earl was not disposed to be lenient. Accordingly an application for an extension of the six months' period was submitted to the court, to which the Earl replied by filing his own Chancery bill in August 1708. While trying to reach some private accommodation, Richard's lawyers formally attacked the bill as technically defective. When by the end of 1708 all hope of reaching agreement outside court had disappeared, Richard's chief counsel succinctly outlined future policy: 'our business is to get time and weary the enemy with expense at his own charge'.[29] Nor were they unsuccessful. Not until December 1710 was a decision reached on the Earl's bill. Moreover, Richard was then allowed two further years in which to pay the legacy. If unpaid by then, he was to be denied equity of redemption on his reversion, and the property was to pass to Katherine.[30]

The minor successes of Richard's lawyers consoled rather than encouraged him. Legal expenses drained his meagre resources, while the constant threat of ultimate defeat, and all that that implied, sapped his morale. By December 1708 he was desperately short of money and attempting to secure salaried employment. He sought the help of his cousin, Lord Downe, and of his friend and neighbour, Sir Arthur Kaye of Woodsome. From December 1710 the latter, recently returned as Tory M.P. for Yorkshire, made concerted efforts to secure Richard a post in the civil service. The two corresponded regularly and when a 'favourable juncture' appeared Richard travelled to London to make himself readily available. At one stage he had hopes of a post in the Stamp office, which reputedly carried an annual salary of between £300 and £400, but his own disappeared in a flood of applications. He then pursued jobs in the Customs office and the 'Salt duty' but these too failed to materialize. Indeed, his endeavours were counterproductive for, after narrowly avoiding nomination in 1712, he was appointed in the following year to the prestigious, but expensive, and therefore uncoveted, post of High Sheriff of Yorkshire. Far from promising to alleviate his difficulties, this threatened to exacerbate them.[31]

Fortunately Richard's lawyers further deferred the date by which the legacy had finally to be paid. On 19 November 1713, however, he was ordered to pay £1,000 in four days, and an additional £4,000 by the following spring. This time, presumably because every conceivable device had already been exploited, there were no further attempts at prevarication. By this stage the sum owed in principal and interest had risen to £7,770. Firstly, Richard raised a mortgage for £2,220. Then in 1714, taking the option created for him by his father before the latter's death, he sold the Lascelles Hall estate; unfortunately, details of the sale price and of the precise amount of property involved in the transaction have not survived, but the proceeds were insufficient to discharge his liabilities. Even after further money had been raised on bonds and from sales of timber, £2,832 remained due on the legacy account. However, relaxing his previously inflexible attitude, the Earl of Westmorland then allowed much longer than officially stipulated for the final discharge of the debt; the last payment was not in fact made until June 1719. Meanwhile, in 1718 the Earl had permitted Richard to enter into the Whitley estate. The opportunity was seized eagerly for the property was no longer subject to the jointure of £350, Dame Frances Beaumont having died in the previous year.[32]

Due to the weight of the charges upon it, the Whitley estate had been run at a loss between 1704 and 1718. Only in 1715 did income exceed outgoings, and then only marginally. By 1718 accumulated deficits amounted to over £1,550, all of which was due to the Earl. That there was little fluctuation in the size of the listed items and that, therefore, deficits were regular phenomena supports Richard's assertion in 1707 that the estate had been burdened with more than it could support. However, Katherine's reply, that resources such as wood, coal, and stone were not being fully exploited, may also have been valid. The accounts contain few items other than those essential to the administration of a rentier's estate. Demesne profits were small and often insignificant and, apart from tax allowances which were deducted from the £900 annuity, the charge consisted entirely of rents. Besides the annuity, the discharge contained none other than unavoidable outpayments. Thus, although there was no improvement in income, and in particular little or no exploitation of natural resources, expenditure was likewise kept to an absolute minimum. Consequently certain requirements, such as running repairs, were not catered for.

TABLE 10
Whitley Estate Accounts, 1704–18

Charge	Rent Arrears	Rent Due	Demesne Profits	Tax Allows.	Total
	£ s. d.	£ s. d.	£ s. d.	£ s d	£ s d
1704		360. 4.11	2.15. 7	46.2.3	409. 2. 9
1705		689.16. 5	106.19. 0	92.4.7	889. 0. 0
1706	32.15. 1	785.11. 2	46.15. 2	92.4.7	957. 6. 0
1707	54. 0.10	821.17. 4	39. 2. 2	92.4.7	1007. 4.11
1708	94.18. 7	820.17. 4	42. 9. 6	92.4.7	1050.15. 0
1709	77. 9. 7	858. 8. 4	38. 2. 8	92.4.7	1092. 5. 2
1710	113. 3.11	840. 5. 1	7. 9.11	92.4.7	1053. 3. 6
1711	85.15. 8	857. 1.11	26. 6. 9	92.4.7	1060.18.11
1712	72. 9. 0	848. 2. 8	42. 0. 6	92.4.7	1054.16. 9
1713	99. 9. 0	857. 9. 8	27. 1. 3	46.2.3	1030. 2. 2
1714	99.14. 6	864. 3. 2	138. 9.10	46.2.3	1148. 9. 0
1715	96. 1. 6	894. 2. 8	138.12. 6	46.2.3	1174.18.11
1716	102. 7.11	866.16. 8	41. 4.10	92.4.7	1102.14. 0
1717	116. 2. 5	866.19. 1	4. 0. 0	69.3.8	1055.15. 2
1718	167.19. 1	866. 5. 4		69.3.8	1103.10. 1

Discharge	Outpayments	Rent Charge	Arrears	Total	Balance
	£ s. d.	£ s. d.	£ s. d.	£ s. d.	£ s. d.
1704	12. 4. 6	450.0.0		462. 4. 6	− 53. 1. 9
1705	112. 5. 6	900.0.0	32.15. 1	1045. 0. 7	−156. 0. 7
1706	107.14. 8	900.0.0	54. 0.10	1061.15. 6	−104. 9. 6
1707	142.17. 2	900.0.0	94.18. 7	1137.15. 9	−130.10.10
1708	140.15. 4	900.0.0	77. 9. 7	1118. 4.11	− 67. 9.11
1709	177.18.11	900.0.0	113. 3.11	1191.12.10	− 99. 7. 8
1710	144.13. 4	900.0.0	85.15. 8	1130. 9. 0	− 77. 5. 6
1711	147.10. 1	900.0.0	72. 9.0	1119.19. 1	− 59. 0. 2
1712	162. 2. 6	900.0.0	99. 9. 0	1161.11. 6	−106.14. 9
1713	180. 4. 7	900.0.0	99.14. 6	1179.19. 1	−149.16.11
1714	159.12. 1	900.0.0	96. 1. 6	1155.13. 7	− 7. 4. 7
1715	167.14. 2	900.0.0	102. 7.11	1170. 2. 1	+ 4.16.10
1716	226. 2. 0	900.0.0	116. 2. 5	1242. 4. 5	−139.10. 5
1717	229.11. 7	900.0.0	167.19. 1	1297.10. 8	−241.15. 6
1718	216. 1. 0	900.0.0	165.18.10	1281.19.10	−178. 9. 9

NOTE: 1704 was a half-year account. The rise in rent due was caused by the letting of demesne property and, from 1707, by the accession of property previously held by Dame Frances Beaumont. Demesne profits include wood sales. Tax allowances represent those taxes paid by the Earl of Westmorland for the property which provided the annuity. In 1718 £1566 was owing to the Earl from this account.

Source: WBE/28–30.

Nevertheless, though the estate remained subject to the annuity for an indefinite period to come and had lacked proper attention for more than a decade, there were several reasons for Richard's eager entry. Dame Frances's jointure having lapsed, it had become possible to manage the property profitably. Also, as Richard wrote to the Earl in May 1718, an 'advance of rents . . . may be made in all or most of the farms which every day's experience confirms me they are capable of'.[33] Exploitation of natural resources might also be resumed, while possession made the raising of capital on loans much easier because occupied land was regarded as much firmer security than land held in reversion or expectancy. Finally, Richard was understandably keen to enjoy his inheritance after years of frustration and delay, anxious dispute and costly litigation.

Richard raised the gross rental of the Whitley estate from £1,350 in 1719 to over £1,700 in 1723, the year of his death. This still proved inadequate for his needs. Although there is no precise indication of the extent of his indebtedness in 1718, there is evidence of his having to incur further debts in succeeding years. In May 1718 he mortgaged all his lands in Kirkheaton to his sister-in-law, Ann Horton, for £1,630. This remained outstanding in August 1720 when the mortgage was re-assigned for £2,000. In April 1723 Richard mortgaged three houses for £1,000, and in June another house for £400. None of these sums was repaid before his death.[34] Complaints to the Earl of Westmorland concerning the aforementioned Whitley estate accounts are a further indication of his acute shortage of cash. Richard argued that the demesne lands and tithe had not been let at realistic rents, that many other rent improvements could have been made, and that the steward who had managed the estate singlehanded throughout had been overpaid. He suggested that the accounts be submitted to a third party for arbitration, presumably hoping to receive some compensation. The Earl refused to agree to this, pointing out that the uncertainty of the lawsuit and the intransigency of Dame Frances during her life-tenancy had both militated against efficient management. Moreover, the tithe was 'a very uncertain affair'; one 'could never let it for a certain rent'. The Earl reminded Richard of the 'noise and clamour' which had resulted from the 'little which we did' to make improvements. Regarding the steward, the Earl questioned whether 'a court or a gentleman' would 'have appointed a steward to manage such an estate for so little as Mr Cooper had'. He maintained that Richard would agree with him if he took a long, reasoned look at the situation, and encouraged him to let 'what is past' be forgotton. However, in the midst of his problems, which following his rent improvements included heavy arrears, Richard found it difficult to reciprocate.[35]

Among the troubles of his last years was a claim from a Mrs Baynes for £400 bequeathed to her by Dame Frances. Initially her lawyer demanded the sum from the Earl of Westmorland on the grounds that the Countess had inherited the whole of her first husband's personal estate. The Earl replied that already there had been vastly more paid than the personal estate amounted to. Accordingly the sum was demanded of Richard, who had inherited from the person who gave Dame Frances the power to grant the legacy in the first place. After being asked to pay without suit, Richard replied that, though he wished to settle amicably, he had to defend himself as best he could. In May 1721 Richard was served with documents supporting the lady's case. His lawyer advised petitioning Chancery that the money be derived from the personal estate. Instead Richard wrote to the Earl, hoping that the latter would interpose between himself and Mrs Baynes. When this proved unavailing he told the Earl bluntly that the personal estate had been deliberately undervalued. This too failed so, weary of the courts, Richard quietly forwarded £400 to Mrs Baynes in December 1722.[36]

Yet despite his debts and disputes Richard managed to invest some capital in the repair and improvement of Whitley Hall. A letter dated June 1721 discloses that he had recently commissioned a firm of joiners and carpenters, and planned to build a new coach-house.[37] He certainly could not afford such expenditure. No doubt his behaviour was governed by sheer necessity, or by a determination to improve his circumstances before the ever-vigilant gaze of neighbouring gentry.

Perhaps understandably in view of his previous testamentary conflicts, Richard Beaumont died intestate in November 1723. It is difficult to estimate his current indebtedness but clearly it was considerable. At least £5,875 of his debts were discharged between 1723 and 1731, when £9,400 remained unpaid. At his death, therefore, he owed in excess of £15,000. In the words of his wife, he had been 'rendered incapable of making of that provision for' his children 'as was in any degree suitable to their family and relations'.[38] Nevertheless, he had conducted a stubborn holding operation in the hope that a solution to the problems which had accompanied a wealthy inheritance would be found by grateful and less careworn successors.

4. LONG MINORITY AND SHORT SUCCESSION 1723–43

The administration of Richard's estate was granted to his widow, Susannah Beaumont. As Richard's heir was only seven years old in 1723, Susannah, as his guardian, controlled family affairs until her own death in 1731. Her major tasks were financial: the payment of the Countess of Westmorland's annuity and the repayment of her husband's debts. She also had to provide for a large family, having produced four sons and eleven daughters in twenty-three years.

The minority undoubtedly alleviated current problems; at such times it was easier to keep expenditure within bounds. Unfortunately tenants' difficulties forced Susannah to lower the rents improved on her husband's entry to the estate. Although the gross rental was £1,725 and £1,719 in 1725 and 1726 respectively, it was reduced to below £1,600 by 1731. She compensated for this by raising more than £400 through timber sales. Moreover, Susannah was quickly successful in her efforts to discharge debts. Between 1723 and 1731, besides paying £321 in funeral expenses and miscellaneous bills, she personally disbursed at least £4,344 in repayments of principal and interest. She also discharged all but £951 of the £6,519 due for the Countess of Westmorland's annuity between 1723 and the latter's death in 1730. Further loans proved unnecessary, though relatives and friends came to her assistance on at least two occasions. Her sister, Ann Horton, repaid most of a debt of £900 in 1729, while in that same year Dorothy Wilkinson of Whitley repaid a further £200. Despite these efforts, £9,400 of Richard Beaumont's debts remained unpaid when Susannah died in 1731. By then, however, the death of the Countess of Westmorland had greatly improved the family's financial circumstances. After expressing the hope that her eldest son, Henry, would find himself better able to provide for his brothers and sisters than his parents had been Susannah entrusted her children to the care of their aunt and her sole executrix, Ann Horton.[39] Thereafter the latter was fully responsible for the conduct of family affairs till the end of the minority in 1738.

Her endeavours, together with the means at her disposal, are fully revealed in the accounts which are extant for the entire period of her guardianship.[40] The rental was still by far the major source of income, amounting to more than two-thirds of the total charge. There were only minor fluctuations in rents due. These were the result either of alterations in the amount of property let in any one year, of the purchase of property which was subsequently let,[41] or of changes in the rents of individual properties – though there was no general improvement in rents during this period. Fluctuations in rent receipts were much more marked, ranging from £1,503 in 1732–3 to £1,835 in 1737–8, and due largely to movements in rent arrears. The largest totals, in the period 1736–8, reflect not only falls in current arrears, but also substantial repayments of old ones. Indeed, during this two-year period more old arrears were repaid than new ones became due, total arrears falling from nearly £500 to below £150. This was a considerable achievement on Ann Horton's part because during the following twenty-five years the total of arrears due in any one year fell below £250 on only two occasions. Of the other items on the charge, the most significant was the income from sales of timber, which was regularly felled at Lepton. There was also a small but fairly regular income from Whitley tithes, and occasional sundries. The latter included receipts from the sale of stone, from small timber purchases by the tenants from the steward, and in 1737–8 from the sale of 'peats and turfs at Meltham'. The two remaining items to be charged were the current balance of the demesne account and the previous year's balance on the general account, if the former was, and the latter had been, in surplus.

The demesne account was continuously in surplus in the years after 1731–2. Income from this source fell broadly into two categories: rent from those parts of the demesne which

Table II

Whitley General Accounts, 1731–8

Charge	Rent Arrears	Rent Due	Tithes & Sundries	Wood	Demesne Balance	General Balance	Total
	£ s. d.	£ s. d.	£ s d	£ s. d.	£ s. d.	£ s. d.	£ s. d.
1731–2	194.14. 4	1617. 4.10¾	12. 1. 8	200. 0. 0			2023.19.10¾
1732–3	249. 3.11¾	1616. 4.10½	20. 0. 3		87. 7. 0	23. 4. 0	1998. 0. 8¼
1733–4	362.13. 6	1612.11.10¾	12. 0. 6	250. 0. 0	53. 1. 7	28. 3. 4	2319.10. 9¾
1734–5	389. 0. 8	1623.19.11¼	14. 9. 0	200. 0. 0	55. 6. 0	2. 4. 2	2284.19. 9¼
1735–6	407. 7. 7	1620.12.11	11. 7. 0	200. 0. 0	78. 4. 7	479.16. 5½	2797. 8. 6½
1736–7	498. 8. 5	1622. 7.11	9.18. 0	19. 0	54.12. 0	182. 9.10¼	2368.15. 2¼
1737–8	357. 8. 7	1623. 7.11½	13.12. 9	60. 0. 0	63. 1. 2	120. 5. 6¼	2237.16. 0

Discharge	Rent Arrears	Disburse-ments	Salary	Demesne Balance	Total	Balance
	£ s. d.	£ s. d.	£ s. d.	£ s. d.	£ s. d.	£ s. d.
1731–2	249. 3.11¾	1700. 1. 9	15. 0. 0.	36.10. 2	2000.15.10¾	+ 23. 4. 0
1732–3	362.13. 6	1587. 3.10¼	20. 0. 0.		1969.17. 4¼	+ 28. 3. 4
1733–4	389. 0. 8	1908. 5.11¾	20. 0. 0		2317. 6. 7¾	+ 2. 4. 2
1734–5	407. 7. 7	1377.15. 8¾	20. 0. 0		1805. 3. 3¾	+ 479.16. 5½
1735–6	498. 8. 5	2096.10. 2¾	20. 0. 0		2614.18. 7¾	+ 182. 9.10¼
1736–7	357. 8. 7	1871. 0.10¾	20. 0. 0		2248. 9. 5¾	+ 120. 5. 6¼
1737–8	146. 1. 7	1761.16. 1¾	20. 0. 0		1927.17. 8¼	+ 309.18. 3¾

NOTE: Rent Arrears in the Charge are old rent arrears; those in the Discharge are new totals of arrears.

Sources: WBE/I/5–11.

were let, and the proceeds of sales of temporary grazing rights and of the products of the family's home farm. Besides taxes and assessments, demesne disbursements included the cost of labour, of seed and manure, and of various repairs to the property. Although initially there was much activity on the demesne, both aspects of income declined from 1734, arrears forming a large proportion of the charge thereafter. This was because Whitley Hall was never fully occupied from Susannah's death until the end of the minority.[42] Nevertheless, a good deal of money was spent on the upkeep of the Hall in the form of leading, glazing, masonry, and carpentry; the garden and orchard were also improved. Neither the demesne's position as a residential focus of the estate nor its potential as a farming unit were fully developed. But the property was kept in a constant state of repair and, in all but one of the seven years before 1738–9, the demesne account contributed a surplus to the general account.

The largest single item on the discharge of the General Account was 'Disbursements'. Of the eight sub-sections into which these were divided in a subsidiary account, the first, 'accidental' payments and those 'by order', was a miscellany. It included such items as the cost of fencing and walling, the purchase of equipment for the coalmine, and in 1737–8 the latter's repair after a roof fall. It also embraced repairs to leased property, fees for 'viewing' parts of the estate, and a few small legal expenses. Next came those taxes and assessments on leased property which the family, and not their tenants, paid; never amounting to more than £11 a year, these indicate that the family continued to do little to alleviate the tax burden imposed on their tenantry. 'Rent collecting' expenses were even smaller; tenants were given due notice of collection days, when they were also provided with dinner and ale. 'Annual outpayments' of £41 consisted solely of the cost of 'putting out' eight poor boys each year as apprentices; this local charity had been established in 1704 by Richard Beaumont's will. A further column contained the wages of those servants who remained at Whitley Hall during the two years following Susannah's death. The three remaining categories were much the most substantial. There was the cash forwarded from the estate to William Elmsall, the family's banker.[43] Though mainly concerned with the discharge of debts, he was also involved in providing for the children, making payments 'by order' either to Miss Horton or to others with whom they were staying. Additional money spent on education and maintenance increased with the children's age. It was least in the earlier years when they lived in the country but later, when Henry for example spent some time in London and Bath, it steadily increased. Finally, 'debt and interest' payments made by Ann Horton herself were comparatively small during the first four years because then William Elmsall was responsible for the bulk of repayments. Once she ceased to employ him the amount which Miss Horton expended in this way increased dramatically, and averaged over £1,400 a year in the three years from 1735–6.

Besides a solitary deficit from the demesne account and the steward's salary, raised from £15 to £20 a year in 1732–3, the only item on the discharge other than disbursements was the total of new arrears. As pointed out above, both new and old arrears were greatly reduced towards the end of the minority. This contributed to the greater achievement of a constant surplus on the general account between 1731 and 1738. The amounts were nominal during the first three years, but from 1734–5 onwards combined surpluses amounted to more than £1,000. None of this required drastic changes in the organization of the estate, or in the policies by which it had previously been administered. Nor, when reliance on the rental was heavy, were there more than sporadic increases in rent. Nevertheless, between 1731 and 1738 debts fell by nearly £8,000.[44] This dramatic improvement in the family's financial position was primarily due to the minority's low level of non-productive expenditure. In this latter respect the period contrasted sharply with that before 1723, and to a lesser extent with that before the death of the Countess of Westmorland in 1730. There was little household expenditure at Whitley and, more significantly, no conspicuous expenditure of any kind. Particularly after 1730, the long minority provided the family with an opportunity of retrenchment following Richard Beaumont's troubled career which his widow and sister-in-law used to great advantage. In so doing they provided Henry Beaumont with a secure base from which to launch his career when he came of age in the autumn of 1738.

TABLE 12
General Accounts, 1738–43

Charge	Arrears £ s. d.	Rent Due £ s. d.	Previous Balance £ s. d.	Others £ s. d.	Total £ s. d.	Balance £ s. d.
1738–9	146. 1. 7¼	1623. 7. 4½		14. 7. 9	1783.16. 8¾	+148.10. 0
1739–40	303. 2. 0¾	1622. 4.10½		17. 5. 9	1942.12. 8¼	+ 96. 6. 4¾
1740–1	220. 2. 1	1636. 2. 4½		42. 4. 6	1898. 8.11½	+ 22.10.11¾
1741–2	291.17. 7	1645.14.10½		22. 9. 5½	1960. 1.11	+ 79. 6. 1
1742–3	210. 6.10	1686. 3.10½	79.6.1	19.18. 6	1998. 3. 3½	+ 48. 0. 7½

Discharge	Arrears £ s. d.	Salary £ s. d.	Disbursements £ s. d.	Demesne Balance £ s. d.	Total £ s. d.
1738–9	303. 8. 0¾	20. 0. 0	1165. 8. 7	139.10. 1	1635. 6. 8¾
1739–40	225.12. 1	20. 0. 0	1367. 8. 5¼	233. 5. 9¼	1846. 6. 3½
1740–1	302.11. 1½	20. 0. 0	1221. 8. 8¼	331.18. 2	1876. 7.11¾
1741–2	221.14. 4	20. 0. 0	1290.15.10¼	348. 5. 7½	1880.15.10
1742–3	488.11.11½	20. 0. 0	1065.19.10	375.11. 8½	1950. 2. 8

NOTE: In 1739–40, 1740–1, and 1741–2 the previous year's surplus was not placed on the Charge

Sources: WBE/I/12–16.

Henry Beaumont's term as head of the family was short for he died unmarried in October 1743, shortly before his twenty-sixth birthday. Although by December 1738 his predecessors had reduced the family debts to a total of £1,650, Henry opted for a further period of comparative restraint. Change when it occurred was not drastic, but merely the predictable result of authority having become vested in an owner-occupier rather than in a non-resident guardian. Not only was there no increase in sources of income, but existing sources yielded less than previously. No wood was sold and the demesne account was continually in deficit. Income consisted solely of rents, rent arrears, and a few sundry items. There were in fact more increases than decreases in rents due, but both were sporadic and bore little relation to actual receipts, which fluctuated wildly between rapid rises and equally precipitous falls. The difference between the highest and the lowest totals of rent receipts was over £300, while totals of rents due rose by only £60 during the same period. Thus, there was an increase in the irregularity of rent receipts plus an overall decrease in their size. This resulted in large reductions in the total charge. Not once during these five years did it reach £2,000, whereas in six of the seven years prior to 1738–9 it had exceeded that sum. To balance the general account it was necessary to achieve similar decreases in the discharge. Henry managed this, despite the fact that rent arrears were unpredictable, and that each year the discharge carried a large and rising deficit from the demesne account. As the only other items on the discharge, besides this and the totals of arrears, were the steward's salary and disbursements, cuts were made in the latter. During Henry's tenure they were at an annual average of £1,221 as against £1,756 during Miss Horton's guardianship. This proved sufficient to produce an average annual surplus on the general account of £78.

Of the changes which Henry was forced to make and which he allowed himself, a definite shift of policy in regard to the demesne was perhaps most important. Before 1738 most of it had been leased. It was now taken back in hand and both its residential and productive aspects developed. Income from demesne rents soon disappeared to be replaced by farming expenses. There were subsequently few if any sales, most of the produce being consumed by the household at Whitley. Secondly, a considerable amount was spent on making Whitley Hall a more comfortable place in which to live. As the property had long been unoccupied, there was much scope for such expenditure. The accounts tell of the employment of several craftsmen and many labourers. Besides masonry, carpentry, and smithwork, there was extensive roof repair. As a result of these developments the demesne account altered radically. The size of its charge became almost insignificant, while the discharge increased rapidly, producing a sizeable annual deficit, which featured in the general account. In regard to general disbursements, taxes, the cost of rent collecting, and annual outpayments were virtually unchanged. On the other hand 'accidental' payments were much larger and included various items which reveal more of Henry's policies. A great deal was spent, for instance, on providing adequate walling for the woods on the estate. This, together with a lack of wood sales, preserved resources from which his successor was later greatly to benefit. Furthermore, not a year went by without additions or repairs to the premises occupied by tenants. Some household expenses, including an occasional tribute to current fashion, also fell into this category. In 1740–1 a Mr Cook was employed in 'making and laying some pipes in the Park to convey the water into the gardens'. However, the money provided for Henry's personal use – nearly £4,500 over five years – was by far the largest item among the disbursements. All we know for certain about this expenditure is that much of it went on London bills. Some satisfied further household needs and paid for the property in South Crosland and Netherfield bought for £315 in 1742.[45] The total sum involved illustrates the profound difference between a family economy during, and after, a minority. In further contrast with the period under Miss Horton, debt and interest payments, at a total of £132, were negligible.[46]

Consequently Richard Beaumont's debts had still not been fully discharged at Henry's death. Moreover, the estate was burdened with substantial additional liabilities for the future. Heeding the plea made by his mother in her will, Henry settled portions of £1,000 each on his younger brother and his five sisters soon after his succession, none of which was paid before his death in 1743.[47] Debts apart, Henry Beaumont achieved much with fairly slender resources and over a limited period. Besides expanding the estate and providing for younger contemporaries, in five years he re-established the home farm, repaired the Hall, and improved tenants' household property. By the time of his premature death active family life had at last been restored to Whitley. After a long and fortuitous period of recuperation the Beaumonts' affairs were once again being conducted with some of the ease and confidence evident at the turn of the century.

5. THE GREAT IMPROVER 1743-64

Henry Beaumont was succeeded by his twenty-four-year-old brother, Richard, who, living until 1764, had a much greater opportunity than his elder brother had had of directing the family's concerns. Indeed, Richard exerted a much stronger and more personal influence on the family's affairs than any other of its members during this period: he lived more adventurously than any of his predecessors, and transformed Whitley Hall and its environs by a policy of wholesale improvement. From 1743 the style of life at Whitley became radically different and the family emerged dramatically from the modest, and often straitened, circumstances in which they had lived for nearly forty years. Again, the major features of their financial and economic situation can be identified from a full series of accounts. A glance at these indicates that the scope of Richard's activities was quite unprecedented in the family's history. There was a marked rise in both the number and the size of fluctuations on both the charge and the discharge of the general account. In particular, the sums charged under the heading of 'cash received of Richard Beaumont and others for his use' often amounted to more than the total income which had been available to his predecessor. On the discharge side, disbursements rose dramatically and fluctuated wildly; in addition the deficit on the demesne account sometimes exceeded the amount of rent due annually from the estate. Although there was a tendency during the first decade for the general account to be in surplus, and a tendency during the second for it to be in deficit, the balancing sums were small and technical, and constitute a thoroughly inadequate guide to the reality of the family's

TABLE 13
General Accounts, 1743–64

Charge	Arrears £ s. d.	Rent Due £ s. d.	Cash £ s. d.	Previous Balance £ s. d.	Others £ s. d.	Total £ s. d.
1743–4	478. 4.11½	875.11. 2¼	70. 0. 0	48. 0. 7½	429. 0. 0	1900.16. 9¼
1744–5	310. 1.11	1722.18. 5¼	443. 3. 7		87. 5. 0	2563.18.11¼
1745–6	397.18. 3	1729. 5. 4½	1598. 0. 0		71. 4. 8¾	3796. 8. 4¼
1746–7	503. 1. 2¾	1757.13. 4½	1459. 5. 9	147.16. 2¼	37. 3. 4¼	3904.19.10¾
1747–8	431.16. 4	1760. 1. 4¾	2539. 5. 0	106. 5. 5¼	34.15. 0	4872. 3. 2
1748–9	386.13. 0¼	1773.11. 4½	2000.10. 0	264. 8. 6	295.14. 3¼	4724. 9. 2
1749–50	446. 0.10	1779. 2.10½	1684.15. 0	263. 0. 0	145. 2. 6¼	4318. 1. 2¾
1750–1	433. 3.10½	1781.12. 5½	819.14. 0	79.17. 5¼	91. 7. 4	3205.15. 1¼
1751–2	408.10. 2	1783. 8. 5	4267.12. 0	440. 5. 7½	147. 4. 3	7046.17. 5½
1752–3	529. 0. 5	1814. 8. 4½			1. 8. 0	2344.16. 9½
1753–4	284.11.10	1786. 4.11	134.17. 0	16. 8.11½		2205.13. 9
1754–5	369.13.10	1881. 0. 5½	495.12. 2			2762.15. 5
1755–6	410.13. 8	1900. 2.11	745.10. 6			3056. 7. 1
1756–7	557. 3. 8	1892. 7. 4½	814. 7. 1	27. 7.10		3291. 5.11½
1757–8	584. 2. 1½	1900. 2. 4½	850. 7. 6			3334.12. 0
1758–9	699.15. 9	1900. 4.10½	5950. 0. 0			8550. 0. 7½
1759–60	777.14. 6½	1904.17. 4½	781. 8.11			3464. 0.10
1760–1	726.18. 8	1909.17.10½	742. 3. 4			3378.19.11½
1761–2	651. 1.10	1910.11.10½	855. 8. 0			3417. 1. 8½
1762–3	643. 4.11½	1910.11.10½	2131.15. 6¾			4685.12. 4¾
1763–4	571. 1.10	1909. 9.10½	2146.19. 7			4627.11. 3½

NOTE: The full title of the third column is: 'cash received of Richard Beaumont and others for his use'.

TABLE 13
Continued

Discharge	Arrears	Disbursements	Demesne Balance	Previous Balance	Others	Total	Balance
	£ s. d.	£ s. d.	£ s. d.	£ s. d.	£ s. d.	£ s. d.	£ s. d.
1743–4	308.16.11¾	1197. 1. 2	371.15. 0½		28.15. 5	1906. 8. 7¼	− 5.11.10
1744–5	397.12. 3¼	1630.19. 0¼	474. 1. 9½		74.10. 6	2577. 3. 7	− 13. 4. 7¾
1745–6	503. 1. 2¼	819.15.11¾	2265. 7. 3¾	13. 4. 7¾	47. 3. 0	3648.12. 2	+147.16. 2¼
1746–7	428. 8. 4¼	1169. 1. 1¾	2153. 9.11½		47.15. 0	3798.14. 5½	+106. 5. 5¼
1747–8	386.13. 0¼	2374.15. 1¼	1801.10. 6½		44.16. 0	4607.14. 8	+264. 8. 6
1748–9	446. 0.10	1461.18. 4½	2337.10. 4		215.19. 7½	4461. 9. 2	+263. 0. 0
1749–50	433. 3.10½	2378. 0. 4	1384.16. 7		42. 3. 0	4238. 3. 9½	+ 79.17. 5¼
1750–1	408.10. 2½	980. 0. 3¼	1340.12. 0		36. 7. 0	2765. 9. 5¾	+440. 5. 7½
1751–2	529. 0. 5	4941.16. 0¾	1044.13. 7¾		431. 5. 3¾	6946.17. 5½	+100. 0. 0
1752–3	284. 0.10½	1660.18. 2¼			397. 4. 6	2342. 3. 6¾	+ 2.13. 2¾
1753–4	356. 9.11	1811.16.10½			20.18. 0	2189. 4. 9½	+ 16. 8.11½
1754–5	410. 3. 8½	2338.17. 2			60. 4. 6	2809. 5. 4½	− 46. 9.11½
1755–6	557. 3. 8	2405. 5. 7½		46. 9.11½	20. 0. 0	3028.19. 3	+ 27. 7.10
1756–7	584. 2. 1½	2699.10. 5			20. 0. 0	3303.12. 6½	− 12. 6. 7
1757–8	699.15. 9	2661.10. 3½		12. 6. 7	20. 0. 0	3393.12. 6½	− 59. 0. 7½
1758–9	777.14. 6½	7784.13. 3		59. 0. 7½	20. 0. 0	8641. 8. 5	− 91. 7. 9½
1759–60	726.18. 9	2796. 5. 1¾		91. 7. 9½	20. 0. 0	3634.11. 8¼	−170.10.10¼
1760–1	651. 1.10	2556.10. 5½		170.10.10¼	20. 0. 0	3398. 3. 1¾	− 19. 3. 2¼
1761–2	643. 4.11½	2878.14. 7½		19. 3. 2¼	20. 0. 0	3561. 2. 9¼	−144. 1. 0¾
1762–3	571. 1.10	3982. 7. 3¼		144. 1. 0¾	23.10. 0	4721. 0. 2	− 35. 7. 9¼
1763–4	370. 5. 8½	4224.15. 8½		35. 7. 9¼	20. 0. 0	4650. 9. 2¼	− 22.17.10¾

NOTE: In 1752–3 and 1753–4 the previous year's surplus was not placed on the Charge. The figures for 1743–4 are comparatively low because, due to reorganization, they refer to only part of a year. Further rearrangements in 1752–3 led to the disappearance of the separate account of the demesne at Whitley (see reference 48).

Sources: WBE/I/17–37.

financial circumstances. This is only revealed by a detailed examination of the major column in the charge, and of Richard's expenditure. Together with the absence of his executors' papers, the vagueness of many entries in the accounts hinders any attempt to arrive at precise conclusions; but surviving records do reveal in broad outline the pattern of both his income and his expenditure.[48]

During these years there was an overall increase of nearly £200 in the amount of rent due annually. This was largely the result of further purchases of real estate, and of Richard's inheritance of property at Mitton and Grizzlehurst following his second marriage in 1748. Although at the time of his death Richard was planning a general improvement of rents, there were very few rent increases in earlier years.[49] Rent receipts fluctuated and arrears were high, particularly after 1756. However, periodic drives to collect arrears were not unsuccessful and trends in rent receipts, while not particularly encouraging, were relatively unimportant compared to the fluctuations in total income. The amount due for tithes was as small and uniform as the arrears in its payment. Sundry receipts were virtually insignificant, except in 1744 when £418 was raised from wood sales: for eight years thereafter arrears in wood payments made a small contribution to the charge.[50] Other items comprised surpluses from previous general accounts and, in the four years from 1748, modest surpluses from the Mitton demesne account.

Clearly, however, the 'money received of Richard Beaumont and others for his use' was mainly responsible for the size of, and the fluctuations in, the total charge. In most cases individual sums were merely listed as having been forwarded to the steward either by Richard himself or by another named person. Despite this, it is possible to identify the nature of most of this income. At least £2,884 of it was derived from sales of wood: initially these were from timber stands at Lepton but from 1753 most of the felling occurred on the Mitton estate. Portion money also appeared under this heading. In 1745 Richard married Judith Ramsden of Crowstone. Full details of the marriage settlement are unavailable, but a draft deed relating to jointure lands refers to Judith's 'additional portion' of £3,500, for which Richard was to provide an additional jointure of £300.[51] However, only £2,278 of the money in this category can definitely be identified as Judith's portion; the remainder was probably among the sums forwarded by Richard himself. Judith soon died and in 1748 Richard took Elizabeth Holt as his second wife. The latter's portion consisted both of property at Mitton and Grizzlehurst, and of an unspecified sum of money.[52] Her guardian contributed £117 to this section of the accounts; once again further sums may have come via Richard himself. Moreover, when Richard sold part of the Mitton estate for £5,210 in 1764, £2,125 of the purchase price appeared under this heading. Only about £20 of this money is attributable to sales of produce from the farms at Whitley and Mitton. But, as the charges of the demesne accounts are noticeably small, it is possible that some of the unattributable sums were also derived from these sources. Alternatively, while it is clear that Richard engaged in a substantial amount of direct farming, this may merely have met household requirements. There is no doubt, however, that most of the income in this category consisted of borrowed money. Not only is a mortgage for £3,150 raised in 1752 easily recognizable, but many other sums are listed as having been forwarded 'on bond'.[53] Moreover, the individuals who provided these loans appear in subsequent years among the disbursements in the discharge as receivers of debt and interest payments. It is impossible to arrive at a reliable estimate of the sum total of Richard's loans, but most of the money was borrowed on bonds at interest rates of $4\frac{1}{2}$ per cent or 5 per cent. He complained constantly of a shortage of cash and his creditors were numerous and ever-changing.[54] Thus, even though the rental rose steadily, the family's traditional source of income was quite unequal to Richard's demands. Two lucrative marriages in four years also failed to meet his needs. The nature and scope of his activities forced him to borrow repeatedly and heavily. As a result debt repayments and interest charges gave a further boost to expenditure which was already very large.

The discharge of the general account commenced with new arrears. Owing perhaps to the tax payments required of tenants, these reached substantial proportions during the course of this period but, as noted above, they returned to a lower level by 1764. The steward's salary remained virtually the same throughout the period, while sundries were infrequent, the first two items being payments to a Mr Osborne for veterinary services during the cattle plague which was rampant in Yorkshire at that time. The remainder were rent allowances made during that difficult period. From 1757 deficits from previous accounts appeared regularly in the discharge. They resulted from huge general and demesne disbursements. By far the largest items of expenditure were house, tradesmen's, and workmen's bills, money forwarded to Richard himself, and debt and interest payments. Despite the fact that the accounts often hide almost as much as they reveal, it is possible to trace not only the immediate, but also the longer-term results of these enormous outlays.

A great deal of money was devoted to the improvement of the estate. Though mainly concerned with the Hall and demesne, Richard extended and improved the rest of his property. Between 1745 and 1753 he was involved in four land transactions, two of which were at the expense of his own debtors. In May 1745 he purchased thirty-three acres in Kirkheaton for £860, and in November of the following year a small holding in Lepton for £21. He paid £100 for a local fee farm rent in 1751, and £32 in 1753 for an exchange of property in Whitley. Moreover, Richard built a number of houses, cottages, and farm buildings for his tenants, even providing one of them with a new fulling mill in 1749–50 at a cost of £80. In 1751–2 a total of £561 was spent on the complete rebuilding of the steward's farm house and outbuildings in Lepton. Also, in 1758 the roads on the estate were extensively repaired. This programme was not as impressive as that carried out during the same period by the Hothams, but by 1764 most of the family's property was either in good condition or under active consideration for repair or rebuilding.[55]

Richard Beaumont was also keenly interested in the exploitation of coal and timber resources. Besides a gamekeeper, he employed two men to protect his timber. Their work, which involved the marking and enclosure of woods as well as felling, carriage, and replanting, was a regular source of expenditure which, nevertheless, brought handsome returns. In regard to collieries, of which there were by now three on the estate, Richard revised the family's traditional policy. In return for a constant supply of fuel to meet his own needs he provided the colliers with board and wages as well as equipment. In 1743–4 he met the cost of repaving one mine, and later financed the opening of another. When 'a large party and servants' travelled into Lancashire after his second marriage in 1748, Richard paid men for 'trying for coal at Grizzlehurst'. All this indicates that he had more than a rentier's interest in mining, but there is no firm evidence that he derived income from selling coal. On the other hand the accounts do reveal that he greatly expanded farming operations at Whitley which, at the very least, must have considerably reduced household expenditure. Besides barley, wheat, oats, rye, and clover, the demesne produced peas, beans, lentils, and turnips. And yet much was spent each year on additional corn, straw, and hay for his animals; labour and manure were also regular items of expenditure. The steward

TABLE 14

Disbursements, 1743–64

	Debt & Interest Payments	Money to R.B.	Others	Total
	£ s. d.	£ s. d.	£ s. d.	£ s. d.
1743–4	139. 9. 6	386.16.10	670.14.10	1197. 1. 2
1744–5	56. 2. 0	747. 5. 2	827.11.10¼	1630.19. 0¼
1745–6	438.15. 0	142.15. 0	238. 5.11¾	819.15.11¾
1746–7	236. 5. 0	775.16. 6	156.19. 7¾	1169. 1. 1¾
1747–8	1570.13. 6	571. 3. 0	232.18. 7¼	2374.15. 1¼
1748–9	888. 2. 6	402. 0. 0	171.15.10½	1461.18. 4½
1749–50	1853.19. 6	289.15. 6	234. 5. 4	2378. 0. 4
1750–1	480. 0. 0	414.18. 0	85. 2. 3¼	980. 0. 3¼
1751–2	3449. 5. 8	1409. 1. 0	83. 9. 4¾	4941.16. 0¾
1752–3	302. 0. 0	1055.12. 6	303. 5. 8¼	1660.18. 2¼
1753–4	472.14. 6	929.10. 8	409.11. 8½	1811.16.10½
1754–5	1011. 5. 0	400. 0. 0	926.12. 2	2337.17. 2
1755–6	1278. 1. 0	447.15. 0	679. 9. 7½	2405. 5. 7½
1756–7	1058. 3. 0	643. 4. 6	998. 2.11	2699.10. 5
1757–8	1639. 0. 0	480. 0. 0	542.10. 3½	2661.10. 3½
1758–9	6276. 8. 0	549.12. 0	958.13. 3	7784.13. 3
1759–60	1402. 5. 6	396.11. 6	997. 8. 1¾	2796. 5. 1¾
1760–1	1126.15. 4	514.11. 0	915. 4. 1½	2556.10 5½
1761–2	1825. 9. 1	219. 0. 0	834. 5. 6½	2878.14. 7½
1762–3	1971. 6. 2	1211. 8. 6	799.12. 7¼	3982. 7. 3¼
1763–4	2806. 2. 6	647. 0. 0	771.13. 2½	4224.15. 8½

Sources: WBE/I/17–37.

attended most of the local markets and fairs where he acquired cattle, sheep, poultry, and horses. In two years, 1744–5 and 1750–1, he purchased fourteen and twenty 'Scots' bullocks respectively, while on a number of occasions he bought between twenty and fifty sheep. Clearly, mixed farming was practised on a substantial scale.

However, most of Richard's expenditure was devoted to the improvement of the Hall and gardens at Whitley. Throughout this period, but especially after his marriages in 1745 and 1748, large amounts of money were spent on labour and materials, and many different craftsmen – including plumbers, masons, carpenters, plasterers, and others – were employed. The accounts tell of 'a chimney-piece carried from London', of huge quantities of 'slate from Elland Edge', of 'trees in baskets' brought from Pontefract, and of tons of earth being moved to facilitate planting. An exceedingly fine plaster ceiling, depicting a harvest scene, was installed in one of the main rooms at Whitley Hall. The dining room was fitted with a magnificent fireplace, and the master bedroom panelled in oak. A temple and hermitage were built in the grounds, and 'a fine avenue of beech trees' planted between the main gate and the Hall entrance. The diary of a local clergyman, the Revd. J. Ismay, vividly describes how far this work had progressed by 1760:

Being called upon to see a sick person at Liley near Whitley Hall . . . I was easily prevailed upon to take a view of the house and gardens . . . We were conducted all through the apartments which abound with many pictures. . . . The saloon is a noble room . . . the room on the west contains a good billiard table, and that on the east a fine carpet. . . . The situation of this house is indeed most beautiful; to the south there is a spacious plain and lawn in the front, containing a bowling green and grassy slopes which yield a fine mountainous prospect. The Hall stands on an eminence and its beautiful situation is much improved by the works and adornments of art. The gardens abound with avenues, greenhouses, walks, and basins. There is a terrace walk to the temple and hermitage, flowering shrubs, serpentine paths, and the new road to the north; all are very beautiful and have a good effect.[56]

In the midst of these magnificent surroundings Richard and his family lived in considerable style. They ate and drank prodigiously. A celebration dinner at Whitley in 1749 comprised thirty-three separate dishes,[57] while in 1760–1 a single wine order included thirty gallons of Madeira. When Richard tired of his billiard table, his bowling green, his new pair of chaise horses, or of following the local hunt, he diverted himself at Scarborough and York races. While there, at Eton visiting his prospective heir, or in London, he and his wife purchased large quantities of shoes, clothes, and jewellery. Added to this were the sums distributed to local charities. Besides occasional gifts to the poor, Richard opened a subscription to the infirmary at York. He also contributed to the cost of building a school at Crosland and a chapel at Longwood and towards the end of his life erected a new family vault in the parish church at Kirkheaton.

As a result of this relentlessly heavy expenditure Richard quickly added to the £1,000 or so in debts which he had inherited from his brother. Indeed, he was only able to maintain his high level of expenditure by frequently changing his sources of credit. Such a policy could not continue indefinitely when total debts increased rather than diminished. Although debt and interest payments never fell below £1,000 a year from 1754–5, and twice very considerably exceeded this sum, Richard's financial situation was becoming increasingly difficult by the early 1760s. In 1764 he sold part of the Mitton estate for £5,210.[58] Despite the large repayments which this facilitated, Richard owed in excess of £8,000 at his death a few months later. Moreover, at this stage the estate still owed at least £2,000 to Richard's surviving sisters, while none of the generous portions provided for his own children had yet been paid. Owing to the lawsuit the family had been forced to reduce the size of portions and had in addition got a generation behind in paying them – a problem which was undoubtedly exacerbated by Richard's costly programme of improvement. Nevertheless, his optimism remained undaunted to the end, for he bequeathed £1,000 to his widow and provided a further £2,000 for his younger children. His will also requested his executors to sell more of the Mitton estate to discharge his debts as speedily as possible.[59]

Ironically, as in the period before 1704, solid achievements contained the seeds of future difficulties. In a letter of 6 June 1749 Mr Creyke of York, with whose family Richard had spent much of his childhood, had offered him some advice: do not 'be persuaded', he had written, 'to enter into any expensive projects of building or making gardens as you have now a happy prospect of an increasing family . . . it will be more for your honour and satisfaction to provide for' any children 'in a manner suitable to their birth than to be under a necessity some years hence to sell your eldest son to a person who may only have money to make an alliance convenient'. This was a tactful allusion, not just to the possible long-term effects of the lawsuit, but also to the ambitious developments which were already under way at Whitley. Many years later Richard's eldest son and heir endorsed the letter with the bitter comment: 'the advice of a sincere friend not attended to'.[60] However, although in improving Whitley Hall and the estate Richard Beaumont undoubtedly overreached himself, his activities were only partly responsible for the decline in the family's fortunes which occurred in the half century after his death. Following the long period of enforced neglect after 1704, an investment programme was virtually essential if the recovery in family fortunes which had preceded his succession was to continue. It was very difficult in mid eighteenth-century England to maintain or improve family status without indulging in this type of capital expenditure. Moreover, a decline in status, with its own economic consequences, was difficult to justify on purely financial grounds. In particular, it reduced the possibility of success in the marriage market of the kind that Richard himself achieved. Furthermore, Richard was careful to refurbish not only the circumstances in which he and his family lived, but also the general condition and management of his estates. In order to advance on a much broader front than any of his predecessors he had to borrow, and to be prepared to remain in debt, but this was common practice among his contemporaries. As soon as he began to fail, prematurely, in 1762 he made great efforts to stabilize family finances. If he had lived long enough to implement the general rent improvement which he planned, the result of these efforts would doubtless have been more than a partial reduction in outstanding debts.

As it was, Richard Henry Beaumont did inherit a difficult situation. Not only were there numerous debts and settled payments to discharge, but the recurrent expenditure involved in the upkeep of the new Whitley Hall was considerable. His major problems, however, were unrelated to these factors. In the first place his mother, Dame Elizabeth Beaumont, survived her husband for nearly three decades, receiving throughout that lengthy period a jointure of £500 a year. Secondly, Richard Henry Beaumont himself was temperamentally quite unsuited to the task of managing his inheritance. Still a minor in 1764, he lived an eremitical life at Whitley and Mitton after coming of age, self-confessedly disinclined to become involved in estate affairs and preferring instead to spend his time poring over books and manuscripts. His activities as an antiquarian earned him the honorary degree of M.A. from Oxford University and a Fellowship of the Society of Antiquaries. However, although he served one term as High Sheriff of Yorkshire in 1793, he was fundamentally as uninterested in county affairs as he was in landownership and estate management; and when he died unmarried in 1810 he owed nearly £13,000 and his affairs were in complete disorder.[61]

The endeavours of the Whitley Beaumonts were confined throughout this period within a fairly narrow compass. They were not active politically, and only during the Civil War did they become involved in public events. There are few indications of their participation in local administration. None of them was gainfully employed. The family had no trading or commercial interests, and made no ventures in the sphere of public finance. Even though their estate was rich in coal, only latterly did they show any interest in directly exploiting these resources. Their life was centred on a compact and slowly expanding estate: its development and management were their primary concern; its produce, profits, and security were all they had. In these circumstances they supported Charles I financially, fought for him, and brushed aside the consequences of their behaviour without being seriously hampered by them. Half a century later they coped long, arduously, but none the less successfully, with a lawsuit whose cost was in every respect enormous. Finally, before the last traces of this dispute had disappeared, they embarked on developments at Whitley which were equal to those undertaken by any of their contemporaries of equal social standing. How, and why, were they able to achieve so much?

Of all the features of their history none is more distinctive than their demography. At no time during the seventeenth and eighteenth centuries was a deceased head of the family succeeded by a son who had obtained a majority. As a result the succession passed either to a minor, or to the cadet branch of the family at Lascelles Hall. This often had a markedly beneficial effect on the fortunes of the Whitley Beaumonts. When a few years of quiet recuperation were necessary after periods of misfortune or costly development, as in 1723 or 1764, these were provided in the form of minorities when conspicuous expenditure was at a minimum. Even when not particularly desirable, minorities were useful, as in 1668 and 1692. Moreover, when debts and future commitments demanded greater resources, as in 1631 and 1704, these were to some extent provided by the Lascelles Hall branch of the family, whose property was merged with that at Whitley. Conversely, the two branches were divided in 1668 when several years of prosperity had suggested that this would not endanger the fortunes of either.

The benefits which accrued from this demographic pattern were consistently reinforced by firm and careful estate management. Of these four families the Beaumonts engaged in the most direct farming. Their home farm at Whitley reduced household expenditure and, particularly before 1668 and between 1738 and 1764, often achieved rather more than this. Moreover, although they too found the potential for rent improvements restricted by the lack of upward movement in agricultural prices, they lost no time in increasing rents where this was possible; they also considerably reduced their own costs by requiring their tenants to pay all the taxes levied on leased property. This policy was further toughened by a refusal to make free allowances of small timber to tenants for repair work. The family's ability after 1723 to mount a slowly expanding programme of major repairs and improvements to their property benefited the tenantry, as did veterinary assistance and rent allowance during the cattle plague. Nevertheless, the relatively high level of rent arrears in all the years for which records are available suggests that their primary aim was to derive as much rent as possible from their estate. There is little evidence, however, that their efforts to maximize estate income were stimulated by imagination or enterprise. Beyond appointing stewards, who themselves farmed locally, they did nothing to promote more efficient farming among their tenants. They benefited substantially and increasingly from the woods, quarries, and pits on their property but for most of this period were reluctant to become more directly involved in the production and marketing of these resources. Their major achievement as landowners was the steady, piecemeal expansion of the Whitley estate; even this was largely offset by the sale of the property at Lascelles Hall in 1714, though in the circumstances this could not, apparently, have been avoided.

Far from acting as a deterrent, a fundamentally conservative outlook encouraged their efforts in the marriage market where, however, they met with only mixed success. Within the comparatively short space of ninety years, in 1656, 1698, and 1748, three of the Beaumonts married heiresses. Two of these marriages were very beneficial, particularly that of 1748 which, though followed by a long widowhood, added valuable property to the Whitley estate. But the marriage of 1698 – an achievement in itself, whose results could so easily have been different – proved disastrous, providing the family with a bill of well over £30,000 in the next thirty years. The reason for this stemmed not so much from the fact that the marriage was barren, nor from the Countess of Westmorland's long survival of her first husband; but rather from the remarkably generous settlement which Richard Beaumont provided for his wife at his death in 1704. Thereby he diverted a huge volume of resources away from a family which had never been unduly anxious to maintain strict control over the whole of its patrimony. In the difficult period which ensued the problem was one of retrenchment rather than survival. Later, with the help of a lengthy minority, the Beaumonts lived comfortably and, latterly, in some luxury. Thus, even when prices were depressed, rent movement sluggish, and income opportunities outside agriculture unsought or unavailable, diversification was not essential to success. Both the Beaumonts' achievements and the more varied endeavours of others had a common basis in landed property.

IV

THE CONSTABLES OF EVERINGHAM
AND RASEN

THE contrast between the two families examined so far is clear-cut. The history of the Hothams unfolds on a relatively grand and often dramatic scale. In every respect the more substantial of the two and almost without exception individually driven in search of public success, they were a family to be reckoned with throughout the East Riding and, indeed, beyond. The Beaumonts on the other hand, partly because of their lesser means but also through choice, led a humdrum and largely anonymous existence. Except during periods of minority, they were never long or far away from the confines of Whitley Hall. Though not uneventful, their history until 1743 was characterized by the mundane: it was precisely this that Richard Beaumont then attempted to break away from.

Although initially this may seem to have been impossible, our next family, the Constables of Everingham Hall in the East Riding, had much in common with both the Hothams and the Beaumonts. Their income was broadly on a par with that of the Hothams for they were substantial landowners in Yorkshire and Lincolnshire. However, because of the fiscal and other penalties which resulted from their recusancy, their manner of life was often at or below the level afforded by the Beaumonts. Members of the family were barred from public office, so of necessity they spent much time on or near their estates. Their property was not rich in timber or mineral resources; rents and the profits of direct farming were their only permanent sources of income. It was therefore a substantial but narrowly based economy which, owing to the family's recusancy, was frequently under siege down to the early decades of the eighteenth century.

One could easily exaggerate the difficulties which the Constables had to overcome. Government policy towards recusants was generally much harsher in theory than in practice; and, together with various friends and acquaintances, the family soon became adept at eluding or mitigating the legal, fiscal, and other consequences of their nonconformity. Nevertheless, they were at times under severe financial and economic stress, and were obliged to part with a considerable amount of property in the century or so before 1720. Thereafter the penal laws fell progressively into abeyance, though this was not primarily responsible for the family's economic recovery. The basis for this was laid during the second half of the long career of Sir Marmaduke Constable who, because he remained unmarried, did not have to provide for a wife and children. Consequently, while enjoying a comfortable and indeed adventurous existence, he amassed sufficient personal estate to enable his successor to purchase land which more than compensated for earlier property losses. In fact by 1760 the Constables' affairs were in far better shape than those of either the Hothams or the Beaumonts.

1. THE CRISIS 1640–60

The Constables of Everingham were merely one of several branches of the Constable family in the East Riding of Yorkshire. Their most famous ancestor, Sir Robert Constable, led the Pilgrimage of Grace and was primarily responsible for the family's tenacious adherence to the old faith during the late sixteenth century. In the early seventeenth century some members of the Everingham branch conformed to the established religion, but they soon reverted to open Catholicism. In 1613 the head of the Everingham family was described as a 'very noted man' with an annual rental of £3,000. His successors, however, got into financial difficulties and were obliged to alienate substantial amounts of real estate. By 1632, when Philip Constable succeeded, they owed £3,656, besides being liable for a further £400 a year in rent charges and life annuities. Following his conviction for recusancy in that year, Philip was fined £250–£260 a year until 1642. Although considerably reduced in previous decades, his estates produced an annual rental of £1,850 in 1640, at which point he was still justifiably regarded as 'rich' and 'of the higher class'.[1]

Philip Constable's house at Middle Rasen in Lincolnshire adjoined an estate of some 3,000 acres, while the Yorkshire estate consisted of 3,000 acres near Everingham Hall and in Holderness in the East Riding, 1,000 acres at Drax in the West Riding, and a house in York. This property was as varied in type as it was scattered. That at Everingham, Rasen, Thorpe, and in Holderness was still semi-feudal in organization, with a multiplicity of small, unenclosed holdings occupied by farmers, husbandmen, and cottagers; many tenants held their property from year to year and performed a variety of customary services for their landlord. On the other hand each of the family's manors of Wholsea, Arras, and Gardham was farmed by a single tenant, partly enclosed, and leased for a term of years; Drax was similarly divided into five independent farms. The Constables also held two leases: one of the tithes of Weighton, Shipton, and Arras, and the other of the tithes of Hayton, Bielby, and Storthwaite, both of which they sub-let at a large profit. Finally, the family held a reversionary interest in leases at Acklam and Woodhouse Grange, the lessors being the Master and the perpetual chaplains of the Savoy hospital in London.[2]

The family was Royalist as well as Catholic. Their political allegiance was confirmed by the free grant of a baronetcy in July 1642 and Sir Philip Constable's were among the first estates to be sequestered by Parliament. He remained in England throughout the wars, in which three close relatives were killed fighting for the King. Whether he himself was militarily active is uncertain, though his age probably prevented this. Both his homes were damaged in the hostilities and, after residing briefly in York, he sought refuge in Newark Castle. On its surrender in 1646 he attempted to compound and was eventually allowed to do so. However, this decision was quickly reversed and his estates re-sequestered in 1650–1. Attempting to modify this penalty, Sir Philip's eldest son, Marmaduke, claimed part of the Lincolnshire property under a settlement of 1619. When this failed he leased his title to a creditor and unsuccessfully petitioned the authorities on the latter's behalf. The Sequestration Commissioners leased the Yorkshire estate to Sir Philip's sons or to tenants who held in trust for them, but the Lincoln-shire estate was let to an army officer. While the family received the statutory fifth from their east Yorkshire property, the rents which they were obliged to pay for it were only just below its full value. Thus, they maintained a tenuous and uneconomic control over only part of their estates.[3]

Sir Philip's daughter, Katherine, married Edward Sheldon of Steeple Barton in Oxfordshire in 1649. In the following year Marmaduke married Anne, daughter of Richard Shirburne of Stonyhurst in Lancashire. Both families were also Catholics. Though Katherine received a portion of £3,000, Marmaduke's bride was provided with £4,000. The entire Constable estates were settled on trustees to the use of Marmaduke, and his male heirs in succession, after Sir Philip's death. Marmaduke assumed control at Everingham, Sir Philip retired with his daughter to Oxfordshire, and Robert Shirburne, Anne's cousin, came to east Yorkshire to act as chief steward of the estate.[4]

The family's situation worsened when Sir Philip was included in the third Treason Act in 1652. His name had appeared in drafts of previous acts but, after frantic petitioning, had been removed. During debates on amendments to the third act Sir William Constable of Flamborough, Puritan, Regicide, and Colonel in the Parliamentary army, twice divided the House in an attempt to save his relative, but to no avail. Sir Philip's estates were forfeited to the Commonwealth and put up for sale. Marmaduke immediately looked for ways in which potential ruin might be averted. As the 1619 settlement had entailed the estates on him after his father's death, and as only Sir Philip had been convicted of treason, he asked the government to declare that the sale was for Sir Philip's life only. The authorities agreed in March 1653 after Marmaduke had taken the 'Engagement'. He then argued that, as the land in Holderness had been granted by letters patent, it ought merely to be subject to a composition fine. The act specifically catered for this and the claim was allowed. He next ensured that the forfeited estates were sold to someone who was content to pose as the owner while allowing him to manage the property and receive the profits. His accomplice was John Rushworth, who purchased the estates with money provided by Marmaduke, and held the property on his behalf. Rushworth, a friend and distant relative, and a skilled operator in this complex business, collaborated with others who had similar objectives and comparable experience; moreover, his activities were shielded by a

long and conspicously successful career in Parliament's service.[5] He was able to contract for the purchase of the whole
property. Richard Shirburne obtained large loans from the
London money market, and by June 1653 Rushworth had paid
half the purchase price. The formal deed of sale was signed and
sealed on 7 June. A series of private legal manoeuvres completed the fabrication. Sir Philip, Marmaduke, and Rushworth
vested the estate in three Catholic trustees who became responsible for the accumulated debts for 999 years. The trustees
immediately leased the property back to Marmaduke and
Rushworth for the same period minus ten days. Sir Philip ceded
his life-estate to Marmaduke, and Rushworth formally authorized the existing stewards and bailiffs to continue their
activities.[6]

For two years all went well. However, in 1655 it was reported
that some of the profits from the estate were accruing to Sir
Philip. A bill for the 'discovery' of his estate was filed in Chancery and he, Rushworth, and the main tenant in Lincolnshire
were interrogated. Later, in a letter to the local Major-General,
Rushworth denied any approach by Sir Philip to himself but
agreed that at the request of Sir William Constable of
Flamborough, he had acted on behalf of Richard Shirburne's
grandchildren. There was no further action. The family's position was perhaps more secure after this public scrutiny than it
had been before. Certainly they took great care to maintain the
façade in every detail. Lands were surrendered to Rushworth
and courts held in his name. As Robert Shirburne regularly
drafted the replies of the Everingham constable to the ques-
tionnaires circulated by the latter's superiors the family was also
able to survive further inquiries concerning their recusancy.
The final hurdle before the Restoration was the Act of 1659 for
the banishing of certain delinquents. Sir Philip was exempted
on health grounds and obtained a letter of protection after
undertaking to live 'peaceably and quietly'.[7]

The family also coped, albeit arduously, with the pressures
which these developments brought to bear on their economy.
The long sequestration before 1649 must have considerably
reduced their income, which consisted solely of estate revenue.
Composition brought further problems, Sir Philip allegedly
having to pay £4,000 in goods for arrears in the fine which had

accrued since the outbreak of hostilities. In 1650 Marmaduke raised rents in Yorkshire from £1,163 a year to £1,407, and in 1651 to £1,442. With £684 from Lincolnshire this produced a gross annual rental of £2,126. The official valuation which followed the second sequestration later in 1651 estimated that leased property was annually worth £215 less than Marmaduke was asking for it. Thus, he made heavy demands of his tenants long before his financial position reached its nadir in 1653. After the second sequestration Marmaduke was forced to borrow heavily in London. He retained part of his property via leases from the commissioners either to himself or to his tenants, but the cost was enormous. In one case he paid £617 annually for land which he valued at £636 a year. These rents were regularly reviewed, the £617 being raised to £673 in 1652. As tenants were forbidden to make more than proportionate increases when sub-letting, Marmaduke was driven further into debt. The sale which followed the Treason Act gave him full control over most of his property, but the purchase price with which he had to provide Rushworth was £7,557; the composition for Holderness amounted to an additional £759. As a result total debts rose to £15,880 which at 6 per cent carried annual interest charges of £952. This last sum accounted for about half the family's gross annual income.[8]

Marmaduke resorted to the enclosure of part of the Lincolnshire estate, thereby clashing with the parson of West Rasen. When, despite this opposition, the enclosure was completed rents there were raised. Sales of timber also yielded substantial income at this stage. While now free to sell property, Marmaduke in fact expanded the estate between 1653 and 1655, acquiring three holdings for a total of £1,370. Two were in Yorkshire and had belonged to his tenants; the third, in Lincolnshire, was a farm which Sir Philip had previously leased. The transactions were facilitated by Marmaduke's ability to mortgage parts of the newly acquired property in providing some of the purchase price; timber sales provided further capital. The only contemporary sale was of a small farm in Acklam for £200. Meanwhile, the rental fluctuated constantly. In 1653 the tenant of Gardham was evicted because someone else agreed to pay a much greater rent. This apparently occurred at Arras too and, in the face of tenants' pleas of inability to pay, rents were also increased at Everingham and Wholsea. Yet, despite purchases and rent increases, the gross rental in Yorkshire was £1,004 in 1655 compared with £1,442 in 1651. Tithe leases, which previously had been sub-let at great profit, had not been removed from sequestration; also rents had been so high in 1651 that either Marmaduke or the commissioners had subsequently reduced them. Unfortunately this decrease occurred at the time of greatest need. Although Marmaduke severely pruned expenditure in Yorkshire to £1,100 in 1655 (£600 for interest charges and £500 for general disbursements), this was greater than available estate income. Accordingly, he again improved rents in Yorkshire in 1656, this time by £80, to produce a rental of £1,084. This still failed to create a favourable balance, and was some £358 less than the Yorkshire rental for 1651. During this same period the Lincolnshire rental rose by a mere £20. Scattered evidence suggests a simultaneous contraction of production on the home farm. Nor could heavy demands on relatively meagre timber resources have continued indefinitely.[9]

Not surprisingly, Sir Philip and Marmaduke arranged to sell their least profitable property, namely the land in Holderness. The Treason Act, which had allowed Marmaduke to compound for this, required existing rents to remain unchanged. There were also rent arrears of up to three years' standing. The property was sold in small parcels between 1656 and 1659 for a total of £1,448. Shortly before the Restoration sequestration of the tithe and other leases was lifted. The fall in the rental which followed the sale of Holderness was more than offset by these additional sources of income. Nevertheless, the gross annual rental remained lower than it had been in 1651, and overall there was only a slight increase in the family's gross income between 1640 and 1660. This contrasted sharply with the enormous increase in their expenditure which they only survived by incurring large debts. In 1660 some £12,042 of these had still to be repaid.[10]

One should not overestimate the family's difficulties during these years. Although their Catholicism was a distinct disadvantage, recusancy was abolished as an offence in 1650. The authorities were more tolerant of religious unorthodoxy during the Interregnum than either before or afterwards. Professional and political disabilities remained but they were able to travel widely both at home and abroad. Marmaduke visited the Continent on at least three occasions between 1640 and 1660; his two brothers and a sister continued their education there, eventually becoming Benedictines.[11] However, the estate was confiscated for most of the decade after the outbreak of civil war, and home life was disrupted for much of that period. The sale to Rushworth left huge debts, and Marmaduke could never have been entirely sure that the fabrication would not be uncovered and dismantled. Yet he was relatively untroubled by the authorities after 1653, his economy withstood the pressure imposed on it and, despite the heavy debts, his estate remained as large in 1660 as it had been in 1640. Several factors other than his own prodigious resourcefulness were in his favour. In confining its punishment to Sir Philip Parliament kept to the letter of its own law, something which did not always occur. This provided Marmaduke with a basis upon which to plan in the midst of rapidly changing circumstances. A mortgage market sufficient to meet his needs was available in London, and in the Shirburnes he had relatives who were familiar with its operations. Finally, his estate was large enough, both to provide creditors with adequate security, and slowly to erode his debts while still catering for everyday needs. For the time being at least ownership of property had triumphed over a variety of political, religious, and economic problems.

2. MONEY AND FRIENDS 1660–74

Apart from the occasional acknowledgement in high places, the Constables were not rewarded for their sufferings on the King's behalf. Encouraged by Charles II's public statements, they looked for an early relaxation of the penal laws but were disappointed, not least because Sir John Hotham headed the East Riding peace commission. At York assizes in 1660 high constables were reminded of recent 'great neglect' and given warrants 'for putting the laws against papists into execution'. As usual Robert Shirburne prepared a report for the local constable to submit. After declaring that there were no recusants in the constabulary and that, in any case, absence from church was permitted by the royal declaration of 1660, he went on to criticize outside interference in local matters. The Everingham constable refused to endorse the document and reported in his own 'True Account' that Marmaduke, his wife, and all their household except Henry the blacksmith were papists; but there were no further proceedings. Circumstances worsened following the Act of Uniformity. In 1663 the East Riding justices ordered presentments of all papists, together with their servants and those of their children who were nine years of age or over. On this occasion the local constable submitted a favourable report which, however, was overruled. Later he was probably among those punished because they had 'wavered', knowing some 'to have deeply suffered for the King'. Marmaduke, his wife, and a bailiff were among the 400 presentments, and Marmaduke was one of several 'of quality' who were indicted. At his trial the jury brought in a verdict of *ignoramus* but, on being sent back by the judge, found him guilty on the same evidence. This was his first conviction for recusancy. Contemporary Treasury records indicate that few convictions were followed by fines and there is no evidence that Marmaduke was so punished on this occasion. In 1668 Robert Shirburne asked a sympathetic York ecclesiastic for help should trouble arise from a recent archiepiscopal visitation. Neither Sir Marmaduke (Sir Philip had died in 1664) nor his lady had been presented, but both they and the Everingham churchwardens had been summoned for 'clandestine practice'. He was assured that 'no prejudice shall come unto them', nor did it.[12]

In many respects the family were completely unhindered in the practice of their religion. A priest lived at Everingham after the Restoration and held regular services there. He and other family chaplains in the East Riding were aided by a roving mission. Members of the family travelled freely at home and had no difficulty in obtaining passes to go abroad. They circulated Catholic news and broadsheets, had no qualms about undertaking executorships or administrations, and even presented incumbents to the rectory at Everingham. When Sir Marmaduke's wife died she was buried in the chancel of one of the main churches in York while the Minster bell tolled for her. In the face of official proceedings they could 'fence' or prevaricate 'as well as most' and were confident that their enemies 'may show their malice but shall not hurt'. They were severely scornful of any Catholic who yielded to pressure and felt compassion only 'for the poor people who want both money and friends'. In so doing they acknowledged the main sources of their own strength and safety.[13]

After 1660 the family was involved in several legal disputes which reveal something of the background against which they undertook the major task of discharging their debts. The first reflects the apparent willingness of certain individuals to take advantage of their difficulties; they were after all good reasons for regarding them as easy prey. In 1650 Sir Philip had temporarily assigned his interest in the Savoy leases to James Blackbeard, one of his creditors, allegedly in order to prevent their inclusion in a second sequestration. Later Blackbeard and two accomplices, maintaining that the leases had been purchased outright in 1650, entered the properties. By 1664 Sir Marmaduke had regained Acklam and, though the subsequent arbitration award is unrecorded, also retained Woodhouse.[14] Other disputes suggest, however, that faced with the continual necessity of making ends meet the Constables were prepared to boost their income and reduce their expenditure by any means at their disposal. Thus, after demanding a suit fine from a neighbouring landowner at Drax and yet refusing to pay tithes to him, they were defeated in court and forced to accept a lease of the tithes at an annual rent of £20.[15] They also disputed with the prebendary of Weighton concerning their lease of tithes there. The latter charged them with being in arrears with their rent and with farming certain tithes not mentioned in the lease. Unfortunately the decision of arbitrators is again unrecorded.[16] Of much greater substance was a running battle throughout the 1660s with John Davenport, the parson of West Rasen, concerning their enclosures in Lincolnshire. Accusing them of having enclosed glebeland, Davenport entered the property and cut hay at random. Subsequently he led local farmers in defence of their common rights with the result that Robert Shirburne experienced difficulty in securing tenants. Sir Marmaduke was forced to make substantial concessions in an out of court settlement in 1671, though by the agreement many acres remained enclosed.[17] Finally, Sir Marmaduke disputed with Richard Shirburne junior. By a family settlement of 1649 Shirburne senior had reserved the power to devise £3,000 from the estate which then passed to his son. By his will of 1667 he granted the Constables £2,600, gave them his entire personal estate, and made them his executors. Shirburne junior accused them of unduly influencing his father on his death bed. Certainly the will bears the shaky signature of a dying man. Yet Sir Marmaduke retaliated against non-payment of the legacy by distraining on Shirburne's Lancashire estate. Under the arbitration of Lord Langdale in 1668 the Constables received £1,750.[18]

The need to maximize income and minimize expenditure was the major influence on estate management. In 1660 Robert Shirburne agreed that the York house was let to a good tenant, but 'if it were at liberty I believe it would yield a better rent'. In 1661 he wrote to Lady Rudsham asking for arrears in her payments of tithe at Hayton. The Drax rental was improved in that year, and when one tenant failed to pay the whole of his rent in 1663 Shirburne insisted that he make it up 'by hay, cattle, or something'. In 1664 the Everingham tenants were refused permission to pasture part of the townfields, and oats were sown to prevent them doing so. Shirburne's attitude to their rent arrears was unequivocal: 'if' they 'will not give security for the future payment of their rents more certainly, they must not take it unkindly if it is required they give present caution for this year, and leave their farms at Ladyday next'. The tenant of Gardham was constantly in difficulties. Though 'it is not usual to sue a tenant so quickly for his rent', Shirburne threatened to prosecute him for non-payment of arrears. The rent was lowered but by 1666 the tenant was still in arrears. He maintained that the rent was still too high and that, if he was forced to leave the property, nobody would 'farm it almost at any price'. The family agreed to do 'what is conscionable [sic] in these hard times' but were shortly writing of 'the bad end' which 'is made with Halliday', and agreeing that they had 'better get something than lose all'. Thus, attitudes towards tenants' problems were increasingly uncompromising. The family assumed control over farming of the common fields at Everingham and Rasen, reduced rents only as a means of cutting their own losses, and did not tolerate arrears. Other means of increasing income included timber sales. In 1670 several oaks and ashes at Everingham were put up for sale; though valued at £280, Sir Marmaduke hoped to sell them for £320. Profits from direct farming, however, were poor. In 1666 Robert Shirburne complained that 'goods do scarcely give half the value they did three years since'. By 1670 the home farm at Everingham had been considerably contracted, while that at Rasen was apparently discontinued.[19]

TABLE 15

The Constables: Income, Expenditure & Debts 1662 & 1664

1662

Income	£	s.	d.
Yorkshire	1200.	0.0	
Lincolnshire	700.	0.0	
	1900.	0.0	

Disbursements			
Debt of £3680 paid annually in rent charges	598.	0.0	
Interest on debt of £6590	407.	8.0	
Annually in annuities	290.	0.0	
Annual outpayments	85.	0.0	
1 steward & 2 bailiffs	52.	0.0	
Servants' wages	78.	0.0	
	1510.	8.0	

'There remains for ourselves only'	389.12.0	
'Other debts for which we pay no consideration'	780. 0.0	

1664

Yorkshire Rents £1220 –	Interest on £9000 debts	504. 0.0
	Rent Charges	305. 0.0
	Life Annuities	338. 0.0
1147		1147. 0.0
73		
	Servants' Wages	60. 0.0
	Others	116.13.4
		176.13.4 –
		73. 0.0
		103.13.4

Lincolnshire Rents £600 –
Outpayments   192
             408
             103.13.4
             304. 6.8 'remains to ourselves for
                            housekeeping, clothes etc.'

Sources: DDEV/56/408, 443.

There are no extant statements of gross income during this period, but there are reliable statistics of its major component, the rental. This rose by £332 between 1664 and 1671. An additional £212 from Lincolnshire resulted, despite the dispute with Davenport, from enclosure. The situation in Yorkshire was less straightforward. There the gross rental fell from £1,220 in 1664 to £1,100 in 1670, mainly due to the reduction of the rent at Gardham by £60 a year. But in 1671 the rents of Wholsea, Thorpe, the York house, and the tithes were increased. These increases, together with the rents of Wood-house which were by then available, produced a Yorkshire rental of £1,352, £252 more than the previous rental and £132 more than in 1664. Thus, in 1671 the gross rental of the entire estate was £2,152, a mere £26 a year more than in 1651. This fluctuating income was unequal to the task of discharging debts which in 1660 totalled £12,042.[20]

Numerous arrangements for discharging debts had been made: besides mortgages and bonds, there were life annuities and annual rent charges. This complex situation arose from the need in 1652–3 to raise large sums of money at short notice. Life annuities were extremely costly if individuals lived longer than expected. Furthermore, although rent charges and annuities were a means of gradually reducing debts, fixed capital repayments were inconvenient in years when income declined. Moreover, because the family contracted numerous debts and granted many separate securities, it was often difficult to provide a new creditor with acceptable security when an impatient one called for his money. Eventually a more drastic solution was devised whereby property was leased to groups of businessmen who assumed responsibility for repaying an agreed schedule of debts, using the income from the leased property to this end. Debts dominated expenditure and reduced the family to a shoestring budget. In 1662, for example, the gross rental amounted to £1,900. Of this £407 was devoted to interest charges, £598 to rent charges, £290 to life annuities, £130 to wages, and £85 to sundries. Taking no account of mortgage capital or debts of £780 on bonds, this left 'for ourselves only £389'. Similar remainders in 1664 and 1673 were £304 and £385 respectively.[21]

The Constables survived this parlous situation largely

TABLE 16
The Constables: Income, Expenditure & Debts 1668, 1670, 1673

1668		£	s.	d.
Yorkshire Rents £1105	Interest on £7516	470.	0.	0
1014	Annuities	200.	0.	0
91	Rent Charges	200.	0.	0
	Outrents	93.	0.	0
	Assessments	51.	0.	0
		1014.	0.	0

No interest paid on debts of £818.19.7

1670				
Yorkshire Rents £1100	Interest on £6430	400.	6.	0
	Annuities	200.	0.	0
	Rent Charges	200.	0.	0
	Outpayments	93.	0.	0
		893.	6.	0

No interest paid on debts of £480.0.0

1673			
Yorkshire Rents	927.	7.	8
Lincolnshire Rents	602.	12.	0
	1529.	19.	8

Expenditure			
Interest	140.	0.	0
Annuities	234.	0.	0
Rent Charges	200.	0.	0
Towards other Debts	400.	0.	0
Outrents	133.	5.	0
Assessments	38.	3.	4
	1145.	8.	4

Sources: DDEV/56/408; 58/132.

because of substantial assistance from Richard Shirburne senior and his wife, Elizabeth. In 1661 the Shirburnes purchased Kingerby Wood near West Rasen for £600 and settled it on the Constables after Elizabeth's death. By her will the latter also left the family many goods and chattels. Most of all, however, they needed cash. One of the loans raised in 1653 had been a mortgage on Gardham for £3,000. In 1664 the property was sold to a Mr Sheldon for £3,200. But he merely acted as trustee for Elizabeth Shirburne, who provided the purchase money, allowed the Constables to retain future profits from the property, and devised it to them after her death. Furthermore, before he died her husband authorized his steward 'to pay over surplus moneys' to Sir Marmaduke. Together with the capital acquired through Richard's will, these developments enabled Sir Marmaduke to reduce his debts to £6,430 by 1670.[22] In the following year a further large reduction was made possible by the marriage of Sir Marmaduke's son, Philip, to Margaret Radcliffe, daughter of the future Earl of Derwentwater. During 1671–2 the whole of Margaret's portion of £4,000 was devoted to discharging debts.[23]

In June 1674 Sir Marmaduke handed over control of family affairs to his newly married son. He leased part of the estate to two businessmen who undertook to repay remaining debts, which amounted to less than £3,000, during the succeeding seven years. Taking an annual income of £150 from the estate for himself and his wife, he went into semi-retirement.[24]

3. MIXED FORTUNE 1674–98

For several years after Philip Constable's marriage the family lived in uncertainty. Would their Catholicism remain unpunished and comparatively unhindered, and would they be able to maintain and complete the discharge of their debts? In 1672 Charles II issued his Declaration of Indulgence which suspended the penal laws. This was soon withdrawn and followed by a vigorous anti-Catholic campaign. However, Philip avoided conviction for recusancy, and remained untroubled by the authorities until 1678. Moreover, his financial situation continued to improve. In 1677 he and his wife moved into Everingham Hall and Sir Marmaduke went to live in the house at York. The latter reserved the right to use several apartments at Everingham, while Philip paid him £220 for farm stock and an annual rent of £156 for the Hall. These arrangements indicate that there was still no slack in the family economy. Annual expenditure was higher with two separate units to support, and in 1675 annual income had been reduced by a failure to renew the lease of Woodhouse. In addition the York house was mortgaged for £150 in 1678. However, a contemporary memorandum states that between 1672 and March

1679 debts amounting to £2,628 were discharged. By then, therefore, nearly all the family's creditors had been satisfied.[25]

This achievement was preceded, and inevitably overshadowed, by the outbreak of the Popish Plot controversy. The anti-Catholic campaign which followed was more ferocious than any of its predecessors and, unable to avoid involvement, Philip Constable was severely punished. Having been presented as recusants by the constable of Everingham, he and his servant were imprisoned in York Castle by order of the East Riding justices in March 1678. An order of the House of Lords allowed him to pass 'quietly over the seas' in March 1679. In April Sir Marmaduke also fled abroad where he died in August 1680, a 'papist fled from justice'. Meanwhile, Philip had returned and, after refusing to take the oaths, was again imprisoned at York in July 1680. Together with Lord Dunbar and Sir William Langdale, he was named in the Papists, Removing and Disarming Bill which was published in December. He remained confined until 1683 when he petitioned the King 'for a pardon'. He reminded Charles of his family's service to the Royalist cause and of the 'total ruin' which had consequently overtaken them. The petition was apparently successful and Sir Philip, as he had by then become, was released. As the King continued to issue anti-recusant proclamations in order to disarm his critics, the circumstances of Catholics remained distinctly unfavourable.[26]

Sir Philip's imprisonment coincided with, and in some ways caused, a further deterioration in his economic position. The loss of Woodhouse was followed by a similar failure to retain the lease of the tithes of Weighton, Shipton, and Arras. Moreover, some rents – at Wholsea, Arras, and Gardham – had to be lowered owing to the inability of the tenants to pay them. Consequently, the gross rental in Yorkshire, which had totalled £1,352 in 1671, fell to just over £1,000 in the two decades after 1680. There was a parallel decrease in the Lincolnshire rental which, after reaching £814 in 1673, fell to £647 in 1687. Sir Philip may have taken some of the Lincolnshire property into his own hands, but it seems that there too rent reductions were mainly responsible for the fall in income. No property was sold. Thus, in the period 1680–1700 the family's average gross rental was £1,697 a year as against £2,152 a year in 1671. Nevertheless rent arrears persisted. There were also new items of expenditure. Sir Philip had apparently returned from the Continent in 1680 in the belief that he could live unmolested in Lincolnshire; before his second imprisonment he repaired the Hall at Middle Rasen. Soon after his release in 1683 he was engaged in similar work at Everingham. The only evidence of his paying recusancy fines dates from 1685 when he paid £120 in two instalments, but he probably began payments after his release from prison, and may have been fined from the time of his conviction in 1678. He once again had to borrow, and raised £600 on bonds during 1681–3. In 1684–5 income amounted to £1,927 and must have included further loans, the proceeds of heavy wood sales, or both. During the same period expenditure totalled £1,935.[27]

Thus, the family's position at the end of Charles II's reign was far from promising. It changed dramatically, however, with the accession of James II in 1685. Following the new King's suspension of the penal laws, Sir Philip received a warrant allowing him to travel freely, and dispensing him from the oaths and 'from all penalties, notwithstanding former statutes'. He was not slow to exploit his newly acquired respectability. In April 1687, perhaps with a view to overriding tenants' objections, he successfully petitioned for a licence to keep deer at Everingham, and for permission to enclose some 300 acres at Gardham in order to establish a warren. Moreover, he was one of six Catholic J.P.s appointed in the East Riding where, predictably, there was a renaissance of Catholic life and worship. In 1687 Bishop Leyburn confirmed sixty-two local Catholics in the family chapel at Everingham. It was equally natural for Sir Philip to live ostentatiously, if only by borrowing a further £500 on bonds during the first six months of the new reign. In May 1686 he mortgaged the manor and farm at Gardham to Thomas Day, an 'artisan skinner' of York, for £1,000. Yet he received no lucrative office or unexpected financial reward from James II with which to offset these growing debts. For the second time in half a century the family's position rested precariously on the success or otherwise of the King. Once again his failure severely harmed their own fortunes. Soon after the invasion of William of Orange Sir Philip, accompanied by two servants, fled to France.[28]

He felt able to return after a few months. Although an Act of Toleration was passed in 1689, it specifically excluded Catholics. Probably because of a further refusal to take the oaths Sir Philip was again imprisoned at York in 1690. In August he petitioned for release on the grounds that he was suffering from 'complicate diseases'; he was set free on promising to behave well and to appear 'when and where required'. Later he sought treatment at Greenwich hospital but was required to give security in June 1692 for a subsequent appearance before the Court of King's Bench. There he entered into an additional recognizance for his future behaviour. For the next four years the authorities remained satisfied with his conduct.[29]

Sir Philip continued to find it necessary to borrow. Between 1689 and 1691 he raised £300 on bonds and borrowed a further £500 from Thomas Day. Following a third loan, of £500, from Day in 1692 the mortgage was converted to cover the total debt of £2,000. A London acquaintance granted Sir Philip another mortgage, for £424, in 1694. This borrowing was due neither to a further decrease in income nor to a sudden rise in family expenditure. As Sir Philip's mother had died in 1679 no jointure had had to be paid to her, while the deaths of his own wife and of two, and possibly four, of his seven children no doubt further reduced costs. In 1693, for example, the education and maintenance of his son and daughters cost only £94; the question of the provision of portions for the latter had yet to arise. Annual outpayments were high, amounting in 1693 to £237, £118 of which comprised annuities to various relatives. Moreover, Sir Philip incurred certain extraordinary items of expenditure (fines for the renewal of leases for example) following his return from France. Without doubt, however, the main cause of his growing indebtedness was direct taxation. From 1689 war with France necessitated substantial increases in national revenue. The unpopular hearth tax was replaced by poll taxes, assessments, and a variety of other levies. The militia tax, paid solely by recusants, was revived, while non-jurors were obliged to pay poll taxes and assessments at twice the normal rate. The list of outpayments for 1693 contains militia taxes and, although Sir Philip managed to avoid several payments of poll tax, both single and double, the Treasury eventually discovered this and forced him to pay some of his arrears.

He avoided double payment of the assessment in 1689, but from then onwards an increasing proportion of his property, and by 1693 the whole of it, was taxed at the double rate. Unlike other taxes, which had a cumulative effect, the assessment was itself very heavy. In 1689–90 the Yorkshire estate paid three assessments totalling £233. During 1689–91 £370 was paid from the Lincolnshire estate on the same account. In 1691 when Sir Philip's gross rental stood at £1,715, he was assessed at £275; in that year he spent £771 or over 40 per cent of his income on taxes, outrents, and servants' wages. In 1692 the assessment was replaced by the levy of a pound rate on annual income, the provision relating to double payment remaining in force. In

TABLE 17
Sir P. Constable's Finances in 1691 & 1693

Income	1691	1693
	£ s. d.	£ s. d.
Everingham	312. 3. 2	311. 7. 8
Thorpe	135.13. 4	133. 0. 0
Hayton	40. 6. 8	40. 7. 0
Storthwaite	12. 0. 0	12. 0. 0
Bielby	35. 0. 0	Unlet
Arras	79. 0. 0	70. 0. 0
Gardham	120. 0. 0	120. 0. 0
Wholsea	38. 0. 0	38. 0. 0
Acklam	73. 4.10	73.14.10
Drax	223.14. 0	223.14. 0
Rasen	681.15.11	681.15.11
	1741.17.11 −	1703.19. 5 −
	771.10. 7	1161.10. 8
	970. 7. 4	542. 8. 9
Expenditure		
Outpayments	468. 7. 0	236.14. 0
Assessments	274.10. 3	494.11. 8
Servants' Wages	28.13. 4	110. 5. 0
Other Wages		27. 0. 0
Repairs		80. 0. 0
Sons & Daughters		84. 0. 0
Interest		129. 0. 0
	771.10. 7	1161.10. 8

Sources: DDEV/58/139, 141.

1693 £494 of Sir Philip's gross rental of £1,700 was devoted to this new tax. Other outpayments, which included wages, repairs, children's maintenance, and interest charges, totalled £667. The £542 left 'to me to live upon myself and children' was clearly insufficient.[30]

Sir Philip's indebtedness increased as a result of the marriage in 1698 of his daughter, Anne, to William, second son of another recusant, Sir Thomas Haggerston of Haggerston in Northumberland. If she outlived her husband, Anne was to receive a jointure of £600 in return for her portion of £3,000. Sir Philip's marriage settlement had set aside only £1,500 as a portion, but the Haggerstons offered Sir Philip a life annuity of £100 if he doubled this sum. Though it may have clinched the match, this arrangement was a losing gamble on Sir Philip's part for he died less than eight years later. Moreover, he was unable to pay the portion; down to his death and beyond interest at 6 per cent (£180 a year) was paid on it. Neither of the two mortgages was redeemed. Excluding those on bonds about which there is no evidence, total debts amounted in principal to £5,994 by the end of 1698.[31]

In these circumstances – stable income, and rising expenditure and debts – Sir Philip was embroiled in further trouble with the authorities. Together with the Langdales' family chaplain, he was arrested at Dilston in Northumberland, home of the Radcliffes, in March 1696. After being brought to London 'on suspicion of treason' he was imprisoned in a 'little pitiful' room in the Tower 'to be kept until discharged by due course of law'. However, he was set free in May without having been brought to trial. Thereafter, Sir Philip made strenuous efforts to solve his financial problems. One memorandum tells of 'goods taken down and pawned'; among them were 'all the chairs and tables belonging the dining room and withdrawing room', a 'trunk with your worship's wearing clothes', and 'all the chairs, tables, and stands with bedposts and sides belonging the three best lodgings rooms'. In 1697 Sir Philip's London agent, William Heath, pawned 'a double silver tankard', a 'pair of candlesticks', and 'twelve spoons'; this silverware was redeemable on payment of £15. To add to his difficulty in obtaining credit, Sir Philip was accused by the Treasury in 1698–9 of having evaded payments of the poll tax. The charges related specifically to the Yorkshire estate and to a house which Sir Philip had let in London, but a preliminary investigation of payments in Lincolnshire aroused suspicions there too. Letters from Heath to Sir Philip reveal that, although most of the levies had been paid, few of them had been at the double rate. The Barons of the Exchequer threatened to appoint a commission of inquiry into his affairs in Lincolnshire unless Sir Philip success-fully refuted the charges. The latter wished to avoid this at all costs, firstly because he had in fact evaded double payment at Rasen, and secondly because the local under-sheriff was a notorious anti-Catholic who was likely to punish tax evasion severely. Accordingly he bought the silence of both the national and the local tax officials, and paid 'what was missing' only in Yorkshire.[32]

Following this period of wildly fluctuating circumstances, Sir Philip's economic position was characterized by three unsatisfactory and related features. Although his estate had remained stable in size after a period of slow but definite contraction, the income derived from it had continued to decrease owing to the growth of arrears and the enforced reduc-tion of certain rents. Together with heavy direct taxation, these developments had forced him to become steadily more in-debted. However, as his personal situation became more vul-nerable, he found it increasingly difficult to raise new loans. This prevented him from shelving current problems in the hope that future circumstances would be more conducive to their solution. More drastic methods of solving his difficulties had to be adopted.

4.   A CONTRACTING ESTATE 1698–1716

In March 1698 Sir Philip leased his Lincolnshire estate to Messrs H. Pullein and W. Knight for seven years. Leases had long been used in evading recusancy exactions; this one also tightened up the property's administration. The lessees covenanted to pay the rent punctually and to submit a copy of the rental each half year; they were also to be responsible for general maintenance and for the transport of materials for the repair of the Hall. Sir Philip agreed to pay for repairs and to meet the usual outrents and taxes. Unlike the majority of agreements between landlords and stewards (the lessees may

1. Sir John Hotham, 2nd Bart. (1632–89) in 1654
(Lord Hotham)

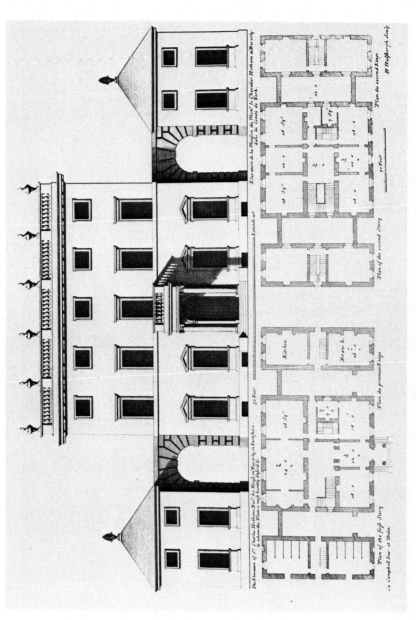

The Elevation of Sr Charles Hotham Bar.^t his House in Beverley in Yorkshire, to whom this Plate is most humbly Inscrib'd.

Plan of the first Story.

Plan of the second Story.

Elevation de la Maison du Mon.^r le Chevalier Hotham a Beverley dans le Comté de York.

Plan du premier Etage.

Plan du second Etage.

A. Campbell Inv. et Delin.

H. Hulsberg Sculp.

Kitchin

Brew h.

2. The Hotham House in Beverley: Plan and Elevation

3. Sir Charles Hotham, 5th Bart. (1693–1738)
(Lord Hotham)

4. Sir Thomas Beaumont, Kt. (c. 1605–1668)
(Leeds City Library)

5. Richard Beaumont (1670–1723)
(National Portrait Gallery)

6. Improvement at Whitley Hall: the Fire-Place in the Dining Room
(Kirklees Metropolitan Library)

7. Everingham Hall as recently renovated to conform to Carr's original work
(*Dr R. B. Wragg*)

8. Mary, née Bright, Marchioness of Rockingham (1736–1804)
(National Portrait Gallery)

have farmed demesne land but clearly acted in the latter capacity) the lease gave Sir Philip legal control (a strong guarantee of
efficiency) over the strictly defined responsibilities which he
delegated. In return he financed the improvement of the Hall,
where the two men and their families may have lived, and paid
them a joint salary of £10 a year. If the lessees farmed demesne
land, he also lost its annual rent. But, as farming operations at
Rasen had long been restricted, there was no question of his
losing the profits of a thriving home farm.[33] At about the same
time the administration of the Yorkshire estate was similarly
rationalized along lines proposed by Francis Stansfield, who
first appeared as steward there in 1699. The estate was then let
for just over £1,000 annually, though rents were 'seldom less
than £300 or £400 in arrear'. Stansfield suggested that full-time
staff be reduced from five to three, and that additional labour be
employed casually to 'serve Sir Philip for one month in the year
whilst he stays in the country'. These economies would facilitate the payment of an annual salary of £100 to Stansfield
himself, in return for which he undertook 'to secure and pay Sir
Philip his half year's rent . . . within three months after the same
became due', and 'to plant . . . good fruit trees' and '1,000 trees
in the park'. Sir Philip accepted his proposals and in 1702 leased
the park, six closes, and three rooms in Everingham Hall to
Stansfield for seven years at an annual rent of £65.[34]

These two leases catered both for the possibility of another
imprisonment and for Sir Philip's preference for living in
London.[35] Stansfield's accounts, the first continuous series
among the family papers, are those of a professional steward of
the type increasingly employed by landowners from this period
onwards. The Lincolnshire men did not fall within this category but were more capable than their employer of managing
the estate efficiently. Stansfield collected many old arrears but
did not prevent the accumulation of new ones, which included
land tax payments as well as rents, for some time between 1693
and 1702 Sir Philip had required tenants to pay the land tax.
Heavy arrears signified the failure of this policy and, after he
formally undertook to resume tax payments in 1702, arrears
were trivial. Meanwhile, Sir Philip had been forced to reconcile
himself to another necessity, namely the loss of Gardham, the
mortgage on which was foreclosed by the Day family in 1701.

TABLE 18

F. Stansfield's Yorkshire Estate Accounts, 1699–1706

Charge	Rent Receipts £ s. d.	Sales £ s. d.	Arrears £ s. d.	Previous Balance £ s. d.	Sundries £ s. d.	Total £ s. d.	Balance £ s. d.
1699–1700 1 yr.	1075. 1. 2	89. 1. 6	147.18. 8		3. 0. 0	1315. 1. 4	− 8.15. 7½
1700–1 1 yr.	798.10. 2	1247.16. 4	399. 3.10		6. 0. 0	2451.10. 4	+ 74.13. 7
1701–2 1 yr.	1033.18. 6	37. 3. 6	452. 8. 8	74.13. 7	97.13. 0	1695.17. 3	− 32.16.11
1702–3 1½ yrs.	1619.12. 9	7. 7. 0			15. 0	1627.14. 9	− 4. 3. 3
1704–5 1½ yrs.	1553. 5. 7	10.16. 0			7.14. 0	1571.15. 7	−235. 7. 8½
1705–6 1 yr.	1037.13. 6	6. 6. 0			1. 2. 6	1045. 2. 0	−216.19. 5
1706 ½ yr.	498. 4. 3	5.11. 0			50.18. 0	554.13. 3	−324.10. 1½

Discharge	To Sir P.C. £ s. d.	Previous Balance £ s. d.	Arrears, Allowances, Taxes £ s. d.	Debts & Interest £ s. d.	To Heath £ s. d.	Others £ s. d.	Total £ s. d.
1699–1700 1 yr.	149. 7. 0		533.19. 0½	149. 0. 0	50. 0. 0	481.12.11	1363.16.11½
1700–1 1 yr.	395. 6. 8	48.15. 7½	618. 0. 0	644.14.10		669.19. 7½	2376.16. 9
1701–2 1 yr.	433.13. 0		184. 9. 1	160. 0. 0	100. 0. 0	850.12. 1	1728.14. 2
1702–3 1½ yrs.	306. 0. 0	32.16.11	314. 6. 0	80. 0. 0		898.15. 1	1631.18. 0
1704–5 1½ yrs.	94.15. 0	4. 3. 3	313. 6. 7½	120. 0. 0		974.15. 5	1807. 3. 3½
1705–6 1 yr.	215.12. 6	235. 7. 8½	185. 3. 9		300. 1. 0	503.17. 5½	1262. 1. 5
1706 ½ yr.	41. 2. 6	216.19. 5	130. 2.10½		122. 0. 0	490.18. 7	879. 3. 4½

Sources: DDEV/56/18–24.

This was the first major alienation of property since the sale of land in Holderness in the 1650s. Had circumstances not prevented him from acquiring an alternative source of credit, Sir Philip would no doubt have assigned the mortgage and retained the property. However, the full proceeds of the alienation – £3,200 – cleared not only the mortgage to the Days but also three bonds and the mortgage of 1694.[36] In 1701–2, for the only time in seven years, the accounts were in surplus. The decrease of £120 a year in the rental following the sale was partially offset by an improvement of £46 a year in the Everingham rental and by the letting of the York house for £43 a year. Nevertheless, the accounts quickly assumed a set pattern whose main feature was an annual and rising deficit. A major expense was the cost of the tour to France and the Low Countries during 1701–3 which was arranged for Sir Philip's son, Marmaduke. Lack of money dictated a much abbreviated version of the conventional grand tour. Sir Philip paid Mr Charles Janvers £40 a year 'to travel with, accompany, and assist my son', gave Marmaduke £20 'at parting', and sent him £240 'while abroad'. The rest of his expenses, totalling £400, were borrowed. In fact in the period 1701–5 Sir Philip and Marmaduke borrowed a total of £2,280 on bonds and £400 on mortgage.[37] Meanwhile, estate income continued to decline. The York house remained unlet from 1704, while the proceeds of the tithe lease were unpredictable. An even greater problem was Sir Philip's inability or reluctance to reduce his personal expenditure.

In 1705 Sir Philip settled his entire estate on trustees to the use of Marmaduke and his male heir, subject to the raising of £2,000 to reduce his debts which, with the exception of his daughter's unpaid portion of £3,000, were immediately converted into a single mortgage. In the last year of his life he felt able to spend £70 on a coach, though unable to travel to Yorkshire in it 'for want of money'. Moreover, the wages of his London agent, who had served him for thirty years, were in arrears.[38] At his death in 1706 he left his son greater financial problems and a smaller estate than he himself had inherited. The financial arrangements for his daughter's marriage, his son's tour, and his own undignified visits to the pawnshop contrast sharply with his predecessors' frugality. Together with his delegation of responsibility for estate affairs, they suggest a degree of fatalism on Sir Philip's part. This resulted not only from numerous difficulties – heavy taxation, repeated imprisonment, and lack of credit-worthiness – but also from a feeling of isolation in the face of them. He was neither as personable nor as popular as his son proved to be, nor was he surrounded by relatives, friends, and accomplices as his father had been. The Radcliffes supported him but only from a distance, whereas the Shirburnes had both lived and worked at Everingham. Heath gave valuable service but never matched either the confidence or the competence of Rushworth and his colleagues. Moreover, the career of no other head of the family was as subject to radical changes of fortune. As a result the circumstances which his son inherited derived from something more than the pressure of events for, bewildered and dispirited, Sir Philip decided to live at a certain level, whatever the consequences.

TABLE 19

M. Constable's Review of his Finances, 1705

Income	£ s. d.,
Yorkshire Rents	1025. 9.10
Lincolnshire Rents	672.18. 0
	1698. 7.10
Expenditure	
Taxes & Outpayments	539.11.11
My Father	600. 0. 0
Stewards & Bailiff	120. 0. 0
6% Interest on £1,000	60. 0. 0
Other Relatives	286. 0. 0
	1605.11.11
Remains:	92.15.11

Source: DDEV/59/22.

Sir Marmaduke was twenty-three years old at his succession. On reviewing his financial situation he found that over half his income was earmarked for expenditure before it reached his hands. Of a gross annual income of £1,698, £906 was due in taxes, wages, outpayments, and interest charges. £792 remained upon which to live, and with which to discharge debts of £5,500. From the outset Sir Marmaduke took firm control of the management of his affairs, cancelling the arrangements with

Messrs. Stansfield, Knight, and Pullein. Henceforward each estate was administered by a single steward who submitted accounts at half-yearly intervals. Policy was directed towards the elimination of the 'waste and superfluity' which had been apparent in Sir Philip's lifetime. Using money forwarded to him by Stansfield in 1705–6, Sir Marmaduke discharged one debt of £580 but for some time thereafter was unable to make further repayments. During 1706 he was preoccupied with his father's bills and had to borrow on bond to pay them. In 1707 he cleared £188 of the deficit on Stansfield's account, but covered the rest of the sum with a promissory note and made a further loan on bond. Following the death of his brother-in-law in 1708 he determined to provide Anne Haggerston with half of her unpaid portion. In order to do so he had to take out a mortgage for £1,500, having previously been obliged to re-assign the mortgage of 1705. Fortunately both sums were forthcoming from Thomas Radcliffe, younger son of the 1st Earl of Derwentwater.[39] Down to the close of the decade Sir Marmaduke continued to be troubled by lack of capital. As a result little was available for purely personal needs and it took him several years to establish himself.

Once this was achieved, however, he exhibited a more relaxed attitude to life. From 1710 there was a significant rise in the sums annually made available to him from the estate. In that year he embarked on a six months' trip to Northumberland and Durham. He also engaged the services of Anthony Wright of Covent Garden, a Catholic banker. Besides servicing debts, the latter forwarded cash and goods from London, accounted for his client's legal business, and provided up-to-date news and expert advice. Naturally Sir Marmaduke was also in touch with the agents of some of his creditors, one of whom in 1713 proclaimed himself 'desirous to promote your happy settlement'. He went on to recommend a Mrs Clifford who 'will be in all respects one that is beyond all exceptions and qualified to make you as happy as any man living. Her person is fine and humour sweet, and £6,000 is her portion and may be more.' Although this sum was more than sufficient to clear his debts, Sir Marmaduke did not pursue the recommendation, preferring the more carefree life of a bachelor. He met current commitments, repaired some of the houses on his estates, left

Wright's account in moderate surplus, and spent the rest of his money on the usual pursuits of a country gentleman. Living well but within his means, he took out no further mortgages and left the discharge of existing ones to the future. This attitude was reinforced by the fact that he suffered little on account of his Catholicism, despite his father's record and his own close association with the Radcliffes and the Haggerstons. There was some stiffening of official policy after 1708 but, far from being convicted, Sir Marmaduke remained completely untroubled by the authorities. Although as a precaution trustees were still used in all legal transactions, by this time one wing of Everingham Hall had been converted into a chapel. There would appear to have been no hindrance to the private practice of Catholicism there.[40]

These comfortable circumstances were greatly disturbed by the Jacobite rebellion of 1715, the north-eastern branch of which was led by Thomas Forster and the Earl of Derwentwater, who joined forces at Greenrig in Northumberland on 6 October. After a month of aimless wandering through the north they were surrounded at Preston on 13 November and induced to surrender. The Earl was subsequently impeached and beheaded. Sir Marmaduke took no part in the rebellion for by 5 October, owing to his known association with the Earl, he had been placed under house arrest by the Lieutenant-Governor of Hull. Later he refused to take the oaths and was imprisoned in Hull and then in York until the end of 1716. Whether or not he would have taken up arms had he been free to do so is uncertain. Apparently, however, he had foreknowledge of events. In June 1715 he had vested his estate and the task of repaying his debts in trustees, one of whom had been Derwentwater himself. Shortly afterwards he drafted a will, leaving £1,000 to the Earl and naming him as one of four executors. In August Sir Marmaduke also renewed his lease of Acklam. Moreover, these events coincided with marked fluctuations in his estate accounts. During 1715 efforts were made to boost estate income by collecting arrears and increasing miscellaneous sales. Simultaneously expenditure was kept to a minimum, allowing unusually large sums to be forwarded to Sir Marmaduke and his banker. From August 1715 to January 1716 Wright's accounts list disbursements totalling £2,885, the purpose of which is unspecified. Neither this money nor that forwarded to Sir Marmaduke was devoted to the estate or to repaying debts. The combined sums are far in excess of the likely cost of his imprisonment. One suspects, though there is no proof of this, that the money was spent in furthering the Jacobite cause.[41]

TABLE 20

Money Passed to Sir Marmaduke by his Stewards, 1707–30

	£ s. d.		£ s. d.		£ s. d.
*1707	204. 5. 7	1715	1315. 4.10	1723	874. 3. 2
*1708	282. 0. 0	*1716	1162. 3. 7½	1724	693. 6. 9½
*1709	340.17. 0	*1717	280. 0. 0	*1725	574.15. 9
1710	487.11. 0	1718	631.13. 2½	1726	716.16.10
1711	565. 0. 0	1719	770.18. 2	*1727	1090. 0. 1
1712	644.16. 6½	*1720	511.10. 8	*1728	862. 0. 0
1713	721. 6. 8½	1721	836.15. 7½	*1729	758. 5. 0
1714	808. 5. 0	1722	685. 0. 0	1730	620. 0. 0

NOTE: * indicates incomplete accounts – therefore figures represent a minimum

Sources: DDEV/56/30, 48–96, 168–198.

Whatever the reason for it, this expenditure considerably exacerbated Sir Marmaduke's fiscal problems, which further deteriorated when Anne Haggerston demanded the remainder of her portion. Despite large wood sales in 1716, Sir Marmaduke was unable to provide £1,500 from his own resources, so he raised a mortgage for £2,000. As a result his debts in principal rose to £5,500, exactly the amount which he had inherited in 1706. Having no male heir, and being therefore free to dispose of his property, he chose to raise capital by selling parts of his estate. Firstly he sold Middle Rasen; the purchase price is unrecorded but the annual rent previously received for the property had totalled £101. The second sale was of the farm at Wholsea for £1,000; hitherto this had been let for £44 annually.[42] Following the failure to renew profitable leases and the rent arrears and reductions of the period 1680 to 1700, alienation of three freehold properties constituted a very serious deterioration in the family's economic situation. In the short space of sixteen years more than £200 disappeared from the annual rental. Because the debts incurred in the mid seventeenth century had been almost totally discharged by 1680, these property losses did not represent the long-term results of earlier difficulties. They were due instead to successive adversities from the Popish Plot episode to the abortive rebellion nearly forty years later. These dealt a severe blow to the morale of many Catholic families in the north.[43] In the case of the Constables their effects were also economic.

5.   RECUPERATION 1716–30

In Yorkshire the loss of Wholsea was accompanied by further decreases in the income from the estate. The Everingham rents were reduced by £40 annually, probably because Sir Marmaduke took more land into his own hands. There was also a slight reduction in the rent from Acklam, while tithes again proved difficult to sub-let. By Michaelmas 1717 most of the usual items of expenditure had reappeared among the disbursements, which also included large sums spent on the repair of the Hall. However, despite these developments, the account was on the whole in surplus. In 1716 £880 was forwarded to Sir Marmaduke and, while the figures dropped in the two following years, there was a marked recovery in 1719. In Lincolnshire the loss of Middle Rasen was somewhat mitigated by increases in 'casualties'. The account was regularly in surplus and Sir Marmaduke continued to be supplied annually with large amounts of cash. These and the proceeds of his sales enabled him to make loans: £300 to the purchaser of Wholsea and, in 1717, £1,333 to his nephew, Sir Carnaby Haggerston. In 1718 he discharged the mortgage for £2,000 prior to entering a new and increasingly popular field of economic enterprise – the stock market.[44]

After 1688 successive governments were stimulated by the cost of the French wars into devising various means of attracting public loans, one of the most successful devices being the lottery. The sum paid for lottery tickets constituted a loan for which interest was returned, winning tickets receiving additional interest. By January 1720 Sir Marmaduke had purchased £1,000 worth of tickets. In that year the South Sea Company took over much of the National Debt in return for various concessions, persuading holders of annuities or lottery tickets to convert them into Company stock. Sir Marmaduke was attracted by the scheme and Wright soon converted all his lottery tickets. From 128½ per cent in January the price of stock rose to 890 per cent in June, and touched 1,000 per cent in July. By 25 June Sir Marmaduke had been congratulated on his 'success in the South Sea affair', and had sold his stock at what must have been a resounding profit. At the end of July 1720 the 'Bubble' burst and the price of stock fell rapidly. Sir Marmaduke regarded this as a purely temporary development and determined to invest again when the price had further declined. In August he 'bought some lottery tickets which are to be subscribed into the South Sea'. This second investment was of £1,058 at 400 per cent. The expected recovery failed to materialize and by November the price had dropped to 135 per cent. Sir Marmaduke retained his stock until the end of 1722, hoping by the receipt of dividends to avoid overall loss. The price at which he then sold is not recorded, but over eighteen months his investment brought a return of £13 in dividends and other accretions.[45]

Other aspects of his affairs progressed more smoothly. In 1719 the mortgage for £2,000, raised in 1716, was assigned to his banker. Between 1719 and 1722, besides large sums forwarded from the estate, Sir Marmaduke had substantial repayments from Sir Carnaby Haggerston at his disposal. In 1723 he lent Robert Watson, the purchaser of Wholsea, a further £1,500 on mortgage. Three years later he discharged the mortgage for £1,500, originally raised in 1708 and assigned in 1717. Only the mortgage to Wright remained unpaid. The number of begging letters which Sir Marmaduke received during these years pays eloquent tribute to a steady rise in his fortunes.[46] Albeit at the cost of contracting his economic base, the sales of 1716 undoubtedly strengthened his financial position. Indeed, for someone with neither wife nor family to support, his estate income was more than adequate for current needs, provided he remained free of damaging entanglements with the authorities.

In the aftermath of the rebellion persecution of Catholics subsided. By 1717 Sir Marmaduke felt able to appoint a priest, John Bede Potts, to his Everingham staff. Previous experience as cellarer at Lambspring Abbey qualified him to act as steward, a post which provided him with some disguise. The events of 1715 did not deter Sir Marmaduke from maintaining contact with both the Haggerstons and the Radcliffes, and he lent financial support to Lady Derwentwater. In succeeding years he was troubled by the authorities on only one occasion, in 1722, when he and his cousin, Cuthbert Constable of Burton Constable, were summoned to Beverley to take the oaths. Sir Marmaduke may have agreed with Cuthbert that 'the consequences cannot be worse by not appearing than by appearing'. There were no repercussions and his cousin's hope that 'we shall not meet in prison' was fulfilled. Two pieces of contemporary legislation particularly concerned recusants. The first was an act of 1714 for the registration of non-jurors' estates at the quarter sessions. Sir Marmaduke complied after refusing to take the oaths in 1715. An act of 1723 for raising £100,000 from papists' estates indicated the uses to which that of 1714 might be put. The sum to be levied was divided between the counties according to the amount of registered 'papist estate' in each. Sir Marmaduke and his friends were apprehensive, particularly as most taxation of this kind was levied on landowners. However, allowances were made in assessing the levy for leases or annuities to Protestants and an 'appeal day' was held in each locality. In August 1723 Sir Marmaduke's steward in Lincolnshire urged him to attend that at Caister 'if your Honour thinks fit to appeal of the two mortgages'. There are no details of the amount of Sir Marmaduke's assessment or of his payments. As usual, despite the fact that Yorkshire bore the heaviest levy, there were many evasions. Only two-thirds of the tax was ever collected, and that not until 1743.[47]

Apart from such hindrances leading Catholics led a fairly untroubled, if truncated, life. Barred from every type of office, they formed a race apart among landowners. All Sir Marmaduke's relatives, correspondents, and employees, including his banker and his lawyers, were Catholics. His only regular non-Catholic associate was Mr Draper, a local huntsman. Life was narrow in other respects. Sir Marmaduke was a confirmed bachelor, 'a strong abettor for liberty'. As he employed at least five people in the management of his concerns he himself spent little time in this way. Unlike his father, he did not keep a London house and was reluctant to linger in the capital when he visited it. His movements coincided with the 'season' only when he attended provincial race meetings. He visited Lincolnshire infrequently, spending most of the year in the rambling Hall at Everingham or in the suite at Farnham provided for him by the Haggerstons. Known chiefly as a 'keen sportsman', much of his time was taken up in hunting and shooting. However, Catholicism did not prevent Sir Marmaduke and his friends from living well. Their purchases included wine from France, Italy, and Spain, olives and anchovies from Bordeaux, pointers from Majorca, horses from Spain, and seeds, stockings, and snuff from France. They reduced costs by ordering jointly and by purchasing shares in merchant vessels, though not 'stinting you to price that you may send us the very best'. Payments were usually made by bills of exchange but on one occasion, following a grain shortage in Alicante, they sent a shipload of corn. The animals and seeds purchased abroad enabled Sir Marmaduke to pursue his twin passions of breeding and forestry, and he patronized a tree nursery at Scorborough from which he supplied his estate.[48] Thus, his life was unashamedly rather than necessarily provincial, but lived within narrow limits and with a few close friends and relatives. Though not without enjoyment or luxury, there was little scope for enterprise or ambition.

His private affairs continued to progress in the late 1720s. In the period 1727–30 he made further loans to Robert Watson after the latter had redeemed his mortgage for £1,500; he also purchased three properties. One of these was in Gardham but the size and price of the transaction are unrecorded. He also bought properties in Bielby and Everingham for a total of £120. Inquiries concerning additional property in Acklam were unsuccessful. Much the most important development of this period, however, was further enclosure in Lincolnshire. In 1721 tenants there had been 'very earnest . . . to have my leave to lay down two of their cornfields from ploughing to pasture'. Once again the opposition of the parson of West Rasen delayed the implementation of the scheme. Enclosure did not begin until October 1727 and was completed in eleven months at a cost of £233. Thereafter rents at West Rasen, previously 'so much underlet . . . in the opinion of all that know it', were increased by £178 a year.[49] This more than compensated for the fall in estate income which had followed the sales of 1716.

Early in 1726 Sir Marmaduke sustained an injury while

hunting which greatly altered the future pattern of his life. Subsequently he spent several months in Bath receiving treatment but his condition did not improve sufficiently to permit him to hunt again. Henceforward, deprived of a favourite pastime, he spent much of each year in London. In 1728 a correspondent's wish that 'you are able to follow the foxhounds' was coupled with the hope 'that you have no occasion to seek health in foreign parts'. However, Sir Marmaduke had become increasingly dissatisfied with life in England, not least with the circumscribed lot of the Catholic, and left for the Continent in May 1730. Ostensibly his trip was for a short period of treatment at the health resorts but, once abroad, he remained there for many years. Although recent activities had produced various estate improvements, Sir Marmaduke's property was in one respect in great need of attention at his departure. Many of the houses and cottages on the estate were in a bad state of disrepair; in 1727 the roof of his own bedroom at Everingham had collapsed after a rainstorm. While he was away Sir Marmaduke hoped that all would be 'put ... in good order by degrees'.[50] At least, or so he thought, the *status quo* could be maintained during his absence.

6.   AN ABSENTEE LANDLORD 1730–46

During the spring of 1730 Sir Marmaduke was in London preparing to go abroad. He appointed Robert Usher as deputy to Potts and sent him to Everingham with a list of instructions. The Lincolnshire estate was administered by Thomas Champney, one of the tenants. Similar arrangements operated at Drax and Arras, while Usher supervised the rest of the Yorkshire estate. All these individuals took their orders from Potts, who was directly responsible to Sir Marmaduke. Each year during the latter's absence £1,000 was forwarded from the estate to Wright, who passed credit to various European agents as directed by his client. Whether an additional sum provided by Wright in October 1730 was forwarded annually is not known; nor is there any indication of its size. By October 1730 Sir Marmaduke was in Rotterdam, having already visited Flanders, Holland, and Germany. 'The pleasure I have had in my journeys is inexpressible, and [I] repent [of] nothing so much as sitting at home so many years idle.' Before leaving he had told

Potts: 'its impossible for me at the distance I shall soon be at to answer or determine every little accident that may occur in my little affairs, so must leave them to your prudence and discretion'. The significance of this remark was reduced by Sir Marmaduke's failure to give any reliable information regarding the length of his trip. At no stage had he definite long-term plans, and his letters were either confusing or contradicted by his actions. Thus, in December 1730, having ordered the replacement of dead tree shoots, he said that nothing was to be 'done anew till my arrival'. He then said that a return to England was 'far from my thoughts at present'. In 1733 he spoke of 'steering my course homewards' after seeing a little more of Italy. In March 1735 he reported that he would soon be in London while, during the following August, 'I now think of my return to my native country'. In 1737 he indicated that he was approaching home, and in 1739 expected to be in London by the following spring. Finally, in 1742 he planned to return but not to remain in England. In fact he stayed abroad until 1744, Potts having died in 1743.[51]

In his letters Sir Marmaduke either recommended that certain matters be left until his return or delegated responsibility for all his affairs, large and small, to Potts, asking the latter not to trouble him with queries. Potts, on the other hand, looked to Sir Marmaduke for decisions and, grasping at any suggestion of his early return, frequently failed to act upon them. Moreover, Sir Marmaduke was an irregular correspondent. Although he wrote forty-six letters to Potts, there was none between November 1733 and December 1734, and between August 1735 and December 1736. These long silences encouraged rumours which made Potts frantic with worry. In 1735 he was 'glad to see your hand again, it being reported that you were cast away at sea'. In 1737 the rumour was that 'you are either dead or would never return'. Soon there were 'many and different opinions'. Potts himself travelled to Flanders in 1733 for a meeting of his Congregation but did not meet Sir Marmaduke, who was then in Italy. In 1736–7 Potts missed three similar meetings on the grounds that his responsibilities did not allow him to travel. The death of Usher in 1739 prevented him from complying with a request from Sir Marmaduke that he visit him in Cambrai. But a journey to another meeting of the Congregation brought the two men together in July 1741. This was the only occasion on which they met between 1730 and Potts's death and, not surprisingly, the latter grew 'tired of my charge of moneys'. He finally became incredulous: 'will you never return home'; why do [you] 'prefer foreign company before your own interest?'[52] Without doubt Potts had to work in exceedingly trying circumstances largely due to Sir Marmaduke's carefree behaviour.

Yet Potts's temperament greatly exacerbated his difficulties. He lacked confidence and felt 'incapable of undertaking the management of your affairs'. Permanent anxiety distorted his judgement. Writing of a dispute over rent arrears, he proclaimed that he would rather pay the sum himself than have 'so much concern about it'. His spirituality was of questionable help, being of an almost masochistic type which expected, if it did not welcome, difficulties. 'There is no place without them and the very best are not free from them in one respect or another.' He was painfully shy and unaccustomed 'to go about with how do you [do] and the like'. When Sir Marmaduke urged him to get out and about Potts replied: 'it leads to many sins which a solitary chair is not subject to'. Moreover, in the limited contact with others which he allowed himself Potts was neither personable nor liberal. He reported a servant for being out till 1 a.m. at Christmas time, and moved the fellow's bedroom so as to be aware of his movements. When Potts suspected that bricklayers were raiding the orchard he deprived them of their accommodation in the Hall garret. His relations with both servants and tenants deteriorated to the point where real difficulties arose; one suspects that Potts's manner and attitudes were largely responsible for this. If possible, he simply avoided tasks which he considered beyond him, yet was extremely scrupulous about quite insignificant matters. On most occasions Sir Marmaduke either ignored or soothed him: 'never any more make use of the word *sorrow* . . . it is too expressive for such trifles'. However, in 1741 Sir Marmaduke at last apologized: 'I am sorry you meet with so much trouble on my account. It was never designed upon when I left home'.[53] But he did not allow concern to alter his chosen way of life.

Circumstances were made even more difficult by illness and death. Usher was disabled from a fall in 1737 and died two years later. A replacement was appointed but soon dismissed because neither Potts nor Sir Marmaduke wished to employ a married man, especially one whose wife was a non-Catholic. A second replacement, James Marrow, also died before Sir Marmaduke's return. Potts's own condition steadily deteriorated following a bad fall from a coach when returning from Cambrai in 1741. He was unable to wear shoes for months afterwards and by July 1742 had ventured only two miles from Everingham since his return. After his death in 1743 Fr Rogers, chaplain to the Gascoignes, collaborated with Wright and Sir Carnaby Haggerston in an effort to keep Sir Marmaduke's affairs in order.[54]

Sir Marmaduke was certainly a strict landlord. Though allowing tenants to hold half a year's rent in hand, he did not tolerate further arrears. When Potts reported that widow Anna Bell was having difficulty in paying her rent Sir Marmaduke ordered him to 'quit her of her cottage, and all others that do not' pay. In 1732 he asked Potts to warn the Lincolnshire tenants that ejection would follow interference with his timber. When tenants trespassed and refused to obey the court Sir Marmaduke ordered them to 'be punished as far as possible it can be carried'; and after one tenant had destroyed a wall in his tenement in order to introduce a second door he was 'proceeded against with the utmost severity'. On digging turf from demesne land another individual was not spared 'one half inch' but fined at 6*d.* per square yard of turf dug; 'let him burn out of hand the turf he has pared and spread the ashes on the same ground'. The fact that properties were occasionally 'called in the markets' indicates Sir Marmaduke's eagerness to avoid having land 'in hand'. Nevertheless prospective tenants were carefully vetted. A young man, 'having a very indifferent character, and being of an idle temper, was not admitted to be your tenant, most of his neighbours apprehending that he would soon make an end of all, and his wife be thrown upon the town'. Ironically Champney was forbidden to let property to absentee tenants, properties 'inhabited by servants' having been ruined 'during my father's time'. Once admitted, the good tenant could expect certain signs of favour; when a property became vacant it was Sir Marmaduke's 'will that your tenants be served first'. However, despite this and the severe punishment of wrongdoers, tenants were constantly troublesome. They stole, poached, organized hare-coursing on the estate, and 'drew the staple out of the park gate to let your bull into his closes to serve his cows'. When penalties for failing to perform drainage duties were omitted from the court rolls, tenants ignored local custom until their insertion placed them 'under a necessity to keep' ditches 'well dressed'.[55] Though behaviour was rarely extreme, there was a steady incidence of recalcitrance.

Certain developments seem to have been the direct result of Sir Marmaduke's absence. For example, neglect of customary services was apparently unprecedented. 'Your cottagers have been extreme obstinate; none of them would come to your assistance except poor Samuel Cook.' Again, 'your whelps in Town are very poor; none keeps them well but Thomas Deane'. Absenteeism was perhaps exploited when a tenant claimed Sir Marmaduke's permission to do something, for instance to plough ley, to which Potts took exception. Moreover, rent arrears grew steadily until Sir Marmaduke maintained that he had never known them so high. Potts pointed to unfavourable harvests and price fluctuations as reasons for this, excusing his own inability to enforce payment as much as that of certain tenants to pay. 'If we did proceed according to your directions we should be obliged to turn off your chief tenants.' He threatened distraint, while Sir Marmaduke recommended 'prudential severity'. Potts began to lose control of the situation after Usher's death. 'Neither fair nor foul words can prevail with some.' When a boundary dispute broke out in 1741 he maintained that tenants were 'resolved to ruin one another'. Frustration occasionally provoked him to extremes. 'I shall discharge widow Emerson of her cottage the next Ladyday because she is about marrying an old shoemaker from Cranswick, for we do not want old cottagers but such as are able to work whenever called upon.' In regard to arrears Sir Marmaduke eventually reverted to ordering distraint 'without mercy' and immediate eviction, but with as little effect as before.[56]

Nowhere are the difficulties which arose during, and because of, Sir Marmaduke's absence more evident than in the case of building and repair work. Examples of the ruinous condition of much of his property abound. In May 1731 a Lincolnshire tenant alleged that his house was unsafe. In November 'Thomas Young will either have his repaired with barn and stall this year, or will go off next year'. Two months later there were 'sad outcries at Rasen concerning their houses'. Three were 'very ruinous', Champney's having 'two props and must have a third'. By November 1732 Daniel Decow's house at Drax had three props 'and must yet have another'. It fell during the following summer and 'nothing but providence preserved the inhabitants' lives'. In 1736 a shop in Everingham collapsed, and in 1737 the walls of another house would withstand no more than 'the first or second push'. In 1739 one tenant's house was so 'very ruinous that he is afraid to lie in it'. Sir Marmaduke's 'absolute orders' in this respect had been 'to put all in good order by degrees'. Some repairs were carried out and a few new buildings were erected, but no attempt was made to deal with the situation 'by degrees'. Indeed, Potts acted as if no such orders had been given, often desiring, for example, that 'you give orders to cast up clay'. He repeated such requests, despite Sir Marmaduke's frequent delegation of full authority: 'Champney has built nothing because no order to make brick, and you yearly expected home'. Complaints became so numerous that 'no-one can be favoured in this without giving offence to the others, so everyone must rest quiet till your return'. Sir Marmaduke's grumbles about the size of disbursements encouraged Potts to evade the issue of repairs and rebuilding. In 1736–7 he survived queries about the number of 'houses you have repaired or built again', but two years later Sir Marmaduke was surprised 'to hear after so long absence that I have any farmhouses upon my estate in bad repair'. He ordered a major effort but Potts was 'of the opinion that the repairing and rebuilding some tenements are an encouragement to others to let their places run in ruin in hopes of a like favour'. Thus, Potts painstakingly evaded his responsibilities. For his part Sir Marmaduke eventually recognized the connection between the size of rent arrears and the amount of ruinous property. In 1741 tenants were 'not to be in arrears more than I allowed; also keep in good repair their houses'. When Fr Rogers wrote to Sir Marmaduke after Potts's death some houses were being repaired, but only because previous neglect had left some tenants in extreme difficulties.[57]

Sir Marmaduke had hoped 'to avoid all . . . law in my absence' but disputes arose both at Drax and West Rasen. The first concerned the family's fishing rights on certain stretches of the Ouse. Their previous monopoly was challenged and encroachments made. In Lincolnshire a neighbouring landowner aired unrecorded grievances by cutting river banks and flooding Sir Marmaduke's land. The latter was determined to defend his interests 'with all the vigour' that could be 'set in motion'. Potts interpreted the word 'avoid' differently and attempted to persuade Sir Marmaduke to return, while taking very little positive action himself. The West Rasen dispute was settled by the Commission of Sewers but that at Drax, after being settled out of court, reopened because, according to Potts, of rumours that Sir Marmaduke was dead. Sir Marmaduke finally accepted his deputy's fear of involvement and postponed action until his return.[58] Here also Potts's lack of fibre and Sir Marmaduke's determination to remain abroad were damaging. After Potts's death inaction became near confusion. Clearly, the *status quo* of 1730 was not maintained.

However, although the estate was neglected, Sir Marmaduke's general financial and economic circumstances did not decline. Income from the tithe lease steadily decreased but the amount was small in relation to gross annual income. Rent arrears grew but were never as high as during Sir Philip's lifetime. Concern stemmed as much from their appearance as from their size. Besides paying for his travels, the money annually forwarded to Sir Marmaduke was devoted to the purchase of books, paintings, and sculptures. These were later sent to England and formed a valuable part of his sizeable personal estate. Much surplus income was loaned. By 1744 Sir Marmaduke had lent a total of £5,000 to Sir Carnaby Haggerston. He lent others a further £600 on bonds. In 1737 Wright was directed to invest 'in some of the public funds'. At least £3,000 was invested in East India bonds, though total investment was probably larger than this. Sir Marmaduke made no attempt, nor was he pressed, to discharge his mortgage debt of £2,000 after assigning it yet again in 1732. He made inquiries concerning the availability of land in Acklam and, on various occasions, discussed with Potts the advisability of buying property in Sancton, Hartswell, Weighton, and Shipton. At various times he asked whether Robert Watson could be induced to sell the property at Wholsea which he had purchased from Sir Marmaduke in 1716.[59] All this was to no avail and no further purchases were made.

By 1740 Sir Marmaduke was exhibiting an old man's anxiety to bring his affairs into order, showing particular interest in this connection in the fortunes of the Haggerston family. The Constables and the Haggerstons had been related since 1698 when Sir Marmaduke's sister had married William Haggerston, the father of Sir Carnaby. Their affairs were more closely linked in 1730 when, by a new will, Sir Marmaduke left all his real and personal estate to Sir Carnaby's second son, William. William Haggerston travelled to the Continent in 1743 to be educated in his great-uncle's self-confessed 'whimsical manner'. The settlement which Sir Marmaduke executed in 1744 left his entire estate to William and his heirs male in succession after Sir Marmaduke's death, provided William assumed the name of Constable. Only necessity brought Sir Marmaduke back to England. Writing from Cambrai in 1741, he complained of 'pure idleness ... not knowing where to go to see what I have not before. Travelling is almost done when we find no variety.' But even when the desire to travel had waned Sir Marmaduke preferred to live on the Continent. There was no revival of interest in his estate affairs after his return. In March 1745 he asked one of his servants to 'represent more lively to me the situation of my affairs ... in Yorkshire', and added: 'this will be the last that I shall trouble myself with them'. Having no desire to live at Everingham, he probably returned to the rooms at Farnham which the Haggerstons had previously reserved for him, where he spoke of passing 'the rest of my days quietly'. But in that year of the second Jacobite rebellion he was a marked man and, sometime during the autumn or winter, he was imprisoned in York castle. He escaped before the end of the year and fled to the Continent, dying in Paris on 15 June 1746.[60]

In his long, solitary career Sir Marmaduke achieved considerable, if relatively unspectacular, success. From a vulnerable position in 1706 he contrived to leave a solid inheritance to William Haggerston. 'When I was in debt', he wrote to Sir Carnaby, 'I was never easy till I had £1,000 in my pocket. By that means I was master to live as I pleased, pay everybody punctually their own, and as that increased discharged the incumbrances I had upon my estate as fast as I could.'[61] Interesting though it is, this provides a rather flattering explanation of his strategy. Although the estate remained the bulwark of his economy, he was not an enterprising manager. Initially very careful, he became much less strict once he had established himself. At no time did he farm on a marketable scale. Moreover, apart from the improvements which followed the Lincolnshire enclosure, he brought about no rent increases on his property. Although agreements with tenants were reasonable, he dealt severely with the slightest transgressions and was harsh with cottagers and labourers. During his absence abroad he allowed estate affairs to get out of hand. Fortunately, the consequences were less substantial than his own neglect. In several respects his situation differed from that of his predecessors. Except for the period of the first rebellion, it was much easier to live as a Catholic in England after 1706 than it had been previously. Sir Marmaduke was also able to use the new investment opportunities provided by the stock market. Above all, despite his extensive travels, his bachelor status kept expenditure well within his means. He had no direct heir but was able to assist his chosen successor's family as his own capital resources accumulated. He recouped some of the acreage sold in 1716 and, by requiring his personal estate to be devoted to the purchase of additional property, more than replaced earlier losses. None of these achievements, moreover, prevented him from leading the kind of life which he most desired.

7. A MINORITY 1746–52

Together with his younger brother, Edward, William Haggerston remained on the Continent until he came of age in 1752. Sir Carnaby hired a Jesuit, Fr Fleetwood, to act as their travelling companion. Meanwhile, as William's guardian and one of three executors named in Sir Marmaduke's will, Sir Carnaby assumed control of the Constable family's affairs. In 1746 he travelled to Everingham to take stock of the situation. He drew up twenty-two instructions for Chorley, the new steward. Sir Carnaby ordered, firstly, a comprehensive survey of the houses, cottages, and fences in both Yorkshire and Lincolnshire. Where building or repairs were necessary, work was to be 'well done'. Rent increases were left to Chorley's discretion: 'if farms are very low, if the tenants can be brought to advances they may be, but always so as they may still remain good farms'. In fact, as Chorley soon discovered, there had been virtually no rent increases, and a number of rent reductions, in Yorkshire since 1670. Moreover, the size of the estates, and with it the rental, had been steadily decreasing for many years. The York house had somehow drifted out of the family's possession while, although the lease of Acklam had been renewed in 1745, it proved impossible to renew the remaining tithe lease which had lapsed at Sir Marmaduke's death. Yet Chorley did not increase rents. Sir Carnaby did not allow him discretionary powers in regard to rent arrears. He was 'to allow no tenants to run in arrear further than the time given them for payment'. Another aspect of policy was the redevelopment of the home farm at Everingham. Cattle and sheep were bought and turnips, oats, barley, and potatoes planted. The pond was stocked with fish, the orchard and plantations expanded, and a stud developed.[62]

During 1748 both Yorkshire and Lincolnshire experienced severe outbreaks of cattle plague. By October the West Rasen estate was in the midst of its second outbreak, 'more fatal than the former', and in Everingham and Thorpe 347 head of cattle had perished out of a total stock of 769. Chorley attempted 'by all ways and means to prevent' tenants from 'leaving their farms' and 'not to lessen rent if it can possibly be prevented, though there may be one or two exceptions'. He suggested that the only way of achieving these aims was to discharge those rents which remained unpaid for 1748, 'taking their bonds' for the same 'payable to Mr Constable the day he shall come of age'. The scheme proved acceptable both to Sir Carnaby and to the tenants. It only remained 'to persuade' the minor 'not to take' the bonds when he assumed control of his inheritance.[63]

A second untoward development concerned William's tour. Fr Fleetwood complained 'of the dearness of all things' and soon began to draw more from Wright's contacts than the annual allowance of £330. Although he promised to manage 'as frugally as possible', the cost of the tour continued to rise. Moreover, William himself began to cause trouble. He was under the impression 'that in case my brother happened to die that not only the real estate but every farthing of the personal went to another person'. Maintaining that he could immediately 'dispose of his personal estate', he asked Wright for a statement of his account, a draft of £500, and a copy of Sir Marmaduke's settlement of 1744. When Wright failed to comply William drew on him for £500 'that he may make as tolerable a figure as some of his countrymen do'. Meanwhile, Fleetwood continued to exceed the allowance; in June 1750 Chorley informed Sir Carnaby that during the year ending March 1750 he had withdrawn £815. Sir Carnaby was thoroughly alarmed. After slightly increasing the allowance and demanding that it only be withdrawn monthly, he accused Fleetwood of undertaking several journeys purely for his own benefit. Convinced that the priest was responsible for William's behaviour, Sir Carnaby announced his intention of employing another guardian. Fleetwood denied these charges and maintained that the brothers were becoming increasingly intransigent as they grew older. While acknowledging that the withdrawal of the £500 was entirely his own idea, William reported that Fleetwood had stimulated his doubts about the settlement. Asserting that the allowance was totally inadequate, he suggested that neither he nor his brother needed a guardian, certainly 'not one of the same sort of persons'. In fact Fleetwood was not replaced but remained abroad until William's return. In the meantime the latter was allowed to 'go where he pleases . . . provided he kept within any bounds', but this continued to prove difficult to enforce. Sir Carnaby was greatly relieved when the tour came to an end.[64]

Meanwhile, estate affairs were progressing satisfactorily. Further outbreaks of cattle plague did not affect the Constable estates and the home farm at Everingham was steadily developed. Sir Carnaby's major concern was to deploy the proceeds of Sir Marmaduke's personal estate in purchasing property to add to William's inheritance. In 1751 he heard that the Duke of Leeds wished to sell his estate at Seaton Ross near Everingham and asked 'if it can be had reasonably'. He bought the property in 1752 for £12,000, only £70 more than the value of the personal estate. Let at old rents it was worth £430 annually, but it was estimated that this sum could easily be raised to £490. Seaton Ross was considerably more valuable

TABLE 21
Sir M. Constable's Personal Estate

Credit	£	s.	d.
Balance of Various Accounts	2558.	0.	6
Principal & Interest due	7586.	0.	0
5 India Bonds sold for	530.	14.	7
Miscellaneous	381.	3.	6
	11055.	18.	7

Debit			
Legacies to Executors	£60.	0.	0
To Sir C. H. in trust	630.	0.	0
To B. Salvin's children	1000.	0.	0
To Servants	138.	7.	2
Miscellaneous	147.	8.	4
	1975.	15.	6

Balance due to Sir Marmaduke	9080.	3.	1 −
Death-Bed Legacy	150.	0.	0
	8930.	3.	1
Acklam Lease Valued at	1400.	0.	0
Plate, Pictures, Books etc.	1600.	0.	0
Made good for Seaton	70.	0.	0
	12,000.	3.	1

Sources: DDEV/56/484b; 58/118.

than any other single property which the family owned, or had owned, and represented the major result of Sir Marmaduke's achievements. In June 1752 William Haggerston-Constable came of age and returned to claim his inheritance. At the same time the accounts of Sir Marmaduke's personal estate were finalized. Cash in hand, debts owing to the deceased, and the proceeds of the sale of remaining East India bonds amounted to £11,056, but Sir Marmaduke's numerous bequests reduced this to £8,930. Both the lease of Acklam and Sir Marmaduke's books, paintings, furniture, and plate 'ought to have been sold'. However, Sir Carnaby thought a sale 'troublesome', and that they 'ought not to go out of' the family. He offered them to William 'at the appraisement'; the latter paid £3,000 for them plus £70 to make up the purchase price of Seaton Ross.[65] Thus, initially the demands on William's purse were heavy. But as a result a valuable inheritance remained intact, Sir Marmaduke's will was respected, and the Yorkshire estate greatly expanded.

8. A NEW ERA: 1752 AND BEYOND

William Haggerston-Constable's first concern after assuming control was to raise the £3,070 which he owed to Sir Carnaby. Sir Marmaduke's mortgage debt of £2,000 was also outstanding. However, William's early decision to build a new Hall at Everingham made redemption of this mortgage impossible; when the current creditor called for his capital it was again reassigned. Occasional references to the construction of the building do not allow an estimate of its cost, but apparently no expense was spared. William hired John Carr, the most famous of Yorkshire architects, while the reputation of some of the craftsmen, such as Daniel Shillito the carver, was firmly established throughout the north. Work on what came to be regarded as one of the finest Georgian country houses in the county began in 1756 and was not completed until 1764.[66]

The inauguration of this project coincided with, and was no doubt partially responsible for, the first major rent increases (the 1727–8 enclosures apart) for nearly a century. In 1756 the Lincolnshire rents, which then stood at £680 a year, were raised to £1,150. Excluding Seaton Ross, the Yorkshire rents, which in 1746 had been £928, were raised to £1,138 a year by 1759. The latter figure included a slight decrease in rents at Everingham; this stemmed from the expansion of the home farm, which by 1759 was making a substantial contribution to annual income, both directly and indirectly. Furthermore, although when Seaton Ross was purchased a rent improvement to £490 a year had been postulated, its annual rental was in fact raised to £505. These increases met with some opposition. Thomas Champney, 'having been forty-eight years in your family's service and now turned seventy years old and not able to work', complained that William had 'laid more' on his farm 'than on any' in West Rasen. Having warned his landlord that 'you are likely to be a great deal advanced in the land tax if you go on by the new raisement', he suggested that, in order to deceive the land tax commissioners, there should be a return to the age-old system of large entry fines and nominal annual rents. However, the land tax had long ceased to bear any relation to property values, and his suggestion was ignored. In the one area, Drax, where the commissioners made inquiries about rent increases, the 'tenants refused to inform'. Champney quietly forgot his threat to seek another farm 'in my old age' and remained a Constable tenant. The comments of local clerics, who were discomfited by William's offer of money but no land for a lease of Everingham tithes, reveal why he was able to effect such large rent improvements. They feared that a fixed money payment would rapidly decrease in value 'if lands and the produce of them advance for the next forty or fifty years as they have done'.[67]

For his part William spent £233 on property repairs in 1759–60 at a time when other expenditure was soaring. Indeed, the large increases in annual income did not cover his expenditure. In 1759–60 gross income amounted to £3,071 while gross expenditure totalled £4,134. Excluding the mortgage assignment, he was forced to borrow £3,380 between 1757 and 1764. By 1766 only £1,019 of this had been repaid. However, this indebtedness was not prolonged for by his marriage in 1758 to Lady Winifred Maxwell, only daughter and heiress of William Maxwell of Nithsdale, he became entitled both to a dowry of £6,000 and to the barony of Herries in Scotland. By the marriage settlement offspring also became entitled to the barony of Nithsdale, which meanwhile was set aside to provide a jointure for the bride's mother; and then one for the bride or groom if either survived the other. Owing to the attainder of the bride's grandfather the Constables did not inherit Herries. Moreover, William Maxwell was also short of cash and, after handing over £1,000 of the dowry in 1758, gave security for payment of the rest of the sum. This remained unpaid for several years, but the credit probably brought William Constable's finances into technical surplus and, if the building of the new Hall was partly motivated by a desire to improve his marriage prospects, the investment was an undoubted success.[68]

By the 1760s the fortunes of the Constables were rising rapidly. Expenditure decreased as the new building neared completion and, though many debts remained unpaid, they were more than offset by money owing to William. The marriage produced three sons and two daughters but the establishment of family life at Everingham in no way lessened the vigour with which William had previously conducted his concerns. Capital for further investment soon became available and during the next two decades at least £766 was devoted to the purchase of additional property.[69] Moreover, by 1780 almost the whole of the Yorkshire estate had been enclosed by act of Parliament. As a result further large increases were made in rents. William Constable was quick to take advantage of the new opportunities which an industrializing economy and a growing population provided for agriculturalists; and a new and much more prosperous era in the family's history ensued in the late eighteenth century.

Both current circumstances and future prospects were much brighter in 1760 than they had been in the 1640s. Yet the period from the mid seventeenth to the early eighteenth century was the most turbulent in the family's history. A variety of factors ensured that problems which at times threatened to engulf them failed to do so.

In the mid seventeenth century, while land remained the most acceptable form of security for a loan, there was a rapid expansion of the mortgage market. The Constables experienced little difficulty in raising huge and extended loans which they used in purchasing their own property from the Treason Trustees. Vital to the success of this operation were the efforts of John Rushworth and his associates, which nullified the worst effects of Sir Philip Constable's inclusion in a Treason act. Equally important at a later stage was financial help from the Shirburnes, which enabled the family to discharge debts after strenuous efforts to maximize income and minimize expenditure had produced little more than the capital needed to meet interest charges. Moreover, during this earlier period the Constables did not hesitate to transfer as much as possible of this financial pressure from themselves to their tenants. In addition to repeated rent increases, intolerance of rent arrears, distraint, and evictions, they pushed through an enclosure plan in Lincolnshire which, unlike its early eighteenth-century successor, did not have the full support of the tenantry there. By 1670 rents throughout the estate were as high as circumstances permitted following three decades of extremely tough management.

Except on the property enclosed in Lincolnshire in the 1720s, there were virtually no rent increases between 1670 and 1745.

The same period witnessed the loss of six properties – three freehold and three leasehold – which brought about a substantial reduction in recurrent income. The family withstood these and other setbacks because alienation of the freehold properties greatly reduced their debts; and also because they remained in possession of a substantial estate. Its profits financed a brief but successful foray in the stock market; gradually discharged most of the debts which were outstanding; and, albeit somewhat indirectly, financed the purchase of Seaton Ross and other lands, which more than made up for earlier property losses. Meanwhile, although a policy of burdening them with the whole of the land tax was quickly withdrawn, the tenants undoubtedly suffered from decades of neglect, both enforced and avoidable. Substantial improvement in their circumstances after 1745 went hand in hand with renewed increases in rents. However, as far as both the family and the estate were concerned, these later rent increases constituted a base for positive development rather than, as in the past, a means of staving off difficulties.

Although an uncompromising attitude towards their tenantry, particularly customary tenants such as cottagers, was a characteristic feature of the Constables' activities, several other factors made important contributions to their achievements. For example, unlike that of each of the other families considered in detail here, at no stage was part of the Constables' property settled on more than a single heir. Settlements did not go so far as to prevent alienations of property. Sir Philip and Marmaduke Constable together arranged the sale of Holderness in the 1650s, while the fourth baronet's lack of a male heir allowed the sales of property which followed the Jacobite rebellion of 1715. Sir Marmaduke was dubious as to his father's powers in relation to the mortgage of Gardham which was foreclosed at the turn of the century but, after seeking legal advice, chose not to pursue the matter.[70] Nevertheless, at no stage was partible inheritance considered. Even Sir Marmaduke, who died unmarried and childless, was careful to settle the whole of his landed property and the greater part of his personal estate on his chosen heir. Moreover, wives repeatedly pre-deceased husbands. Thus, although portions and other marital gains played an important part in solving problems, jointures did not have to be paid. Outgoing portions for daughters were likewise paid with remarkable infrequency, partly because few daughters survived to a marriageable age, but also because several of those who did entered religious life. Here again the family's experience was in sharp contrast to that of many of their contemporaries.

Recusants were forbidden to pursue political, military, or administrative careers. The effect which this had on family fortunes cannot be calculated, if only because successive heirs may have chosen not to enter public life had they been free to do so. Exile and imprisonment, however, did lead to some deterioration in their circumstances and morale, while changes in legislation and in the national temper affected their ability to raise loans. Nevertheless, whilst it was a constant source of anxiety and inconvenience, their recusancy did not have an overwhelmingly detrimental effect. This was only partially due to their persistent and highly successful efforts to avoid conviction and punishment. Parliament condemned their political allegiance more than their religion. Moreover, during Charles II's reign existing fiscal sanctions were not implemented by the Treasury. When, after the revolution of 1688, fiscal punishments were incorporated in the national tax system, sanctions were very heavy but only for a relatively short period. Recusants continued to be taxed at a higher rate than others but the sums involved were considerably below what the law provided for and, unlike fines, could be passed on from landlord to tenant. Indeed, at no time during this period were the Constables penalized with more consistent severity than they had been during the decade prior to the Civil War. Even at that stage many of the penal laws had fallen into disuse. This process continued, with a few interruptions, throughout the following century. Leading recusants had fewer opportunities than others, which caused intense frustration, and to a large extent lived apart from the rest of the community. But their circumstances became progressively easier and, generally speaking, the bark of officialdom was much worse than its bite.

V

THE BRIGHTS OF CARBROOK AND
BADSWORTH

BESIDES throwing into sharper focus some of the contemporary economic difficulties associated with land, not least the distinctly mixed fortunes of many of their tenants, the history of each of these three families provides evidence of the growing prosperity of various other individuals who were below the ranks of the baronetage, sometimes indeed of the gentry. Though its precise origins remain obscure, the fortune of the Heron family, whose daughter Katherine married the ill-fated Sir John Hotham, the third baronet, appears to have been derived from commercial activity in the mid seventeenth century. It was dispersed following the death of Katherine's father, John Heron, because he was succeeded only by co-heiresses. When Richard Beaumont sold Lascelles Hall in 1714 the purchaser was John Denton of Broadroyd Head in the parish of Denton, whose predecessors had been yeomen weavers in that vicinity. Those who obtained freehold property from the Constables derived their wealth from yet another source. Both the Days and the Watsons, who acquired Gardham and Wholsea respectively, were heavily involved in a lucrative trade in rabbit skins with London: the former as artisan-skinners in York, the latter as farmers (tenanting additional property from the Constables at Arras) in the East Riding.[1] While many parts of the East Yorkshire Wolds were improved during the course of the eighteenth century, the success of these two families serves as a reminder that before improvement fortunes were made there from specialized, though perhaps unsophisticated, types of agriculture. Moreover, as has been noted in an earlier chapter, the rise to wealth of certain individuals and families was both rapid and prolonged. Without doubt the Brights of Carbrook and Badsworth fall into this particular category.

In 1600 Thomas Bright of Whirlow was a yeoman farmer at Bradway near Sheffield. He was succeeded in 1616 by his eldest son, Stephen, about whose early life very little is known. Stephen Bright married a widow, Joan Smale, in 1610 and thereby probably acquired Carbrook Hall. Thereafter that property became the focal point of a rapidly expanding estate. Between 1616 and his death in 1642 Stephen spent more than £10,000 on purchases of real estate in south Yorkshire and north Derbyshire. All this property, much of which was urban and industrial in character, lay within a short distance of Carbrook Hall; its acquisition greatly increased the family's status in the locality. Shortly before his death, being 'a person of £1,000 a year . . . of credit and respect in the affections of the gentry, and of extraordinary merit', Stephen Bright was granted arms as a 'gentleman'.[2]

There are a few indications of how he financed the expansion of his estate. He married twice and presumably received a portion from each of his brides. In 1622 he was appointed bailiff of the Earl of Arundel's huge estate in Hallamshire at an annual salary of £50; and at one stage was reputedly defrauding his employer of rents worth £1,000 a year. Stephen himself was a strict landlord, quick to distrain for non-payment of rents. He was also heavily engaged in the lead trade, not only mining and smelting ore, but shipping it via Bawtry and Hull to markets in London and overseas. No doubt he used profits from all these activities in purchasing property. Moreover, as was true of his successor, some of his purchases were undoubtedly facilitated by the fact that they were from his own debtors. In 1642 the gross annual rental of his estate, which had been negligible at his succession, amounted to £672, and his personal estate to more than £5,500.[3] Stephen Bright settled his entire real estate, except for lands in Totley and Dore, on trustees for the use of his only surviving son, John, and his male heirs. Later he bequeathed portions of £1,500 to each of two surviving daughters, and £40 in life annuities and more than £1,200 in legacies to various friends and relatives. John Bright received the lands in Totley and Dore and, as executor, the residue of his father's personal estate. He also inherited his father's stock in the lead trade and his position as bailiff of Hallamshire.[4] Above all, he succeeded to the whole of the compact estate which his father had accumulated.

Without doubt Stephen Bright completely transformed the

circumstances of his family. Yet his achievements were far surpassed by those of his son, who enjoyed many of his father's qualities as well as the fruits of his success. Owing to their combined efforts the family rose in two generations from the yeomanry to that part of society where gentry mingled freely with aristocracy. Simultaneously their wealth increased from the very moderate to the massive. In Stephen's lifetime progress was uninterrupted; under John it became spectacular.

1.   JOHN BRIGHT'S EARLY CAREER 1642–60

John Bright succeeded shortly before the Civil War. The family was Puritan and, though only twenty-three years old in 1642, John was 'the most active person at Sheffield on the side of Parliament'. After serving briefly as a captain under Fairfax, he was appointed colonel of a foot regiment. He participated in attacks on Selby and Wakefield, helped to raise the sieges of Bradford and Nantwich, and fought at Marston Moor. He laid the siege of Sheffield castle, whose Royalist garrison was commanded by Major Thomas Beaumont, and eventually forced its surrender. Later as Governor he organized several successful forays and skirmishes. During the second Civil War Colonel Bright commanded Cromwell's troops at the battle of Preston and then joined the siege of Pontefract. Despite his youth and comparative inexperience, he was regarded as a brave and skilful officer. He severely criticized the intrigues and ineptitude of the army commissioners, and supported his complaints with numerous suggestions for reform. Membership of various parliamentary commissions convinced Colonel Bright that he was far better equipped to deal with the problems of army administration than the majority of his colleagues. This early, arrogant self-confidence was never undermined by failure. In July 1650, shortly after his regiment had begun to march north against the Scots, he resigned his commission. In April 1654 Major-General Lambert, who had succeeded Bright in his command, offered him a colonelcy of a cavalry regiment. He refused but accepted a foot regiment in 1656. In 1659 he was chiefly responsible for the defeat of the Presbyterian-Royalist rising led by Sir George Booth.[5]

Early in the Civil War Colonel Bright was drawn into Parliament's machinery of government, eventually becoming one of the busiest of public administrators. In 1643 he was appointed to four commissions, including that which dealt with the sequestration of Royalists' estates in the West Riding. Thereafter he served on many other commissions, accumulating wide experience of local government. After his resignation from the army he became even more heavily involved in administration. Besides further committee work, he was sometime Governor of both York and Hull, and served a double term as High Sheriff of Yorkshire. He also became M.P. for the West Riding and, in 1654, Visitor of Oxford University. His natural abilities developed rapidly under the dual stimulus of opportunity and experience, while success enhanced both his confidence and his family's prestige. Although on one occasion Carbrook Hall was plundered during his absence, the demands of his public career did not lead to any discernible neglect of his private concerns. Marriage in 1644 or 1645 to Katherine Lister encouraged him to spend as much time as possible at home. Most of his work for Parliament, both military and administrative, was performed in Yorkshire.[6]

Colonel Bright's career provided him with opportunities for personal gain of which he was quick to take advantage. In particular, his membership of the local committee for sequestrations was a key factor in the expansion of his estate. The sequestration of the Earl of Arundel's property in Hallamshire was followed by large, permanent, and apparently free additions to Bright's own holdings in that area. Later, though his official position should have disqualified him, he obtained leases of Arundel property in Sheffield, including that of a huge ironworks. Though complaints forced him to surrender the latter, he acquired a similar lease of a coalmine in Handsworth. Prior to his major purchase, of the manor of Badsworth, Colonel Bright took part in the sequestration of the property. Moreover, several of his numerous loans appear to have stemmed from information concerning individuals' circumstances obtained during his public duties. Army service provided other opportunities. At one stage he hoped to sell his pay slips at a profit of between 6s and 8s. in the pound, and was offered a profit of 2s. 6d. in the pound. Other receipts were equally unofficial. On his acceptance of a commission to raise militia forces in 1651 the Council of State promised to 'take care for your entertainment when the month's pay for the militia shall be out'. Although, he told Cromwell, his colonel's pay 'was not considerable to me' and 'would not have kept me and two servants', some of the other positions which he held, for example the governorships, were also salaried posts. There remains the possibility that Colonel Bright misappropriated some of the public money which frequently passed through his hands. From 1649 there was a dramatic rise in his income, most of which could only have been derived from public sources. The exact size and cause of this rise are not ascertainable, but at the Restoration he forestalled any attempt to examine his public activities during the Interregnum by destroying those papers which he felt might incriminate him. Clearly, he had much to hide from his political opponents.[7]

Table 22
The Brights: Personal Accounts 1642 & 1648

Stephen Bright 1642	£	s.	d.
Desperate Debts	429.	6.	8
Present Debts	1581.	2.	5
Lead Trade	1874.	0.	0
Stock & Goods	1306.15.0		
Household Goods & Plate	250.	0.	0
	5441.	4.	1

John Bright 1648			
General View of My Stock & Goods	£	s.	d.
Corn Sown – 26 acres	90.	0.	0
Oats & Wheat in Chambers	40.	0.	0
8 oxen & 4 steers	80.	0.	0
6 kyne & 3 calves	40.	0.	0
4 steers, 1 heifer, 1 bull	24.	0.	0
5 horses, 3 mares, 1 filly	80.	0.	0
Malt in Garner	50.	0.	0
	404.	0.	0

Source: BR 111.

In managing his private concerns Colonel Bright was, above all, decisive. The most significant change during the first decade of his career was his retreat from the lead trade, which was completed by 1648. His father had been involved in producing and marketing lead. The ore was mined in the Peak district and smelted there or near the Bright estates at Beauchief and Totley. Fothers and pigs of lead were then transported overland to Bawtry. From there they were shipped by river to Hull, and then by sea to London or the Continent. Accounts show no decrease in production during the war years and, though market changes made sales more difficult, profits were not adversly affected. The reason for Colonel Bright's decision was the slenderness of these profits in relation to the capital investment required to earn them. Profits were slow to materialize owing to the long delay between production and the receipt of returns from sales. Much capital remained tied up in unsold lead and credit to customers. Warehousing facilities on the routes to the markets were expensive. Agents were employed in Derbyshire, Bawtry, Hull, and London; each received either a commission, a salary, or both. Finally, there was the cost of fixed investment in buildings and machinery, and of the wages of miners and smelters.[8] As other activities indicate, Colonel Bright was not apathetic towards industrial or commercial ventures. He merely regarded the family's involvement in the lead trade as a poor business proposition. By withdrawing he released capital for more profitable investment elsewhere.

Some of this capital was re-deployed in a much smaller industrial venture. After inquiring about the possibility of leasing coalmining rights in Handsworth, where he already leased farmland, Colonel Bright obtained an estimate of mining profits there during 'past years'; he secured another, more pessimistic valuation from a recent tenant. In March 1650 he decided to go ahead and, for an annual rent of £30, was empowered 'to get one rib of coal lying in a close belonging to the manor of Handsworth'. £320 was invested in 'setting . . . the coal mine agate' and open-cast production began in February 1652. Within a few years the first shafts had been sunk. Colonel Bright employed a 'banksman' who hired men, paid wages, supervised mining, and sold coal. He was responsible to the bailiff of the farmland leased nearby. The accounts of the two men were interrelated, the bailiff providing the banksman with working capital, while the banksman usually returned profits to the bailiff, who then included them in his charge. Between 1652

and 1660 Colonel Bright received only £156 directly from the
mine, though accumulated rent amounted to £270. Even when
farming profits were added to this sum the venture was only
marginally successful. Numerous factors account for this lack
of profitability. Annual production was never higher than the
1,500 loads of 1655–6, dwindled thereafter, and by 1659–60
had dropped to little more than 1,000 loads. Such small-scale
production did not justify attempts to open markets beyond the
immediate locality where, however, demand never overtook
supply. An annual average of 175 loads remained unsold and a
gradual reduction in price, which further reduced profits, failed
to boost sales. Moreover, besides rents and initial capital
investment, running costs were relatively heavy despite the
small scale of operations. Employees were numerous; apart from
the colliers who received both quarterly and board wages,
'sinkers' were frequently hired and 'draughtsmen' employed
permanently. Then there were the wages of the banksman and
the bailiff; in particular the latter received a commission
amounting to half the net profits of the mine. Finally, casual
disbursements on items such as tools and timber were not
inconsiderable. The difficulty of achieving profits led to frequent changes of banksman and bailiff; before 1660 no less than
five individuals served in these two capacities. All these problems irritated Colonel Bright. Nevertheless, because his
involvement was small and associated with the more successful
farm at Handsworth, he continued mining for many years after
the Restoration.[9]

Loans on bonds and mortgages proved a much more profitable avenue of investment. Indeed, most of Colonel Bright's
available capital was invested in loans or in purchases of real
estate, which two activities were frequently inter-connected. It
is not possible to discover exactly how this came about –
whether for example mortgages were foreclosed – but several
purchases were made from debtors who, overwhelmed by fiscal
problems, discharged their debts to Colonel Bright by selling
property to him.

Stephen Bright had been owed £2,010 at his death. £800 of
this was due from a Mr Barker, who earlier had sold him a
moiety of the manor of Ecclesall. In 1646, when Barker owed
Colonel Bright £1,029, he discharged his debt by selling the

second moiety to him for £1,344. This sale and the gradual repayment of smaller sums reduced Colonel Bright's loans to modest proportions – £377 in 1647. However, from 1649 a dramatic increase in resources, alluded to above and only partially due to his withdrawal from the lead trade, produced a steep rise in both the number and size of his loans. During the following three years he lent a total of £8,880 to six individuals on mortgages. In 1653-4 he himself required capital for the purchase of Badsworth, but between 1655 and 1660 he lent a further £9,000 to seven other people. Apart from these sums, there were numerous smaller loans. The figures reveal a marked change in his fortunes at a time when the money market was rapidly expanding. Though spending most of his time in Yorkshire, he had good contacts in the London financial world, and was frequently solicited for advice as well as capital. His rates of interest varied, the most savage being the 50 per cent required of John Jackson in 1658 on a loan of £3,000. Much lower rates produced steady returns on investment in a sphere where overheads were virtually non-existent.[10] Moreover, Colonel Bright knew from experience that, if one chose carefully, a loan might lead to the purchase of its security; it was this possibility which most interested him.

The expansion of his estate was Colonel Bright's primary aim throughout his career, and he made considerable progress in this regard before the Restoration. Although full details of his first wife's portion are unrecorded, her widow's jointure included land in Craven worth £92 a year which was added to the rental of the Bright estates in 1645. It was joined a year later by the second moiety of Ecclesall. In 1648 Colonel Bright purchased a messuage, two cottages, and a close in Ecclesall for £200. This was offset in 1649 by the sale of closes nearby for £200. Even though no transactions are recorded, further additions in Carbrook and Ecclesall followed the sequestration of the Earl of Arundel's estate. Increases in rents due there – from £320 in 1640 to £816 in 1660 – resulted not from rent improvements but from the accumulation of property. The individual transactions mentioned above could not alone have been responsible for this rise, particularly as some property in this locality was sold during the same period. Colonel Bright's most important acquisition in these two decades was the manor of

Badsworth and adjoining lands in Skelbrook and Ackworth, which he purchased for £8,600 in 1653. This provides a further indication of the contemporary increase in his resources. The property, comprising 1,400 acres near Pontefract, had belonged to Thomas Dolman, a Catholic Royalist whose name had been included in a Treason act. Like Sir Philip Constable Dolman engaged the assistance of John Rushworth. Unlike Sir Philip he was compelled to sell his major property in order to save the rest of his estate. Colonel Bright left Carbrook to live at Badsworth soon after the purchase, and in 1655 acquired a close and several parcels of arable there for £38. Subsequently Badsworth became the focal point of a second estate which he established at some distance from his initial base in south Yorkshire. The final purchases before 1660 were of a house and land in Eckington, an annual rent charge of £100 from the manor of Halifax, and Westwell Hall and lands in Derbyshire. The terms of the first two transactions are unrecorded, though the rent charge was purchased from Sir Arthur Ingram who was among Colonel Bright's debtors. Originally purchased by Stephen Bright, Westwell Hall had passed to his widow and her daughter, Martha, in 1642. The latter married William Lister and, in return for an additional portion of £1,000 to his stepsister, Colonel Bright reobtained Westwell with its annual rental of £110. He made two further sales in this same period. In April 1653, anxious to raise money for the purchase of Badsworth, he sold property in Edale to his cousin, James Bright, for £2,480. When James died shortly thereafter Colonel Bright inherited the property, worth more than £170 annually, as his next heir. In the same year he sold lands in Totley for £950.[11]

Thus, by various means Colonel Bright substantially increased the size of his estates. His gross annual rental was roughly three times greater (£1,641) in 1660 than it had been (£583) in 1642. As he leased out most of his property tenants' rents comprised his major, private source of income. The size of rents fluctuated somewhat, especially during the Civil War. In 1646 rents at Craven and Carbrook were increased, while those at Edale and Totley were reduced. After two or three years when circumstances altered, rents returned to their former levels. Existing rents generally remained stable, and the rise in the gross annual rental was almost entirely due to the rapid expansion of the estate. Throughout this period part of the property, firstly at Carbrook and then at Badsworth, was farmed directly. Moreover, in 1646 Colonel Bright took a lease for an annual rent of £50 of lands in Handsworth and Bolsterstone, and appointed a bailiff to supervise direct farming there. A few scattered accounts, which are all that remain to record what were fairly large-scale farming operations, reveal not only that quantities of several types of produce were sold at Carbrook and Handsworth, but also that after 1655 food was sent from both farms to Badsworth for Colonel Bright's personal use. Thus, direct farming both reduced his costs and made some contribution to his annual income.[12]

A final factor in Colonel Bright's success during this period was the quality of his management. The chief manuscripts relating to the development of his private affairs are two pocket books.[13] Significantly, the earlier of these was first used by Stephen Bright. The latter's managerial abilities had been both recognized and improved by his appointment as bailiff of Hallamshire; the books indicate that his successor inherited them. Besides annual lists of rents due, they contain lists of debts, both 'present' and 'desperate', accounts of dealings in the lead trade, particulars of plate, stock, and goods, and notes of executorships, trusteeships, and settlements. The ordered, almost compulsive detail of these accounts suggests that Colonel Bright enjoyed being a businessman and they leave no doubt that he was a meticulously efficient one. Although he must have employed a number of individuals, particularly during the wars and after his purchase of Badsworth, no one other than Colonel Bright himself appears to have acted in an overall administrative capacity. The professionalism with which he ordered his immensely complex affairs only became a common feature of business and estate management long after his death.

2.   SIR JOHN BRIGHT'S LATER CAREER 1660–88

On John Rushworth's advice Colonel Bright destroyed many private papers at the Restoration to prevent the government from examining his previous activities. However, the Act of Indemnity of 1660 pardoned all offences arising from earlier hostilities and, far from being punished, he was honoured by the new administration. In August 1659 he had helped to crush Sir George Booth's Presbyterian–Royalist rebellion, and early in 1660 had been appointed to commissions for raising militia and defending the Commonwealth. Yet in July 1660, less than two months after Charles II's return, he was created baronet. In September he was appointed to the committee which supervised the disbanding of the army. His subsequent receipt of a royal pardon for his rebellion and treason was a pure formality. Not only did Sir John emerge from the Restoration physically unscathed and with his social status increased, but also his economy, which had benefited so greatly from Royalists' misfortunes, in no way suffered following the change in the political situation. Nevertheless, Sir John's life after 1660 was quite different from before. He served two terms as Deputy-Lieutenant for the West Riding, and in 1668 became Lieutenant-Colonel of the local militia. With these sole exceptions he devoted himself exclusively to private affairs from 1660 onwards.[14] He spent most of the rest of his life at Badsworth, becoming increasingly influential in the business life of landowning circles in Yorkshire. Having farming and industrial interests, and being very active in both the money and property markets, Sir John was looked to for advice on all these matters and, not surprisingly, was in great demand as a trustee. The admiration, envy, and respect of his contemporaries resulted from, and was further justified by, his success. Bringing wide experience and proven abilities to bear on his concerns in new, leisured circumstances, he directed a second and equally spectacular rise in his fortunes, the main feature of which was another enormous increase in the size of his estates.

Sir John continued to invest most of his available capital in the money and property markets. From 1660 records of his loans are more difficult to interpret than previously, but they leave no doubt that he greatly increased their number and size. By the 1680s he was among the chief creditors in the West Riding. An undated letter of the 1660s indicates explicitly that, as before, his policy was to interrelate lending and purchasing wherever possible. According to his nephew, John Bright of Gray's Inn: 'Mr Gerrard is very willing to give you 8 per cent knowing the good hands he is to fall into, if you agree the security for £1,500 which I do not see but may be good. I dare prophesy further it must be sold in a few years. He is an honest gentleman of himself but has a plague of a wife which forces him to expenses.'[15]

Sir John's first large post-Restoration loan, of £2,500 in 1661, was to Sir Edward Rhodes of Great Houghton, formerly Stephen Bright's debtor and a fellow Parliamentarian. Rhodes discharged some of this debt in 1664 by selling property in Great Houghton to Sir John for £1,720. He then leased the land back from Sir John, paying the rent and the rest of the loan in annual instalments of £250. In 1669 and 1670 his son sold more property in the same vicinity to Sir John for a total of £1,860. Together with the purchase in 1662 of a large farm in Milnehouse for £650, and in 1670 of a smallholding in Great Houghton for £92, these properties substantially increased Sir John's holdings in the vicinity of his new home. He was determined to expand and consolidate the Badsworth estate. His most complicated transaction in the 1660s was the purchase of a large estate at Kinsley and Cockhill, which also lay near Badsworth. This highly desirable property had originally belonged to a Mr Monson but on his death had been shared equally among his five daughters. In a sustained and skilfully conducted campaign between 1661 and 1670, involving many transactions, Sir John purchased the entire estate for a total of £8,210. At least two of the vendors discharged their debts to him by selling their share of the property. Moreover, Sir John was accused of tricking four of the owners into low sale prices; certainly the price of the last transaction was considerably higher than the others. While concentrating on the Badsworth estate, Sir John took several opportunities of adding to his property in south Yorkshire. In 1667–8 he acquired a farm and close in Brightside for an unknown sum and a house in Pitsmoor for £120. In 1671 he bought three closes and a wood in Thrifthouse for £65 and a farm in the same area for £100. He also sold two houses in Sheffield for £430 in 1671, and two cottages there for £8 in 1675.[16]

Besides the loan to Sir Edward Rhodes, Sir John lent £1,500 to a Mr Wombwell in 1661 and £1,000 to Sir Hugh Smithson. These were merely the largest of numerous advances which by the mid 1660s totalled between £5,000 and £10,000. Most repayments of principal were preceded by annual interest payments but in several instances debts were repaid in the form of annuities. Before 1670, by which time total debts had fallen to around £1,500, Sir John used repayments in the purchase of the property at Kinsley and Cockhill. During 1670, however, there was a sharp increase in his loans; indeed, he himself became so short of cash as a result that he raised £1,580 on mortgage to complete the purchase from the fifth Monson daughter. Thereafter Sir John's major debtor was the wildly extravagant Sir John Jackson of Hickleton, who by 1679 owed him a total of £10,300. After Jackson's death in that year the trustees of the Hickleton estate repaid one mortgage, but were only able to discharge further debts by selling the manor of Billingley and property in Milnehouse to Sir John for £4,000. Despite this, Sir John remained among the trustees' largest creditors. In order to supplement his supplies of cash he decided to sell Westwell Hall, the most detached of the properties on his Sheffield estate. But he attempted unsuccessfully to drive a hard bargain and eventually dropped the idea. Nevertheless, during the 1670s the debts owed to him by, among others, Jackson, Sir Matthew Wentworth, and Sir John Kaye grew steadily. Income from annuities for the discharge of loans amounted to £526 in 1680 alone. By 1682 Sir John would appear to have been owed around £20,000.[17] Subsequently he granted many further mortgages and when he died in 1688 he undoubtedly had a considerable fortune invested in this way.

Because most of his liquid capital was so invested there were no additions to the estates between 1671 and 1680. However, from 1680 there followed a third and final period when Sir John's estates, particularly in the Badsworth area, were greatly extended. He bought a house in Rotherham for an unknown sum and a farm in Ackworth for £320. In 1681 he purchased the manor of Billingley from the Jackson trustees. He also bought fee farm rents worth £104 annually from two London businessmen for £1,760. In 1683 Sir John purchased closes in Ackworth for £280, and in the following year two properties in Totley. The latter were subsequently let for £82 a year. Also in 1684 Sir John acquired a moiety of the manor of Barnby for £2,300. Besides a house, cottages, and farms, this property included a large ironworks. In 1685 he bought eight closes in

Great Houghton from local merchants for £770, and finally in 1687 he effected an exchange of small properties in Ecclesall. A career spanning nearly half a century and primarily devoted to the acquisition of real estate ended in a flurry of purchases. As a result his gross annual rental rose from £673 in 1642 to £3,210 in 1687.[18] At no time, even at the height of his public career, did this most successful of Yorkshire landowners cease to be active in either the money or the property markets.

After the Restoration coalmining continued at the Handsworth pits. However, not only was there no attempt to broaden the scope of activities there, but it proved difficult to maintain operations at their former, modest level. The situation slowly deteriorated until 1684 when mining ceased. Although by then the mines had been worked for more than thirty years, they had contributed an almost insignificant sum – slightly more than £500 – to Sir John's resources. The venture was hampered by a variety of difficulties. While average production after 1660 was somewhat less than previously, the market also contracted, and large amounts of coal remained unsold for lengthy periods. As there was no comparable fall in costs, profit margins were reduced and accounts were occasionally in deficit. On one occasion a pit caught fire; on another a roof collapsed. Severe drainage problems, which were never overcome, caused long halts in production. There were also labour difficulties. Thomas Stacy, the bailiff, was unequal to the demands of the post. Moreover, in his view the average collier was 'but a beggar'. So too were the banksmen, because the mine could not provide a salary which would have attracted a better sort of person to the job; as before, there were frequent changes of personnel. Furthermore, by the end of the 1670s the coal seams mentioned in the original agreement were nearly exhausted. As relations with the neighbouring landowner were bad, mining was discontinued in 1684. Although Stacy grew steadily more apathetic and incapable, Sir John nursed the project to the very end. Against involvement on the scale of earlier ventures in the lead trade, he neither hoped for nor expected substantial development at Handsworth. Yet, albeit only slightly, the mine diversified his economy.[19] It is perhaps significant that in 1684 he leased the right to mine coal on his newly-acquired property at Billingley. In the same year he purchased Barnby with its

TABLE 23
Production, Sales & Profits at Handsworth Pits, 1652–84

	Production (In Loads)	Unsold (In Loads)	Banksman	Net Profit To Sir J. B.
				£. s. d.
1652–3		220		27.10. 0
1653–4		135		24. 0. 0
1654–5				22. 0. 0
1655–6	1535		R.H.	35. 5. 0
1656–7			R.H.	15. 0. 0
1657–8	1261	150	R.H.	32. 8. 6
1658–9	1026	225	R.T.	6. 0. 0
1659–60	1044	173	G.B.	5.11. 9
1660–1	887	12	G.B.	6.14.10½
1661–2	1021	120	G.B.	3. 0. 1
1662–3	1036	120	G.B.	6. 9. 5
1663–4	1028	119	G.B.	11. 2. 0
1664–5	1107	474	G.C.	36. 7. 9
1665–6	1052		G.C.	11. 7. 6
1666–7	1212		G.C.	25. 0. 0
1667–8	1202		G.C.	30. 0. 0
1668–9	1223		G.C.	25. 0. 0
1669–70	1001		G.C.	15. 0. 0
1670–1	1026	414	G.C.	NIL
1671–2	861		W.H.	20. 0. 0
1672–3	819	356	W.H.	NIL
1673–4	723	24	W.H.	NIL
1674–5	738	72	J.S.	10. 0. 0
1675–6	1087		J.S.	15. 0. 0
1676–7	1099		W.H.	25. 0. 0
1677–8	947		W.H.	25. 0. 0
1678–9	958		W.H.	18. 0. 0
1679–80	1042		W.H.	22. 0. 0
1680–1	1045	95	W.H.	11. 0. 0
1681–2	1028	117	W.H.	20. 0. 0
1682–3	716		T.J.	NIL
1683–4	209		T.J.	11.10. 6
				515. 7. 4½

NOTE Gaps in the first two columns mean that figures are not available. Column 3 illustrates the frequency of changes of banksman.

Source: BR 55.

large ironworks and immediately began to reconstruct the furnaces. There is no evidence, however, that production commenced before his death.[20]

After 1660 Sir John derived his financial resources firstly, and foremostly, from rent receipts. The large rise in his gross annual rental was due almost entirely to his purchases, and only marginally to increases in rents. The Kinsley and Cockhill estate is the only property where a significant rise in existing rents appears to have taken place, and even this may have resulted from purchases or from the leasing of demesne which had previously been farmed directly. Direct farming was another but decreasing source of income. Sir John's accounts corroborate other evidence that this was a difficult period for Yorkshire farming. In 1670 he either drastically reduced or completely closed the farm at Badsworth, leasing it thereafter for £200, and then for £240, a year. In 1674 he reduced the Carbrook farm and in the 1680s had difficulty in finding a tenant for it at £30 a year. By then farming had also ceased at Handsworth and Bolsterstone.[21] Interest payments were a third source of income. No accounts of these have survived but there are indications of the rates which Sir John charged and of the manner in which he treated his debtors. Although his rates were usually below 8 per cent, they fluctuated between 2 per cent and 15 per cent. His policy apparently was to treat each request for a loan according to individual circumstances. There was certainly no correlation between rates of interest and the size of loans. He could be severe and, on occasion, distrained goods and chattels in lieu of unpaid debts and had recourse to the courts. But both the rates which he charged and the correspondence which he had with some of his debtors suggest that normally he was sympathetic rather than stern, if only because he had designs on the security of many of his loans. The latter were so large that interest payments must have made a substantial and annual contribution to his income.[22]

A large proportion of Sir John's resources, however, came from marriage portions. On the death of his first wife, Katherine, in 1663 he ceased to enjoy the profits of the property at Craven which had formed part of her portion, but in succeeding years he contracted three further marriages. In 1672 he married Elizabeth, daughter of Sir Thomas Norcliffe; no details of her portion are recorded and she died in 1674. Then in 1682 at the age of sixty-three Sir John married the twenty-three-year-old Frances, daughter of Sir Thomas Liddell and widow of Thomas Vane. Her portion included a jointure but again further details are unavailable. However, when Frances died a few months later Sir John was granted letters of administration over her estate. Almost immediately, in June 1683, he married for the last and most lucrative time. He was more than thirty years older than Susannah, daughter of Michael Wharton, whose portion amounted to £5,000. Contemporaries congratulated Sir John's 'mettle' in venturing 'upon girls'; they also maintained that he 'had thirteen or fourteen thousand pounds by his wives'.[23]

Those who came into contact with Sir John recognized the qualities upon which most of his remarkable success was based. On returning to Ravensworth Castle from Badsworth in 1669, for example, Sir Thomas Liddell found 'this place . . . much defective since I saw the beautiful order of your family'. Until afflicted by the gallstones which eventually killed him, careful management formed an essential part of his economic strategy. Typical of the order and detail of his personal accounts is the note of 1 April 1682 that he was then owed £700 as his father's executor; Stephen Bright had died forty years earlier. Sir John demanded similar standards of efficiency from his employees. Thomas Stacy, for instance, had to submit detailed accounts and reports of the small mining concern at Handsworth. Moreover, although the family – the Liddells – of the young man with whom Sir John's daughter, Catherine, became involved was one of the wealthiest in the north, Sir John insisted on conducting meticulous investigations and lengthy negotiations, involving considerable travel and expense, before he approved a marriage settlement. Such thorough preparation and careful consideration of tactics were hallmarks of Sir John's conduct of business affairs. He was quite capable of taking risks, as his absorption of the Arundel property and purchase of Badsworth indicate, but when, as in the Kinsley and Cockhill episode, circumstances provided him with time for thought as well as action, he operated with consummate skill. Because of the lack of comprehensive accounts it is impossible to examine in detail Sir John's expenditure or investments other than his purchases, loans, and industrial concerns. One encounters the occasional interesting particular, such as the bill dating from 1669–72 for £78 for repairs to Pitsmoor Hall, or the accounts dated 1679–80 of the building of houses, a mill, and a wheel at Ecclesall. But there is no indication of the relationship which such expenditure bore, for instance, to personal or family expenditure. There is one glimpse, however, of the effect which increasing wealth had on Sir John's standard of living. In 1657 his collection of plate was valued at £160; by 1685 it was worth £1,211.[24] Moreover, both his own and his daughter's marriages indicate a substantial rise in the family's social status. His achievements were partly private but mainly public before 1660, and vice versa thereafter, but so great were they that their main effect – a steady increase in the family's property and prestige – was constant.

In one respect, however, and it was no fault of his, Sir John's plans remained unfulfilled; he was unable to pass on his great wealth to a son. Despite four marriages, Sir John had only four children and was pre-deceased by three of them. His sole surviving heir was his first daughter, Catherine, who married Henry Liddell of Ravensworth Castle. Eventually, following a variety of settlements, he left the greater part of his property to their second son, John, provided he added the name of Bright to his own. By this means Sir John ensured that his would not be amalgamated with other property, and that it would remain under the, albeit hyphenated, name of Bright. Yet in two respects his final disposition of property was most unfavourable to his successor at Badsworth. Firstly, he left Carbrook and Edale to his nephew, John Bright of Gray's Inn; in 1687 the annual rental of this property was £696. Secondly, Sir John was even more generous to his last wife, Susannah. Not only did he provide her with an annual jointure of £1,000 after his death, but he also gave her several recently acquired properties for life, including Barnby, land in Totley, and the fee farm rents purchased in 1681. She also received a legacy of £2,500 and much of his personal estate.[25] The arrangements made for his wife are more explicable than Sir John's disposition of Carbrook and Edale. At sixty-three he was old enough to be Susannah's father when he married her; no doubt his generosity was proportionate not only to the size of her portion, but also to his and others' surprise that the match was made. By 1687, when Sir John made his will, these considerations had been enhanced by age and also perhaps by the care which he received from his young wife during his last, painful illness. On the other hand Sir John came to his decision concerning Carbrook and Edale as early as 1672, long before the death of his second son. At that stage he could not have regarded his nephew as a substitute for the children who eventually pre-deceased him. Whatever the reasons for his final dispositions, the fiscal difficulties which bedevilled his successors stemmed directly from them. Susannah was as hardy as she was lucky. She remarried soon after Sir John's death and lived until 1737, drawing considerably more than £1,000 a year from the Bright estates for the rest of her life. Meanwhile, Carbrook and Edale passed permanently from the possession of the main branch of the family.

Sir John Bright died in September 1688 aged sixty-nine. His funeral was one of the events of the year in Yorkshire. After lying in state his remains were carried to Badsworth church by 'twelve knights, baronets, and gentlemen'. The mourners were splendidly dressed, and later sumptuously fed, at Sir John's expense. As they pondered on his achievements the minister gave him a 'great character' in his panegyric.[26] Without doubt those achievements were undermined by Sir John's settlement of money and property on his wife and nephew as well as on his grandson. Although John Liddell-Bright inherited substantial property, he was deprived of the profits of more than half Sir John's large estates. Consequently he and his successors encountered problems which Sir John had striven, and been glad, to avoid. Yet nothing can obscure the extent of Sir John's personal success. In retrospect his career appears as one of inexorable progress, if not in one sphere then in another. He was occasionally ruthless and unscrupulous, and had great good fortune. Before the Restoration his achievements stemmed to a large extent from opportunities provided by political developments. However, Sir John grasped these and brilliantly exploited them. Although his interests were varied, he concentrated on meeting the contemporary demand for capital, and on expanding his estate. Landownership was not only a means of increasing social prestige, of which his family had comparatively little at his succession, but also the safest insurance against political or financial misfortune. The latter was an important consideration for someone who enjoyed sudden favour and success, by no means all of it strictly on merit. His efforts were sustained by an impressive combination of personal qualities. Few of his neighbours matched the breadth of his interests or the range of his experience. Few of them possessed his flair for organization or had so clear an idea of what they were about. He, and to a lesser degree Stephen Bright, presided over one of the most remarkable family success stories in seventeenth-century Yorkshire.

3. STRUGGLE FOR SURVIVAL 1688–1735

Although as a younger son John Liddell-Bright was lucky to inherit property, his fortune was mixed. He was not entitled to any of Sir John's huge personal estate, and only succeeded to part of his real estate. While the 1687 rental of Sir John's property had amounted to £3,210, his successor's rental totalled only £2,310 in 1695. Moreover, the latter stood charged with huge jointure payments; one of £400 a year to Lucy Bright, Sir John's daughter-in-law, and another of £1,000 a year to his widow, Susannah. Thus, clear income from Liddell-Bright's rental amounted to only £900 annually.[27] In fact his situation was even more precarious. The rental was his only major source of income, and the larger jointure only lapsed after his death. Lucy Bright died in 1708 but Susannah lived on to the ripe old age of eighty-six, by which time Liddell-Bright had been dead for two years. During a long career he was harassed by various problems, most of which originated in the difficult situation which he inherited.

Liddell-Bright was a minor when Sir John died in 1688. In August 1690 he was granted a pass to travel to Holland for what was probably a tour to complete his education. During his minority affairs in Yorkshire were supervised by his parents and by Sir John's executors. He returned to England in or before 1694 when he became engaged to Cordelia, only daughter of Samuel Clutterbuck of Ingatestone in Essex. A successful marriage offered to alleviate his fiscal problems and this match certainly promised to be lucrative. Samuel Clutterbuck had been a wealthy merchant in London and by his death in 1692 had acquired real estate in Essex, Kent, and London, and was possessed of a considerable personal estate. He had bequeathed £13,000 to his widow, Dame Anne, £5,000 to his eldest son, Thomas, and £6,500 each to his younger son, John, and his daughter. The marriage agreement stipulated that Cordelia's portion should amount to £8,000, although initially Liddell-Bright was to receive only £2,000 of this sum. The remainder was to be vested in trustees until he had purchased real estate equal to its value. If for any reason Cordelia was unable to enter into her jointure after Liddell-Bright's death, this property was to be to her use for 500 years before finally becoming vested in his heirs. This represented a compromise between Liddell-Bright's need to obtain the largest possible portion and the Clutterbucks' desire, in view of his financial circumstances, to safeguard Cordelia's future. An opportunity of making a sizeable addition to his estates was welcome, especially as he was free to choose the property to be purchased. Accordingly, in September 1697 he bought the manor and lands of Bamforth in Derbyshire for £5,881, thereby adding £206 to the annual rental of his Sheffield estate.[28]

Subsequently Liddell-Bright maintained that the £8,000 portion had been granted over and above Cordelia's legacy of £6,500.[29] On this basis, he alleged, he and his wife received considerably less from the Clutterbuck estate than was their due. Meanwhile, John Clutterbuck, who like his father had gone into trade, claimed that he had received almost none of his £6,500. Attempting to mollify her younger son, Dame Anne Clutterbuck, her husband's sole executrix, granted him two houses in Queen Street, London, which were worth £70 annually in 1697. In the following year as security for the receipt of his entire legacy Dame Anne conveyed to John £1,983 of his father's trade debts, and also mortgages which Samuel had granted to Sir Peter Glean, but which had never been redeemed. She then attempted to obtain repayment of these debts. What success Dame Anne had regarding the trade debts is not clear, but after a long struggle she was successful in regard to the mortgages. As Sir Peter Glean was dead she exhibited a Chancery bill in 1698 against his heirs, charging them with various obstructions and petitioning for foreclosure of the equity of redemption on the mortgages. The case was eventually heard at the Exchequer bar and in July 1702 a verdict in

Dame Anne's favour was pronounced. The court calculated that £3,747 remained due on the mortgages and, when the debtors failed to repay this sum, ordered that the mortgaged property be put up for sale. Until it was sold the property became vested in Dame Anne and, reinforcing her earlier transactions, she conveyed it to John Clutterbuck in 1703.

In the meantime Dame Anne had gone to live with her daughter and son-in-law at Badsworth, leaving John in charge of her affairs in the south. Following the transaction of 1703 she considered that the latter had received much more than his share of her estate. Perhaps with a view to dealing with Liddell-Bright's claims, as well as 'to prevent any disputes that may happen about the small estate I shall leave', she appointed him the sole executor of her will of January 1704.[30] When Dame Anne died later that year the mortgage suit automatically lapsed, and Liddell-Bright assumed responsibility for the disposal of the remainder of the Clutterbuck estate. John Clutterbuck quickly and successfully petitioned that the suit be revived. When the Glean property was sold in 1705 for £4,200 he duly received his £3,747. Part of the residue was devoted to legal costs, about which there were claims and counter claims; the remainder passed to Sir Peter Glean's heirs. The suit finally closed in July 1708.[31]

In the intervening period a further dispute, between Liddell-Bright and John Clutterbuck, had come before Chancery. Both parties were in financial difficulties and coveted what remained of the Clutterbuck estate. In his will Samuel Clutterbuck had stated that, should his personal estate prove insufficient to discharge all his legacies, those which had been paid should be 'proportionately abated'. In 1707 Liddell-Bright invoked this clause in Chancery in an effort to extract money from John Clutterbuck who, he claimed, had received far more than his due. He alleged that, besides the houses in Queen Street, the trade debts, and the Glean mortgage moneys, John had received £500 for an apprenticeship fee, £2,000 to pay for a business trip to Turkey, mortgages worth a further £2,000, and jewels and furniture of unknown value. He also charged John with obstructing his efforts to draw up accounts of his executorship, and with receiving various moneys knowing them to be due on the same accounts. Finally after claiming £8,000

over and above his wife's legacy, he submitted that more than
£2,000 of the combined sum remained unpaid and that, in his
view, it ought to be paid by John Clutterbuck. The latter
rejoined that £2,569 of his legacy remained unpaid. Moreover,
while acknowledging receipt of the Glean mortgage moneys and
the houses in Queen Street, he denied having received other
mortgages and maintained that he had had to write off his
father's trade debts. As the money for his apprenticeship fee
and his Turkish trip had been paid during his minority, he
argued that they constituted his lawful maintenance and formed
no part of his legacy. In his view his father's personal estate had
been more than sufficient to discharge all the legacies. It had
not done so, firstly because his brother, Thomas, had received
extra money to facilitate the purchase of a post in the Six Clerks'
Office, and secondly, because his sister, Cordelia, had been
given an extra £1,500 to bring her portion to £8,000. Clutterbuck vehemently denied that the portion was meant to be
separate from the legacy, charged Liddell-Bright with
exaggerating the size of Dame Anne's estate, and denied
obstructing his executive duties or concealing moneys belonging to the estate. He also maintained that Dame Anne had
intended to name him as her executor. In acting otherwise he
could only feel that she had been of unsound mind when
drawing up her will, or that it had been forced on her. There is
no reference to further proceedings, nor is there any indication
of an out of court settlement. The suit probably lapsed following John Clutterbuck's bankruptcy, which was declared later in
1707. Subsequently – with what success is unknown –
Liddell-Bright had to convince the Commissioners for Bankruptcy that no debt was due from him to Clutterbuck. The only
other reference to the matter dates from Michaelmas 1709 when
Liddell-Bright's lawyer expressed the hope that there would be
'no more danger' from Clutterbuck, 'he being gone'.[32]

This perhaps indicates that the Brights feared the strength of
their opponent's case. However, as with most uncompleted
lawsuits, it is almost impossible to separate fact from fiction.
More relevant is the extent to which Liddell-Bright's marriage
and his subsequent involvement in the turbulent affairs of his
wife's family affected him financially. A number of facts are
unknown: the cost of Liddell-Bright's lawsuit and the result of

the bankruptcy proceedings into which he was drawn. Moreover, although Dame Anne's estate was reputedly small at her death, its value is unrecorded, as are the details of its ultimate disposition. Nevertheless, some aspects of the situation are clear. Liddell-Bright received the costs of his participation in the Glean mortgages dispute. On his own admission he received at least £12,000 from the Clutterbuck estate prior to exhibiting his bill in Chancery in 1707. In view of John Clutterbuck's bankruptcy he could not have obtained the residue of his claim from the source from which, he argued, it ought to have come. Finally, he and his family stood to gain more from the disputed estate on account of his executorship. The evidence suggests, therefore, not only that he did not lose from his marriage, but that his gains were probably very considerable.

Yet Liddell-Bright's general financial circumstances, far from improving, grew steadily worse while these disputes were in progress. By the turn of the century he was considerably in arrears with payments of Dame Susannah's annuity. Until 1695 he paid the annuity promptly, despite being confronted with huge rent arrears. But by 1701, when arrears remained high, he was £2,548 behind in his annuity payments. Timothy Kiplin (one of his stewards) attempted for a time to placate Sir John Newton, Susannah's second husband. There was a limit, however, to what Kiplin could achieve. The arrear rose to nearly £1,300 during 1704. The fact that Sir John discovered several mistakes unfavourable to him in Kiplin's accounts, and that he himself needed cash to complete a building project, eroded his patience. When the situation had not improved by September 1705 he threatened to exact his due by means 'which would not be more disagreeable to Mr Bright than myself'. Unfortunately, there is a gap in the correspondence during the period when Liddell-Bright was in dispute with John Clutterbuck, but accounts show that in November 1710 £2,060 was due for the annuity. Newton's patience was exhausted and he demanded that Liddell-Bright pay promptly or expect severe consequences. The result of this threat was an agreement signed by both parties in November 1711. Liddell-Bright promised to devote the rents from all his properties except Badsworth firstly to the payment of the annuity, and only thereafter to his own needs.

Henceforward the situation changed dramatically. Despite persistently heavy rent arrears, expenditure was almost totally dominated by payments to Sir John. An account dated April 1716 indicates that arrears in the jointure had been cleared, and that current payments were being made punctually. Liddell-Bright also fell into arrears with Lucy Bright's jointure of £400. Although she died in 1708, he did not forward the last instalment to her executor until March 1710.[33]

It proved impossible for Liddell-Bright to meet these huge demands on his resources without borrowing heavily. In October 1705 he mortgaged Bamforth for £500. He borrowed an additional £700 in November 1707 on the same security. The deeds of both transactions recite a previous mortgage for £1,000. Moreover, accounts of interest payments in 1707 reveal that he raised a further £1,000 on bonds. By 1710 his creditors were demanding repayment and the mortgages were assigned to a new source of capital.[34] The fact that his circumstances worsened despite the money which he received from his marriage suggests that he had extraordinary items of expenditure other than the two jointures. Yet there is no indication that he had to make substantial payments following his dispute with John Clutterbuck. However, there was another avenue of possibly heavy expenditure.

At the general election of July 1698 Liddell-Bright stood as one of three candidates for the borough of Pontefract, which sent two members to Parliament. He came second in the poll, thirty-six votes behind Sir John Bland but only two votes ahead of the loser, Mr Monkton. The latter petitioned the parliamentary Committee of Privileges and Elections, charging Liddell-Bright with 'corrupt and illegal practices' during the contest. No action was taken so in November 1699 Monkton renewed his petition. In its report of the following January the Committee declared Liddell-Bright duly elected. However, the full House of Commons disagreed and issued a writ for a new election. Liddell-Bright again defeated Monkton but only, according to a majority of the aldermen and burgesses, as a result of flagrant malpractices by the mayor. As the Committee of Privileges and Elections failed to take up the matter again, Liddell-Bright continued to sit at Westminster, but was not returned at the next election in 1710.[35] The history of the

Hothams illustrates the heavy cost of electoral struggles after 1688, and borough elections were particularly bitterly contested. There seems little doubt, though there is no proof, that the events described above involved Liddell-Bright in expenditure which he could ill afford. Significantly, these events coincided with the first manifestations of Sir John Newton's impatience. Moreover, from 1701 onwards Liddell-Bright's life became almost exclusively centred on Badsworth. Subsequently, even in matters of the utmost importance, he preferred others to conduct his London business for him, loudly proclaiming his 'taste' for 'a country life'.[36] His preference was stimulated by lack of money and also, no doubt, by his experiences. Together with the cost of rent arrears, of jointures, and possibly of his dispute with John Clutterbuck, political ambition swallowed the money which he obtained from his marriage, drove him into deficit, and forced him to borrow. Although he balanced the annuity account in 1716, other debts remained outstanding.

Before these problems arose he made the best of the circumstances which he had inherited. He avoided the costs of maladministration by appointing stewards to each of the two parts of his estate. Also by August 1693 a considerable amount of direct farming was in operation at Badsworth. If this was not on a marketable scale, it at least reduced household expenditure. In January 1698 Sir Henry and Dame Catherine Liddell gave their son a rent charge of £30 a year from property which had previously formed part of Sir John Bright's estate. A year earlier Liddell-Bright had purchased property in Pontefract for £399, possibly for electoral purposes. Soon afterwards he bought two houses there for an unrecorded sum, but sold them almost immediately for £70. In 1702 he purchased a close adjacent to property which he owned in Sheffield for £50, and in 1704 bought a parcel in Ackworth for £37. Earlier he had exchanged certain lands in the Croft field at Billingley; so his resources were sufficient in these early years to permit some expansion and consolidation of the estate other than the acquisition of Bamforth. Even at this stage, however, Liddell-Bright could not afford to be benevolent; his tenants were required to pay all taxes, even the heavy land tax of the war years.[37]

As problems increased he was forced to maintain a very tight

control over his expenditure, especially following his agreement
with Sir John Newton in 1711. Because his tenants had great
difficulty in paying existing rents he could not look to rent
increases for assistance. Meanwhile, he had little if anything to
spare for repairs and improvements. Had it not been for income
from wood sales he would have sunk even further into debt.
Fortunately Liddell-Bright's Sheffield estate had plentiful supplies of wood and he was able to sell in bulk to John Fell, one of
the south Yorkshire ironmasters whose timber consumption
was both large and continuing. Between May 1710 and April
1717 he raised £1,187 from such sales. Total receipts from this
source were probably considerable. With this extra money
Liddell-Bright avoided falling further into debt and maintained
current accounts in small but persistent surplus. From time to
time he had opportunities of improving his estate without adding greatly to his expenditure. Thus, after purchasing another
small parcel in Little Houghton Ing in 1713 for £5 7s. 6d., he
was a party in 1716 to three exchanges of property in Billingley
whereby he acquired nearly 100 acres of land in the townfields.
These transactions appear to have been followed by enclosure
for rents at Billingley were soon increased by £72 a year. So,
although Liddell-Bright may have been handicapped and frustrated by lack of money, as a landowner he was not reduced to
inactivity by it. Besides more mundane pursuits, he was a
'famous breeder of beagles, spaniels and foxhounds . . . in this
line of business he was an acknowledged master and his dogs
were in great demand'.[38]

Liddell-Bright's marriage produced four sons and three
daughters. The eldest, Thomas, came of age in 1716. By a
family settlement in November of that year he vested the whole
of his real estate after his death in trustees for his male issue and
their heirs in order, and in default for his right heirs. Thomas
received Great Houghton for life and, on Dame Susannah
Newton's death, was to receive a further £200 a year from
Badsworth and Ecclesall. Portions to a total value of £12,000
were to be raised for the other children from the whole estate
except Great Houghton. Liddell-Bright reserved the right to
make more detailed provision in this regard by future deeds or
in his will; otherwise each portion was to be £2,000. Finally, the
power to provide jointures for future wives was allocated to

both father and eldest son.[39] In the prevailing circumstances the provision for younger children was by no means insubstantial, though it was somewhat unconventional to provide equally for sons and daughters. However, their portions were not in immediate demand, and the early death of Susannah Newton was probably, though mistakenly, expected. Meanwhile, to devise an annual income of more than £300 from Great Houghton before her death exacerbated fiscal problems. But, if the family was to maintain itself socially, and if Thomas was to be afforded an opportunity of marrying well, some provision for his separate maintenance had to be made as soon as he attained his majority.

At this point Liddell-Bright became involved in yet another legal dispute. This too stemmed from his marriage in that it concerned his purchase of Bamforth in 1697, the money for which had come from Cordelia's dowry. No doubt wishing to avoid the costs and delay of Chancery proceedings, he agreed that the matter be put to arbitration. As a result records of the case are scanty, but it appears that a significant amount of land thought by Liddell-Bright to have formed part of his purchase had not in fact been scheduled in the documents recording the transaction. He accused the vendors of wilful negligence and demanded retribution. The arbitrators deliberated for more than a year. However, their award, which is not recorded, was one with which Liddell-Bright and his lawyers were extremely pleased. Yet within a few months he sold Bamforth for £5,727, £154 less than he had paid for it in 1697. Among the many points which remain unclear is whether the arbitrators stipulated that he should sell the property and, if so, why. By March 1717 Liddell-Bright had apparently decided to sell or realized that the arbitrators would recommend that he do so. His pleasure at the award suggests that besides the purchase money he received substantial damages. Although his father criticized him for accepting such 'a modest price for £250 a year', the money enabled him to discharge his debts.[40] Moreover, at the close of 1717, for the first time for many years, he had a substantial amount of capital available for investment. He was soon corresponding with his father about the use of these newly acquired resources.

Sir Henry Liddell thought them 'too large to lie idle' and

suggested that he invest in the funds. Liddell-Bright readily agreed and, sending £3,200 to London, asked his father to invest this for him. Faced with this responsibility, Sir Henry's enthusiasm waned but he agreed to 'act as for myself and not without advice of the most judicious I know in these matters'. A letter of August 1718 reveals that Liddell-Bright then possessed £3,500 worth of annuities, and that though 'stocks . . . fall, yet ours continue above what we bought at'. He also purchased lottery tickets, though to what extent is not clear for there is no formal account of his London business, and it is impossible to ascertain the purpose of individual remittances. However, his sale of plate in December 1718 perhaps indicates that he too had contracted the current fever for this type of investment. Although he purchased a further thirty lottery tickets in the following March, his annuities had by then greatly fallen in value, and he contemplated selling them to avoid further loss. Despite his father's advice to the contrary, 'for 'tis expected they'll rise', Liddell-Bright sold some annuities in April 1719, losing 'near 10 per cent'. The sale of an additional £1,000 worth fetched no more than £918. Soon afterwards, despite having permitted his father to raise a loan partly on their security, he exchanged the remainder of his holdings. There seems little doubt that this first venture into the stock market was a dismal failure, but worse was to come. During the following year the South Sea boom got under way. In August 1720 when South Sea stock reached its highest point before its collapse Lord Lonsdale, who was then acting for Liddell-Bright in London, invested £1,000 of the latter's capital in the fourth and final subscription without obtaining prior permission to do so. Within days its price plummeted and Lonsdale was 'extremely concerned you are not likely to have any advantage from your subscription'. In fact Liddell-Bright was threatened with a severe loss and Lonsdale repeatedly offered to reimburse him. Whether this offer was taken up is not known. The correspondence closes in October 1721 with Liddell-Bright feeling at least 'more than safe in the lottery'. Estate accounts reveal that by then a shortage of cash had once again forced him to borrow.[41]

Most income from the Sheffield estate consisted of rents; most expenditure of payments to Liddell-Bright or to others for

TABLE 24

J. Battie's Sheffield Estate Accounts, 1715–35

	Income				Outgoings			
	Rents	Others	Total	Balance	To J.L.B.	Interest	Others	Total
	£ s. d.	£ s. d.	£ s. d.	£ s. d.	£ s. d.	£ s. d.	£ s. d.	£ s. d.
1715	892.11. 6		892.11. 6	+ 22. 5. 3	823. 5. 0		47. 1. 3	870. 6. 3
1716	898. 8. 0	58.13. 5	957. 1. 5	+154.16. 3	620. 0. 0	38.10.0	143.15. 2	802. 5. 2
1717	924. 6. 6	11. 9. 3	935.15. 9	+ 75. 1. 9	770.13. 4	57.10.0	32.10. 8	860.14. 0
1718	692. 8.11	15.18. 6	708. 7. 5	+165. 2. 7	502. 0. 0		41.14.10	543.14.10
1719	631.10. 2	12. 7. 0	643.17. 2	+ 75. 6. 2	545.15. 0		22.16. 0	568.11. 0
1720	720. 8.11	34. 2. 0	754.10.11	+118.19. 5	609. 4. 0		26. 7. 5	635.11. 5
1721	678. 7.10	144.11. 6	822.19. 4	+ 98. 5. 3	678.10. 0	7.10.0	38.14. 1	724.14. 1
1722	586.19. 9		586.19. 9	+120.17. 4	390.14. 0	30. 0.0	45. 8. 5	466. 2. 5
1723	601. 7. 1		601. 7. 1	− 93. 0.11	461.10. 0	15. 0.0	31.16. 2	508. 6. 2
1724	652. 4. 0		652. 4. 0	+126. 6. 4	463. 0. 0	22.10.0	40. 7. 8	525.17. 8
1725	587. 3. 8		587. 3. 8	+ 5. 2. 7	495. 0. 0	15. 0.0	72. 1. 1	582. 1. 1
1726	694. 3. 5		694. 3. 5	+ 64. 3. 6	596. 0. 0		33.19.11	629.19.11
1727	805. 9. 8		805. 9. 8	+153. 6. 1	550. 0. 0	22.10.0	79.13. 7	652. 3. 7
1728	707.12. 7		707.12. 7	+241.11.10	378. 0. 0	45. 0.0	43. 0. 9	466. 0. 9
1729	685. 8. 1		685. 8. 1	+223. 5. 6	425. 0. 0		37. 2. 7	462. 2. 7
1730	668. 5. 9	4.13. 9	672.19. 6	+209. 0. 6	383. 4. 9	22.10.0	58. 4. 3	463.19. 0
1731	675.17. 8		675.17. 8	+194.18. 7	449. 0. 0		31.19. 1	480.19. 1
1732	713. 6. 4	24. 4. 5	737.10. 9	+ 41.13. 2	622.10. 3	45. 0.0	28. 7. 4	695.17. 7
1733	673.12. 9		673.12. 9	+ 20. 0. 0	622.13. 0		30.19. 9	653.12. 9
1734	678.18. 3	12. 6	679.10. 9	+156.10. 1	443. 0. 0	52.10.0	27.10. 8	523. 0. 8
1735	384.16. 1		384.16. 1	+240.13. 5				144. 2. 8

NOTE: As John Liddell-Bright died in 1735, only part of that year's income was due to his executors. There are no details of expenditure for 1735.

his use. Throughout these twenty years the account was in surplus, sometimes very considerably so. Surpluses were paid to Liddell-Bright, except in 1715–16 when the money was included in the following year's income. Fluctuations in rent receipts resulted from three factors. The sale of Bamforth in 1717 reduced the amount of rent due. Secondly, existing rents at Ecclesall were raised by £40 a year in 1725; as the property was professionally surveyed in that year, this may have been due to reorganization or enclosure.[42] Finally, in 1718–21 and 1727–8 the steward obtained large payments of rent arrears. From £638 in 1715 arrears fell to £20 in 1728; thereafter the annual total of arrears remained below £50. Other receipts (mainly for grazing rights) were few and small, but in 1721 the steward received £100 from wood sales, £25 for clay, and £10 for 'a parcel sold in Hedge Hogs'. Expenditure was dominated by payments to Liddell-Bright. Other payments included interest charges from 1721 onwards, chief rents, the cost of providing tenants with dinners twice yearly, and taxes. As most tenants were obliged to pay all taxes, both local and national, the amount paid by the steward in this respect was small. The latter, John Battie, received an annual salary of ten guineas and the wood warden, Fowler, one of £2. Throughout this period almost nothing was spent on repairs or improvements to property or premises. Liddell-Bright's policy was to extract a maximum amount of income from the estate at minimum cost and nothing prevented him from achieving this aim.

Overall Timothy Kiplin's accounts of the other half of the estate were in substantial surplus. Except in 1720 and 1722 surpluses were forwarded annually to Liddell-Bright; in those years they were retained as income on succeeding accounts. Only in the last account of the series was a fairly substantial deficit recorded. There is no indication of whether this adverse trend continued. Here too rents constituted the major source of income, though there were marked fluctuations in receipts. Existing rents at Billingley were improved in 1716, while subsequently Great Houghton did not appear on the rental, having become vested in Thomas Liddell-Bright by the family settlement of that year. Moreover, like his opposite number at Sheffield, Kiplin was very successful in reducing rent arrears – in his case from £336 in 1715 to £20 in 1723. The other major

item of income was the money sent from Sheffield by Battie.
However, only some of this came to Kiplin, the rest being
directed to Liddell-Bright or to others for his use. Of the
substantial amounts received from sales all but £60 in 1717 for
'beasts and wool' came from wood sales. In 1721 and 1723 other
income came in part from the surpluses of previous accounts.
However, both then and in 1718 it also consisted of sums
received from various individuals. There is no way of discover-
ing of what these sums consisted; they may have been payments
for wood or beasts, or they may have been loans. The expenditure section of Kiplin's accounts graphically illustrates the
extent to which Dame Susannah Newton's annuity continued
to dominate family finances. Payments to her formed the largest
single item in either series of accounts. Interest payments in
1715 and 1717 were for those debts which were finally cleared
following the sale of Bamforth. In 1718 £206 was disbursed for
wood, clients' demands in this regard only being met by sub-
contracting. Other expenditure came under the heading of
'Family Payments', concerning which the accounts yield few
details. Besides annual outpayments from the estate, they must
have included the bulk of domestic expenditure. They also
comprised the cost of Cordelia Liddell-Bright's stay in London
in the early 1720s and the expenses connected with the schooling of one of her brothers at Sedbergh.

These accounts undoubtedly present an incomplete picture
of Liddell-Bright's circumstances. From 1723, just at the point
where Kiplin's account recorded its first sizeable deficit in
nearly a decade, there is only a partial account of the smaller half
of the estate. The almost total lack of information relating to
Badsworth is doubly unfortunate. Rents due there fell from
£567 in 1718 to £449 in 1722, and were only £526 in 1732. In
January 1732 a correspondent informed Liddell-Bright: 'I hear
there is a great call for woollen manufactures. I hope your wool
will thereby advance in price.' In the absence of the sale of part
of Badsworth this information indicates that he was engaged in
direct farming there. Other sources hint at further developments. For £28 in 1735 Liddell-Bright purchased a parcel of
land adjacent to his 'enclosed lands ... in Badsworth'.
Moreover, in 1752 the rector of Badsworth, speaking of the
period before 1748, said that: 'I found that such quantities of

TABLE 25

T. Kiplin's Badsworth Estate Accounts, 1715–23

Income	Rents	From Battie & J. L. Bright	Sales	Others	Total
	£ s. d.	£ s. d.	£ s. d.	£ s. d.	£ s. d.
1715	1242.13.7	50. 0.0	381.12.0		1674. 5. 7
1716	920. 9.11		103. 5.0		1023.14.11
1717	967.17.10	300. 0.0	325. 0.7	28. 6. 4	1621. 4. 9
1718	954. 3. 2	270. 0.0	1. 0.6	207. 5. 0	1432. 8. 8
1719	872.17. 6	100. 0.0	264. 6.0	20.17. 0	1258. 0. 6
1720	864.14.10	308. 0.0		4.18. 6	1177.13. 4
1721	858. 7. 2	437.16.6		253. 3. 4	1549. 7. 0
1722	863. 7.10	477.14.5		18. 2.10	1360. 5. 1
1723	865.10. 2	200. 0.0		262. 4. 7	1327.14. 9

Outgoings	To Sir J. Newton	Interest & Incidental	Family	Total	Balance
	£ s. d.	£ s. d.	£ s. d.	£ s. d.	£ s. d.
1715	1233.18. 0	75. 0.0	200.14.6	1508.12. 6	+ 165.13. 1
1716	542. 0. 1		381. 0.0	923. 0. 1	+ 100.14.10
1717	941.19. 6	200. 0.0	470. 0.9	1612. 0. 3	+ 9. 4. 6
1718	770. 0. 0	206. 0.0	459.11.0	1435.11. 0	− 3. 2. 4
1719	900. 0. 0		358.13.3	1258.13. 3	− 12. 9
1720	707. 0. 0		318. 2.6	1025. 2. 6	+ 152.10.10
1721	1097.14. 9		339.19.4	1437.14. 1	+ 111.12.10
1722	892.19. 5		418. 0.5	1310.19.10	+ 49. 5. 3
1723	1000.15. 7		405.14.4	1406. 9.11	− 78.15. 2

Sources: BR 158–165.

land had of late years been enclosed from the common corn fields and laid down to grass that the tithes of corn ... were reduced in their value.' Scattered rentals suggest that this enclosure took place between 1732, when rents due at Badsworth were £526, and 1740, when they amounted to £715. It would appear, therefore, that Liddell-Bright initiated, if he did not complete, a substantial amount of enclosure at Badsworth. Together with direct farming, this resulted in a large increase in his income from that part of the estate. Furthermore, although estate accounts indicate that wood sales provided much income, they do not reveal the full extent to which timber resources were exploited. According to Battie's accounts, sales of wood from the Sheffield estate were negligible in the 1720s. Another source, however, records the receipt of £1,671 between 1720 and 1728 'for spring wood sold out of Ecclesall woods'. In 1719 Liddell-Bright was faced with heavy demands for wood which he was only able to meet because he had timber supplies in places other than Ecclesall. In that year he agreed to supply another ironmaster with wood from Great Houghton, and in 1720 was engaged in valuing wood at Wincobank near Sheffield. Kiplin's receipts may have included money from sales from these properties, but may not have been fully inclusive of such sales. It is at least certain that wood sales were much greater than the estate accounts suggest. Finally, there remains the further possibility that other sources of income were excluded from those listed in these accounts.[43]

Despite its inadequacies, available information permits one to draw firm conclusions about Liddell-Bright's performance as a landowner. Clearly, he pursued a variety of policies which enabled him to maximize his income. Besides exploiting timber resources on a large scale, he greatly reduced rent arrears without paying more than a trivial proportion of the taxes levied on his property. Expansion, consolidation, and enclosure produced a substantial increase in his rental. He spent little on repairs but from the outset of his career afforded efficient supervision of his estates. He also practised a considerable amount of direct farming at Badsworth; in later years at least this was on a marketable scale. All this points to his being capable and energetic. Contemporaries certainly respected his abilities as a landowner. His brother, George Liddell, frequently solicited his advice on matters of estate management. And when Lord Irwin went abroad for two years he asked Liddell-Bright, who agreed, to manage the huge Temple Newsam estate during his absence.[44] Yet although successful landownership eased his financial difficulties, it did not solve them and, within a few years of the sale of Bamforth, he again became indebted. The size of this second series of loans was never great but they remained unpaid at his death. Moreover, by 1731 Liddell-Bright was once more experiencing difficulty in paying Dame Susannah Newton's jointure. By this time he was a sick as well as an impecunious man, whereas 'Lady Newton who is old enough to be your mother ... has neither gout nor stone nor other distemper but old age'. In spite of his many efforts, Liddell-Bright was unable to solve his balance of payments problem simply because he failed to outlive this remarkably resilient woman. Furthermore, at his death in 1735 the portions of his younger children had yet to be paid. He was evidently confident of future prospects because, though a son had died young since 1716, he disposed in his will of the full £12,000 then set aside for younger children. There was, indeed, some justification for confidence: Dame Susannah's death was inevitable, and his prospective heir, Thomas, had married a local heiress in 1734. The latter's fortune consisted not only of real estate, but also of £16,000 in cash. She had still to receive most of this in 1735 but that she would eventually do so was not doubted. For the present it remained necessary to exercise restraint and Liddell-Bright's will restricted the cost of his funeral to £50.[45]

Between the death of Sir John Bright in 1688 and that of his fourth wife in 1737 a sum in excess of £55,000 was paid in jointure moneys from the revenue of the Bright estates – which had an annual income of between £2,300 and £3,000 throughout the same period. In meeting these demands John Liddell-Bright avoided selling any of the property which he had inherited. Indeed he was able to add to and improve it. A lucrative marriage, however troublesome, proved very helpful. For the rest he had to tighten his belt and set about increasing his income as best he could. In achieving this he survived at least one period of extravagance – his venture into politics – and another of downright misfortune – his flirtation with the funds.

He also weathered a host of other difficulties, most of which stemmed from his marriage to Cordelia Clutterbuck. For assistance he looked to the mortgage market and to his abilities as a landowner. He bequeathed liability for the unpaid portions of his younger children to his successor, but this was much less of a financial burden than he himself had inherited. His experiences illustrate the inherent strength of a real estate economy at a time when long-term credit was readily available. Moreover, his personal achievement, though not without blemish, was considerable.

4. THE AFTERMATH 1735–52

Thomas Bright waited until middle age before marrying Margaret Norton in 1734 and succeeding his father in 1735. His wife's portion, both actual and prospective, was not only large but particularly valuable from the Bright's point of view because, besides cash, it included property adjacent to Badsworth. By his will of 1729 Margaret's uncle, John Lowther, had left her a moiety of his estate of Ackworth Park. He also bequeathed legacies of £5,000 each to Margaret and her sister, Dorothy; when the latter died young Margaret became entitled to the entire £10,000. By her parents' marriage settlement Margaret was provided with a portion of £4,000; she also received a legacy of £2,000 by the will of her great-grandfather. Thus, her fortune comprised the moiety of Ackworth Park plus £16,000.[46]

Payment of Dame Susannah Newton's annuity of £1,000 ceased at her death in April 1737. Furthermore, those properties which Sir John Bright had granted her for life – Barnby, Totley, and the fee farm rents purchased in 1681 – then reverted to Thomas Bright, adding £320 to his annual rental. None of these developments, however, prevented the family's history from being one of continuing financial difficulty. At his death in 1739 Thomas was 'greatly indebted'; even after the sale of personal estate £5,200 of his debts remained undischarged. In addition the portions of his brother and sisters had still to be raised. Several factors were responsible for this situation. Outgoings continued to be very heavy. Besides the money devoted to the discharge of John Liddell-Bright's debts, the Newton annuity had to be paid until April 1737. From 1735 onwards interest at an annual rate of $4\frac{1}{2}$ per cent on unrealized portions had to be disbursed; this alone amounted annually to £495. Moreover, Margaret Bright was unable for many years to claim most of her huge fortune. She was entitled to the moiety of Ackworth Park only after the death of her aunt, Mary Lowther, who lived for many years after John Lowther's death. Furthermore, the property was burdened with John Lowther's debts, with miscellaneous legacies of £1,210, with a life annuity of £100 to a Mr Shippen, and also with a legacy of £6,000 to Mary Lowther. These heavy liabilities had precedence over Margaret's own legacy of £10,000, while Mary Lowther's longevity prevented her succession to the property. Thomas Bright died before the latter became possible.[47]

However, before her marriage Margaret had received the legacy of £2,000 from her great-grandfather and, following a Chancery lawsuit which ended in 1737, her portion of £4,000 was paid. Thomas's annual income from the estates rose by £200 on his marriage; he inherited the other properties in 1735 and 1737 respectively. In the light of these developments the outpayments listed above do not in themselves account for his 'great' indebtedness in 1739. There are two possible additional explanations. After his succession he may simply have lived extravagantly; the lack of contemporary accounts makes it impossible either to verify or to deny this. Secondly, his income before marriage may have been insufficient for his needs, resulting in indebtedness prior to the rise in his income outlined above. Between 1716 and 1734 his sole annual income was £300 from property in Great Houghton. Had his father had more money there is no doubt that he would have been considerably better provided for.[48]

Yet Thomas's debts and the unpaid portions formed only part of the difficult situation inherited by his successor. The only issue of Thomas and Margaret's marriage was a daughter, Mary, so in 1739 the Bright estates passed to Thomas's younger brother, John, by the settlement of 1716. At that point the property became burdened with Margaret's jointure of £500 a year. Moreover, taking advantage of a right vested in him in 1716, Thomas had granted Mary a portion of £5,000 by his will.[49] This too was to be raised from the Bright estates. By 1739, therefore, the property had become liable to annual outpayments in interest and jointure moneys of some £995, and for unrealized portions amounting to £16,000. If John Bright died childless, and he was unmarried in 1739, the estate would pass for the first time to a woman, Mary Bright. The fact that she was likely to inherit the residue of her mother's as yet unrealized fortune after the latter's death in no way compensated for the fact that the Bright estates would pass out of the family at Mary's marriage.

Although John Bright succeeded in 1739, responsibility for the unpaid debts and portions became vested by Thomas's will in three trustees, of whom John was one. The others were Dame Margaret, Thomas's widow, and his uncle, Sir Henry Liddell, later Lord Ravensworth. Their first task was the payment of Thomas's legacies, which were small, and the discharge of his debts, which were substantial. Only after this was completed could they proceed to raise portions, firstly for John Liddell-Bright's younger children, and then for Mary Bright, who was still a minor. The trustees seem largely to have ignored Thomas's will. Realizing that the proceeds of the sale of his personal estate would be insufficient to cover his debts, Thomas had stipulated that real estate should be sold to complete their discharge. The trustees did not even sell all his personal estate; they retained £350 worth of it at Badsworth. They also avoided the sale of real estate, converting £5,200 of Thomas's debts by borrowing £1,200 on bonds, and by raising two mortgages – one for £3,000 and another for £1,000 – on the security of the property which had reverted to him in 1737. Despite this increase in total indebtedness, they felt sufficiently unconcerned to lend £500 at interest in 1740. This lack of urgency persisted. Although the bonds and the £1,000 mortgage were redeemed before John Bright's death in 1748, the other mortgage was assigned and remained unpaid until 1755. Inevitably this caused further delay in the raising of portions. None of the £12,000 due by the 1716 settlement had been raised by 1748; by then John Bright was dead and his sisters were well into middle age.[50]

Unfortunately, the estate accounts which deal with the decade following Thomas Bright's death are far from complete. They indicate that income from the Sheffield estate at least was maintained at a high level. They reveal no general increases in

TABLE 26
Bright Estate Accounts, 1739–50

Income	Rents	Wood	Others	Total
	£ s. d.	£ s. d.	£ s. d.	£ s. d.
1739	1994.18. 9	100. 0. 0		2094.18. 9
1740	2108.18.10	87. 7. 0	100. 0.0	2296. 5.10
1741	2066.13. 6		20. 0.0	2086.13. 6
1742	2040.12.10	172. 0. 0	20. 0.0	2232.12.10
		Sheffield Estate Only		
1743	651. 2. 0		20. 0.0	671. 2. 0
1744	730.12. 7	62.10. 0	32. 4.0	825. 6. 7
1745	733. 8. 4	421. 0. 0		1154. 8. 4
1746	679.13. 1			679.13. 1
1747	693. 8. 5		25.19.0	719. 7. 5
1748	763. 6. 7	29. 0. 0	12.0	792.18. 7
1749	688.17. 5	235. 0. 0	201.12.0	1125. 9. 5
1750	713.10. 0	225. 0. 0	26.10.8	965. 0. 8

Outgoings	London	Country	Total	Balance
	£ s. d.	£ s. d.	£ s. d.	£ s. d.
1739	825. 0. 0	1077. 8. 8	1902. 8.8	+ 192.10. 1
1740	967.10. 0	1115.19. 9	2083. 9.9	+ 212.16. 1
1741	1150. 0. 0	844. 0. 8	1994. 0.8	+ 92.12.10
1742	950. 0. 0	1238.13. 2	2188.13.2	+ 43.19. 8
	To J.L.B.	Sheffield Estate Only		
1743	200. 0. 0	307. 4. 3	507. 4.3	+ 163.17. 9
1744	200. 0. 0	315. 4. 0	515. 4.0	+ 310. 2. 7
1745	500. 0. 0	323. 2. 2	823. 2.2	+ 331. 6. 2
1746	200. 0. 0	303. 4. 5	503. 4.5	+ 176. 8. 8
1747		260.15. 5	260.15.5	+ 458.12. 0
1748	589. 4. 9	203.13.10	792.18.7	
1749	300. 0. 0	800.12. 3	1100.12.3	+ 24.17. 2
1750	450. 0. 0	490. 9. 8	940. 9.8	+ 24.11. 0

Sources: BR 137–148.

rents, though arrears, which were mainly responsible for fluctuations in receipts, were never very high. There was a steady income from the sale of grazing rights and large sums continued to accrue from wood sales. Because these accounts deal very summarily with outgoings, it is impossible to analyse John Bright's personal expenditure. He apparently dictated policy to the other trustees, as was perhaps inevitable, and his extravagance and/or lack of urgency were responsible for the slow rate at which liabilities were reduced. As Dame Margaret's jointure was accounted for separately, the only regular outpayments besides taxes and salaries were interest payments on loans and portions. By this time these amounted to between £700 and £800 annually. With a high income, no family, and in the light of his father's experience, John ought to have been able to make principal repayments in excess of £2,500, but failed to do so. Perhaps his sisters were content to receive annual instalments of interest, though this is difficult to believe of Catherine who married in 1743. The slow rate at which capital sums were realized probably accounts for her marrying a doctor, and for her sisters remaining, and dying, unmarried. When John himself died childless and unmarried in 1748, the estates passed to Mary Bright who was still a minor.[51]

In that year Dame Margaret Bright was married again, to Sir John Ramsden of Byram. She and Lord Ravensworth were now jointly responsible for the discharge of debts and the raising of portions. But in practice Sir John, as Mary's guardian and the husband of one of the trustees, took charge of family affairs. The payments problem which confronted him was formidable. With Mary Bright approaching a marriageable age progress towards a final solution was more than ever necessary. Judging property to be the most valuable part of Mary's prospective fortune, Sir John eliminated the sale of real estate as a means of raising capital. He too turned instead to the mortgage market. In 1749, after paying John's small legacies, he raised a mortgage for £2,000. This covered John's own portion which he had bequeathed in equal shares to his three sisters. Sir John then raised a further mortgage for £3,000 which he granted to Anne Bright as her portion. In May 1750 he paid £1,000 of Cordelia's portion of £3,000 from the estate revenues; she continued to receive interest on the remaining sum. Finally, in December 1750 Sir John raised another mortgage for £3,000 which Catherine Wintringham received as her portion.[52]

All these mortgages were raised on the security of the Badsworth estate. More importantly, they were at an annual interest rate of 4 per cent, $\frac{1}{2}$ per cent less than the previous rate on the unrealized portions. The cost of the family's inability to provide these capital sums was thereby lowered. Albeit belatedly, John Liddell-Bright's younger children received their due and his real estate remained intact. However, Sir John reserved the right to discharge remaining debts by the sale of property. Thus, within a short period he was responsible for a marked improvement in the family's situation. Fortunes remained dogged by the results of Sir John Bright's final dispositions, but at least their lasting effects were mitigated and measureable progress made. Moreover, future prospects took a dramatic upward turn when Mary Bright caught the eye of one of Britain's most eligible bachelors.

5. A NEW DEPARTURE 1752–6c

In May 1751 a contemporary noted that 'Lord Rockingham had made some visits to Miss Bright and very probably it would be a match'. Having succeeded his father in the previous year, Charles Watson Wentworth, 2nd Marquess of Rockingham, was then twenty-one years old. His main estate was at Wentworth Woodhouse in south Yorkshire where, under Rockingham's father, Flitcroft had begun to build a huge palladian mansion. He also owned extensive property at Malton in the North Riding, at Milton and Great Harrowden in Northamptonshire, and in County Wicklow in Ireland. Net annual income from these estates amounted to £14,000. Within a century his family were to become, if they had not already done so, the twelfth largest landowners in the United Kingdom.[53]

Mary Bright was regarded as one of the wealthiest heiresses in the north, but Rockingham's lawyers were somewhat dismayed when they discovered that her fortune was more prospective than actual. The Bright estates were burdened, not only with Dame Margaret's jointure and with the remainder of Thomas Bright's debts, but also with the mortgages raised to pay portions, and with the remaining £2,000 of Cordelia Bright's portion. All these had precedence over the raising of Mary Bright's own portion of £5,000. Moreover, property might yet have to be sold to discharge these debts and, by Thomas Bright's will, Mary Bright was only entitled to the residue of any purchase money after her mother's death. In addition Dame

Margaret had sold her reversion to the moiety of Ackworth Park. As Mary Lowther was still alive £12,000 was still owing to Dame Margaret by John Lowther's will. This had been settled on Mary Bright but she was only entitled to it if she or her issue survived her mother. Fearful that the marriage negotiations might break down, Sir John and Dame Margaret Ramsden agreed that, irrespective of the strict terms of the trusteeship, Mary should immediately after the marriage enjoy the profits of most of the Bright estates subject, nevertheless, to Dame

TABLE 27

Badsworth Estate Accounts, 1750–60

Income	Rents	Last Balance	Total	Current Balance
	£ s. d.	£ s. d.	£ s. d.	£ s. d.
1750–51	1447.13.11½	37.14. 6	1485. 8. 5½	+ 32. 9.11
1751–52	1647.17. 5½	32. 3. 6	1680. 0.11½	+ 58. 1. 9¾
1752–53	1648. 8. 0½	58. 1. 9¾	1706. 9.10¼	+ 84.14. 9¾
1753–54	1448. 1. 7	84.14. 9¾	1532.16. 4¾	+ 59.16. 5¾
1754–55	1548. 5. 9½	59.16. 5¾	1608. 2. 3¼	+ 356. 7. 7¾
1755–56	1548.18. 4½	356. 7. 7¾	1905. 6. 0¼	+ 287. 5. 4¾
1756–57	1552.17. 1	287. 5. 4¾	1840. 2. 5¾	+ 344.10. 4¾
1757–58	1548. 5. 9½	334.10. 4¾	1882.16. 2¼	+ 331.10. 9¾
1758–59	1649. 1. 4½	331.10. 9¾	1980.12. 2¼	+ 365. 7. 1¼
1759–60	1548. 2. 1	365. 7. 1¼	1913. 9. 2¼	+ 427. 4. 8¼

Outgoings	To Rockingham	Extraordinary	Rest	Total
	£ s. d.	£ s. d.	£ s. d.	£ s. d.
1750–51		1280. 0. 0	172.18. 6½	1452.18. 6½
1751–52	300. 0. 0	1160. 0. 0	161.19. 1¾	1621.19. 1¾
1752–53	1396.10. 0	63.10. 0	161.15. 0½	1621.15. 0½
1753–54	1300. 0. 0		172.19.11	1472.19.11
1754–55	1100. 0. 0		151.14. 7½	1251.14. 7½
1755–56	1400. 0. 0	52.10. 0	165.10. 7½	1618. 0. 7½
1756–57	1330. 0. 0		175.12. 1	1505.12. 1
1757–58	1200. 0. 0	126. 5. 1	225. 0. 3½	1551. 5. 4½
1758–59	1330. 0. 0	83.18.11	237. 6. 2	1651. 5. 1
1759–60	1300. 0. 0		186. 4. 6	1486. 4. 6

NOTE: Extraordinary Payments 1750–2 were to Sir John Ramsden.

Sources: WWM.A. 746–755.

Margaret's jointure and to the portion debts. They were to retain those properties which had reverted in 1737 and to hold responsibility for the discharge of Thomas Bright's debts. In return Lord Rockingham granted Mary £500 a year in pin money from his estates, and £2,000 from his estates and £1,000 from the Bright estates as a jointure after his death. The couple were married on 26 February 1752 when Rockingham was twenty-one and Mary Bright sixteen years of age.[54]

Sir John Ramsden sold Barnby in 1755 to clear the remaining mortgage for £3,000 of Thomas Bright's debts. The residue of the purchase price of £6,400 passed to Dame Margaret by her first husband's will. Meanwhile, interest payments on the other debts continued. A mortgage for £600 of the remaining £2,000 of Cordelia's portion was raised in 1757 on the security of the Badsworth estate. This and the other mortgages were assigned to new sources of capital from time to time but none were redeemed for many years after 1760.[55] Interest payments were by now comparatively small in relation to total net income from the Bright estates, and negligible when compared with Lord Rockingham's earnings. Full accounts of the Bright estates minus Dame Margaret's jointure lands and the property which had reverted in 1737 are extant for the period 1750–60. Income continued to be derived mainly from rent receipts, which fluctuated only as a result of movements in arrears. However, large sums continued to be raised from wood sales in Sheffield. As it had long been a non-residential property, expenditure at Sheffield had always been small. Miscellaneous expenditure there, which consisted almost exclusively of annual outpayments, rarely exceed £60 annually. Interest payments on debts, which amounted to around £400 a year throughout this period, were discharged from this account. The residue, including surpluses not added to subsequent accounts, were paid to Sir John Ramsden before the marriage, and to Lord Rockingham thereafter. With the major exception of interest payments the pattern of expenditure at Badsworth was very similar to that at Sheffield. Miscellaneous outgoings were higher because Badsworth Hall was not let and had to be maintained. Besides annual outpayments, they included £65 a year for house servants' wages and £25 a year for the upkeep of the gardens. There were also extraordinary items, such as the post fine of £64 for Badsworth manor in 1752–3, and a bounty of £53 to a tenant in 1755–6 to cover his losses from cattle plague. Other items covered the cost of Lord Rockingham's short and infrequent visits to Badsworth. After his marriage the remaining income, by far the greater part, was sent to him in cash. Thus, the Bright estates became part of the vast economic network of one of the nation's chief rentiers. These accounts were the last vestige of their separate identity, which quickly disappeared after Mary's marriage. From 1760 both properties were administered from Wentworth Woodhouse.

TABLE 28
Sheffield Estate Accounts, 1750–60

Income	Rents	Wood & Misc.	Total	Balance
	£ s. d.	£ s. d.	£ s. d.	£ s. d.
1750	713.10. 0	251.10.8	965. 0. 8	+ 24.11. 0
1751	711. 6. 2	27. 9.0	738.15. 2	+ 271.13. 0
1752	686. 3. 2	2. 8.0	688.11. 2	− 23. 4. 7
1753	695.11. 2	1. 7.0	696.18. 2	+ 237. 2.10
1754	704.12. 5	6. 7.0	710.19. 5	+ 13. 4. 0
1755	699.10. 8	13.0	700. 3. 8	+ 57.14. 0
1756	690. 7. 3	688.17.0	1379. 4. 3	+ 3.16. 6
1757	703. 2. 8	350.17.6	1054. 0. 2	+ 13.16. 3
1758	746.10.10	301.12.6	1048. 3. 4	+ 35.14. 9½
1759	732.16. 8	500.19.0	1233.15. 8	− 7.13.10
1760	689. 2. 8	17.6	690. 0. 2	+ 298.10. 7

Outgoings	Interest	To Sir J.R.	Rest	Total
	£ s. d.	£ s. d.	£ s. d.	£ s. d.
1750	442.15. 8	450. 0.0	47.14. 0	940. 9. 8
1751	400. 0. 0		67. 2. 2	467. 2. 2
1752	400. 0. 0		311.15. 9	711.15. 9
1753	400. 0. 0	To Rockingham	59.14. 4	459.14. 4
1754	400. 0. 0	262.10.0	35. 5. 5	697.15. 5
1755	400. 0. 0	200. 0.0	42. 9. 8	642. 9. 8
1756	400. 0. 0	910. 0.0	65. 7. 9	1375. 7. 9
1757	400. 0. 0	600. 0.0	40.13.11	1040.13.11
1758	405.11. 9	500. 0.0	106.16. 9½	1012. 8. 6½
1759	400. 0. 0	800. 0.0	41. 9. 6	1241. 9. 6
1760	339.13. 5		51.16. 2	391. 9. 7

Sources: WWM.A. 699–718.

Besides being rich, Lord Rockingham was successful. In 1751 he had been appointed Lord Lieutenant of the East and North Ridings, and Lord of the Bedchamber to George II. In 1760 he was dubbed a Knight of the Garter. During the ascendancy of the Earl of Bute after 1762 he led a section of the Whig opposition. In 1765 he formed his first administration which, however, only survived for a year. After a further and lengthier period in opposition he again became Prime Minister in 1782, only to die in July of the same year. Though there is no evidence that this process began before 1760, the gross annual income from the Bright estates nearly doubled between Rockingham's marriage and his death. This was largely due to the contemporary rise in food prices which enabled landlords greatly to increase their rents. However, Rockingham earned a formidable reputation as an efficient and improving landowner, being elected to a Fellowship of the Royal Society for his services to agriculture. Arthur Young 'never saw the advantages of a great fortune applied so nobly to the improvement of' estates as at Wentworth Woodhouse. By the turn of the century the gross income from the Bright estates was four times what it had been in 1752. Mary survived both her husband and her mother, dying in 1804. Eventually she had succeeded to the residue of Dame Margaret's fortune. As her own marriage was childless the Bright estates, together with the rest of the Rockingham property, passed to her nephew, William, Earl Fitzwilliam.[56]

There were three distinct phases in the history of the Brights of Carbrook and Badsworth during this period. Before 1688 they met with almost unqualified success. Between 1688 and 1752, faced with a variety of difficulties which rendered their financial situation somewhat precarious, they tackled their problems with varying degrees of skill and resolution without finally solving them. Mary Bright's marriage in 1752 provided a solution, but only at the cost of annihilating the family's separate identity.

The careers of Stephen and Sir John Bright were remarkably successful. They support the view that the land market remained active throughout the seventeenth century. Throughout the entire period 1619–88 the Bright estates were steadily expanded. Moreover, this process was far from haphazard, being simultaneously one of consolidation. Once established in the Sheffield area, Sir John acquired and developed a country estate elsewhere with comparable success. As significant as the accumulation of real estate was the manner in which this was brought about. Activity in the money market frequently preceded purchases of substantial amounts of landed property. The full effects of the recognition of the equity of mortgage redemption only manifested themselves towards the end of the century. In the meantime Sir John took full advantage of the prevailing uncertainty. Both father and son were lucky in their gains at the expense of the Arundels. Moreover, by fighting on the victorious side during the Civil War Sir John reaped benefits which were substantial and permanent. But, besides stemming from good fortune and the flow of events, the success of both men reflected their abilities. Both their private and public activities reveal vigour, skill, and purpose in breadth. Only Sir John's venture in the coal trade can be described as a comparative failure. This was due more to the deficiencies of his situation and of the age in which he lived than to any lack of enterprise on his part. Despite heavy transport costs, Sir John farmed directly but was quick to reduce his commitments in this respect according to current market conditions. Both he and his father were chiefly rentiers. Even without rent improvements, the buying and leasing of land was for them a safe and most lucrative form of investment. Apart from being economically worthwhile, such investment also brought social prestige. Their careers illustrate that there was no surer method of increasing status than by acquiring real estate. Socially the rise in their fortunes was proportionate to their success as landowners.

Once a large estate had been accumulated good management could overcome serious and protracted financial difficulties without either loss of property or much diminution in prestige. John Liddell-Bright was able to boost his income because rent increases had been few during previous decades, and because there was scope for the rationalization of existing tenancies. Moreover, he and his successors took great advantage of their ability to supply fuel to local ironmasters, while home farming was indirectly, if not directly, profitable. A tight control over expenditure resulted in the imposition of an unusually heavy tax burden on the tenantry. But few of the resulting rent arrears were written off and many were collected in succeeding years. Additional capital was raised in the mortgage market. Though interest payments increased costs, repayment of principal could be, and was, postponed indefinitely. By the eighteenth century the discharge of debts by the sale of real estate was a last resort. Only in 1755, after decades of financial stringency, did the Brights sell Barnby. They could have avoided doing so even then but it was expedient to sell property which had only reverted to them some fifty years after Sir John Bright's death, and which, consisting of ironworks, was not an integral part of their economy. Thus, the history of the Brights after 1688 shows that a landowner, if he owned a moderately sized estate, had no need, unless he was over ambitious or faced with crushing problems, to look beyond his landed property for a means of maintaining his position. If they arose, opportunities for diversification sometimes demanded skills and experience which were not forthcoming, as was the case when John Liddell-Bright ventured into the unfamiliar world of pure finance.

The debts which remained from preceeding generations were of little significance to someone of Lord Rockingham's vast wealth. Unfortunately, however, Mary Bright's marriage to him resulted in the disappearance of the Brights as a separate family entity. This was ironic, firstly because marriage into the aristocracy was in one sense their greatest achievement, and secondly because marriage had been an important factor in the rise of their fortunes. The money and property which Stephen and Sir John Bright gained by their marriages were very substantial. John Liddell-Bright's marriage immersed him in legal difficulties but also provided him with much-needed capital. Thomas Bright married very successfully too. Even though his wife's inheritance took a long time to materialize, the promise of it encouraged Rockingham to marry Mary Bright. But a bride's fortune had to be matched by suitable provision for her jointure. If she pre-deceased her husband, as was the case with at least five Bright wives, the jointure was never paid. However, there was no means of telling for how long a widow might live and, therefore, for how long a jointure might remain payable. After 1688 the Brights suffered heavily in this respect. By granting property for life, a large legacy, and a heavy jointure to Dame Susannah, Sir John Bright made huge demands on his successors, especially as his daughter-in-law's jointure remained payable for twenty years after his death. Moreover, Dame Margaret received a jointure of £500 for decades after Thomas Bright's death, while waiting to succeed to her own inheritance.

Nevertheless, the major criterion by which the success of a marriage was judged was whether or not it produced a male heir. The Brights' failure to do so on the two occasions when it mattered most played a crucial part in their history. Whether Sir John Bright would have settled the whole of his estate on a son and heir had he been able to do so is uncertain, for he arranged for Carbrook and Edale to pass to his nephew even before the death of his two sons. Yet Sir John frequently revoked settlements and the final disposition of his property would almost certainly have been less disadvantageous to the main branch of the family had he not been forced to regard a daughter's child as his male heir. Thomas and John Bright's failure to produce male heirs was even more significant. There was then no viable alternative to the estates becoming vested in an unmarried daughter and niece and, therefore, to their passing out of the family on her marriage. The only consolation in this situation, and it was disproportionately small, was that of all factors in a family's fortunes procreation was the least predictable and the least manageable.

VI

CONCLUSION

I. THE IMPACT OF THE INDIVIDUAL

After a succession of detailed studies of particular families the prevailing impression, almost inevitably, is of the extent to which personal behaviour influenced dynastic fortunes. The previous four chapters consist largely of a record of individual triumphs, mediocrities, and failures, so firmly did the performance of their respective leaders govern the policies pursued and the circumstances enjoyed by these families. Nor is there reason to suppose that the production of further case-studies would create a substantially different impression.

To emphasize a single factor such as the impact of the individual is, of course, to run the risk of distorting or over-simplifying historical reality. Individual baronets or their successors, though very much in the forefront of family affairs, often remain shadowy figures. The sources only rarely permit the clear delineation of personality traits; and character cannot be analysed by picking up an action or an opinion here and there and tying them in a bundle. Moreover, although character and personality can be assumed to have had a pervasive influence on behaviour, it is also true that no man, perhaps more especially in economic and social matters, was an island. Some individuals can clearly be seen in the process of changing their circumstances; but, even in what is otherwise a detailed history, it is difficult to identify the extent to which circumstances changed individuals. And yet no one passed through time and its accidents and remained unchanged. It is, therefore, hazardous to attempt to draw too fine a distinction between character on the one hand and circumstance on the other. It is nevertheless necessary to consider the question of the impact of the individual at some length and in the context of the Yorkshire baronetage as a whole.

The one factor which has been most commonly discussed in

this connection is the use of strict settlements from the mid seventeenth century onwards. This undoubtedly limited the ability of many owners to alienate, encumber, or otherwise mismanage real estate; and did so not just because strict settlements created merely life-tenancies, but also because they restricted a life-tenant's powers of leasing or mortgaging his property. As research has progressed, however, it has tended to suggest (and the present evidence would support this) that the spread and the consequences of the use of strict settlements have been the subject of some exaggeration and misinterpretation.[1] This has resulted partly, perhaps, from the concentration of much early work on the fortunes of aristocratic landowners; if the peerage adopted strict settlements quickly, and thereafter executed them with a high degree of consistency, it does not necessarily follow that less substantial landowners behaved in a similar fashion. Even in the case of the peerage, however, the full significance of certain factors has only recently been appreciated. For example, opportunities for evading or negating settlements arose regularly and, in any case, could be created without undue difficulty; the pattern of events within families often rendered the strictest of settlements obsolete; and, although strict settlements facilitated, indeed encouraged, primogeniture, there was no absolute conjunction between the two. For many decades after their introduction strict settlements were used widely but by no means universally. As late as the nineteenth century there remained, especially in more remote areas, a substantial amount of property to which they had not been applied. Some property by its very nature could not always be included in settlements, however strict – long-term, undervalued, and therefore lucrative leases from the Crown and other institutions, for example. Moreover, as three of the case-studies illustrate, voluntary dispersals of freehold property were not uncommon. Some of this property never reverted to the main branches of families; and where the reversion of property was provided for and did take place, it often came about only after a lapse of many years.

The case-studies provide several instances in the post-Restoration period of settlements which were less than strict, some considerably so; as well as instances where, under the pressure of events, settlements were either modified or reversed. Sir John Hotham, the second baronet, planned to leave certain properties to his second son, Robert. But the latter's death, followed by his own, and then by the decline and death of Sir John's eldest son, necessitated a complete reformulation of policy under which the entire estate devolved on a cousin. The Beaumonts split their estate in 1631 and again in 1668. Whitley and Lascelles Hall were later reunited, but only in circumstances which eventually led to the latter's alienation. Because he accumulated property throughout his career, and married four times without being able to produce a direct male heir, Sir John Bright executed numerous settlements, repeatedly altering his dispositions as his circumstances changed. In the end he divided his estate between a grandson and a nephew, though settlement was strict in each case. Although alone of these four families the Constables consistently endeavoured to implement strict settlements, they nevertheless relinquished four freehold properties between 1650 and 1720, and apparently resisted the alienation of only one of these. Whether purchased property was strictly settled, or for that matter settled at all, depended entirely on the policy of the purchaser; until it was settled it was alienable at will. The eventual need to re-settle property, which arose at least once in every generation, provided owners with the opportunity to exclude property from settlement if the freedom to dispose of it in some other way was judged to be necessary. The case-studies also indicate that the purchase, reversion, or inheritance of property in between settlements was frequently sufficient to meet such needs. Sir Charles Hotham, the fourth baronet, raised his mortgages partly on the security of the property at Filingdales, which reverted to him after the death of Durand Hotham, and of all his eleven children. Following Dame Susannah Newton's death her jointure lands were available to the Liddell-Brights, while after his second marriage in 1748 Richard Beaumont was able to raise substantial loans on the security of Mitton and Grizzlehurst. As indeed happened in the last two of these cases, such property could also be sold. Even where an entire estate was subject to strict settlement, as was the case with the Lascelles Hall property until 1705, a life-tenant could conspire with his son, if the latter was of age, to break the entail. Only by this means was Richard Beaumont junior able at short notice to raise a substantial part of Lady Westmorland's legacy by the sale of Lascelles Hall in 1714. Alternatively, a life tenant could achieve the same aim independently by private act of Parliament.

As long as a strictly settled estate passed directly from father to son it was likely to pass from one life-tenant to another. Failure in the male line, however, which occurred relatively frequently in the late seventeenth and early eighteenth centuries, often meant that it passed instead to a tenant in tail, who was free to dispose of it as he or she wished. Moreover, where owners, Sir John Bright for example, despaired of producing a male heir, they might feel disinclined to leave their entire estate to a single beneficiary: in such circumstances, besides permanently settling property on more than one person, they not infrequently settled property temporarily on a widow as an additional jointure. The dispositions of Sir Thomas Beaumont indicate that, for quite different reasons, other landowners arranged partible inheritance. Thus, property could be settled strictly or otherwise without an entire estate being included in a single disposition. Even where all property devolved on one life-tenant, the extent to which his freedom, or that of his successor, was limited was never great; and depended on a wide variety of factors, both actual and possible. The situation differed from family to family; from one generation of a family to another; and, not uncommonly, from one decade to the next.

Enjoyment of the benefits of various new departures in the field of finance was also largely dependent on the way in which individual owners managed their affairs. The reduced severity of the law relating to mortgages made them much less fraught with risk than had been the case in the sixteenth and early seventeenth centuries. Rates of interest fell gradually, and credit facilities became more diverse, more sophisticated, and more readily available both in London and in the provinces. Following the early, turbulent years of their existence, the funds eventually became a highly acceptable investment alternative, particularly during periods when returns on investment in land were low. All these developments enabled capital accumulation or the liquidation of debts to be dispersed over more than one generation, and if necessary over several, and thereby provided landowners with greater time, flexibility, and security in the management of their financial affairs, The manner in which the Constables emerged from the parlous situation which confronted them in 1653 illustrates what was possible when families faced their problems with skill and determination. If these qualities were absent, however, an entirely different scenario might quickly develop. Later, under Sir Philip Constable, the family's fortunes again deteriorated, partly because repeated involvement with the authorities undermined the confidence of creditors, but also because the third baronet lacked the will and the ability of his predecessors. The long career of Sir John Bright reveals how easy it remained for ambitious creditors to undermine the circumstances of feckless debtors. Interest rates far in excess of the legal maximum were demanded and obtained, and much property was alienated in the pursuit of solvency. Potentially beneficial developments in this area perhaps encouraged some individuals to overreach themselves. Once confidence in their ability to retrench began to be eroded, the process was difficult to halt, even under a new family regime. A more equitable situation at law persuaded many of those who were hard-pressed to defend their interests in the courts; as Richard Beaumont discovered, it was usually possible by this means to delay the final day of reckoning. Thereby, however, they ran the additional risk of incurring heavy legal costs with no guarantee of ultimate success on the point at issue.

As the tasks associated with the management of land and of money became more complex and varied many landed families began to delegate responsibilities for particular aspects of their affairs. The employment of growing numbers of stewards, attorneys, bankers, and their subordinates not only brought the business of individual owners under closer control, but also created greater continuity between owners and their successors. Wrights, the Covent Garden bankers, for example, managed important aspects of the Constables' financial affairs for many decades after 1710. Richard Chorley, who succeeded Potts as chief steward at Everingham, worked under both Sir Carnaby Haggerston and his son, William. William Wight served in a similar capacity on the Hotham estates for more than three decades from the early eighteenth century. Returns on investment in such services were undoubtedly high. None of the stewards on these four estates was paid on commission; apart from the £100 a year which Sir Philip Constable briefly paid to Francis Stansfield, their annual salaries ranged from as little as £15 to only £40, and were remarkably low in relation to the range of duties which they performed. This level of salaries, however, suggests that these men were neither as experienced nor as competent as might at first appear. All of them, some clearly more so than others, expected and needed firm guidance. The huge estates of the wealthiest owners required, and often obtained, stewards who were both efficient and relatively independent. Owners of less substantial properties were usually obliged to engage personnel who, though perhaps warmly recommended by friends and neighbours, were nevertheless of lesser and unproven ability. It is doubtful, therefore, whether as a body stewards entirely compensated for the uncertainty and neglect which resulted from increased landlord absenteeism. Fully professional stewards did not emerge as a recognizable group within rural society until the nineteenth century. Before then there was no formal training for the post and recruitment was from a very wide and disparate field. While they give an initial impression of careful management, their accounts bristle with makeshift devices, such as too cursorily summarized totals and large categories of miscellaneous expenditure. The complaints of owners bear witness to the fact that accounts were frequently completed long after the period to which they relate. For this and other reasons, for example their tendency to sympathize with the tenants, stewards were widely distrusted. Nor, as Potts's behaviour illustrates, was the employment of a scrupulous individual a guarantee of good management. Whether or not he was reliable, it was usually impossible for a chief steward to keep an eye on the whole of an estate; responsibility for the day-to-day management of outlying properties was almost invariably vested in tenants, who might content themselves with little more than the collection of rents and the payment of taxes. Thus, in this respect also the behaviour and attitudes of owners were of paramount importance. Lack of effective direction on their part automatically placed strain on administrative systems which, in many instances, were not yet equipped to withstand it.[2]

One new development which was of considerable benefit to

many families during this period was the abolition of royal wardship in 1646, and the assumption by the Court of Chancery from 1660 of the jurisdiction over minors previously exercised by the Court of Wards and Liveries. The arbitrary costs of royal wardship disappeared to be replaced by a system under which caretaker responsibilities for estates normally became vested in a panel of trustees instead of in a single guardian. Having been nominated by the deceased parent, trustees could be relied on to have the family's best interests at heart and were in any case answerable for their trusteeship at law. Whereas under the previous system wardship had frequently been granted to complete strangers by a court which was always more concerned to raise revenue than with equitable jurisdiction. Chancery closely scrutinized executors' and trustees' accounts and was empowered, where necessary, to assume full control of the management of a minor's affairs. In discharging their duties trustees were aware that minors, on attaining their majority, might bring actions for mismanagement against them, and many trustees submitted a detailed record of their activities for the approval of the court.[3]

Some families benefited immediately from the demise of wardship in the 1640s. Sir William Savile of Thornhill died in 1644 when Sir George, the future Marquess of Halifax, was only ten years old. When he eventually came of age in 1654 Sir George found himself a wealthy man. 'The early death of his father, leaving settled estates, and his own long minority, had protected in great measure his interests.' The family affairs of Lord Wentworth, Earl of Strafford, provide another example. Excluding salaries and profits from his Irish tobacco farm, Wentworth's annual income had climbed to almost £23,000 by 1639. At his death in 1641, however, his known debts were estimated to amount to £107,000. His heir, who was then fifteen, escaped wardship and kept out of the public eye by travelling abroad. When he came of age the second Earl was forced to sell much property in Yorkshire. None the less the Irish estates remained to form the basis of a revival in the family's fortunes. These distant properties, together with the rest of his affairs, had been managed during his minority by his cousins, the Wentworths of Bretton and Woolley. The demographic factors which produced minorities also resulted in the failure of heirs, male or female. In such circumstances the inheritance to an estate sometimes reverted, or was devised, to a minor, as happened at Everingham following the death of Sir Marmaduke Constable. Minorities occurred in other ways too. Gilbert Stapleton of Carlton died in 1637 leaving several young children. The estate became vested in the future Sir Miles Stapleton, but not because he was the eldest surviving male heir for he had two older brothers. The first of these, however, was certified as a lunatic, while the second surrendered his birthright to Miles in order to become a monk at Douai. Thus, what had originally promised to be a long minority was made even longer by the eventual succession of the third son in 1650. A series of early deaths could greatly lengthen periods of minority. When Sir Thomas Bland died in 1657 his eventual heir, Francis, was fifteen years of age. Francis died in 1663 just after attaining his majority, when his eldest son and prospective heir, Thomas, was but one year old. Thomas died a minor in 1668 and was succeeded by his younger brother, John, who finally assumed control of family affairs in 1684 after twenty-seven years of almost continuous minority. Again, though not continuous, the minorities experienced by the Wentworths of North Elmsall were lengthy, occurred in each of three successive generations, and comprised thirty-five of the eighty-seven years between 1653 and 1740.[4]

The case-studies provide several examples of how minorities provided opportunities for retrenchment, reorganization, or development. Few families experienced them as regularly as the Beaumonts, but both their history and that of the Hothams and the Constables underline the fact that even a single minority could be enormously beneficial. An attempt to measure the incidence of minorities among the larger group of ninety-three families has been hampered by the unsatisfactory nature of much of the evidence relating to their demography, particularly for the earlier part of our period. Material relating to some twenty families is so sparse, at times because families quickly became extinct in the male line, as to be useless. Moreover, records of the relatively few families who were raised to the baronetage in the eighteenth century often provide little, if any, hard evidence for the seventeenth century. It is possible to compensate for this somewhat by extending the period of

TABLE 29
Minorities, 1646–1815

A. *Distribution of Minorities*

Families with 1 minority	21
Families with 2 minorities	31
Families with 3 minorities	9
Families with 4 minorities	3
	64
Families with no minorities	9
	73

B. *Length of Minorities*

1 year	11	12 years	5
2 years	9	13 years	1
3 years	7	14 years	3
4 years	10	15 years	6
5 years	9	16 years	5
6 years	9	17 years	4
7 years	10	18 years	0
8 years	2	19 years	1
9 years	5	20 years	0
10 years	7	21 years	4
11 years	7	? years	7
	86		36
			86
			122

C. *Onset of Minorities*

Pre-1641	6	1726–35	7
1641–46	10	1736–45	7
1646–55	9	1746–55	10
1656–65	6	1756–65	4
1666–75	4	1766–75	4
1676–85	13	1776–85	9
1686–95	9	1786–95	3
1696–1705	6	1795–1805	4
1706–15	2	1806–15	2
1716–25	7		50
	72		72
			122

D. *Total Years of Minority*

0 years	9 Families
1– 5 years	10 Families
6–10 years	14 Families
11–15 years	9 Families
16–20 years	9 Families
21–25 years	4 Families
26–30 years	7 Families
31–35 years	2 Families
36–40 years	2 Families
? years	7 Families
	73

Sources: As in Table 2.

measurement down to 1815. The results, which inevitably indicate the minimum incidence of minorities, are significant. Seventy-three families experienced a total of at least 122 minorities between 1646 and 1815. Only nine families did not experience minorities. Of those who did, twenty-one families had one minority, thirty-one families had two minorities, nine families had three minorities, and three families had four minorities. The length of the 122 separate minorities varied greatly. Seventy-nine lasted for between one and ten years, and thirty-six for between eleven and twenty-one years; seven minorities were of uncertain duration. Periods of minority were spread fairly unevenly over the decades. Yorkshire saw much fighting during the Civil War and several members of these families were killed or mortally wounded in battle.[5] This largely accounts for the higher than average number of minorities which began before 1646 (but continued thereafter). The other decennial figures peak in the period 1676-95 and again in the mid eighteenth century. Finally, there are figures for the total number of years of minority experienced by individual families. Total duration is again uncertain in seven cases. Of the rest, twenty-four families had up to ten years of minority, and thirty-three families between eleven and forty years of minority. There seems little doubt that minorities constituted an important element in the history of a high proportion of this group, particularly in the century or so after wardship's abolition.

However, the benefits of minorities after 1646 derived not so much from the absence of wardship dues, nor primarily from the care with which trustees discharged their duties under the scrutiny of Chancery. More important was the fact that a minority, by definition, was a period during which there was no head of a family of age. Not only was conspicuous expenditure virtually non-existent, but expenditure normally considered essential to the upkeep of a family was greatly reduced. Income declined too if the deceased head of the family had received salaries and other emoluments, but in the vast majority of cases this was more than offset by the reduced outgoings consequent upon his death. Where, as was generally the case, income had come primarily from the estate, a much greater proportion than previously was available for saving or investment. In other words minorities were beneficial precisely because they were periods when control over a family's finances was not vested in a single individual.

None of the foregoing is meant to suggest that landowners were commonly devoid of feelings of responsibility towards the wider interests of their families and estates. The argument is merely that the head of a family had rather more within his power, for good or ill, than is sometimes supposed. In fact few of them lacked a sense of pride in their families' past achievements and current position, a sentiment which did much to make one generation aware of its obligations both to those past and to those yet to come. It was this which dominated Dame Elizabeth Hotham's actions in 1691 when, free to dispose of the family's property as she wished, she left the whole of it to a single heir in the interests 'of the family and the name of Hotham'. Though not always strong enough to ensure such single-minded behaviour, family pride expressed itself in many ways. It was at least partly responsible, for example, for the safekeeping of the large collections of family papers now at the disposal of historians, many of which begin to bulk large from the later seventeenth century. Good management demanded the preservation of much legal, financial, and estate material, but the same cannot be said of the host of more personal documents, which were preserved because of the evidence they provided of a dynasty's past endeavours. Many individuals went further than this and dabbled, albeit amateurishly, in family history. For example, Walter Strickland of Boynton, father of the first baronet, was acknowledged by contemporaries to be 'well versed in antiquity'; later his copious notes were used by Roger Dodsworth and other, more professional antiquaries. The extent to which Strickland pursued his interests was untypical; the interests themselves were not. A person's rank represented the visible evidence in the present of past progress and, among the gentry, families of relatively recent origin, such as the Brights, the Tempests, and the Milners, valued their coats of arms inordinately. Among the personal estate inherited by John Tempest in 1658, for instance, was his father's 'great gold ring having my coat of arms engraven upon it'. Sir John Goodrick, having agreed to contribute to the cost of a new stained glass window in Ripon minster in 1663, instructed the artist to 'take care my arms be placed according to my rank, which are blazoned thus . . .'. There followed a long and precise description of his requirements. Marked success might encourage a curious mixture of hypocrisy and unreason in attitudes to these matters. Sir John Bland, the fourth baronet, felt sufficiently proud of his considerable achievements to accept a copy of a new family pedigree, which traced his descent from most of the ancient potentates of Europe. While at pains to point out that it was 'not by my directions or with my knowledge', he none the less maintained that 'the descent is beyond dispute true'. An obsession with rank and ancestry was by no means the only manifestation of a sense of destiny; nor was the feeling expressed merely at the level of the individual. Each February in the post-Restoration era it manifested itself corporately in the 'annual feast' of the 'principal gentlemen' of Yorkshire at the Merchant Tailors' Hall in York.[6]

Even if they could not look back with pride on their history, and many undoubtedly could, families were exceedingly conscious of their current position in society. When, for example, Richard Beaumont's financial difficulties encouraged him to seek employment in the civil service in 1710, it was recognized by those who made representations on his behalf that he would not wish to hold certain positions, irrespective of their salaries, because they were generally regarded as being unacceptable to someone of his status. If the behaviour of a prospective heir or head of a family appeared to have jeopardized family fortunes, or threatened to do so if it went unchecked, relations or friends were quick to offer unequivocal criticism or advice – witness Mr Creyke's letter to Richard Beaumond in 1748, or Sir Beaumont Hotham's castigation of the mismanagement of his predecessor, the sixth baronet. The bluntest ultimatum on record came from the eighty-nine-year-old patriarch, Sir Thomas Gascoigne, to his son and eventual successor, who was then sixty-two years old himself.

You have plunged yourself so deep into debts and disgraces as must needs bring you present great misery if you escape ruin. And there is no prevention but a private retired life and in the North . . . Commit the care of your affairs at Barnbow to your uncle and brother. Away with Cotch into Cumberland.[7]

Branches of families tended to band together if one or all of them were experiencing difficulties. As we have seen, the Wentworths of Bretton, Woolley, and Wentworth Woodhouse did this with great effect following the Earl of Strafford's execution in 1641. Cuthbert Constable of Burton Constable kept in close contact with Sir Marmaduke at Everingham in the difficult years after 1715, while earlier, and most remarkably, Sir William Constable of Flamborough, Puritan, Regicide, and Colonel in the Parliamentary army, twice divided the House of Commons in an effort to save the estates of the Everingham branch from inclusion in a Treason act. In the case of Walter Calverley, who succeeded to a small and heavily encumbered estate in 1652, it was his maternal grandfather, Sir Walter Pye, who immediately summarized his predicament and offered him assistance.

Look upon your revenue as it is clogged with your mother's jointure, which is a full half of whatsoever your estate can be, and seriously consider if by thrift you may pay it out of your rents. If not, there are but two ways: a good wife or the sale of lands, and the sooner you put either in practice the more will it be for your advantage. You shall have in both my best help.[8]

In the final analysis the family name was literally the most sacred symbol of all. When the failure of heirs necessitated provision for estates to pass to distant relatives, prospective beneficiaries were almost invariably required, if they wished to inherit the property, to change their name accordingly. Liddell became Liddell-Bright; Haggerston, Haggerston-Constable, and then Haggerston-Maxwell-Constable, and so forth. Family pride, therefore, sustained, if it did not always determine, policies. In so far as it motivated individuals, it contributed much to that striving for permanency which characterized the behaviour of many of them.

Nevertheless, a number of families either ruined themselves through excess or were overwhelmed by their problems. The Jacksons of Hickleton, for example, never overcame the financial difficulties into which they fell before the Civil War, despite their ownership of a substantial estate in south Yorkshire. During the minority which followed the death of the first baronet in 1679, trustees sold parts of the estate to Sir John Bright and others in order to reduce the load of debt. Their efforts were brought to nought, however, by the wild extravagance of the second baronet. When he died, unmarried and grossly indebted, at the age of twenty-seven, the succession passed to his half-brother, Sir Bradwardine. In 1704 he sold the rest of the family's property to clear debts and raise life-annuities of £40 each for himself and his half-sister, Lucy, Countess of Londonderry. Two years later he was in prison for debt 'without hopes of getting his liberty' and was 'still under a cloud' in 1712. Glad to obtain a post as a tax administrator, he lived on for many years in permanently reduced circumstances. Although there was a 'probability of his marrying a good fortune if he will but be advised', he remained a bachelor and was the 'last of my family'.[9] The decline of the Reresbys of Thribergh was even more precipitate. Owing to extravagance both at court and in the country, the size of the family's estate was greatly reduced by sales in the early seventeenth century. In addition the mother of the diarist and second baronet, Sir John Reresby, was so upset by his marriage to the daughter of a York barrister, as well as by his refusal to revert to Catholicism, that she settled her own property on his uncle and younger brothers. However, following a long, busy, and careful career, Reresby left his eldest son and heir £1,700 a year in land and £4,000 in cash. Unfortunately, Sir William became addicted to gambling, cockfighting, 'and every other kind of debauchery'; lost one whole property on a single wager; and sold the bulk, if not all, of the rest of his property in 1705. Thereby he was reduced to extreme poverty and for a while acted as tapster in the Fleet prison. Neither he nor the brother who succeeded him in the title married; and when Sir Leonard died in 1748, leaving the Foundling hospital as his residuary legatee, the baronetcy became extinct.[10]

While the Burdett title remained extant throughout the eighteenth and nineteenth centuries, the family lost their estates during the long career of the first baronet, Sir Francis, who died in 1719. In 1643 his father had named Robert Rockley as trustee of the estate during Burdett's minority. Following Rockley's sudden death in the following year Sir John Kaye of Woodsome, who meanwhile had married Burdett's mother, became guardian to the child; and was awarded £120 a year from the estate by arbitrators to meet his expenses. On returning home from the wars and without assessing the situation, Rockley's son unwisely agreed to assume his father's position as trustee, whereupon he was immediately sued by Kaye and other creditors for payment of debts and maintenance. Rockley refused to accede to these demands and took his case to Chancery, where for more than a decade it remained, until he was finally ordered to pay over £7,000. He died in prison for debt in 1679. On coming of age in 1664 Sir Francis Burdett had to face the costs and other consequences of this dispute, but went on to complete 'the ruin of his house by his own extravagance and vices'. Having had three sons and two daughters by his marriage, he produced an even larger family by one Ann Watkins, whom he married after his first wife's death. Before the close of the lawsuit he was several thousand pounds in debt and gradually sold off the whole of his estate in succeeding years. His successor in the title lived in York; and was himself succeeded, first by a son who was rector of Newington in Kent, and then by another son who had emigrated to Florida.[11] The Swales of Swale Hall provide a rather different example of economic eclipse. Never substantial owners of land, they held much of their property on lease from the Crown. Both this land and their ancestral estate were lost at the turn of the seventeenth century following legal action against their leadmining activities in Swaledale. The third baronet, Sir Solomon, was comprehensively defeated in the Court of the Exchequer, spent some time in the Fleet prison for debt, and eventually died poverty-stricken in 1733. He was succeeded in the title by a nephew whose father had earlier turned merchant in Spain, and on whose death without heirs the title became extinct.[12] Another contemporary, Sir William Chaytor, spent no less than seventeen years in the Fleet prison for debt. Originally of Butterby and Houghton-le-Spring in Co. Durham, he had inherited the Croft estate in 1660 on the death of the infant son of his second cousin. However, he was permanently embarrassed financially 'by the great incumbrances left upon his estate by his father who suffered for his loyalty to King Charles I'. In 1688 Sir John Sudbury, Chaytor's major creditor, threatened to use him 'like a teague or a papist'; part of his estate was seized in 1690; and by private act of Parliament in 1695 Chaytor re-settled his property for the payment of debts, and of maintenance to himself, his wife, and his children. This arrangement was to no avail for in January 1700 he was arrested at Croft by sheriff's bailiffs and carried up to prison in London. Whether by better management Chaytor could have avoided this fate is unknown though, perhaps significantly, the following was an old saying which he particularly noted: 'he that is his own pupil has a fool to his tutor'. His wife and all thirteen of their children pre-deceased him; and he was succeeded in the rump of his estate, but not in title, by his nephew, Henry, whose illegitimate grandson was eventually created baronet of Croft, and of Witton Castle in Co. Durham, in 1831.[13]

If his behaviour threatened to prove prejudicial, the prospective heir to a family's fortune could be disinherited. For example, in disposing his huge estate Sir Thomas Osborne, first Duke of Leeds, passed over his eldest son in favour of his grandson. The precise reason for this remains uncertain. It may have been due to the second Duke's known association with Jacobites; or to the public outcry and humiliation which followed his grave misjudgement as a naval commander in 1695. Mistaking a group of merchant ships for the French fleet, he had ordered his squadron back to Milford Haven, thereby allowing West Indian traders and five very valuable East Indiamen to fall into the hands of the French. Because his brother, the future fifth baronet, conformed to the Church of England, the Catholic Sir Francis Hungate of Saxton deprived him of his expected inheritance of the family property by cutting the entail, preferring instead to leave it to two daughters. The survivor of these, Mary, eventually married the Catholic Sir Edward Gascoigne of Parlington.[14]

In the case of the Blands of Kippax Park a disinheritance, though initially effected, was later largely revoked, with disastrous consequences for all concerned. The family's wealth and status were greatly increased under the fourth baronet who, after a lengthy minority, expanded his estate by purchase and, above all, by marriage. His wife, Anne, daughter of Sir Edward Moseley of Hulme Hall, brought him considerable property in Lancashire and Cheshire. By her husband's will she enjoyed both this and the land which he had purchased, but Dame Anne finally devised all of it to their eldest surviving son, John, who had succeeded to the title and to the Kippax Park estate in 1715. At his mother's death in 1734, therefore, Sir John Bland became possessed of one of the most substantial estates in the north of England. Following his own marriage in 1716, Kippax Park was settled on the male heirs of his eldest son, but until Sir John made a will the remaining property, including a number of his own purchases, remained undisposed. By an early will Sir John devised virtually all of this property to his eldest son, John. However, long before he came of age Sir John was convinced that the boy's 'extravagant and idle behaviour' would, if indulged,

ruin the family; and in a new will of 1741 deprived him of all but
the Kippax Park property. Sir John had little room for
manoeuvre because one younger son, Hungerford, was
deformed, while the health of the other, Edward, was precarious.
So, except for Kippax Park, he devised all his property to his wife
for fourteen years on trust to pay debts, maintenance, and generous portions to his daughters and younger sons. On the completion of that term the property was to devolve on a panel of
trustees, who were instructed to settle it on John's eldest son
when that son came of age; and, if possible, to devise remainders
so that the property accompanied the title. John received only
those lands adjacent to Kippax Park which his father had purchased; and his receipt of these was conditional on the payment
of £1,000 which was to augment the portions of his brothers and
sisters. On Sir John's own death in 1743 the sixth baronet and
others challenged these dispositions, but a Chancery decree of
1745 declared that the second will and codicil should stand in
their entirety. The new Sir John's next tactic was to discharge the
incumbrances on his own estate. Once this had been achieved he
set about embellishing Kippax Park and by 1749 had reputedly
spent £8,000 in this way. He then negotiated with his mother to
exchange the Kippax Park estate for the other property denied
him by his father's will. She eventually agreed to this, presumably because Kippax was the family's ancestral seat and, knowing
her son, she feared its irretrievable loss. The two parties executed
a formal agreement in July 1749 and effected the exchange by a
private act of Parliament in 1752. Sir John Bland's subsequent
behaviour was exactly as his father had predicted. He left Kippax
Park unfinished and, 'by his wild dissipation and his unconquer-
able disposition to play', squandered his other property. According to Horace Walpole, who for once it seems was somewhat lost
for words, Sir John was 'good-natured and generous and well-
bred'; but as for gambling, there 'never was such infatuation – I
can call it by no term but *flirting* away his fortune'. Matters came
to a head in 1755. 'He t'other night exceeded what was lost by the
late Duke of Bedford, having at one period of the night (tho' he
recovered the greater part of it) lost £32,000.' To elude his
creditors Bland fled to France, where he lost further large sums
to the infamous Irish adventurer, Theobald Taaffe. Unable to
satisfy Taaffe immediately, Bland provided him with post-dated

bills. When these were immediately presented, and equally quickly dishonoured, Taaffe had Bland arrested. An English banker secured his freedom with an unsolicited advance of £500; but, shamed by the dishonour and with no money to meet his enormous debts, Bland shot himself. His executors were plagued for years by long and intricate lawsuits and, after Sir Hungerford's death in 1756, Bland's sisters themselves fell into dispute. A further act of Parliament in 1764 divided the remaining Yorkshire estate between Elizabeth and Anne Bland; and on the latter's death in 1768 the property passed to a cousin, Thomas Davison, who assumed the family name.[15]

Edward Wortley-Montagu arranged a celebrated and entirely successful disinheritance. He was as miserly as his son was eccentric and extravagant. Moreover, he lived long enough to make his plans stick. A leading landowning industrialist in south Yorkshire and the north-east, Wortley-Montagu never achieved the more public success which initially he coveted. Recalled in 1718 from a brief and unsatisfactory performance as ambassador in Constantinople, he was promised £10,000 and a place to compensate him for arrears of pay and extraordinary expenses. The arrears of £5,000 were forthcoming, but he received neither a post nor further money to defray his costs whilst in office. He sat as an opposition M.P. at Westminster until the late 1740s, whereupon he lost interest in politics, 'hoarding health and money' and constructing elaborate calculations of what the government owed him. His relations with his son were always strained and soon deteriorated to the point of mutual antipathy. As a child the young Wortley-Montagu frequently ran away from school. On one occasion, after being absent for a year, he was found crying fish in Blackwall; on another he was arrested by the British consul in Oporto, having worked his passage there, deserted ship, and then found employment in a local vineyard. In 1730 at the age of seventeen he married a washerwoman, whereupon he was bundled away to a tutorship in the West Indies. The woman was pensioned off but remained Wortley-Montagu's lawful wife until shortly before his death in 1776. It was at this point that his father first determined to disinherit him. On returning from the Caribbean he was allowed £300 a year. He spent several years on the Continent as a university student before enlisting in the allied army. Then in 1746 he joined the diplomatic staff of his cousin, Lord Sandwich, who secured his return as M.P. for Huntingdonshire; and in 1748 was appointed commissioner to the Congress at Aix-la-Chapelle. By this time his annual allowance had been raised to £1,000, on condition that he never occupied the same benches in the House of Commons as his father; and that, elsewhere, they were never in the same city at the same time. As he grew older Wortley-Montagu junior's behaviour became increasingly bizarre. He contracted a bigamous marriage to a woman of doubtful reputation, designed and wore a wig of iron wire (for which apparently he was elected to the Royal Society), and in 1751 was briefly imprisoned in Paris. There was now no question of his being returned again as a county M.P. so, in order to protect him from his creditors, his father got him in as member for Bossiney in Cornwall in 1754. Subsequently, Wortley-Montagu spent most of his time abroad, travelling extensively and frequently communicating his observations to the Royal Society. He went through a further marriage ceremony and several mistresses, turned Catholic and then Muslim, and never failed to provide contemporary gossip-columnists with excellent copy. In 1761 his father left him £1,000 a year, which was to double on the death of his mother; in the following year she left him a guinea. The estates went to Wortley-Montagu's sister who, in her own right, was created Baroness Mount Stuart of Wortley, and whose husband, Lord Bute, subsequently subsidized his curious brother-in-law. The will of 1761 provided for considerable property to descend to the male child that Wortley-Montagu might have by any future, lawful marriage. In 1776, hearing of his wife's death, Wortley-Montagu placed an offer of marriage in the *Public Advertiser* to 'any widow or single lady of genteel birth, polite manners, and five, six, seven, or eight months in pregnancy'. However, having on his way home got as far as Padua, he died suddenly after swallowing a fishbone.[16]

If, as happened in the case of Sir Thomas Robinson of Rokeby, a family's affairs were governed for many years by an eccentric and extravagant individual with no legitimate children to provide for, there was little that anyone else could do to save the ancestral estates. Robinson's career got off to a fine start. He purchased an army commission after returning from an extensive grand tour but gladly relinquished it to his brother in 1727 on becoming, through the influence of the Howards, M.P. for Morpeth. In the following year he married Elizabeth, widow of Lord Lechmere and daughter of Charles Howard, third Earl of Carlisle. Whilst abroad, however, he had cultivated a taste for expensive living, not least in regard to architecture, which dominated the rest of his life and quickly drove him into debt. Besides designing the west wing of Castle Howard for his brother-in-law, Ember Court in Surrey for the Onslows, and the gothic gateway at Bishop Auckland, he rebuilt Rokeby Hall and the bridge over the Tees there, enclosed the park, and indulged in extensive landscaping. In London he soon acquired a reputation for excess in entertaining and by 1742 his precarious financial situation led to his expatriation as Governor of Barbados. Once established in that post, he angered the local Assembly by embarking on expensive construction projects, the cost of most of which he was obliged to meet himself. Following a further quarrel over the command of the island's forces, he was recalled in 1747 but not before he had married, secondly, the daughter of a rich local ironmonger. However, his new wife refused to follow him to England and on his return he resumed the costly habits of an irresponsible bachelor. He bought shares in Ranelagh Gardens, became director of the entertainments there, and built a house nearby where he was a lavish host. A few contemporaries acknowledged his genuine interest in the arts, but most regarded him as 'specious' and 'empty', remarkable only for his great eccentricity and extravagance. Several years before his death in 1776 he was obliged to sell the Rokeby estate. He was succeeded in the baronetcy by his brothers, William and Richard, the second of whom was Archbishop of Armagh and received an Irish peerage on Robinson's death. This title later devolved on a cousin, Matthew, who owned an estate at West Layton in Yorkshire.[17]

Thus, ruinous bad luck, gross extravagance and extreme eccentricity, though relatively uncommon, were far from unknown. All families experienced difficult or embarrassing interludes. The exercise of common sense and good judgement was not the only difference between those who survived and those who were ruined; sheer good fortune also had an important part to play. The financial difficulties of the Chaytors and the Jacksons were at one stage no more severe than those faced by the Constables during the mid seventeenth century. The legal entanglements of the Burdetts were no more serious than those encountered by the Beaumonts in the early eighteenth century. John Liddell-Bright squandered a great deal of money during the early part of his career but later established a pattern of retrenchment which kept his fortune intact. Had his less careful sons been in control for longer this might not have proved the case. Likewise, in the third and sixth baronets the Hothams produced two individuals who, if they had not been so short-lived, might have done considerable damage to their family. It has recently been remarked of Catholic families that their religious allegiance 'was not really determinable for more than one generation'; 'every successive head of a family chose its regime anew'.[18] In a far wider sense this was true of all landed families; indeed it was precisely for this reason that disinheritance was so rarely resorted to. Apart from a natural reluctance to consider this alternative, it posed problems of its own where other suitable heirs were lacking. But, above all, it was nearly always impossible to predict an individual's subsequent behaviour prior to his succession. Whatever the long-term trends, as a result of the behaviour of individuals the fortunes of landed families were, in the short term, subject to sharp fluctuations.

2. MATTERS OF LIFE AND DEATH

On 10 November 1638 Sir Edward Osborne of Kiveton, Vice-President of the Council of the North, wrote a revealing letter to his patron, Lord Wentworth, who was then in Ireland. Osborne's official position allowed him the use of the manor-house at York and eleven days previously his eldest son had been killed there when the chimneys above the child's bedroom fell through the ceiling and crushed him. However, Osborne was less concerned by this than with the still greater tragedy which had so nearly befallen him.

The right hand of mercy was stretched out for the preservation of my two surviving children, whose dead bodies (in all probability) had been added [*sic*] to the heap of these ruins, had the fall stayed but half so long as your lordship has been reading these last four lines, they being at that very time passing through the great chamber to their brother's.[19]

A century or so later Osborne's relief was paralleled by that of the Tancreds of Brampton, who on 29 January 1745 placed the following announcement in *The Yorkshire Herald*.

Last week the lady of Sir Thomas Tancred Bart. gave birth to a son, to the great joy of the family; her Ladyship has had nine daughters, but no son before.[20]

The surviving Osborne children (a single daughter had earlier died in infancy) both endured to a ripe old age. Charles, the junior of the two, eventually died unmarried in 1719 at the age of eighty-six; his elder brother, Thomas, rose to national prominence as Earl of Danby and then Duke of Leeds, and was eighty years old at his death in 1712. Sir Thomas and Lady Tancred went on to produce three further sons, one of whom died young; but the child born in 1745 succeeded his father as fifth baronet and lived until 1784.[21] In fact neither the Osbornes nor the Tancreds experienced much difficulty in reproducing themselves. Each belonged to the small group of families who succeeded in a single, direct, male line throughout the seventeenth and eighteenth centuries.

It was in regard to matters of succession that landed families felt themselves most vulnerable, and with justification for the failure of heirs had long constituted 'the greatest threat to the continuance of great families'.[22] The deepest wish of all but a minority of substantial landowners was to settle at least the bulk of their patrimony on a son. Yet their ability to achieve this was ultimately byond their control. Not one of the case-study families, for example, was able to do so continuously in the seventeenth and eighteenth centuries. With the death of the third baronet in 1691, the Hothams experienced the first interruption for six hundred years in a succession from father to son, or father to son's son.[23] Nevertheless, a cousin was then available to inherit the title and estate, both of which have continued in the male line since then. The Beaumonts were less fortunate, losing their title after only three years on the death, unmarried and childless, of the first and only baronet in 1631. However, although there was a further break in the direct male line in

1704, the Whitley estate passed securely in the name of Beaumont till beyond 1800. Both the Constables and the Brights, on the other hand, were obliged to settle property on the heirs of female issue, compensating for this somewhat by requiring the major beneficiaries to assume an appropriately hyphenated surname. Subsequently, the core of the Bright property was lost to both the name and the family on the marriage of a sole heiress in the mid eighteenth century. Here again, it is essential to view the evidence of the case-studies in the context of the history of the larger group. For not only did the failure of heirs wield a profound influence on the fortunes of landed families, but recent research has indicated that that influence was particularly pronounced during the period with which we are mainly concerned.

In the late sixteenth and early seventeenth centuries the population of England grew substantially; although life expectancy remained low, birth rates increased faster than death rates. From the mid seventeenth century, however, there began a new phase of population history in which mortality rates were generally higher, and fertility rates generally lower, than in the earlier period. Between then and the mid eighteenth century fewer people were being born, and people were dying somewhat earlier, than previously. There was less chance that fathers would produce heirs or, if they did, that those heirs would succeed them. Then, from the middle decades of the eighteenth century, population growth was resumed and entered a new phase which coincided with the industrial revolution. These trends were clearly reflected at the highest social level. There was a rapid natural increase in the numbers of the peerage between 1580 and 1630, but by 1660 this had ceased. Between 1660 and 1730 there was almost exact replacement, followed by a generation of decided decline. The turning-point in this downward trend, when it came, was rapid; the subsequent increase in replacement rates reached a peak in 1800. The general picture is of a high level of fertility in the early seventeenth century which, from about mid century, dropped to a low level of fertility in the early eighteenth century. Mortality rates corroborate this evidence. In general mortality was highest between 1660 and 1672; the heaviest child mortality and lowest expectation of life at birth were found in those born between 1650 and 1674. Indeed, in the century after the Restoration there was a tendency to extinction. Following the revolution of 1688 the peerage were marrying rather late, were not having large families, and were dying fairly early. Again, the eventual reversal of this trend was a rapid one; during the second half of the eighteenth century mortality fell at an unprecedented rate. Among the peerage, therefore, lines of succession were broken more frequently during the late seventeenth and early eighteenth centuries than during either the previous or the subsequent periods.[24]

- Insufficient data prevents a systematic analysis of the demography of baronetage families in Yorkshire between 1600 and 1800. Nevertheless, because a baronetcy was an hereditary title, some indication of the broad pattern of their demography can be obtained from an examination of the rate at which baronetcies became extinct before 1800. Before embarking on this exercise, however, it is necessary to note that in a number of ways the extinction of titles seriously underestimates failures in the direct male line. As in each of the case-studies, baronetcies were normally granted to an individual and 'the heirs male of his body lawfully begotten, for ever'. For a recipient's title to remain in being, therefore, he had to produce at least one legitimate son who outlived him. If, however, he produced more than one legitimate son, the title devolved in turn on his younger sons, in the event of their outliving an elder brother who failed to produce a legitimate male child. Moreover, any legitimate children of these younger sons were eligible in their turn to succeed to the title if the direct male line failed beyond the first generation. For example, the fourth and seventh baronets Hotham succeeded to the title because they were male descendants of the first baronet, though not of their immediate predecessors (who died childless and to whom they were cousin and uncle respectively). It also needs to be borne in mind that, 'according to the pleasure of the sovereign', some baronetcies were granted other than merely to a recipient and 'the heirs male of his body lawfully begotten, for ever'.[25] As many as eight Yorkshire baronetcies were further entailed. Five of the recipients were in fact succeeded by sons: but, under special remainders, the other three (Sir Thomas Wentworth of Bretton, Sir George Cooke of Wheatley, and Sir Thomas Robinson of Rokeby) were succeeded by brothers (in 1675, 1683, and 1777 respectively).[26] Furthermore, a simple count of the number of surviving titles in 1800 would be inadequate, for when they became extinct baronetcies could be, and often were, re-created. By this means cousins of both the Armitages of Kirklees and the Lowthers of Swillington enjoyed titles, though neither was directly descended from the first baronets of those families. Similarly, Sir Metcalfe Robinson of Newby, the first baronet, was succeeded in a title by his nephew, despite the fact that the original grant did not contain a special remainder. In

TABLE 30
The Yorkshire Baronetage
Creations, Extinctions, & Re-Creations, 1611–1800

	A	B	C	D	E
1611–20	13	–	–	5	–
1621–30	8	1	–	3	–
1631–40	4	4	–	3	–
1641–50	19	3	–	3	–
1651–60	12	3	–	6	–
1661–70	15	1	–	9	–
1671–80	3	4	1	–	–
1681–90	3	5	1	1	1
1691–1700	2	1	–	–	–
1701–10	–	5	–	–	–
1711–20	3	1	–	1	–
1721–30	–	2	–	–	–
1731–40	1	3	–	1	1
1741–50	1	5	–	1	–
1751–60	–	3	–	–	–
1761–70	–	2	–	–	1
1771–80	3	3	1	3	1
1781–90	5	2	–	5	1
1791–1800	1	3	–	1	–
Totals	93	51	3	42	5

Key: A. First Creations
B. First Creations, Extinctions
C. First Creations, Successions under Special Remainder
D. First Creations, Persisting Beyond 1800
E. Re-Creations.

Sources: As for Table 2.

the case of the Copleys of Sprotborough a title was re-created for the son of a female descendant of the first baronet; and in 1781 the illegitimate son of Sir John Ingleby of Ripley received a title.[27] Finally, in using extinctions of title as a measure of the failure of male heirs, baronetcies must be carefully distinguished from peerages. Occasionally the latter were also granted with special remainders; four of the twelve families who received peerages did so following the extinction of their baronetcies; and in one of these cases, that of the Wortleys, a peerage was conferred on an heiress.[28]

Table 30 has been constructed with all these considerations in mind. Of the ninety-three first grants of baronetcy conferred on families or branches of families in Yorkshire between 1611 and 1800, no fewer than fifty-one (or some fifty-five per cent) were extinct by the latter date. But for successions under special remainders, this total would have risen to fifty-four. It is also noticeable that all re-creations, and all first grants made after 1720, persisted beyond 1800. In other words the fifty-one extinctions were from among the eighty-two first grants made down to 1720. Moreover, some thirty of the fifty-one extinctions occurred in the century following the Restoration; the remaining twenty-one were equally divided between the preceding and subsequent periods. Another way of expressing this is in terms of the length of the individual baronetcies which became extinct before 1800, as in Table 31. Of the fifty-one first creations, only eleven lasted for over a century; thirty-six lasted for less than eighty years; and twenty-six for fifty years or under. Given the high proportion of creations which were made

TABLE 31

Length of First Creations extinct before 1800

1–10 years	5	71–80	2	141–150	–
11–20	5	81–90	1	151–160	1
21–30	5	91–100	3	161–170	1
31–40	2	101–110	3	171–180	1
41–50	9	111–120	1	181–190	1
51–60	4	121–130	3		
61–70	4	131–140	–	Total	51

Sources: As for Table 2.

before or immediately after the Restoration, this is a further indication of the increased rate at which titles became extinct in the century after 1660. In so far as they reached a peak in the late seventeenth and early eighteenth centuries, extinctions corroborate the aforementioned findings for the peerage. Only slightly more than a third of these families avoided a failure of male heirs; and, as we shall see, the number of those who persistently achieved succession from father to son or grandson was many fewer than this.

Measurement of the extinction of titles, however, is no substitute for a closer examination of demographic fortunes. The fact that rather more than half of these families were unable to retain their titles is indicative of certain broad trends; but this alone constitutes an inadequate guide to the wide variety of their demographic experience. It was possible for a family, the Beaumonts for example, to lose its title very quickly, but then to proceed with only one further break in the direct male line before 1800. Equally, families which retained their titles often did so only as a result of the succession of uncles, nephews, cousins, or grandchildren. In spite of the difficulties which derive from the uneven spread of sources, it would be unsatisfactory not to attempt some quantification of the relative frequency of such different types of experience. In addition an attempt will be made to estimate the influence exerted by demographic factors on the management and disposition of property. For purposes of analysis the entire group of ninety-three families has been subdivided into four categories: miscellaneous (seventeen families), which includes both those cases where reliable evidence is unavailable, and those where titles and families became extinct before 1700; secondly, those (twenty-seven) families where succession was to or through a female line; thirdly, those (thirty-five) families who succeeded in the male line, albeit indirectly; and finally, those (fourteen) families who achieved succession through a single, direct male line throughout the seventeenth and eighteenth centuries.

In the first category are three families who left little or no trace of their experiences before the late eighteenth century, when their titles were created.[29] The remainder of this subgroup provide a sharp reminder of the transitory existence of some members of the order of baronets. No fewer than seven of these individuals or families would probably have remained completely unnoticed were it not for the existence of comprehensive, printed records of the entire baronetage. Some of them apparently owned no real estate, and all were insubstantial; they died unmarried, childless, or both soon after receiving their titles in the seventeenth century.[30] Of the remainder, Sir William Pennyman of Marske, illegitimate son of the grandfather of the first Pennyman baronet of Ormesby, died married but childless and intestate in 1643, when his property passed to the Ormesby branch of the family. Sir George Twistleton of Barlby contracted a childless marriage; and at his death in 1635, six years after his receipt of a title, his property devolved on his uncle, John Twistleton of Drax, ancestor of the future Lord Saye and Sele. The property of the regicide, Sir William Constable of Flamborough, one of the original recipients of a baronetcy in 1611, met a quite different fate. Much of it was sold or mortgaged before his death in 1655. As his marriage had produced only a daughter, who died young, his title then became extinct. His body was exhumed in 1660 and his remaining property, specially exempted from the Act of Grace, was confiscated by the Crown. If this type of experience was virtually unique, another was somewhat more common. Sir John Jackson and Sir William Reresby, who squandered their respective inheritances, both died unmarried, and were both succeeded by brothers who also died unmarried. The titles of the luckless Swales and the Mauleverers became extinct in very similar circumstances.[31] All together the history of this subgroup suggests that lack of substance, extravagance, or a rapid descent into poverty tended to promote extinction by making marriage, and therefore succession, more difficult to achieve. Titles remained saleable commodities in the marriage market only so long as they were underpinned by property. Where property did not exist, or was alienated, matters of succession became largely of academic interest.

Even if successive generations of a family married and had children, it often proved possible to produce heirs only through a female line. This occurred to some twenty-seven of these ninety-three families, though the manner in which they responded, or were able to respond, to the situation varied considerably, with significant consequences for the ownership and management of their property. The least disruptive situation was one in which estates devolved, either immediately or with little delay, on the son of a sister or daughter. This was especially true if that individual's own property lay in the same vicinity as that which he inherited. Sir Francis Boynton of Barmston found himself in this fortunate position in 1656. His mother had been the only daughter of Sir Henry Griffith of nearby Burton Agnes. Her brother, the second baronet, married but had no children, and on his death the entire Burton Agnes property came to Sir Francis. Land inherited in this way was normally a good deal further away from an heir's current home. However, if, like Sir Marmaduke Constable, Sir John Bright, or the Earl of Wandesford, owners settled their estates on younger sons of sisters or daughters who had previously come into little or no land of their own, their successors were generally more than glad to reside on their inherited estate. Even the eldest son of a sister or daughter might feel likewise if his own family's property was insubstantial. This was true of Nicholas Errington of Ponteland in Northumberland, who succeeded to the Carlton estates of his grandfather, Sir Miles Stapleton, in 1707; of Walter Ramsden, son of Thomas Ramsden of Crowstone in the West Riding, who succeeded to the estates of his maternal grandfather, Sir Walter Hawksworth, in 1735; and of William Darby of Sunbury in Middlesex, who inherited his uncle St. Quintin's property at Harpham and Scampston in the East Riding in 1795. In these and other instances of inheritance via the female line a change of name was a prior condition of succession to property. Only by such artificial means could a former association continue to be acknowledged. In some quarters by the late eighteenth century, however, this device was utilized to an absurd degree. The eldest son of the aforementioned Walter Ramsden also enjoyed the fruits of inheritance but, in consequence, was eventually known as Walter Ramsden-Beaumont-Hawksworth-Fawkes. From 1784 the Castlecomer estates in Ireland were presided over by the Hon. Charles Harward-Butler-Clarke-Southwell-Wandesford. The other device, a re-creation of title, was less common but considerably more effective. For example, in 1709 Sir Godfrey Copley preferred to leave his estates to a distance relative of the same name, Lionel Copley of

Wadworth, rather than to his married daughter, Catherine, or her possible heirs. When some years later Catherine had a son, Joseph, by her marriage to a Mr Moyle, Lionel Copley entailed the estates on the child in the event of his own three sons dying childless. Thereby Joseph inherited Sprotborough in 1766, changed his name by act of Parliament from Moyle to Copley, and was finally raised to the baronetage in 1778.[32]

As we have seen, the Blands and the Wortleys, despairing of the behaviour of prospective heirs, limited or disbarred their interest in property and were consequently able to make generous provision for daughters. Although, nevertheless, the wildly extravagant sixth baronet, Sir John Bland, alienated much property and ran up enormous debts, both the title and the bulk of the estate surrounding the family seat at Kippax Park devolved on his brother, Hungerford, when Sir John committed suicide in 1755. However, the deformed Sir Hungerford never married and after his death in the following year Kippax Park was shared by his two surviving sisters, Anne and Elizabeth, who themselves remained unmarried. At Anne's death in 1786 the property passed to a cousin, Thomas Davison of Blakiston in Co. Durham. who thereupon assumed the name of Bland. The Wortleys' experiences, though no less dramatic, came eventually to a more satisfactory conclusion. Edward Wortley-Montagu, appalled at the madcap behaviour of his only son and namesake, left his vast estates to his only daughter, Mary, who soon after her father's death was created Baroness Mount Stuart of Wortley. At her death in 1794 the Yorkshire properties devolved on her second son, who took the name of Wortley. On dying without issue in 1740 Sir William Marwood of Little Busby left his property to Jane, daughter of his uncle, the second baronet. Little Busby would no doubt have passed to her son, who was christened Marwood William Turner, but he died childless and unmarried at the age of twenty-two. Subsequently, instead of settling the property on her only daughter, Jane Turner left it to a cousin, William Metcalfe, who then assumed the name of Marwood. In seeking to resolve his succession problems Sir Marmaduke Asty-Wyvill, last baronet of Constable Burton, found himself in a position which, though not unique, was highly unusual. Both he and his half-brother, the sixth baronet, died without issue, but his half-sister,

Elizabeth, on whom the estate devolved, had married a Revd Christopher Wyvill of Black Notley in Essex. Having little property of his own, Christopher moved to Constable Burton after his brother-in-law's death in 1774, succeeded to the property on his wife's death in 1783, and then by a second marriage had a Wyvill son to whom the estate passed on his own death in 1822.[33] On many occasions, therefore, the worst effects of direct descent to a female – the loss of any real connection between a family and its property – were overcome, albeit after a considerable lapse of time.

The property of some families, including the Brights, descended through the female line on two occasions during this period. Before the mid eighteenth-century developments alluded to above, the Wortley estates had been devised by the second baronet to his illegitimate daughter, Ann Newcomen. Sir Francis Wortley had married but had lived apart from his wife for many years and, although his will was long and bitterly contested, its provisions were finally upheld. Ann married a younger son of the Earl of Sandwich, who subsequently changed his name to Wortley-Montagu. Although their marriage also ended in separation, their eldest surviving son inherited his parents' estates. The Cholmelys failed twice in the male line too. In 1689 the fourth baronet was survived by an only daughter, Mary, who was a widow. However, she already had children by her marriage to another Cholmely, Nathaniel, an East Indian diamond merchant. The estate passed to their eldest son and then to his eldest son. Despite three marriages, the latter was survived by four co-heiresses in 1791, only one of whose husbands felt inclined to change his name to Cholmely.[34]

By one means or another, therefore, many of the above families contrived to maintain some degree of separate identity. However, for several of those whose property devolved directly on heiresses or co-heiresses this proved impossible. Where substantial estates passed intact, or virtually so, to a single heiress, highly successful marriages almost invariably ensued. Mary, sole heiress of Sir John Savile of Copley, married Lord Thomas Howard: their eldest son later succeeded as eighth Duke of Norfolk. Charlotte van den Bempdé married William Johnstone, first Marquess of Annandale; and Mary Bright married Lord Rockingham. Both Elizabeth and Mary, daughters and co-heiresses of Sir John Lewis of Ledston, also married well – to the seventh Earl of Huntingdon and the third Earl of Scarsdale respectively. All Sir John's brothers died young or unmarried, and when one of them left his nieces an estate at Marr, it was decided that one sister should take it and the other, Ledston.[35] However, because inherited property remained for some time distinct from a husband's ancestral estate, and was often inconveniently situated in relation to it, it was commonly regarded as being more readily disposable, should the sale of property become necessary. Once the discharge of his debts became a priority Richard Beaumont did not hesitate to sell parts of Mitton and Grizzlehurst, which he had acquired through his second marriage, in preference to part of Whitley; in his will he encouraged his successor to sell the rest of these inherited and detached properties in order to disencumber the ancestral estate. Shortly after his succession the eighth Duke of Norfolk set off to visit Copley Hall which, although it had been his mother's dowry, he had apparently never seen. But, 'seeing it was under a hill and made but a mean appearance, he turned back and would not give himself the trouble to go to it'. The estate was soon sold to a Mr Walker of Huddersfield.[36] Moreover, in view of the fact that the successful marriage of an heiress inevitably brought about the amalgamation of her property with another, perhaps larger, estate, there was much less incentive than there was with an eldest son to endow her with the whole of a family's patrimony. Even Sir Henry Griffith, whose daughter's in-laws were his next-door neighbours at Boynton and Barmston, sold off parts of the Burton Agnes estate before his death. Sir Thomas Wentworth-Blackett, who owned enormous properties in Yorkshire and Northumberland, was sufficiently keen to avoid their total dismemberment to leave virtually all of them to one of his three illegitimate daughters. He nevertheless devised the Gunneston estate to William Bosvile of Gunthwaite, only son of his eldest sister, Diana. Other properties, such as those of the Bamburghs of Howsham or the Forsters of Stokesley, were soon dispersed; or, like those of the Paylers and the Brookes, malingered in the possession of an obscure, middle-aged female before eventually being sold or passing to a distant and less substantial relative.[37]

Inevitably, succession via or to a female echoed more basic demographic trends, eighteen of the thirty recorded instances occurring in the century after the Restoration. Moreover, the phenomenon was fairly evenly spread and affected over a third of those families which persisted for more than a generation after the mid seventeenth century. Its consequences were both substantial and multifarious. A number of families disappeared completely; much property was brought on to the marriage or land markets, or both; the structure of management on many properties was changed; and, on those properties which became detached through female inheritance, the profile of management was considerably reduced.

The third and largest sub-group contains the thirty-five families who achieved succession through the male line, albeit indirectly, throughout the seventeenth and eighteenth centuries. In twenty-three families succession passed to the brother of a previous incumbent on at least one occasion; in a similar number of instances succession passed to an uncle, nephew, or cousin on at least one occasion. Eleven families experienced both of these alternatives. Again, there was a noticeable increase in the frequency of indirect succession during the century after the Restoration: only nine of the thirty-five families maintained direct succession within this shorter period. For the Chaytors, the Burdetts, and the Robinsons of Rokeby breaks in the direct line were unimportant, for by the time they occurred there was little or no real estate for successors to inherit. The influence which indirect succession exerted on the fortunes of the remainder was exceedingly varied, and by no means always disadvantageous. Continuity was greatest where breaks in the direct line were infrequent and did not result in an extinction of title. In the case of the Boyntons of Barmston, for example, succession from father to son and then to grandson was broken only once, in 1731, when the twice-married third baronet, Sir Griffith Boynton, died without issue. His title and estates passed to a cousin, Sir Francis, who knew the property well, having been born and brought up there during his father's lifelong tenure of the rectory at Barmston. The Grahams of Norton Conyers failed but once in the direct male line, in 1730, when Sir Bellingham, the third baronet, died unmarried less than two years after inheriting the title and

estate. However, his brother and successor, Sir Reginald, was
then only twenty-six years old and, having had little time to
develop other interests elsewhere, quickly took up where his
brother had left off. This also occurred at Whitley in 1743 when
Richard succeeded the short-lived Henry Beaumont. Both the
titles and the estates of the Goodricks and the Pilkingtons
devolved on brothers on only a single occasion, their predecessors having failed to marry or have children. There was little
discontinuity if a younger brother inherited the estate, even
where titles became extinct after one generation because of the
absence of a special remainder. This happened to the Saviles of
Methley, who thereafter achieved unbroken succession in a
direct male line until beyond 1800.[38]

In certain respects indirect succession was sometimes positively beneficial. If the next male hair enjoyed property of his
own, the total size of a family's estate was increased. This
occurred in the case of the Beaumonts, for example, on the two
occasions when the Whitley and Lascelles Hall properties
devolved on a single heir. Under the seventh baronet Hotham,
who succeeded his nephew, the South Dalton estate was amalgamated with other property in the East Riding inherited
through his wife. Secondly, where a direct line was broken by
an incumbent's failure to marry, the next heir greatly benefited
from the consequent reduction of settled charges on the estate.
A succession of bachelors or the long survival of a single
bachelor resulted in the disencumberment of property and left a
successor with substantial, if not complete, control over income
and expenditure. When William Haggerston-Constable took
over at Everingham in the 1750s, for instance, there were no
outstanding charges for portions or jointures, nor had there
been for some time past. The Stapletons of Myton were among
the few families who were presided over by successive
bachelors. The fourth baronet, Sir Miles, died in 1752, having
produced a single daughter, Ann, who died unmarried in 1770.
Both the fifth baronet, Sir Bryan, who held the estates until
1772, and the sixth, Sir John, who succeeded him until 1785,
died unmarried and childless. The property then descended to
a further brother, Martin, whose son became the eighth baronet
in 1801. The experiences of the Armitages of Kirklees comprised an extreme version of this same pattern, producing not

just a reduction in settled charges, but also frequent changes of regime, and eventually a deliberate severance of the link between the title and the estate. Sir John Armitage, the second baronet, produced a large family of whom six sons and three daughters were still alive at his death in 1677. It was much to the family's advantage, therefore, that his eldest son and heir, Sir Thomas, died a bachelor in 1694. Moreover, he was succeeded by a brother, Sir John, who also remained unmarried and lived on until 1732. Both title and estate then passed to yet another unmarried brother, Sir George, till 1736. However, while in that year the title devolved on an unmarried cousin, the estates were vested in another cousin who already had children. When the first baronetcy became extinct in 1737 the holder of the estates petitioned for a re-creation of title, which was granted to him in the following year. He also was succeeded by a bachelor son in 1747, and then finally by another, married son and parent of sons in 1758.[39]

The choice which confronted some families was a good deal more momentous than that which faced the Armitages. The estate and title of the Kayes of Woodsome were split on the death of the third baronet, Sir Arthur, in 1726. Had Sir Arthur produced and been survived by a son, the family would have inherited the Lister estates at Thornton. In 1745 these passed instead to Sir Arthur's nephew and successor in the baronetcy, who changed his name to Lister-Kaye. Meanwhile, Sir Arthur had preferred to settle the Woodsome estate on his only daughter, Elizabeth, who in 1722 married Viscount Lewisham, eldest son and heir of the Earl of Dartmouth. Thus, while the Lister-Kayes occupied Thornton and ancestral property at Denby Grange, Woodsome Hall and the estate were tenanted until the Dartmouth family moved there in the late nineteenth century. Likewise Sir John Hewett, the third baronet, deprived his nephew and successor in the title of the family property at Waresley in Huntingdonshire, to which his grandfather had moved from Headley Hall in Yorkshire. From 1737 holders of the baronetcy resided at Potton in Bedfordshire. The most sensational disposition was that made by Lord William Wentworth, third baronet of Wentworth Woodhouse and second Earl of Strafford. When he died without issue in 1695 all his peerage honours became extinct, except for the barony of Raby which, together with the baronetcy, devolved on his cousin, Thomas. Before his death, however, Wentworth left his huge estate to his sister's younger son, another Thomas, whose own son was subsequently created Earl of Malton and then Marquess of Rockingham. In 1711 Baron Raby (the fourth baronet) was created Earl of Strafford but this was little consolation for his earlier deprivation of property, which provoked a long-standing rivalry and animosity between the two families.[40]

While landowners without male children often contrived to maintain the link between title and property, they were often free from settlement restrictions and inclined to share their estates between more than one heir. In so doing they usually exercised considerable discrimination, being careful to maintain the integrity of individual properties, and rarely dividing the whole into equal parts. However, though the core of an estate was generally kept intact, nephews or cousins were not infrequently deprived of at least some of their predecessor's property. Moreover, that which they inherited tended to be encumbered with legacies, annuities, augmented jointures, or a combination of all three. In addition the actual possession of property might be long delayed while preceding life-interests ran out. William Haggerston-Constable found himself in an exceedingly favourable position on his accession. Not only had his uncle's bachelor status extinguished settled charges; but, because many earlier female relations had entered nunneries, and because his mother had been the only daughter of her generation, there were no other collateral males on whom Sir Marmaduke might have settled part of his property. Sir John Bright, on the other hand, left Carbrook and Edale, worth £700 a year, to John Bright of Gray's Inn; and, in addition to her jointure of £1,000 a year, left his widow a legacy of £2,500 and considerable property for life, which, due to her longevity, John Liddell-Bright never possessed. Richard Beaumont of Lascelles Hall found himself in a similarly difficult position in 1704. His predecessor's mother enjoyed a life-interest in Whitley, income from the estate was totally committed to the discharge of jointures or annuities, and was also charged with £7,100 in legacies. In both these cases the provision for widows acknowledged the likelihood of their remarriage. However, even where widows did not remarry, there was no automatic diversion of their share to their husbands' successors. Though not necessarily hostile or indifferent, widows were inevitably less close to their husbands' brothers, nephews, or cousins than they would have been to their own children. At her death in 1713 Lady Belasyse, whose husband had been succeeded by a nephew in 1700, devised all her considerable personal fortune away from the family. The widow of Sir Thomas Frankland, the third baronet, did likewise, despite surviving him for thirty-six years without remarrying, during which time she possessed the whole of the Thirkleby estate and amassed a personal fortune of some £35,000.[41] Finally, many indirect heirs had little expectation or experience of landownership on the scale provided by their inheritances; and between 1680 and 1699, and again between 1720 and 1739, regimes within these families changed with greater frequency than they had done between 1640 and 1659, when deaths and injuries sustained during the civil wars had increased mortality. On the whole, therefore, indirect succession tended to dislocate rather than to perpetuate management policies; to increase rather than to reduce the burden of settled charges on estates; and, at least in the short-term, to divide rather than to consolidate property.

A mere fourteen of these ninety-three families achieved succession in a single, direct male line throughout the seventeenth and eighteenth centuries. In most of these cases fathers occasionally outlived eldest sons, so that succession passed either to younger sons or to grandsons. Only three families – the Inglebys of Ripley, the Winns of Nostell, and the Stricklands of Boynton – succeeded from father to eldest or only son for two hundred years. Not surprisingly, members of all three families enjoyed a tendency to longevity. Although their titles were created in the mid seventeenth century, each was headed by only their fifth baronet in 1800; and thirteen of the fifteen individuals who succeeded to their titles died aged fifty years or over. In one case, however, this remarkably consistent record depended for its preservation on the succession of an illegitimate child. Sir John Ingleby, the fourth baronet, died unmarried in 1771 but not before he had produced two illegitimate sons by Mary Wright. He devised his property to the eldest of these, John, who was granted a re-creation of title ten years after

his father's death. Moreover, the Winns were relative newcomers to the ranks of the landed classes, purchasing Nostell
from the Royalist Sir John Wolstenholme in the 1650s. Thus,
among those families who owned substantial estates throughout the seventeenth and eighteenth centuries the demographic performance of the Stricklands of Boynton was
unequalled.[42]

3. THE RISE AND FALL OF ESTATES

If many of those families who failed in the male line strove
assiduously to maintain some connection with their property,
or at least to perpetuate the memory of that connection, it is not
surprising that the chief policy of those who survived was to
safeguard and preserve their estates. Like Richard Beaumont of
Lascelles Hall after 1704 or successive generations of the Constables of Everingham, most landowners were prepared to util-
ize every other means of achieving solvency before selling the
core of their property. A severe reduction in living standards,
protracted legal involvement, the avid pursuit of job and other
opportunities, intricate arrangements for the raising of loans
and the payment of debts, visits to the auction room and the
pawnshop – all these stratagems were generally adopted before
resort was had to major sales, even though the latter may have
afforded more immediate financial security. However, there
were a number of individuals whose reckless behaviour ran
counter to all that landed society held sacred. Despite earning
the opprobrium of their more sober contemporaries, they either
precipitated their families' decline or brought about their total
ruin. Incapacity or ill-luck were no less common. While their
worst effects were often mitigated with the help of friends or
relatives and by more able and fortunate successors, and seldom
led to a dramatic reduction in the size of a family's estate, they
were nevertheless responsible for bringing much land on to the
property market. In addition inheritance patterns did not
diminish, and probably increased, the number of detached and
outlying properties; and many landowners chose to alienate
these in the pursuit of other, more pressing needs. Nor was
there a shortage of purchasers. Substantial landowners were
joined by others, both from within and from outside landed
society, either in the piecemeal accumulation of property

adjacent to existing holdings or in the more dramatic expansion of ownership. In glossing over some of the less impressive interludes in the history of landed families, antiquarians and genealogists have often faithfully reflected the attitudes of contemporaries, for in difficult times this is what many landowners themselves tended to do. But, if the experiences of this group are in any way indicative of more general trends during this period, the degree to which the higher levels of landownership were characterized by continuity would appear to have been exaggerated. The overall impression is of a busy land market, by no means all of whose activity further substantiated the position of the landed élite.

If through panic, despair, or a failure to extend credit any further, land was sold, it was usually chosen carefully from among property which was outlying, which least complemented the rest of the estate, or which had come into the family relatively recently through marriage, inheritance, or purchase. Where they did take place, major sales of ancestral property were not soon forgotten. Sir Thomas Beaumont's father, Richard, was obliged to alienate much of the Lascelles Hall estate during the early seventeenth century in order to provide for the five daughters of his second wife's first marriage. Later Sir Thomas devoted much of his considerable activity in the land market to repurchasing this property, and by 1668 most of it was again in the family's possession. In 1671 Sir John Reresby regretted that purchases of lands in Mexborough included 'none of those sold by my father'. At the same time he attempted to regain land in Derbyshire which his great-grandfather had lost through not claiming equity of redemption on a mortgage. Although they refused to part with the property, the descendants of the mortgagee felt sufficiently sympathetic to Reresby's case to pay him £500 in compensation. For years after selling Wholsea in 1717 Sir Marmaduke Constable pestered Potts with queries concerning the property, which he clearly hoped to re-purchase. After a considerable lapse of time the Pennymans of Ormesby were successful in a similar endeavour in 1770, when for £47,500 they purchased an estate which included property sold by a predecessor for £3,500 during the Interregnum. In 1733 the estate of William Wombwell of Wombwell was divided equally between his two daughters and co-heiresses, Margaret and Elizabeth, one of whom married a Mr St. Leger and the other Sir Charles Turner of Kirkleatham. Turner bought St. Leger's share for £40,000, and later sold the entire estate back to St. Leger and another party for £105,000. When the property was subsequently sold off in small parcels the major purchaser was a member of a cadet branch of the Wombwell family, George Wombwell, whose successful career as a merchant and sometime Chairman of the East India Company was recognized by the grant of a baronetcy in 1778.[43]

In the century after 1660 it became imperative for landed families to hold on to the acreage which they possessed. As long as rent levels remained relatively stable, loss of property inevitably brought about a reduction in what for most families was the sole permanent source of income. In the prevailing circumstances a reduction in income was difficult to reverse and threatened a family's substance and way of life at their very roots. Moreover, if progress was achieved – in politics, the marriage market, or in terms of a family's standing in the local community – it could not be sustained for long without a growth in permanent income and, therefore, an expansion of the estate. The case-studies indicate that each of the four families concerned achieved a substantial increase in permanent income between 1660 and 1760. It is equally clear that, in addition to inheritance, purchases of property played a major part in this. Other sources of income became available but were without exception enjoyed only temporarily and spasmodically. They concentrated on this particular avenue of productive investment, not just because they were essentially conservative in economic matters; but also because irrespective of the purely financial rewards of such investment, it produced a steady increase in their status and prestige. As the eighteenth century progressed monetary returns from other types of investment rivalled, and in some instances overtook, those obtained in the land market. However, the manner in which estates were expanded bears witness to a keen appreciation of the non-quantifiable rewards of investment in landed property, which ensured its primacy.

Particularly at the level of the baronetage, landowners were less interested in the mere accumulation of property than in the possession of compact estates. If they were in the process of establishing themselves, they looked not just for land but for property which had all the accoutrements appropriate to life as a country gentleman. If already established, they were concerned to acquire as much land in the vicinity of their estate as possible. Power and influence were more readily associated with the possession of unbroken tracts of land in clearly defined areas than with sizeable but scattered acreages. In addition compactness increased the efficiency and capacity of management and reduced administrative costs per acre. As a result consolidation was a characteristic feature of estate expansion. Inevitably, even where large amounts of capital were available for investment in this way, the process of consolidation was gradual and cumulative. Owners and their representatives were constantly tuned to the latest hints and gossip of future sales; and ready, if necessary, to seek out and cajole hesitant or secretive vendors. When large properties came on to the market neighbouring landowners were automatically assumed to be interested in buying them. But the filling in or rounding off of estates also required numerous purchases and exchanges of smaller properties. Over a long period the Legards, for example, were singularly successful in this latter respect, for when their estate was finally sold in 1911 all but two farms out of a total of over 6,500 acres were contained within a single ring fence round Ganton. However, the consolidation of estates was far advanced a century earlier, especially in the East Riding. By the first decade of the nineteenth century there were few small estates on the Wolds, 'the larger proprietors in general having purchased the property of the smaller. . . . The owners likewise of most of the estates have had the opportunity in a long series of years of concentrating their property, and many of them consequently possess large estates in this Riding'. Among the families to whose activities in this respect the writer drew particular attention were the Legards, the Boyntons, the St. Quintins, and the Stricklands.[44]

The case-studies provide much evidence of this process in action. Owing largely to his numerous marriages, the property of Sir John Hotham, the first baronet, was scattered over a wide area from the moors of north Yorkshire to Holderness in the south of the East Riding. Between 1659 and 1750 his successors made no fewer than seventeen purchases of property. Fifteen of these were of land or premises situated within a ten-mile radius of Scorborough or South Dalton, while each of the remaining two purchases consolidated existing property at Wilton in the vale of Pickering. The Hothams' only sales during this period were of their Beverley house and of property adjacent to it. In the period 1639 to 1764 the Beaumonts made twenty-five purchases. None of them cost upwards of £1,000, eight were for sums of less than £100, and without exception purchased property was situated in or near Lepton and Kirkheaton. Apart from the unavoidable alienation of Lascelles Hall in 1714, their few sales were of outlying properties at Sandal, Crosland, and Mitton, all of which either financed other purchases or contributed to the discharge of debts. Moreover, despite their considerable misfortunes between 1640 and 1720, over the period as a whole the Constables contrived to spend far more on purchases of property than they raised from sales. In 1654, in the midst of a parlous financial situation, they went still further into debt by purchasing for a total of £1,170 farms in Arras and Middle Rasen which bordered on property which they already held there. Seaton Ross, bought for £12,000 in 1752, was only a couple of miles from Everingham and in size and value more than compensated for earlier losses. Finally, between 1619 and 1755 the Brights were involved in fifty-three purchases, nine sales, and five exchanges of property; as well as in unspecified but substantial assumptions of parts of the Arundel estate in the Sheffield area. They concentrated initially on consolidating their holdings in and around Sheffield. And then, when increased status stimulated the desire for a more conventional, rural estate, Sir John Bright built up a further closely integrated property centred on Badsworth. The majority of their few sales were of land and premises in Derbyshire. The purchases of these four families were financed in a variety of ways: in repayment of debts, and from portions, loans, salaries, recurrent estate income, and from the proceeds of sales of wood and other property. The only feature common to almost all the transactions was that the property which was acquired consolidated existing holdings.

The memorandum book of Sir Walter Calverley provides a reliable indication of his endeavours in this connection. In 1652, as outlined earlier, Walter Calverley of Calverley succeeded to a small and heavily encumbered estate. By dint of retrenchment and property sales he survived until 1662 when, as his grandfather had suggested, a successful marriage solved his immediate financial problems. His wife, Frances, was the sole heiress of Henry Thompson of Bromfield in Cumberland and of Esholt near Calverley in the West Riding. Shortly before his death in 1691 Calverley directed that the Cumberland estate should be sold to pay for the outstanding portions of his two daughters. His son, the diarist, devoted several years to meeting this requirement before concentrating on the consolidation and embellishment of the Yorkshire estate. Besides building and landscaping at Esholt, he made thirteen purchases of property between 1694 and 1718 for a sum total of over £8,500. His purchases included farms, mills, tithes, houses, and other land, some of which had earlier been alienated by his maternal grandfather. All the property lay in or near Calverley and Esholt and investment capital was derived from rents, interest on loans, sales of wood, the residue of the money received for the Cumberland estate, and from the portion of Calverley's wife. The property acquisitions of Sir John Reresby were also exclusively devoted to consolidation. In his case capital was scarce: for several years much of his estate provided jointures for his mother and grandmother; and, although his bride's portion was 'not £1,200', Reresby stubbornly refused to 'choose somebody of a greater family and fortune'. In 1659, at the cost of 'all arrears due to me from my mother as guardian to me during my minority' (some £2,000), he acquired a beneficial lease of lands in Thribergh, which earlier had come to his mother as her husband's sole executrix. Reresby was much disgruntled by this hard bargain but, as he himself explained, 'those lands were so very necessary to me that I could not well improve or make advantage of the rest of my lands in Thribergh without them'. A decade later his luck changed when he obtained a grant of half of the estate of Mr Bromley, the Earl of Strafford's butler, who had committed suicide and whose property, therefore, was forfeited to the Crown. Reresby carefully negotiated the receipt of that half of the land which lay in his own lordship. The remainder of his acquisitions were all much smaller, comprising lands, houses, or closes in Thribergh or in nearby Mexborough and Bradmarsh. On one occasion, for £225, he was able to extinguish an annual rent charge of £36 from the estate which had earlier been contracted by Sir George Reresby.[45]

Other printed works, in particular abstracts of wills, provide further evidence of strategic estate expansion. Over a long period the Legards competed with one of their neighbours, a Mr Coundon, to acquire property in Bennington. On the latter's death in 1715 Sir John Legard purchased all the deceased's holdings there from his widow and eldest son. Sir Godfrey Copley, the second baronet, not only built a new house at Sprotborough, but 'added to the estate by purchases in the vicinity' at Scawsby Hall, Bilham, and elsewhere. The will of Sir John Bland, the fourth baronet, indicates that he greatly increased the size of the Kippax Park estate by purchasing lands in Allerton and Brigshaw, 'which he laid to the same and enclosed the whole with a wall'. The will of his successor speaks of similar purchases: besides those near Kippax for which the fifth baronet asked his eldest son to pay £1,000, there was a 'close of land which he purchased' and 'then inclosed in his Park, and the two meadows adjoining'. Sir James Pennyman, the third baronet, who lived at Thornton Hall in Cleveland, devised to his heir 'lands by me purchased in Thornton, Stainton, and Maltby', a 'rent charge in Stainton', 'my lands in Middleham which I bought of Mr Digby, lands called the garths bought of Mr Kilvington, and Ten Mile Hill bought of Humber Smith'. A farm which he had purchased in East Upsall in Cleveland was similarly disposed of before his death.[46] While, however, isolated sources are occasionally revealing, it is difficult to appreciate the singlemindedness with which the consolidation of property was pursued without the detailed scrutiny of individual estates. Only a thorough study of all the available documentary evidence will reveal the full scope of any family's activities in the property market. Smaller transactions in particular are often impossible to identify in any other way, while also relevant are those instances where attempts at purchase or exchange were unsuccessful. The piecemeal acquisition of holdings adjacent to an estate was an unspectacular and, of necessity, a protracted phenomenon. Nevertheless it played a significant part in both the expansion and the improvement of landed estates during this period.

Considerably more dramatic was the growth of estates

through marriage and inheritance, of which this group of families provides plentiful examples. A major reason for the rise of the Lowthers of Swillington 'has been the abilities of the younger sons and the fact that the property acquired by them has eventually fallen to the head of the house'. Sir Francis Boynton not only expanded but also greatly consolidated his holdings in the vicinity of Barmston on inheriting the Burton Agnes property in 1656. Following the death in infancy of the son of his second cousin in 1660, William Chaytor of Butterby in Co. Durham succeeded to the Croft estate in the North Riding, which he subsequently made his home. On the death of his father-in-law, Sir Thomas Widdrington, in 1664 Sir John Legard came into the manor and estate of Kidlands in Northumberland. The Milbankes acquired property at Dalden Tower in Co. Durham, apparently through the first baronet's marriage to a daughter of Ralph Cocke, merchant and alderman of Newcastle upon Tyne. In 1689, three years before his accession to the baronetage, John Wentworth of Brodsworth came into the large estate of his cousin, Thomas, at North Elmsall. Sir Thomas Frankland, the second baronet, inherited a considerable estate at Chiswick in Middlesex from his uncle, the Earl of Fauconberg. Sir Edward Gascoigne of Parlington substantially increased his family's landed income by marrying Mary, heiress of Sir Francis Hungate of Saxton. In 1748 Richard Beaumont's second marriage brought him the Holt family's property at Mitton and Grizzlehurst, while four years later the Bright estates were amalgamated with those of Wentworth Woodhouse on Mary Bright's marriage to Lord Rockingham. As a result of his marriage to Frances Thompson Sir Beaumont Hotham inherited further property in the East Riding shortly after succeeding his nephew in the title and estate at South Dalton. And Sir John Ingleby of Ripley, first baronet of the second creation, eventually came into a substantial property at Kettlethorpe in Lincolnshire following his marriage to Elizabeth, daughter and heiress of Sir Wharton Amcotts.[47]

Some families were spectacularly successful in accumulating property through marriage and inheritance. The Blands joined this select group briefly following the fourth baronet's marriage to Anne, daughter and heiress of Sir Edward Moseley of Hulme

Hall, until the sixth baronet dissipated the inheritance. Having in the early seventeenth century also inherited a large property in Lancashire, the Belasyse family of Newburgh later made further substantial additions to their estates through marriage. In 1700 Thomas Belasyse, the first Earl of Fauconberg, was succeeded by his nephew who had inherited through his mother an estate at Sutton in Cheshire. Then in 1726 the latter's son and heir married into more than £2,000 a year from the St. Thomas's Priory estate in Staffordshire. Marriage to the Blacketts of Wallington and Hexham in Northumberland transformed the circumstances of two of these families. The Calverleys' connection with the Blacketts began in 1707 when Sir Walter, the diarist, married Julia, daughter of Sir William Blackett, the first baronet. In 1729 their son, another Walter, married the illegitimate daughter and sole heiress of Sir William Blackett, the third and last baronet; and, having by act of Parliament assumed the name of Blackett, came into the Wallington and Hexham estates as well as other property in Newcastle. However, this marriage was childless and on Sir Walter's death in 1777 part of the property devolved on Sir Thomas Wentworth of Bretton, whose mother had been the seventh daughter of the first Blackett baronet. The core of the Sledmere estate (containing property in no less than fifteen parishes and townships in the East Riding) came to the Sykes family as a result of the marriage in 1704 of Richard Sykes and Mary, daughter and co-heiress of Mary Kirby, although possession was only enjoyed from 1748 following the death of Mary's brother, Mark. By then both Richard and Mary Sykes were long dead, and it was their son and heir, Richard, who first occupied Sledmere. Later in the century Sir Christopher Sykes's marriage to Elizabeth, daughter of William Tatton of Wynthenshawe, brought a further valuable inheritance from her brother.[48]

Over a very long period of time the Gowers, originally of Stittenham, were the most successful of all families in the marriage market. Sir Thomas Gower, the second baronet, took as his second wife, Frances, daughter of Sir John Leveson of Haling in Kent and of Lilleshall in Staffordshire. Sir Thomas was succeeded by his grandson as third baronet until 1689; but it was Sir Thomas's youngest son, William, the fourth baronet, who inherited a huge estate in Staffordshire from his great-uncle, Sir William Leveson, in 1691; and took the additional surname of Leveson shortly before his own death in December of that year. As Sir William's wife, Jane, eldest daughter of the first Earl of Bath, was predeceased by her nephew, the last Earl, the Leveson-Gowers also became co-heirs to the very considerable Bath estates in 1711. Meanwhile, the first Baron Gower had died in 1709 but not before marrying the daughter of the wealthy Duke of Rutland. Their eldest son, the first Earl Gower, married three times: to a daughter of the Duke of Kingston, the widow of Sir Henry Atkins Bart., and finally to the daughter of the Earl of Thanet, who had previously been married to Lord Lucas. His son, the second Earl, married Elizabeth Fazakerley of Penwortham in Lancashire, who enjoyed a fortune of £16,000; and then in 1748 Louisa, daughter of the first Duke of Bridgewater; and in 1786 was created Marquess of Stafford. In the previous year his son and eventual successor had married Elizabeth, Countess of Sutherland, who owned half of that county. Soon afterwards Stafford inherited the Bridgewater estates, thereby becoming the largest landowner in the country, a position he quickly improved on by purchasing the other half of Sutherland from Lord Reay. In 1833 he was further advanced in the peerage with the title of Duke of Sutherland.[49]

No single individual, however, obtained more through inheritance than Sir Hugh Smithson, descendant of a London merchant who had received a baronetcy from Charles II. In 1733, aged eighteen and still an undergraduate at Oxford, he succeeded his grandfather in the title and the estate at Stanwick. In addition to this property, which was worth 'better than £4,000 a year', his predecessor's elderly first cousin had named him heir to 'very near if not quite £3,000 a year more' from property in Yorkshire and Tottenham. Smithson's expectations rose still further in 1740 on his engagement to Lady Elizabeth Seymour whose grandfather, the Duke of Somerset, was to give her a portion of £10,000. Cajoled by the Duke of Leeds, who acted on Smithson's behalf, Somerset grudgingly agreed to the match; and on the death of his aged relative in September of that year, two months after his marriage, Smithson duly inherited the Yorkshire and Tottenham properties. Later his wealth was further and spectacularly increased by developments which could not have been foreseen at the time of his marriage. For in 1744 Lady Smithson's brother, Lord Beauchamp, died on his nineteenth birthday, making her heiress to much of the huge Percy estates. Somerset, who meanwhile had conceived a violent dislike for Smithson, then petitioned the Crown for the earldom of Northumberland, with a remainder to Sir Charles Wyndham but none to Smithson. However, allying with his father-in-law, Lord Hertford, Smithson persuaded George II to delay granting the patent. Following Somerset's death in 1748 the earldom was given to Hertford with a remainder to Smithson. The latter succeeded his father-in-law in the title in 1750, and was created Earl Percy and Duke of Northumberland in 1766. He died twenty years later, having by successive strokes of good fortune reputedly increased his landed income to some £50,000 a year.[50]

However, although inheritance, marriage-related or otherwise, was clearly a significant factor in the expansion of many estates, the common experience was both less dramatic and more diverse than these examples alone would indicate. In the first place genealogies and other, older printed works are often inadequate or positively misleading in describing sole surviving female issue as heiresses or co-heiresses. In a purely genealogical sense this may of course be correct, though it is frequently wrong to infer from the description that such women received property from the deceased. In many instances, as we have seen, property was devised to more distant relatives in the male line, with female issue receiving only money from the estate. In such circumstances the portions of a deceased's daughters or sisters were commonly more substantial than they would have been had their brothers or other, close male relatives survived; and might consist of annuities instead of, or in addition to, capital sums. The fact remains, however, that dispositions of property were considerably more varied than is often supposed and, consequently, few entirely safe assumptions can be made in regard to them. Many would be beneficiaries were disappointed, not just by the operation of chance factors which made remainders redundant, but also by the deliberate choice of those whose property they coveted. For example, when William Savile, son and heir of the Marquess of Halifax, married

Elizabeth, only daughter of Sir Samuel Grimston, in 1687 he must have hoped that eventually he would inherit the large Grimston estates. In fact the Saviles had to content themselves with Elizabeth's substantial legacy, for Sir Samuel left the property to a great nephew. Moreover, particularly if it was situated at some distance from a family's ancestral estate, it was not uncommon for property, once it had been inherited, to be settled on someone (a younger brother or younger son) other than the eldest son and heir of a beneficiary. Thus, Sir Griffith Boynton, the fifth baronet, inherited through his mother considerable property at Otteringham which he gave to his younger brother, Francis, who later sold it. Alternatively, if the incumbent of an estate inherited a large landed fortune elsewhere, his original property might deliberately be kept apart from his subsequent inheritance. After inheriting the Campsall estate on his marriage to Ann Frank in 1694 Sir George Tempest of Tong, in collaboration with his eldest son, Henry, cut the entail on his ancestral property and arranged partible inheritance. Henry, who succeeded to the baronetcy, took Campsall, while the Tong estate passed to Nicholas, his younger brother. Again, in 1755 Sir William Lowther, third baronet of Marske, inherited the rich estates of Sir James Lowther, fourth baronet of Whitehaven. At Sir William's death, unmarried and without issue, in the following year the Cumbrian estates, which were entailed, passed to the fifth baronet of Whitehaven. However, as well as 'thirteen legacies of £5,000 each to his friends', Sir William left Marske to the Wilsons of Dallam Tower; and Holker in Lancashire, which he had inherited through his grandmother, to his maternal cousin, Lord George Cavendish.[51]

Even when property devolved on female issue it was not always shared equally between them or, indeed, shared at all. Sir Thomas Wentworth-Blackett, for instance, left one property to a nephew, and the rest of his estates to the eldest of three illegitimate daughters. Each of his other daughters received merely life-annuities from their elder sister's property. On the other hand, where property was shared the problems associated with its division, together perhaps with its remoteness from a husband's estate, sometimes encouraged its sale. For example, on the death in 1685 of Sir Samuel Marrow of

Berkswell in Warwickshire, both that property and the manor
and advowson of Birmingham, which he had also owned,
became equally vested in each of his five daughters and co-
heiresses. Sir Arthur Kaye of Woodsome married the eldest
daughter, Anne, in 1690 and, although all the parties were keen
to sell their interests, it proved difficult to arrange an equitable
division. Sir Arthur eventually obtained the lordship of Birmingham in the right of his wife, and sold it soon afterwards.
The expectations aroused by a prospective inheritance might
also be eroded by life-interests and other sources of inconvenience and delay, as in the case of the Pennymans of Ormesby. By
his marriage to Mary, sister and co-heiress of Sir Michael
Wharton of Beverley, in 1692 Sir James Pennyman, third
baronet, brought his family within reach of a huge inheritance.
However, there were other co-heiresses and, though Sir
Michael died in 1725, the bulk of his property was not divided
until 1775, by which time the sixth Pennyman baronet occupied
Ormesby. A division 'so as each share might lie together' was
finally allocated by lots drawn from a jar by an 'indifferent
person' (Sarah Palethorpe, a thirteen-year-old from Newark),
and was subsequently ratified by private act of Parliament.[52] As
Lord Rockingham and his lawyers discovered to their dismay
during the negotiations prior to his marriage with Mary Bright,
much of a prospective wife's fortune might be in expectancy
rather than in possession, and might continue to be so for some
considerable time to come. In the interim parts of it were liable
to be diverted elsewhere by unexpected births, survivals, or
deaths.

Furthermore, an inheritance in possession usually ceased to
be enjoyed by a husband's family if he failed to have children by
his marriage to the heiress. Even had their marriage been more
congenial, this would have been the case with the property of
the second wife of Sir Charles Hotham, the fourth baronet, for
their only child died in infancy. Likewise the Beaumonts lost all
claim to the huge Stringer estates on the death without issue of
Richard of Whitley in 1704. Where, as in this case, they outlived
their husbands, heiresses required their inheritance for future
forays in the marriage market. If an heiress bought a successful
first marriage by conceding the right of her husband's family to
eventual enjoyment of her property, irrespective of whether

there was issue of the marriage, as did Katherine Heron on her marriage to the future third baronet Hotham, she nevertheless usually retained possession of it for life. Thus, although the third baronet died in 1691, Katherine's property did not revert to his family until her death nearly forty years later in 1728. Some heiresses retained merely life-possession of property, despite marrying only once and having children by that marriage. The already substantial resources of Sir John Goodrick of Ribston were boosted considerably by his marriage in 1731 to the illegitimate Mary Johnson, who inherited for life the Bramham Park estate which her father, Lord Bingley, had been granted for his services to the Crown. At her death in 1792, however, that property did not pass to her grandson, who had succeeded Sir John in 1789.[53] Moreover, marriage settlements invariably provided heiresses with lucrative jointures which were enjoyed even when widowhood was terminated by remarriage; and, like Richard Beaumont and Sir John Bright, doting husbands often augmented jointures by devising large legacies and annuities to their widows. Much depended on whether wives outlived husbands and, if so, for how long. But even where possession of an inheritance was permanent, some families paid dearly for the property which they inherited.

An important consideration in this last connection is that, precisely because so much was at stake, marriage settlements, wills, and other transactions involving the transmission of property from one family to another were notoriously subject to legal disputes. John Liddell-Bright and Richard Beaumont of Lascelles Hall were not alone in spending half their careers agonizing over the outcome of such disputes; nor were theirs the only families who spent considerable sums, either in an attempt to ensure success or in consequence of failure. Perhaps the most protracted dispute concerned part of the Lancashire property which came to the Lowthers of Marske following Sir William's marriage in 1697 to Catherine, daughter and heiress of Thomas Preston of Holker. The family at Holker were a younger branch of an old-established family of Prestons of Preston Patrick in Westmorland, who, by Crown grant, also enjoyed the manor of Furness. Eventually both Preston Patrick and Furness devolved on a younger brother of the senior branch of the family, Thomas Preston, who was a Catholic priest, but who on his succession to the property renounced his orders and married. On the death without male issue of his wife in 1673, however, he re-entered religious life overseas, leaving his Westmorland estates to his daughters and Furness to the Jesuits. Thomas Preston of Holker, who was descended from a younger brother of the original grantee, at once claimed Furness. Although following a lengthy lawsuit Furness was declared to be forfeited to the Crown, Charles II granted Preston a lease of the property for seven years. This was extended to twenty-one years by William and Mary in 1690, and then in 1695 by a further fifteen years to commence in 1711. Thomas Preston died in 1696 and Sir William Lowther, his son-in-law, in 1705, leaving a six-year-old heir, Thomas Lowther, whose guardian was his grandmother, Thomas Preston's widow, Elizabeth. In 1710 a Richard Woolaston obtained a lease of the manor of Furness from Queen Anne and thereupon brought ejectment orders against the tenants. Elizabeth Preston initiated a costly lawsuit in defence of the minor's interest and, following an appeal to the House of Lords, was successful. She capitalized on this in 1715 by petitioning for a thirty-one year lease of the property, which was finally confirmed by letters patent in 1717. Of shorter duration, though no less remarkable, was the dispute in which Sir Henry Goodrick of Ribston, the fourth baronet, was involved after his succession in 1705. His aunt, Dame Mary Goodrick, and Eleanor Glanville, a distant relative by marriage, contested Sir Henry's right to certain properties which his uncle and predecessor had inherited, and which Sir Henry then enjoyed by his uncle's will. Sir Henry managed to retain these properties and later, to his consternation, was by her will named as heir to Eleanor Glanville's substantial estate in Somerset at her death in 1709. Glanville's son immediately challenged her disposition, maintaining that, latterly, she had thought that her children were bewitched by fairies. After the examination of over a hundred witnesses at Wells assizes in 1712, the will was upset on the grounds of the testatrice's insanity and Sir Henry lost the property.[54]

Particularly where it resulted in an estate being split, litigation was a factor in the sale of property. For example, in 1720 after a lawsuit of twenty-two years' duration, the Keresforth estate of the younger branch of the Armitage family, whose heir succeeded to the Kirklees estate in 1736, was divided between John Armitage and William Collier, who had married an Armitage widow. Both parts of the property were subsequently sold. Thomas Belasyse of Newburgh, fourth Viscount of Fauconberg, had a similar experience. In 1726 he married Catherine Betham, sole heiress by his will of 1712 of William Fowler of St. Thomas's Priory near Stafford. Fauconberg took the name of Fowler and came into more than £2,000 a year. However, in 1727 a later will which revoked that of 1712 was discovered. A long suit in Chancery eventually culminated in an appeal before the House of Lords where, in 1733, it was determined that Fauconberg should give up one half of the inherited property. He thereupon lost all interest in that which remained to him and quickly sold it.[55]

For a variety of reasons, therefore, any estimate of the extent to which families from this group benefited from the inheritance of property is fraught with difficulty. Having been largely created in the early and mid seventeenth century, the baronetage was in numerical decline during the first half of the eighteenth century. While extinctions of title did not constitute an impediment to continuing success as landowners, the adverse demographic trends of the century after the Restoration were in several families not offset by indirect succession, while extravagance and generally less propitious economic circumstances led others into decline. Consequently, before the mid eighteenth century the group as a whole was tending, through economic decline and the failure of heirs, to relinquish some of its property, including some of that which it had gained through inheritance. This, however, is not the whole story. It is necessary to draw a distinction between short-term and long-term gains. A number of families sold inherited property, which was often inconveniently situated in relation to their main estates, in order to tide themselves over financial difficulties or to finance developments elsewhere; others settled it on younger brothers, younger sons, or other relatives. Moreover, although a general failure of heirs boosted gains from inheritance in the longer term, in the short term much property remained in the possession of life-tenants and subject to a variety of capital charges; as well as being liable to legal complexities, which also encouraged sales. As in all periods the most substantial landowning families did best, success in one generation breeding further success in the next. For some ten per cent of those who survived beyond the mid eighteenth century the inheritance of property before then was a major factor in their increase in wealth. Perhaps twice that number made substantial, long-term additions to their estates, with as many again making less impressive, and often temporary, gains.

None of the foregoing is meant to suggest either that estate expansion was most commonly on a piecemeal basis or that only a few estates grew rapidly during this period. Many estates were considerably expanded, not because of frequent interventions in the land market, nor through inheritance. The evidence suggests that a third factor was also of considerable importance, namely the sale of large properties by members of the aristocracy or gentry to other members of these groups. One of the problems associated with the concept of the rise of great estates during the post-Restoration period is that it has fostered the assumption that all, or most, substantial landowners were then in the process of expanding their holdings. Even if this is qualified to acknowledge the effects of demographic developments, it remains an inadequate reflection of reality. Throughout the period and for other reasons much property passed from some substantial landowners to others. For some of the vendors such transactions reflected financial or other difficulties which were eventually overcome; for others they spelt ruin. Whatever the circumstances, a significant number of families established themselves as substantial landowners, or became major landowners, because other families were involved in the reverse process. To some extent, of course, this pattern was common to all periods before the general decline of large estates in modern times. Judging from the experiences of this group, however, it was not least pronounced in the years from the mid seventeenth to the mid eighteenth centuries.

In the first place, while a majority of Royalists survived the Civil War and Interregnum relatively unscathed or at least without substantial loss of property, it is clear that many of them incurred heavy debts. Some Royalists serviced and discharged these debts by a variety of means including the sale of small outlying properties, such as the land in Holderness sold by the Constables in the 1650s, or South Hall and the manor of Cranswick sold by Sir Thomas Williamson to the Hothams in 1660. In other cases, however, disencumberment was judged to be impossible without sizeable alienations. The growth of Sir John Bright's estate owed much to the misfortunes of Royalists. He acquired, in circumstances which remain obscure, much Arundel property in Sheffield; and commenced separate development elsewhere with the purchase for £8,600 in 1653 of 1,400 acres in Badsworth, Skelbrook and Ackworth from the Catholic Royalist, Thomas Dolman. The latter subsequently moved to his less imposing holding near Pocklington in the East Riding, where his family persisted as minor gentry into the eighteenth century. It was these acquisitions in particular which brought Bright into the ranks of the county's substantial landowners where, during the 1640s and 1650s, he was joined by several other major purchasers. In 1649, for example, the Lowthers obtained the Marske estate for £13,000, and in the following year the nearby manor of Oughborough. A few years later their cousins purchased the grange and manor of Round-hay from the Tempests of Broughton; Great Preston, Astley, and Swillington for over £6,000 from Conyers, son of Lord Darcy; and finally property at Garforth and Rothwell. Having paid £10,000 for the Nostell Priory estate in 1629, the Royalist Sir John Wolstenholme was bankrupted by heavy fines in 1650, and sold the property to the Winns four years later. Brian Cooke of Doncaster, creditor to several Royalists, purchased the manor of Bentley in the 1650s; and also that of Wheatley, which became his family's seat and had previously belonged to Sir Robert Anstruther. The Cookes, the Winns, and the Lowthers of Swillington, far from being avid Parliamentarians, were all liberal contributors to the Royalist cause. This did not prevent them, however, from investing the profits of their various commercial interests in the purchase of Royalists' property. Meanwhile, some members of the group were being forced into major sales. James Pennyman, than whom no one in Yorkshire was a more zealous Royalist, sold part of his estate at Ormesby to his major creditor, Sir Gervase Elwes. Henry Calverley was hampered by difficulties unconnected with the rebellion, though in addition his estate, which was in tail, was assessed by the Parliamentary authorities as if it was in fee. Calverley panicked and sold substantial portions of his property. The second Earl of Strafford was shielded from active involvement in the hostilities by his minority and a period of travel abroad. On his return, however, he sold Ledston, Harewood and Gawthorpe (about half his Yorkshire property and worth on his own estimation between £4,000 and £5,000 a year) in order to discharge the remainder of his father's huge debts.[56]

Although the period of the Civil War and Interregnum appears to have been one of marked activity in the land market, there was in this respect no stark contrast between it and the century or so after the Restoration. Owing to their gross indebtedness the entire estates of a number of previously substantial landowning families came on to the market, while many others sold sizeable parts of their property. On the demand side the characteristic feature was for many of these properties to be purchased intact or in a very few lots, not only by established members of the landed élite, but also by successful lesser gentry, or relative newcomers who used non-landed wealth to achieve or to increase gentry status. Among the peerage, for example, there was a perhaps natural tendency for many transactions to be conducted with other members of that group. In the 1670s Sir Thomas Osborne, Earl of Danby, acquired a property in Wimbledon from George, Lord Digby; in 1727 Henry Dawnay of Cowick, second Viscount Downe, sold valuable burgage properties in Pontefract to John Monkton, first Viscount Galway; and when the fourth Viscount Fauconberg determined to sell the St. Thomas's Priory estate in Staffordshire in the 1730s the purchaser was the Duchess of Marlborough. Neither of these last two transactions, however, was in any way indicative of economic difficulty: indeed, besides making considerable gains through inheritance, those families who were raised from the baronetage to the peerage included among their ranks a number of major purchasers. The Straffords, for example, recovered in the late seventeenth century, not least because of the income from their Irish property. In the early eighteenth century the third Earl of Strafford bought a large estate at Stainborough, where he established his seat, as well as both parts of the Armitages' Keresforth estate following its division; while during the course of the century the Wentworth Woodhouse branch of the family virtually doubled their acreage from 9,420 to 17,200, only 3,000 acres of which comprised the Bright inheritance of 1752. The Osbornes of Kiveton in particular not only greatly expanded their holdings but did so by a long series of major purchases, which began in 1636 with the acquisition of Thorpe Salvin from the Sandford family. However, it was during the long and lucrative career of Sir Thomas Osborne, Earl of Danby and then Duke of Leeds, that the family accumulated the bulk of their huge estate in south Yorkshire. In 1673 he bought the manors of Harthill and Woodhall from the Chaworths and, four years later, the adjoining manor of Todwick. Then in 1700–1 he purchased the manor of Wakefield, and those of North and South Allstan, near Kiveton. Later, in 1735, Danby's great-grandson, the fourth Duke of Leeds, obtained the manor of Barnsley; and in 1737, from the trustees of the Coke estate, the castle and manor of Coningsborough. Thereby 'he became the lord paramount, not only in his own immediate district of Harthill and Kiveton, but through a wide extent of country around him'. However, the family fortune was severely taxed by the longevity of the third Duke's widow (his third wife), who outlived him for sixty-three years on a jointure of £3,000 a year; and, following acute financial difficulties in 1745–6, the fourth Duke sold the outlying estate at Seaton Ross in the East Riding to the Constables of Everingham for £12,000. Nevertheless, a century of estate expansion culminated in 1778 when, as a result of his marriage to Amelia Darcy, the fifth Duke's estates were amalgamated with other substantial properties in the North and West Ridings on the death of the Earl of Holderness.[57]

Equally significant, however, was the extent to which successful gentry families at all levels capitalized on alienations of property by members of their own social group. In the decades after the Restoration, for example, besides obtaining Great Houghton from the Rhodes family, and the Kinsley and Cockhill estate from the Monsons, Sir John Bright purchased Billingley and Milnehouse from the Jacksons. The latter's other manor, Hickleton, was bought by the Wentworths of Woolley, untitled but substantial gentry who also acquired property from Sir Francis Burdett. During the same period the Milbankes accumulated Halnaby, Bainingham, and Thorpe; and later, apparently, some of the property relinquished by Sir William

Chaytor of Croft. Other major purchasers towards the end of the seventeenth century were the Inglebys of Ripley, who acquired the Armley Hall estate and other land from the Mauleverers, and Sir Godfrey Copley of Sprotborough who bought Scawsby Hall and land in Bilham. In 1697, in fulfilment of the terms of his marriage settlement, John Liddell-Bright was able to purchase for £5,881 the whole of the manor of Bamforth in Derbyshire from the Ashtons. When he decided to sell the property some twenty years later the entire property again passed intact to other gentry, the Gisbornes. During the first decade of the eighteenth century the bulk of the Reresbys' estate, including Thribergh, Dennaby, and Brinsworth, was purchased by the Saviles of Methley. In 1707 the heavily in-debted Hobys of Hackness Hall near Scarborough finally sold their estate for £31,000 to John van den Bempdé, a rich land-owner of Dutch origin who also had substantial commercial interests, and whose grandson was eventually raised to the baronetage in 1795. In 1714 Richard Beaumont sold Lascelles Hall in one lot to a neighbouring lesser gentry family, and in the following decade the Legards did likewise with their manor and lands at Escrick. The Hawksworths were obliged to sell properties during the early eighteenth century to, among others, the Goodricks of Ribston. Examples from mid century and beyond suggest that this pattern continued. Soon after inheriting the properties at Calverley and Esholt in Yorkshire on the death of his father in 1749, Sir Walter Calverley-Blackett sold them in order to purchase Wallington in Northumberland, which he had also inherited (from his father-in-law) but which, as a result of a Chancery suit, had been ordered to be put up for sale. The Yorkshire properties, sold in two lots, fetched a total of £112,000 from local purchasers – the Thornhills of Fixby (untitled, middling gentry) and Robert Stansfield, gentleman, of Bradford. During this same period Sir Walter was himself a major purchaser from the declining Catholic family, the Swin-burnes of Capheaton in Northumberland. In 1758 Henry Brewster-Darley, current head of a long-established gentry family at Aldby in Yorkshire, mortgaged himself heavily in order to purchase for £23,000 an adjacent estate at Skirpenbeck. This property had been encumbered ever since the death of Sir Watkinson Payler, the last baronet, in 1705 but had remained in the possession of his granddaughter, Mary, until her death in 1756, when the trustees named in her will sold it to discharge debts. One baronet, Sir Lionel Pilkington, simple switched properties, buying the Chevet estate from his brother, who had married the heiress of Cavendish Nevile of Chevet, and selling his ancestral property at Stanley. Another family, the Woods of Barnsley, having gone into economic decline in the seventeenth century, recovered through activity in local commerce and the professions, and, besides inheriting property at Bowling, purchased an estate at Hemsworth in 1769. All this property passed to Sir Francis Wood, created baronet in 1784, whose successor purchased a further estate at Garrowby in the East Riding in 1803. Finally, when some years before his death in 1777 the reckless Sir Thomas Robinson had to sell the Rokeby estate, it too was purchased by a neighbouring gentry family, the Morritts.[58]

While, because of the chronology of creations, study of the baronetage does not provide a balanced view of the flow of non-landed wealth into the property market during the late seventeenth and eighteenth centuries, this group of families contains several examples of that particular phenomenon. Again, some families can be seen to have benefited from the economic difficulties of established members of the gentry and aristocracy. Although John Silvester's family had long been resident in the parish of Ecclesfield in south Yorkshire, he reputedly made his fortune in metal manufacturing in London. Returning to Yorkshire in the late seventeenth century, he and his heir bought Birthwaite and Nether Haigh from Sir Francis Burdett, property at Winterset and Saintingley from the Irelands, an estate at Altofts from the Goodricks of Ribston, and Newland Park (which became the family seat) from the Bunneys. The bulk of this property passed to an heiress, Priscilla, who married John Smith of Ecclesfield, and whose grandson was raised to the baronetage as Sir John Silverster-Smith in 1784. All six of the leading eighteenth-century merchant families in Leeds had departed to solid, prosperous landownership by 1815: two of them, the Milners and the Ibbetsons, purchased much property from Lord Fairfax following his bankruptcy a century earlier. Having previously acquired the manor of Beeston, William Milner, then the largest merchant in

Leeds, bought the Nun Appleton and Bolton Percy estates from Fairfax in 1708, paying only £7,000 for 2,385 acres; his son joined the baronetage within a decade. Milner's contemporary, James Ibbetson, who made a fortune in the woollen trade, bought the Denton estate in Wharfedale from the Fairfaxes in 1717, but also accumulated other property which he left to a younger son, Henry. By the time the latter was created baronet in 1748, his estate was worth well over £1,000 a year; and, following the death of his elder brother, Samuel, the two estates were united under the second baronet, who succeeded in 1761. Although the core of the Sledmere estate came to the Sykes family through Richard's marriage to Mary Kirby in 1704, they used the profits of their Hull merchant house to acquire land before then, and continued to accumulate property sporadically throughout the eighteenth century, obtaining land in Holderness and to the west of Hull, as well as in the city itself. Among their more notable acquisitions was the property at Frodingham Hall which they purchased in 1773 from the Morritts, who sold to defray the cost of their recent purchase of the Rokeby estate from Sir Thomas Robinson. Another Hull merchant, Sir Henry Etherington, was also active in the property market in the mid and late eighteenth century. He bought a Hall and estate at North Ferriby, property at Paull in Holderness, and the manor and lordship of Hatfield in south Yorkshire. Finally, following the break-up and sale of the Wombwell estate due to female succession in 1733, Sir George Wombwell, first baronet of the cadet branch of the family, used the vast profits he had made as a London merchant in its re-purchase.[59]

In the absence of a more comprehensive study of the Yorkshire land market the conclusions to be drawn from this evidence must of necessity be tentative. It would appear, first of all, that both the supply of, and the demand for, landed property remained relatively high throughout this period. Most purchasers were interested in strategic expansion, a tendency which was accentuated by the high land prices of the 1730s and 1740s; but those prices also reduced the reluctance to sell, particularly during those agriculturally depressed decades, and any difficulty in purchasing appropriately situated property would appear to have been only temporary. Secondly, irrespective of the value of particular transactions, there was often a direct connection between moneylending and the acquisition of property. All four of the families studied in detail either bought or sold property in transactions whose primary purpose was the discharge of debts, and in circumstances where the purchasers had previously been creditors of the vendors. This was the chief means whereby the Bright estates were expanded and consolidated during the second half of the seventeenth century; it was also true of a significant proportion of the property transactions in the other case-studies. Thirdly, both purchasers and vendors represented a wide cross-section of contemporary society. The least substantial owner-occupiers were at risk during this period, partly because agricultural profits were harder to come by, but also owing to the interest of larger owners in the piecemeal consolidation of their estates. However, while it highlights this interest, the evidence of the case-studies does not suggest that consolidation was uniformly at the expense of the lower groups in rural society. The status of the vendors in all transactions, large and small, was extremely varied; and ranged from peers and public institutions, through baronets, knights, and other gentry, to substantial farmers, artisans, and smallholders. The incidence of economic decline among the more substantial landowners themselves was far from negligible, and there is ample evidence that the lower social groups contained individuals who were both eager and able to replace them as owners of property. Four of the more substantial sales made by

TABLE 32

The Yorkshire Baronetage: Titles & Estates, 1660–1800

	A	B	C	D	E	F	Total
1660 (1670)	37 (22)	45 (60)	4	0	1	6	93
1700	14	59	6	0	0	14	93
1760	9	43	10	2	2	27	93
1800	0	45	15	1	1	31	93

KEY A Families yet to accede to the Baronetage
   B Families with Title and Estates
   C Families with Estates but no Title
   D Families with Title but no Estates
   E Estates possessed by Female Issue
   F Title extinct and no Estate

the Constables and the Beaumonts (of property at Gardham
1701, Lascelles Hall 1714, Wholsea 1716–17, and at Mitton
1764) were to artisan skinners, lesser gentry, a tenant farmer,
and a maltster respectively. Nevertheless, although the pace of
the development should not be exaggerated, the general drift of
property appears to have favoured the landed élite; and the
present evidence suggests that two factors in particular
promoted this.

The first of these relates to the disposition of property following the failure of heirs. The pattern of the evidence is illustrated
in Table 32, which summarizes developments in regard to both
titles and estates between 1660 and 1800. It must be pointed out
that the Table indicates the minimum incidence of the discontinuity caused by the failure of heirs and of fortunes. The
figures relate only to titles of baronetcy; no distinction is made
between initial creations and subsequent re-creations; and
those baronets who enjoyed their own but not their predecessors' estates, such as the later Hewetts and the Lister-Kayes, or
who were barred by jointures and other life-interests from
entering property, have been included among those with both
title and estates. It is clear, first of all, that although by 1660
ownership of the estates associated with some six extinct titles
had been transferred, the flood of new creations in that year and
during the following decade brought the Yorkshire baronetage
as a group to its greatest strength. However, between 1670 and
1700 the number of extinctions of title and transferences of
ownership more than doubled; and doubled again before 1760.
Further creations bolstered the group until 1700 but in the
following sixty years it steadily declined in size. By 1760 the
number of extinctions of title and transferences of ownership
had risen to twenty-seven, or more than a third of all creations
or re-creations up to that point. After 1760 a better survival rate
and further creations reversed this decline, so that by 1800 the
number of extinctions and transferences had been cut back to
exactly a third of the entire group. In addition one title
remained unsupported by property; and one estate was in the
possession of an untitled female.

While the Table further illustrates the tendency to extinction
during the century after the Restoration, the key question
concerns the fate of the property whose ownership changed.

The number of cases, twenty-seven by 1760, where titles and estates were no longer enjoyed by the families who originally possessed them is exactly the same as the number of instances within this group where succession was to or through a female. Significantly, however, membership of the two groups by no means coincided; and, where it did coincide, the resulting disposition of property was overwhelmingly in favour of other substantial landed families. Six of the former group were either obliged to sell their property before the death of the last male incumbent, or had it forfeited by the Crown. A further six individuals or families owned little, if any, real estate at any stage and became extinct soon after the creation of their titles. On the other hand the bulk, if not all, of the property of eleven families was inherited, either by marriage, will, or other settlement; and either by peerage families, other substantial gentry, or by lesser gentry who, as a result of the inheritance, greatly increased the size of their holdings. This leaves four families, the fate of two of whose property remains unknown. Of the final two families, the Mauleverers sold much property before their extinction; and the Paylers, who were also in financial difficulties long before their extinction, sold the bulk of what remained of their property to the Darleys of Aldby in 1758 following Mary Payler's death.[60] Thus, only rarely did the failure of heirs among the Yorkshire baronetage directly result in substantial properties coming on to the land market. In a number of instances, however, there would appear to have been a connection between the lack or sale of property and the *subsequent* failure of heirs.

Thus, developments in regard to the majority of these families, who were substantial and established members of the landed classes, may be summarized as follows. There was a strong incentive to leave property other than to an heiress. The force of family tradition, particularly in wealthy titled families whose members had usually played a prominent role in local or national affairs or in both, encouraged the arrangement, where necessary, of indirect male succession, which was often followed by changes of name, and sometimes by re-creations of title. In a sense this increased social mobility, for thereby some lesser gentry were afforded unexpected opportunities. The major effects of their succession, however, were that the property concerned remained intact, or at least substantially so; and that it was joined to the property of the beneficiary. Secondly, if, as a result of a failure of direct male heirs, a large estate passed to an heiress, she almost invariably married a substantial landowner, thus ensuring the amalgamation of one large property with another. Moreover, if there was more than one potential heiress, property was not necessarily shared between them; and, even if it was shared, the size of the individual inheritances again often led to highly successful marriages. Although by the mid seventeenth century the growth of the baronetage had the effect of solidifying family traditions, simply by giving many families more to be proud of, it is difficult to argue that any of these developments were peculiar to this period. Substantial families who survived had always gained from inheritance, marriage-related or otherwise; and those who failed in the male line had no doubt often left their property to other males rather than to heiresses. However, the increased rate at which heirs failed in the late seventeenth and early eighteenth centuries gave added impetus to this factor. In addition it may also have altered the pattern of such gains, not by reducing the number of gains through marriage, but rather by increasing those from other types of inheritance.

The other major feature of the evidence here relates to the nature of the transactions in which property was sold. Whether the lesser gentry had a similar demographic experience to that described above is uncertain, though it seems reasonable to suppose that they did. It has been suggested that property inherited from them was more likely to be sold, not only because it was perhaps more heavily encumbered, but also because beneficiaries were generally less capable of discharging incumbrances. In addition there was less incentive for lesser gentry to avoid divided inheritances.[61] The more substantial landowners were always in the market for such properties and it is not difficult to cite instances of their being successful: for example, the Earl of Strafford's purchase of the Keresforth estate and the Hothams' acquisition of the manor of Barghe. However, the present evidence suggests that sales should be viewed in a rather wider perspective. Many substantial landowners sold land and a few alienated their entire estates, either in pursuit of solvency or, particularly where property had been inherited, because it and ancestral holdings were inconveniently situated in relation to one another. The key point about such transactions is that property was rarely split up for purposes of sale. The possible reasons for this are numerous. Demand for larger properties would appear to have been just as high as for smaller ones; while, on the supply side, values tended to rise in proportion to size and compactness. No doubt there was also a natural reluctance to divide property which had previously been consolidated. Moreover, the ingrained reluctance to sell ancestral property encouraged the most hard-pressed landowners to hold out for as long as possible, thus creating the need in the final analysis for quick and substantial transactions, often to major creditors. Here the connection between lending and purchasing is important. Although sources of credit were progressively widened and deepened, during the first half of the period in particular many landowners continued to borrow heavily from other landowners, or from wealthy non-landed men who were anxious to acquire real estate. A final explanation of the size of many transactions relates to divided inheritances. Several examples, above all Sir John Bright's purchase of Kinsley and Cockhill and Sir George Wombwell's acquisition of his ancestral property, suggest that even where property was divided by inheritance, the separate parts often returned to the hands of a single substantial purchaser. The latter's wealth and skill as a negotiator were obviously important factors; but in addition it must often have been in the vendors' interests to sell to the same individual. For many properties could not be split permanently without a consequent reduction in the value and viability of the constituent parts.

Whatever the reasons for it, the results of this phenomenon seem clear. Increasingly the market was dominated by the wealthiest purchasers. Much of the property sold by the larger proprietors went to others within that group; and over all the largest properties passed either to those who already owned large estates, to wealthy lesser gentry who thereby became substantial landowners, or to even wealthier merchants and other outsiders who were eager to emulate the landed élite. Together with the consequences of the failure of heirs and the commitment to piecemeal consolidation, this helps to explain the growth of many existing large estates and the emergence of new ones during this period. Underpinning the entire process was the fact that for most established families the purchase of property was the major avenue of productive investment.

4. A WIDER PERSPECTIVE

The foregoing contains several implications for any assessment of the contribution of these landowners to the development of the wider economy of which their property formed but a part. Although the attitudes and aptitudes of landowners were diverse, the efforts of most members of most families were loosely bound together by a common interest in the furtherance of their dynasty. However, the amount and location of the property owned or controlled by particular generations of a family varied, and even well-laid plans were frustrated or delayed by patterns of life and death. In view of the rate at which heirs failed, of the frequency of changes of regime, and of the number of indirect successions, historians have perhaps underestimated the extent to which the affairs of landed families were subject to discontinuity at the fundamental levels of ownership and management. To the extent that outlying properties were disposed of, management problems became less acute, but the benefits of this were outweighed by other factors which increased the turnover of both property and personnel. While the majority of landed families enjoyed a long period of relative stability and security from the mid eighteenth century onwards, much of the preceding period was characterized by change and uncertainty. Although some families achieved conspicuous success and others died out or were ruined, most held fast between these two extremes, able to maintain their identity and way of life with moderate success, but with no little difficulty none the less.

The self-assurance with which most landowners conducted their affairs in 1760, following a series of political, constitutional, and economic developments which were favourable to their interests, was often lacking a century or so earlier. Then, though in many cases demonstrably capable of managing their concerns efficiently, more landowners were oppressed by the public and private responsibilities which it was their duty, and ultimately their's alone to discharge. Shortly before his death in 1640, for example, Christopher Wandesford drew his son's attention to the 'observation of a very wise man' that 'the happiest condition of life in the kingdom was to be under the degree of a Justice of the Peace, and above the quality of a High Constable'. The events of the Civil War and Interregnum, for many 'the saddest and worst time' in their lives, did nothing to dispel such feelings.[62] Many families remained acutely aware of their collective sufferings and of how nearly they had escaped ruin. In the 1650s Sir Henry Slingsby gravely counselled his eldest son against a too avid pursuit of public success:

In the carriage of public affairs, my advice is that you appear cautious. Many by putting themselves upon numerous employments have lost themselves, though in neighbourly offices to be modestly active manifests signal arguments of piety.

And to his younger son, who was to enjoy much reduced circumstances, he had this to say:

Be it your care by honest ways to improve them; at least to preserve them, which is good husbandry in these days. In a word, if your estate be not sufficient for you, be sufficient for your estate. This was the advice of a wise statist: observe it.[63]

Thomas Fuller, as faithful a recorder as any of the contemporary mood of the landed classes, hoped that 'they may seasonably outgrow the sad impressions which our civil wars have left in their estates, in some to the shaking of their continuement'.[64] For several decades men felt vulnerable to sudden changes of fortune; to developments whose course no one could predict and which were beyond everyone's control. In 1685 Sir John Reresby felt inclined to equate substance with vulnerability, and wished for greater anonymity in return for the personal security which this would afford.

I have seen so many changes, and so many great and little men removed in my time, that I confess it began to cool my ambition, and to think there was a time when every thinking man would choose to retire and to be content with his own rather than venture that and his conscience for the getting of more, and a little left to his family that way was better than more gotten by other means . . . I was convinced that safety was better than greatness, and a good foundation in all conditions the greatest happiness.[65]

This residual unease was reinforced by the economic conditions which prevailed for much of this period. With prices, and therefore rent receipts, depressed from the early 1660s, circumstances for members of the first generation contrasted sharply with those within living memory. Almost a century elapsed before there was a marked upturn in the agricultural conditions which so largely governed the financial prospects of owners of land.

Because it was some time before they came to accept the depression of income from land as a long-term phenomenon, landowners were not quick to react to this incentive to improvement and diversification. Instinctively many first looked beyond their property, to a good marriage or to the rewards of offices or sinecures, for some means of boosting income. In regard to their estates their attitudes were for long characterized by careful and ameliorative rather than enterprising management. Most energy was devoted, for example, to attempts to avoid or collect rent arrears. The latter occurred with monotonous regularity and, on the Beaumont, Constable, and Bright estates, assumed large proportions in the early eighteenth century. Sir Marmaduke Constable tried to solve this problem by allowing his Catholic tenants to hold half a year's rent in hand, though his correspondence with Potts indicates that this policy was only partially successful. He was typical of many owners in denouncing rent arrears in the strongest terms, whilst finding it virtually impossible to do anything about them. Periodically stewards successfully conducted drives to collect long-standing arrears; but there was no ready means, other than the lowering of rents, of reducing current arrears to the point where they were negligible. At times, notably during the cattle plague of the late 1740s, arrears were simply written off. Earlier Sir John Bright persistently refused to do this, though 'desperate debts' from arrears were a cost which eventually even he had to meet. However, during what was generally a difficult period for farmers, suitable alternative tenants were not always readily available. It was both safer and more realistic to be patient with all but the worst cases of arrears, and occasionally to write them off, than to eject or distrain on those tenants in difficulties.

Except where an entire tenantry was under economic duress, judgement of the appropriate action in the face of arrears or other evidence of tenants' difficulties was made no easier by the fact that most substantial landowners became less directly involved in farming as the period progressed. Although the wealthiest of them, such as Rockingham and the Osbornes, established or maintained large home-farms, the remainder increasingly found such enterprises unnecessary or impractical. Even Sir John Bright and the last Richard Beaumont, whose activities in this respect were by no means insignificant, rarely marketed their own produce, and then only in small quantities. While an excess of supply over demand kept prices low, an extensive network of markets and fairs brought an increasing quantity and variety of food to consumers, who as a result grew more reliant on others for their food supply. Where for a time direct farming operations persisted, changes in family circumstances, in the form of minorities, public service, or travel at home and abroad, frequently demanded their contraction or closure. Residence on the estate was rarely unaccompanied by some farming of the demesne, but permanent residence in the countryside became less common and, indeed, was eventually regarded as desirable only when retrenchment was a high priority. It sometimes proved convenient or profitable to establish kitchen gardens, orchards, or decoys, whose products made a welcome addition to the family table and were not difficult to sell. From time to time, however, even these were run down owing to a decrease in the size of a household. Some owners, like Sir Philip Constable in the 1680s, established deer parks on their estates which, apart from their aesthetic qualities, provided venison: but, again, the general trend from the early eighteenth century was for such parks to be diminished in size. Where it was not used to create new lettings, property which became available in this way was often landscaped. By 1760 much of the land which had been farmed directly a century earlier, if not let to tenants, had been utilized in the development of the gardens, shrubberies, and other surroundings without which no eighteenth-century country house was judged to be complete. There was often some delay before permanent tenants were found for new or unused property, but losses were cut by temporary lettings or by the sale of grazing rights. Only rarely was there any reliance on the profits of direct farming, which was practised for convenience rather than out of necessity, and which gradually diminished in scale.[66]

Despite a perceptible retreat from close involvement in the working life on their properties, few landowners could afford complacency. Though largely uninterested in farming practice, they attempted a number of solutions to the problems posed by static or fluctuating rent receipts. In addition to increasing the acreage of their lettings wherever this was feasible, the rationalization of tenures and payments, evident in the preceding period, continued. Except on the largest and most widely dispersed estates, entry fines gradually disappeared from privately owned property. On the Hotham estates in 1711, for example, only the tenants of the outlying property at Filingdales paid fines, most of which were low in relation to their rents. This and the steady decline of duty, boon, and other customary payments and services pay tribute to the on-going conversion of copyhold to leasehold tenures, and to the desire of landlords to maximize the cash income from their estates. Long before the mid eighteenth century the vast majority of tenants paid full economic rents at half-yearly intervals for the property which they occupied. Moreover, the length of leases was steadily reduced in the post-Restoration era. From the 1670s very few leases were granted for more than twenty-one years. Beyond the turn of the century most were much shorter than this, with many leases being for as few as three to five years. Annual tenancies or tenancies at will, widespread in all three Ridings by the early nineteenth century, were by no means unknown; and, particularly in lettings of smaller holdings, there was a move away from leases in favour of the much less elaborate tenancy agreements. To some extent no doubt these developments reflected the unwillingness of many tenants to over-commit themselves, but they also increased the power of landlords over their rent rolls, enabling them to make speedier responses to changes in economic conditions. That rent movement was so slow in such circumstances is a clear indication of farmers' difficulties. Once prices rose in the 1750s, however, the rents of most landowners were not slow to follow them.[67]

Before then, especially where it facilitated a change in land use, enclosure was the means whereby rents were most dramatically increased. Enclosure of the Ings at West Rasen by the Constables in the period 1650–70 enabled a shift from arable to mixed farming, and produced an increase in the rental of over £200 a year. In the 1720s Sir Marmaduke Constable was asked by tenants at West Rasen 'to lay down two of their cornfields from ploughing to pasture'. For an outlay of £233, most of which was paid by the tenants over and above their rents, he secured a further £178 a year in rents, though allegedly the property concerned had previously been under-let. During the following decade John Liddell-Bright raised his rental at Badsworth by almost £200 a year as a result of enclosing common cornfields and laying them down to grass. Enclosure progressed more rapidly on lowland than on upland property but, as at Everingham and West Rasen, its effectiveness was often limited by lack of investment in other, related improvements such as drainage. It was also applied to under-developed property or wasteland, such as those parts of Cranswick taken in by Sir John Hotham in the 1660s. Pursued sporadically and on a piecemeal basis throughout the period, it contributed to an increase in the average size of individual holdings and sometimes enabled the creation of wholly new farms. Landlords were keen to attract substantial tenants on to their property and to encourage those already there. However, as Sir Marmaduke Constable ruefully admitted to Potts, it was easier to achieve this by bringing under-utilized land into cultivation or pasture than by rationalizing the in-fields and reducing the number of small tenants and cottagers. Enclosure of any kind was often difficult to organize or justify when agricultural prices were discouraging. Frequently the subject of bitter dispute, not least with parsons jealous of their tithes, it was best achieved by agreement or on request. The bulk of the enclosures which existed in Yorkshire in 1730 were the product of ages past and, although there was some quickening of enclosing activity from that point onwards, wholesale enclosures remained uncommon for several decades. In the mid eighteenth century many rural properties were akin to those at South Dalton or Methley, where an inner core of common fields was flanked by a patchwork of closes on the surrounding upland or waste. Further out, in areas

unaffected by medieval or later enclosures, property bound-
aries were often marked merely by stones, grass baulks, piles of
turf, or by the line of an ancient road.[68]

Although landlords were sensitive to any reduction in rentals
consequent on an increase in the amount of land in hand, the
failure of tenants occasionally prompted rationalization.
Together with piecemeal enclosure and purchases and
exchanges of small adjacent properties, this led to a gradual
increase in the size of individual holdings. The tendency was to
concentrate on expanding a few, specific farms, at least one of
which was commonly occupied by a steward, agent, or bailiff.
This development is reflected, particularly during the early
eighteenth century, in a proportionate decrease in the total
number of tenants. If this weeding-out process accelerated
during the second quarter of the eighteenth century, it was
earlier promoted by the advent of the land tax. The evidence
here suggests that the extent to which landowners were prepared to shoulder responsibility for payment of the tax has been
exaggerated. It was the Beaumonts' policy throughout this
period to require tenants to pay all taxes levied by Parliament on
the property which they leased. Although as a result they
suffered severely from rent arrears, this also appears to have
been true of the Brights. There is little evidence for the
Hothams during the twenty or so years after 1690 when levies
were at their heaviest. However, many of the leases which they
granted stipulated that tenants were to pay all taxes, and though
the family relaxed this policy on some of their central properties, as late as 1768 Hotham tenants of outlying properties at
Beswick, Wilton, and Filingdales were required to pay the
whole of the tax. The Constables were in a difficult position
because, being Catholics, they were supposed to pay the tax at a
double rate, and did so on several occasions during the 1690s.
Their attempts to foist the tax on their tenants were not completely successful. Rent arrears multiplied and in 1702 Sir
Philip Constable undertook to pay most of the tax, which by
then was usually levied at a single rate on his Yorkshire
properties. By the 1730s Sir Marmaduke had induced his tenants to pay the lower levies, but he paid the higher rates due in
wartime. Perhaps tax payments by tenants were one factor in
the reduction of some of the rents on the Beaumont estate

during the third decade of the century. However, rents which were reduced had been raised only shortly before, reductions were granted reluctantly, and only after evidence of tenants' distress.

The contents of leases and tenancy agreements confirm the impression that landlords were primarily interested in the punctual payment of rents and the preservation of their rights as owners. There were usually strict clauses relating to hedging and fencing, ditching and draining, and the maintenance of soil fertility. Sub-letting was invariably forbidden and the owner's freedom to exploit timber, coal, and other mineral resources was carefully safeguarded. Clauses concerning farming practice, however, were generally both uniform and perfunctory, and only rarely went further than agreement by the tenant to maintain land in the 'best course of husbandry' or 'according to the custom of the country'. In the latter part of the period leases and tenancy agreements began to be printed in batches; and few of them were subsequently endorsed with special requirements. Despite the shortening of terms of lease, good tenants enjoyed security of tenure and many farming families occupied the same property for generations. The more substantial tenants became progressively more independent of their landlords and, if not employed by them in some capacity, were frequently turned to for advice. Sir Marmaduke Constable, while at home more interested in farming matters than many of his fellow owners, went so far as to say that he could 'not believe that any man is obliged to plough his lands unless he has a mind to do so'.[69] Less governed, therefore, by formal agreement, the practical, everyday aspects of life on estates were overseen by stewards, who looked to responsible tenants as well as to their masters for guidance and support. In times of severe hardship tenants could expect to be nursed through their difficulties. In addition to rebates and allowances, houses, farmbuildings, and other facilities were extensively repaired or rebuilt on three of these four properties in the decades before 1760. However, though far from derisory, investment of this sort was in many instances overdue and comprised but a small proportion of owners' total expenditure. In so far as they looked beyond cash flow landlords were largely concerned with the size, location, and organization of their estates. Their direct contribution to agricultural progress was correspondingly modest. The number of both full- and part-time employees was increased, individual holdings were rationalized, and estates as a whole consolidated. While enjoying customary benevolence, tenants were treated with firmness, the emphasis being on the encouragement of the most capable among them. By these means the number of substantial farms and farmers on most estates was increased, though rarely as rapidly as their owners would have preferred. Until rentals resumed a strong upward trend sizeable investment was restricted to the amenities which landowners and their families themselves enjoyed. In other respects development and improvement, though evident, were distinctly unspectacular.

While estate income was largely derived from farmers' rents, many tenants on the Beaumont estates, and also on the Sheffield estate of the Brights, were engaged on either a full-time or a part-time basis in a variety of industrial or servicing occupations. Although on the Bright estate in particular it is difficult to measure rent movement because of the frequency with which holdings were expanded by purchase, the rents of these properties too would appear to have been slow to move upwards before the mid eighteenth century. In addition neither family derived much income from the direct exploitation of non-agricultural resources other than timber. The Brights leased the mining rights on their own property at Ecclesall, and deliberately retreated from the lead trade in the mid seventeenth century. Their activities in that trade and at the Handsworth coal-pits (which they leased partly because of the value of the adjacent farmland) illustrate how difficult it was to run industrial concerns profitably when poor inland communications boosted costs and restricted the size of the available market. Moreover, production methods were little changed since medieval times; while Thomas Stacy, Sir John Bright's manager and partner at Handsworth, was not the only contemporary to draw attention to the problems posed by an unruly, and at times ungovernable, workforce in the coal industry. It was no doubt because of such factors that the Beaumonts chose throughout this period to remain uninvolved in the direct exploitation of the extensive coal deposits on their estates. Instead, like the Saviles and the Dartmouth family at Woodsome, they leased mining rights in return for rents and regular supplies of coal. In south Yorkshire the Wortley-Montagues were the most active lessors, buying out other royalty owners on acquiring a Crown lease of property in Barnsley in the 1690s. But for several decades both they, the Osbornes, and the Wentworths, for example, remained reluctant to become more fully involved in industrial activity. Following improvements in water transport, particularly on the river Don from the 1730s, one can trace a more enthusiastic attitude to the opportunities which ownership of these resources presented. Leasing arrangements became more sophisticated, and rents rose as they were more frequently tied to actual output. The Duke of Leeds took over one mine in 1740–1, and Lord Rockingham another a decade later. Further north direct exploitation was still regarded as too risky, but the Beaumonts steadily increased both the number of their mining leases and the amount of fixed and working capital which they were prepared to invest in the enterprise of others. Organized searches for coal, such as those by Richard Beaumont at Grizzlehurst in the 1740s or later by William Haggerston-Constable at Everingham, became more frequent; though, as in the latter case, they often served merely to underline the flimsiness of contemporary knowledge of geology. Nor were the costs of production and marketing uniformly reduced. As Sir Beaumont Hotham was informed of alum deposits on his Filingdales property in 1768: 'at this very time no alum is sent to London that does not stand the proprietors in £17 or upwards per ton, and the price is only £14'.[70] The development of the heavy industries owed something to the encouragement and financial assistance provided by substantial landowners, though the latter for long remained detached, if not entirely passive, in their attitude towards them. The few who achieved notable success from mining and related activities did so on property along the north-east coast, where conditions, especially as regards transport, were eminently more favourable to both leasing and direct exploitation. Just as the mercantile interest was most prominent in promoting development in the field of transport in Yorkshire, the prime movers in the lead and coal industries were the lesser gentry and substantial freeholders. With the notable exception of the Spencers of Cannon Hall, this was also true of the charcoal iron industry.[71]

Timber, on the other hand, was one resource which was exploited vigorously. The largest purchasers, from the Beaumonts and the Brights, were maltsters and ironmasters; even the small amount of wood felled by the Hothams was sold in the form of firkin staves. The large and regular requirements of industrialists and the eighteenth-century taste for the aesthetically wooded park or demesne were together responsible for significant developments in the management of timber resources. An increasing number of employees were vested with particular responsibility for their preservation and in the eighteenth century many estates established or patronized nurseries from which woods were replenished. Tenants' leases, deeds of purchase, marriage settlements, and the records of legal disputes indicate that owners were acutely aware of the value of timber, if only for purposes of repair or rebuilding. Together with increased demand, improved management produced growth in both the size and the regularity of income from this source. Timber sales were an important additional means of raising capital and bulk sales were particularly common at times of financial difficulty. The Constables sold most timber when their debts were at their highest in the 1650s and 1660s; the Brights in the period 1700–20 when the cost of Dame Susannah Newton's jointure bore heavily on their economy. The Hothams were most active in this respect in the 1720s, following the completion of their costly building project in Beverley, while after 1743 Richard Beaumont sold a great deal of timber in order to reduce the loans which his ambitious schemes necessitated.

If not devoted to expanding or embellishing estates, surplus capital was most frequently invested in the money market. Although the funds attracted an increasing amount of investment as the eighteenth century progressed, the bulk of surplus capital circulated locally. Owners in the north often encountered difficulty in transmitting money and many of the bills of exchange which they or their stewards negotiated merely furnished their own requirements in London and elsewhere in the south. Naturally unwilling to hold much cash in hand, they disposed of large amounts on local bonds and mortgages. Few landowners were as active or as singleminded in this regard as Sir John Bright because few of them enjoyed either his wealth or his business acumen. Most, however, had relatives, friends or acquaintances (including tenants) who required capital on loan and the actual and potential benefits of such investment were keenly appreciated. In addition to the fact that loans often constituted a preliminary to purchases of property, the goodwill earned by lending, either on a person to person basis or via the growing body of attorneys and other individuals who specialized in arranging local exchanges of capital, might subsequently be utilized in borrowing. Moreover, although there was a gradual fall in interest rates throughout the period, it was sporadic and uneven, allowing some creditors to obtain returns in excess of the market average; and while recognition of the equity of mortgage redemption greatly reduced the risks of borrowers, it also increased total earnings from interest payments by encouraging debtors to borrow larger sums, and by indefinitely extending the periods over which money was borrowed. Finally, as the money market expanded capital put out on loan was almost invariably re-obtainable at will because of the ease with which loans on good security were assigned to other would-be creditors.

The importance of this last factor goes far beyond its relevance to activities in the money market and helps to explain why income was so heavily dominated by rents, with intermittent supplementation from interest and dividend payments. As John Bright discovered in 1642, the normal difficulties of disentangling a deceased landowner's affairs were exacerbated by his father's previous involvement, directly and indirectly, in a variety of agricultural, industrial, financial, and other concerns. The proportion of permanent income which was derived from non-agricultural sources other than moneylending rose very slowly, not merely because such ventures were considered to be risky or unprofitable, but also because they tied up capital, more or less inextricably, for long periods. The recurrent needs of substantial landowners frequently demanded at little notice the mobilization of large sums, not all of which could be provided out of recurrent income. Nor, because of restrictions on the use of settled estate, were they always procurable on loan. When rents could be improved only slowly and with difficulty; and when success in the major area of productive investment, the property market, required decisive action, perhaps on an unforeseen scale, it was tempting, indeed prudent, to keep surplus capital in as liquid a state as possible so that it was readily available to meet contingencies.

The variety of these contingencies is well illustrated by the manner in which in-coming portions were spent. In the 1650s Sir John Hotham, the second baronet, used his wife's portion to augment the depleted income from his family's estate. Richard Beaumont appears to have devoted the portion which he received on marrying Frances Lowther in 1676 to the discharge of other settled payments. Sir Charles Hotham, the fifth baronet, used his wife's portion to redeem his father's last and largest mortgage, raised to finance the Beverley house. Portions were also decisive in reducing the Constables' debts. Later both Richard Beaumont and William Haggerston-Constable spent portion money on building and associated improvements at Whitley and Everingham. In only one instance in the history of these four families was a portion deliberately invested in the purchase of additional property. John Liddell-Bright had no choice in the matter for the settlement on his marriage to Cordelia Clutterbuck stipulated that his receipt of £6,000 of her portion of £8,000 was conditional on his acquisition of real estate to that value. Sir John Bright undoubtedly used portion money to finance some of his purchases, but his case was exceptional in that frequent marriage combined with infrequent reproduction brought much capital and few consequent charges, so that he was able to indulge further in his chief preoccupation, the expansion of his estate. It also seems likely that the purchase of South Dalton by the Hothams was financed by the portion which the future third baronet received from Katherine Heron. However, the opportunity for purchase arose unexpectedly; and in the two years before then the whole of the portion had been placed out on loan. Thus, there were no strong conventions regarding the utilization of portions, which met a variety of needs according to the circumstances of those who received them. If marriage negotiations were arduous and protracted, as indeed they often were, it was the size and composition of portions and other related payments which provoked contention, not the question of how they were to be spent.

Charges on an estate could only be broadly estimated; by the time the payment of portions and jointures became due they might exceed what could reasonably be afforded. In the absence of severe financial difficulties there was a tendency for them to escalate as landowners strove to do better for themselves and their children. When, as occurred in most families, the financial scenario of one generation was largely determined years beforehand by the settlements of its predecessors, it is hardly surprising that fiscal capacity often proved to be less than originally anticipated. Moreover, a good marriage was usually bought at the cost, not only of a sizeable jointure for the widow, but also of increased provision for younger children. The subsequent conjunction of long-lived and heavily jointured widows with the need to provide for those children proved particularly embarrassing. Payment of jointures could only be avoided if wives predeceased husbands; but, where widows were sympathetic to the circumstances of their husbands' successors, negotiations for the reduction of jointures, or for their more convenient payment, might meet with some success, albeit at the cost of incurring additional obligations for the future. Thus, in April 1676 Dame Elizabeth Beaumont surrendered her jointure lands, worth £200 per annum, to her son, Richard, and gave him with certain exceptions the furniture and machinery at Whitley. In return he provided his mother with a life annuity of £170 and gave security for the payment of an additional portion of £2,000 to his sister, Ann. Nor was the position in regard to portions entirely inflexible: the payment of principal sums could normally be delayed, provided that those to whom they were due received interest on them. Neither the £4,000 which the aforementioned Richard Beaumont provided for his younger children, nor the £11,000 allocated for a similar purpose by his heir, had to be paid because younger offspring did not survive in the first generation and were not produced in the next. However, payments to the large family produced by Richard Beaumont of Lascelles Hall, who succeeded in 1704, burdened the Whitley estate for many decades. Richard's marriage settlement was executed before his inheritance of Whitley and the provision of portions of £1,000 each for daughters was relatively modest. However, two of these portions, those due to Elizabeth and Everilda, were eventually paid to their children in 1772 and 1780 respectively. Much depended not only on whether younger children were born or survived to adulthood, but also on whether sisters or daughters married; and, if they did, on the extent to which their husbands were able or willing to wait for their money. It seems clear, however, that as the period progressed the payment of a growing number of portions was via loans or by instalments; and that the receipt of many was temporarily postponed or deferred indefinitely.

The Constables were lucky in that Sir Marmaduke's bachelorhood kept their estate free of incumbrances, while all but one of the daughters born before his succession either died young or went into religious life. Yet half that daughter's portion of £3,000 was only paid on the death of her husband in 1708, ten years after her marriage; and when she demanded the remainder in 1716, Sir Marmaduke had to borrow in order to pay it. Although the long minority which followed the death of the fifth baronet in 1738 was a major stabilizing influence on the finances of the Hothams, payment in 1757 of the portions of his two surviving daughters was only achieved by further deferring the receipt by his widow of a legacy of £4,000. The family's major creditor in the 1720s had bequeathed this sum to her; it was eventually paid by the seventh baronet some fifty years later. The affairs of the Brights in the early eighteenth century provide an even more pertinent example of the accumulation of settlement charges. By a deed of 1716 John Liddell-Bright allocated £12,000 for the portions of six younger children: eventually one younger son and three daughters became entitled to £11,000. At his death in 1735 none of their portions had been paid, primarily because Sir John Bright's widow continued to enjoy her huge jointure. John Liddell-Bright's heir, Thomas, married well but most of his wife's inheritance, both real and personal, was prospective and was not forthcoming before his death in 1739, though by then a further £5,000 had been allocated from the estate for the portion of their only child, Mary. Thomas's brother and successor, John, not only failed to pay outstanding portions, despite one sister's marriage in 1743, but ran up large personal debts and arranged for his own unpaid portion to be shared equally between his sisters. By the time of his death in 1748, therefore, the Bright estates were burdened with personal debts, and with interest at $4\frac{1}{2}$ per cent on £11,000, and were shortly to become liable to a further portion of £5,000.

The trustees who succeeded John discharged the portions by raising mortgages. Although the interest on these was only 4 per cent, they remained a charge on Lord Rockingham's estates for many years after his marriage. This was of little concern to someone of his vast wealth, but for many less substantial owners payments of the principal and interest of portions and jointures, or of the loans which replaced them, were becoming a serious problem in the years before estate incomes rose in the mid eighteenth century; if only because they were not the only factors creating disequilibrium between relatively stable incomes on the one hand, and rising patterns of expenditure on the other.

As the case-studies illustrate, most landowners were capable of severely restricting their expenditure when circumstances demanded retrenchment. Although during the early stages of his active career Sir John Hotham, the second baronet, must have found it difficult to balance his budget, there is no record of his becoming indebted. On his visits to London in search of a post in the civil service Richard Beaumont used the 'spare room' offered to him by relatives, 'so that my charge in Town won't be much'.[72] The effect on the family's economy of the enormous penalties imposed on the Constables was greatly reduced by their struggle to keep outgoings to a minimum. The first Sir Marmaduke Constable successfully adapted himself to a situation in which throughout his career he had to live well below the standard to which members of his family had earlier grown accustomed. He finally vacated Everingham Hall to make way for his son's family and retired with his wife to the house in York, where they lived on £150 a year. Though Sir Philip Constable eventually threw caution to the winds, he previously disposed of family heirlooms in the saleroom and the pawnshop in order to make ends meet. Thomas Liddell-Bright received an income of only £300 for most of his life. In the interests of economy his father studiously avoided visits to London and forbade his executors to spend more than a token amount on his funeral. Few individuals, therefore, wantonly ignored the need to curtail expenditure following a decline in disposable income or the accumulation of debts. One reason for the ability to retrench was the small amount of recurrent income which needed to be devoted to running a rentier's estate. Annual dues and outpayments may have been numerous and varied but they were none the less insignificant in relation to the income derived from property. In 1693, for example, the twenty-three un-avoidable outpayments from the Constable estates accounted for only £119 out of a total estate income of £1,700.[73] On all four estates a steady fall in the acreage of property leased from other owners reduced such outgoings, some of which were in any case devoted to covenanted benefactions. Payments of land tax tem-porarily boosted this category of expenditure but, particularly after 1712, much of their burden was assumed by the tenantry. Even if the wages of permanent employees are included, basic running costs rarely exceeded 10 per cent of gross estate income. Consequently, there was considerable scope for economy. Repairs and improvements to property could be kept to an absolute minimum and, above all, by leading a largely private life landowners and their families could restrict personal expenditure.

However, other than at times of financial difficulty, the chief characteristic of general and estate accounts was the huge amount of money which was devoted to purely personal needs. Quite apart from substantial outgoings on plate, furniture, books, and travel, the fifth baronet Hotham persistently spent half or more of his gross income on 'self and family'. A far greater proportion of his sizeable income from office was spent in this way than on the expansion and improvement of his estate. In Richard Beaumont's case, borrowing, largely to meet private needs, often exceeded annual estate income. While, after exercising considerable restraint in the early years of his career, Sir Marmaduke Constable instructed his banker to for-ward well over half his income to defray his expenses on the Continent. Clearly, those who could afford it enjoyed a lavishly appointed lifestyle. In particular many eagerly seized oppor-tunities of entering into areas of expenditure which had pre-viously been foreign to their families. The increase in the wealth of Stephen and Sir John Bright was accompanied by a steady growth in their collection of plate. At his death in 1738 Sir Charles Hotham owned 5,200 ounces of plate, much modern furniture, and a considerable library. Sir Marmaduke Con-stable scoured the Continent looking for paintings and sculp-tures; together with written guidance as to what was suitable for

Potts and the servants to look at and what was not, these were sent back in consignments to Everingham. Nor were such articles quickly disposed of on a purchaser's death. John Liddell-Bright's executors largely ignored his stipulation that the proceeds of the sale of his entire personal estate should be devoted to the discharge of debts, and kept many of his effects at Badsworth. William Haggerston cheerfully afforded a substantial part of the purchase money for Seaton Ross in order to retain Sir Marmaduke's art collection at Everingham. After being professionally valued, such items were carefully preserved and displayed by successors who were only too glad to surround themselves with the evidence of earlier dynastic opulence.

A more peripatetic and cosmopolitan way of life, expensive in itself, undoubtedly provided landowners with greater opportunities for indulging in new tastes and fashions. They met and knew a larger cross-section of contemporary gentry than ever before and, eager to prove their worth by emulation, readily acquiesced in the standardization of behaviour in polite society. Army officers and diplomats spent many years abroad, politicians let or bought houses in London, and many others were drawn south by the growth of the 'season'. The lack of financial caution which characterized Sir Philip Constable's last years had much to do with the fact that he felt, as a recusant, physically more secure in London. Lady Gertrude Hotham grew so used to life in high society that she rarely visited South Dalton after her husband's death, spending more of her time in London or Bath. The medicinal properties of spas were sufficiently respected to leave Sir Marmaduke Constable in no doubt that the injuries of his bailiff, Robert Usher, would be healed by visits to both Bath and Buxton. Moreover, with the increased use of other than merely local educational facilities (Reresby commented that his children 'improved but little in the country')[74] prospective heirs were introduced to wider opportunities at an early age. In the seventeenth century Hotham children were taught at home and at Sedbergh before going up to Cambridge, but by the 1740s were attending Westminster School instead. Whereas Susannah Beaumont's children went to school in York, the next generation were sent to Eton. The wider adoption of the grand tour as the final element in a young man's education was particularly influential, providing him with a breadth of experience which contrasted sharply with the humdrum life on his family's estate. Tours became increasingly elaborate and expensive and many of those who enjoyed them subsequently travelled on the Continent. Sir Marmaduke Constable's first, truncated tour partly motivated his later travels. Following a grand tour in his youth and his official visit to Berlin, Sir Charles Hotham spent £400 on taking his family to France and Minorca. For his tour his son was allowed £800 a year for five years; subsequently, he and his sister, Melusina, both of whom suffered from ill-health, visited a number of German spas in search of a cure for their ailments. William Haggerston-Constable greatly exceeded his allowance while abroad so 'that he may make as tolerable a figure as some of his countrymen do'.[75]

Inevitably, a fondness for the novel and the unusual became increasingly evident in everyday matters at home. In the early eighteenth century the Brights and the Constables imported substantial quantities of food and drink direct from the Continent, and from the 1730s celebration dinners at Whitley were gargantuan affairs with two or three dozen separate dishes on offer. Though first enjoyed for their novelty, the purchase of many items eventually became commonplace. Wine replaced ale as the chief drink of the upper classes, and travel on horseback gave way to the coach and the chaise. Clothes and jewellery were regularly purchased in London rather than in the provinces, and the acquisition of bank and other accounts in the capital brought a wide range of other necessities and luxuries within easy reach.

As the force of external influences strengthened, many landowners grew more critical of their domestic surroundings. Sturdy medieval manor-houses were found inconvenient or unsuitable, while some Tudor mansions, such as that at Everingham, were at best in constant need of repair and at worst dangerously dilapidated. In consequence the period witnessed much building and redevelopment in Yorkshire and other parts of the north, where earlier activity had not been on the same scale as elsewhere.[76] Many families erected entirely new homes, while many more extended and improved existing ones. Nor was such work confined to housing. Stables, gardens, summer-houses, kennels, pheasantries and a host of other amenities were created at considerable expense in an attempt to recreate circumstances experienced and enjoyed elsewhere. Nationally these developments reached their peak during the later decades of the eighteenth century. For many substantial landowners in Yorkshire, however, they constituted the major, single item of expenditure long before then. There was a flurry of activity, especially in the West Riding, around the turn of the seventeenth century; and then, after a brief lull, developments steadily accelerated from the late 1720s and reached a climax during the third quarter of the eighteenth century. Some families extended their activities in this sphere to include a variety of public amenities and, as is clear from three of the four case-studies, the repair and rebuilding of tenanted premises became a matter of priority by or before the mid eighteenth century. In addition the building of great houses and the other improvements associated with them stimulated a wide variety of local trades and, in the form of increased retinues of domestic and other servants, provided additional, permanent employment for large numbers of local workpeople.[77] There is no doubt, however, that the sums expended on these projects far exceeded those devoted to agricultural and other improvements. If, particularly before the mid eighteenth century, investment in the latter was meagre, this was due not merely to the sluggish growth of estate incomes, but also to a singleminded concentration by the vast majority of substantial landowners on purely private rather than on more general developments.

Throughout the county very few great houses were built or substantially improved in the half century after 1640. The earliest activity was at Ledston where between 1653, when he bought the property from the Straffords, and his death in 1671 Sir John Lewis greatly altered and extended the work done on the Hall by several previous owners. In addition he erected a fine turreted and two-storeyed hunting lodge in Ledston Park and built St. John's Hospital, a two-storeyed range of eleven almshouses, in the nearby village of Ledsham. During this same period the Belasyse family of Newburgh founded the Fauconberg Hospital at Coxwold in the North Riding, and in 1676 Sir William Turner erected a similar establishment at

Kirkleatham. In the 1670s the Cholmelys added a magnificent new banqueting hall to their Elizabethan manor house at Whitby. The most notable development in the post-Restoration era was at Ribston where, copying designs adopted in the south a generation before, Sir Henry Goodrick, the second baronet, built an entirely new brick house, fifteen bays in width, in 1674. Not until after 1690, however, did either building or house improvement become more widespread. Among the prime movers were the Fairfaxes who, exacerbating the economic difficulties which eventually brought about their bankruptcy, built at Bolton Percy and at Nun Monckton. In 1693 Sir Brian Stapleton built a stately brick house of seven bays and two storeys at Myton. And between 1694 and 1703 the Duke of Leeds rebuilt at Kiveton Park 'a large new mansion house, well built with all convenience and aggrandisements fit for any nobleman's habitation', and valued at £12,000.[78] During the same period Ingleby Manor and Woodsome Hall were further embellished by the Foulis and Kaye families; Sir James Penny-man of Ormesby built himself a large town house in Beverley; Richard Beaumont made substantial additions, including a new north front, to the hall at Whitley; and, after purchasing Nun Appleton from the Fairfaxes, William Milner demolished the old hall there and built a smaller, more convenient house with some of the materials. During the first decade of the eighteenth century the distinctly regional character of much previous new building rapidly disappeared to be replaced by some of the most fashionable baroque architecture anywhere in the country, with the pace being set by the Earl of Carlisle at Castle Howard, Lord Bingley at Bramham Park (which included magnificent gardens in the French style, later enjoyed through marriage by the Goodricks), and by Sir Edward Blackett, for whom Newby Hall was begun in 1705. From 1709 Lord Raby often employed up to sixty men on the expansion of the house at Stainborough, to be known as Wentworth Castle, and built a new and magnificent east front there. A letter of his in 1710 indicates that in doing so he was mindful not only of what he had seen on his travels, but also of earlier developments nearer home.

I am going on as hard as I can with my building and am at last persuaded to make it of brick and stone as Hampton Court is, and which I am assured will look better than all stone . . . so the new front will be something like that of the Duke of Leeds at Kiveton in our country.[79]

Also impressive, though on a much smaller scale, were the new houses built by the Tempests at Tong in 1702, by Sir Walter Calverley at Esholt between 1706 and 1709, and by Sir William Wentworth at Bretton in 1720. All three properties were surrounded by elaborate gardens, and that at Esholt also had 'waterworks'.[80]

During the second and third decades of the eighteenth century a reaction to English baroque set in and metropolitan tastes were converted to Palladianism. The fact that Lord Burlington, the arch-Palladian, had his country residence at Londesborough in the East Riding did much to convert northerners to the style, as did his design for the highly successful Assembly Rooms at York in 1730. Indeed, the new influence had begun to infiltrate somewhat earlier than this. There is firm evidence from the early 1720s that the Hothams were on friendly terms with Burlington and some years before then the fourth baronet commissioned Colin Campbell, at that stage Burlington's favourite architect, to build the house in Beverley. There is no suggestion that Sir Charles's successor disliked the design of the building, only that he regarded its situation in a busy market town as unfitting for a courtier. Another of Burlington's acquaintances, Sir Thomas Robinson, was both an early convert to Palladianism and a noted amateur practitioner of it. He built his own substantial new house at Rokeby which, after several years' work, was completed in 1731. The major conversion to the new style, however, was that of Lord Malton, who used Burlington's protégé, Flitcroft, on the second part of his vast development scheme at Wentworth Woodhouse. On succeeding to the property in 1723 Malton immediately set out to surpass the recent building activities of his family's major rivals at Wentworth Castle. A west wing in a hybrid style, different from anything else in England, was completed in 1734. Thereafter an east wing, designed by Flitcroft and the largest front in the country, was under construction until after 1750, by which time it was reliably estimated that over £80,000 had been devoted to the entire project. Other major ventures beyond 1730 were at Nostell Priory, where in 1733 Sir Rowland Winn commissioned James Paine, a southern architect and another Palladian, to build a new house on which work continued until the late 1740s; at Wortley Hall, designed by John Platt of Rotherham in 1743; and at Sledmere where, soon after succeeding Mark Kirby in 1748, Richard Sykes began the new house which formed the centre of the even grander edifice later built by Sir Christopher Sykes. Finally, in the period before 1754, Dorothy Pennyman, daughter-in-law of the third baronet, built a new Hall at Ormesby.[81]

To confine attention solely to the building of entirely new houses would be seriously misleading. As Richard Beaumont's activities at Whitley graphically illustrate, the modification and embellishment of existing structures could consume many thousands of pounds, and during the early eighteenth century such projects, often extending as at Whitley over many years, grew so frequent as to become almost commonplace. For example, at Howsham Hall, owned by the Cholmelys, much of the east side of the house was re-structured. John Silvester made substantial additions to Birthwaite Hall, which he had purchased from Sir Francis Burdett; as did Silvester's successors to their main seat at Newland Park. Brough Hall was drastically converted for the Lawsons c. 1730; while at about the same time the Boyntons changed many of the floor levels at Burton Agnes, panelled one room, provided another with a classical ceiling, and later installed chimney-pieces, one of which was from their other house at Barmston. At Kirklees Hall the Armitages built a long west wing and introduced a fine staircase in the 1730s, before concentrating on the lavish decoration of the interior. Following his momentous marriage in 1740 Sir Hugh Smithson embarked on many alterations at Stanwick Park, though only the stables with their fine clock tower remain. In the late 1740s Sir John Bland substantially enlarged the Elizabethan house at Kippax Park to produce a huge façade of thirty-seven bays, and in 1752 the Dawnays commissioned James Paine to remodel Cowick Hall. Many houses were progressively altered over several generations. The Belasyse family installed a new staircase at Newburgh Priory, built a new east front in 1732, a west wing in 1767, and then went on to remodel much of the interior; while at Boynton Hall the Stricklands embellished the interior during the period

1700–4, and greatly altered the exterior in 1730, and again forty years later. Many features at Hawksworth Hall – the decor, bay windows, a billiard room, and a staircase – originated at various points in the eighteenth century, while at Carlton Towers, the home of the Stapletons, the time-span of activity was even lengthier.[82]

Only rarely, moreover, were capital outlays confined to housing. As at Whitley the aim was to surround a house with lawns, gardens, trees, and shrubberies, the whole often being surrounded by a stout wall and fronted by an imposing driveway and gatepiece. At Sledmere two formal avenues led up to the house from the village; and within little more than a year of occupying the property Richard Sykes had planted 20,000 trees – beech, sycamore, wych elm, and chestnut – in the grounds, an activity which he pursued with no less vigour in later years. According to his son, he was so proud of his various domestic improvements 'that he could not endure to hear of strangers going to see Castle Howard and not calling to see Sledmere also'.[83] In many cases, even where houses have survived, their surroundings have long since been superseded, though a variety of relics pay tribute to the grandeur of their total conception: the Turner mausoleum and gateway at Kirleatham, the early Georgian pavilions at Newburgh Priory, the forty-foot obelisk a quarter of a mile from the site of Sir Henry Etherington's house at Ferriby, the summer-house built in 1737 at South Dalton, the pheasantry and chapel erected in the grounds at Bretton Hall in 1744, and the bridge at Nostell which Sir George Savile designed for the Winns in 1763. Nor were such developments confined to demesnes. A succession of costly and elaborate statues and memorial tablets were installed in adjacent parish churches, such as those at Kirkheaton and South Dalton; and several families continued the tradition of providing for, or subsidizing, the erection of various public utilities. The Cross in Beverley's Saturday market-place, paid for by Sir Charles Hotham and Sir Michael Wharton, is the earliest eighteenth-century public building of note in the East Riding; the Penny-mans founded almshouses in Ormesby in 1712, and extended them in 1744 and 1773; Lord Rockingham set John Carr off on his remarkable career as the most illustrious of all Yorkshire architects by lending his patronage to Carr's design for the

grandstand at Knavesmire racecourse, York in 1754–5; and in
the latter year Richard Sykes rebuilt the church at Sledmere at
his own expense. No family contributed more in bricks and
mortar to the welfare of their locality than the Turners at
Kirkleatham. Having founded a hospital there in 1676, they
went on in 1708–9 to provide a Free School of two and a half
storeys with a frontage of nine bays. Then, after rebuilding the
hospital in 1746, they commissioned Carr to repair the church
in 1763, when he also worked on Kirkleatham Hall.[84]

This steady growth of building and associated improvements
came to a crescendo in the 1760s and 1770s. Major projects,
such as those at Everingham and South Dalton, which had
earlier been postponed or delayed owing to the long absence or
sudden death of proprietors, then went ahead, while others
were encouraged to embark on them by the substantial and
long-awaited rise in estate incomes. Besides Everingham Hall
and South Dalton Hall Garth, new houses were erected by Sir
Henry Etherington at Ferriby, the Ibbetsons at Denton, the
Ramsdens at Byram Park, the Vavasours at Hazlewood, the
Wyvills at Constable Burton, and by the Franklands at Thirkleby. Elsewhere the more gradual process of embellishment
remained undiminished, with the most spectacular development being at Scampston Hall where Capability Brown landscaped the grounds for the St. Quintins in 1773.[85]

Whether, given higher levels of income, the later eighteenth
century witnessed a fuller and more wholehearted commitment
to directly productive investment on the part of Yorkshire's
more substantial landowners lies beyond the scope of this
study. It is clear, however, that that commitment was generally
absent between the mid seventeenth and mid eighteenth centuries. Individuals and families were then involved either in a
struggle for economic survival as landowners; in maintaining a
delicate equilibrium between income and expenditure; or were
frankly enjoying a lavish and, in many respects, new life-style.
The net result for most of them was a steady retreat from close
involvement in the working life on their properties; a progress-
ive delegation to others of the responsibility for managing their
estate and business affairs; and a growing absorption with the
more public and conspicuous features of life in high society.

One important consequence of these developments was a

slow but perceptible change in the texture of the landlord–tenant relationship, which became less paternalistic, more distant and more businesslike on the one hand, and more independent and self-reliant on the other. Considerable stress has been placed, and rightly so, on the manner in which landlords cushioned their tenants against the worst effects of periodic depression. This stemmed partly from genuine concern for the plight of the farming community, but was primarily motivated by realization of the consequences for landlords if large numbers of their tenants went bankrupt. Where landlords themselves encountered severe financial difficulties their policies were often tough and uncompromising, irrespective of tenants' circumstances. Overall the most substantial tenant-farmers were favoured and positively encouraged; the least substantial, if not actively discouraged, were regarded with mixed feelings or merely tolerated. The majority of tenants, who lay in between these two extremes, could expect assistance and forebearance during periods of acute, general distress, but at other times were increasingly left to fend for themselves. Where formal agreements between landlord and tenant departed from local custom, it was usually to define landlords' rights more clearly, or to maintain and increase the level of their incomes.

If all this was conducive to agricultural progress, in so far as it promoted the survival of the fittest farmers, there was often little alternative in view of the discontinuity which frequently characterized the formulation and implementation of policy. Patterns of life and death among landowners, as well as vagaries of personality, meant that most estates went through periods of proprietorial inactivity when the profile of management was low; landowners' growing interest and engagement in events outside their immediate localities, and the consequent general reduction in the extent of their direct farming, had a similar effect. At such times the contribution of stewards and other employees was particularly important because in carrying out instructions, generally with commendable efficiency, they prevented any breakdown of management; but only rarely did they achieve significantly more than this. It was only during periods of minority, when considerable sums were available for investment by responsible third parties, that substantial improvements were made in the absence of close proprietorial involvement. Moreover, when estate income was re-invested it was overwhelmingly devoted to the consolidation, expansion and embellishment of holdings, rather than to promoting more fundamental changes in the nature of the economic activities pursued on them. The situation in regard to developments outside agriculture was not dissimilar. With a few notable exceptions, substantial landowners were reluctant to become directly involved in industrial and commercial ventures, and such opportunities as existed on their estates were let to tenants, local freeholders, and lesser gentry. Risks were variously shared according to private judgements and circumstances in a manner which was clearly beneficial to future, broader development.

Essentially conservative behaviour in matters of production was in sharp constrast to landowners' attitudes and record as consumers. By the end of this period they borrowed, as a group, far more than they lent, especially short-term;[86] and as their sources of credit diversified, an increasing variety of other groups benefited from returns on their capital. In relation to their income, and other than at times of acute financial difficulty, the personal expenditure of landowners was always large and frequently lavish; and stricter forms of settlement spread both income and credit across a growing body of dependants whose life-style was similar to that of their paymasters. Their combined outgoings fuelled the growth of a host of consumer industries and services, while the most ambitious projects generated a heavy demand for labour, particularly that of skilled craftsmen and tradesmen. Still more significant was the fact that the landed élite defined a pattern of consumer behaviour for the increasingly prosperous and much more numerous middle ranks of society, acting as a leading sector in the long-term growth of mass consumption. Indeed, opportunities for emulation went further than this: the cycle of success and failure among substantial landowners provided openings as well as incentive to others, who sought the upward mobility which their social superiors had once experienced or continued to enjoy.[87]

REFERENCES

CHAPTER I

1. Quoted in H. A. Lloyd, *The Gentry of South-West Wales 1540–1640* (1968), p. 17.
2. P. Laslett, 'The Gentry of Kent in 1640', *Historical Journal*, IX (1948), p. 156.
3. W. G. Hoskins, *Local History in England* (1959), p. 23 and *passim*; J. Simmons, 'The English County Historians', *THAS*, VIII (1963).
4. D. Spring, 'Introduction' to J. Bateman, *The Great Landowners of Gt. Britain and Ireland* (1971), pp. 7–19; F. M. L. Thompson, 'Land and Politics in England in the 19th Century', *TRHS* 5th series, XV (1965).
5. F. M. L. Thompson, *English Landed Society in the 19th Century* (1963), pp. 327–45; A. D. Carr, 'Deeds of Title', *History*, L (1965), p. 328; N. B. Harte (ed.), *The Study of Economic History* (1971), p. xxvii.
6. L. Stone, *The Causes of the English Revolution 1529–1642* (1972), whose references are designed to provide a guide to the modern historiography of the subject. For the peerage, see the same author's *The Crisis of the Aristocracy 1558–1641* (1965).
7. J. Thirsk, 'The Sales of Royalist Land during the Interregnum', *Econ. Hist. Rev.*, 2nd series, V (1952–3); 'The Restoration Land Settlement', *Journal of Modern History*, XXVI (1954); *The Restoration* (1976); H. J. Habakkuk, 'Landowners and the Civil War', *Econ. Hist. Rev.*, 2nd series, XVIII (1965).
8. H. J. Habakkuk, 'Marriage Settlements in the 18th Century', *TRHS* 4th series, XXXII (1950); 'The Long-Term Rate of Interest and the Price of Land in the 17th Century', *Econ. Hist. Rev.*, 2nd series, V (1952–3); M. G. Davies, 'Country Gentry and Payments to London, 1650–1714', *Econ. Hist. Rev.*, 2nd series, XXIV (1971); M. Beloff, 'Humphrey Shalcrosse and the Great Civil War', *English Historical Review*, LIV (1939). For early 17th-century developments in regard to mortgages, particularly the increasing recognition of the equity of mortgage redemption, see: M. E. Finch, *The Wealth of Five Northamptonshire Families 1540–1640*, *Northamptonshire Record Society*, XIX (1954–5).
9. H. J. Habakkuk, 'English Landownership, 1680–1740', *Econ. Hist. Rev.*, X (1939–40).
10. H. J. Habakkuk, 'Marriage Settlements in the 18th Century', p. 28 and *passim*.
11. H. J. Habakkuk, 'The English Land Market in the 18th Century' in J. S. Bromley & E. H. Kossman (eds.), *Britain and the Netherlands* (1960), p. 165 and *passim*.
12. G. E. Mingay, *English Landed Society in the 18th Century* (1963), pp. 259–60; H. J. Habakkuk, 'England' in A. Goodwin (ed.), *The European Nobility in the 18th Century* (1953).

13. H. J. Habakkuk, 'The Economic Functions of English Landowners in the 17th and 18th Centuries', *Explorations in Entrepreneurial History*, VI (1953).
14. E. Hughes, 'The 18th-Century Estate Agent' in H. A. Cronne, T. W. Moody & D. B. Quinn (eds.), *Essays in British and Irish History* (1949); G. E. Mingay, 'The 18th-Century Land Steward' in E. L. Jones & G. E. Mingay (eds.), *Land, Labour, and Population in the Industrial Revolution* (1967). For the best case-study, see: J. Wake & D. C. Webster (eds.), *The Letters of Daniel Eaton to the 3rd Earl of Cardigan, Northamptonshire Record Society*, XXIV (1971).
15. R. A. C. Parker, 'Direct Taxation on the Coke Estates in the 18th Century', *English Historical Review*, LXXI (1956), p. 247.
16. D. C. Coleman, 'London Scrivenors and the Estate Market in the Later 17th Century', *Econ. Hist. Rev.*, 2nd series, IV (1951); R. Robson, *The Attorney in 18th-Century England* (1959); B. L. Anderson, 'The Attorney and the Early Capital Market in Lancashire' in J. R. Harris (ed.), *Liverpool and Merseyside* (1969); 'Provincial Aspects of the Financial Revolution of the 18th Century', *Business History*, XI (1969).
17. D. M. Joslin, 'London Private Bankers 1720–85', *Econ. Hist Rev.*, 2nd series, VII (1954–5).
18. For the effect on rent receipts of the initial downturn in prices, see: M. G. Davies, 'Country Gentry and Falling Rents in the 1660s and 1670s', *Midland History*, IV (1977).
19. G. E. Mingay, 'The Agricultural Depression, 1730–50', *Econ. Hist. Rev.*, 2nd series, VIII (1955–6). For an example of benevolence of 'almost eccentric' proportions, see: Mingay, 'Thrumpton: A Nottinghamshire Estate in the 18th Century', *Transactions of the Thoroton Society*, LXI (1957), p. 56 and *passim*.
20. G. E. Mingay, 'The Size of Farms in the 18th Century', *Econ. Hist. Rev.*, 2nd series, XIV (1961–2).
21. W. G. Hoskins, 'The Estates of the Caroline Gentry' in Hoskins & H. P. R. Finberg (eds.), *Devonshire Studies* (1952); P. Laslett, 'The Gentry of Kent in 1640'; E. Hughes, *North Country Life in the 18th Century: I. The North-East, 1700–50* (1952).
22. C. Clay, 'Marriage, Inheritance, and the Rise of Large Estates in England, 1660–1815', *Econ. Hist. Rev.*, 2nd series, XXI (1968).
23. C. Clay, 'The Price of Freehold Land in the Later 17th and 18th Centuries', *Econ. Hist. Rev.*, 2nd series, XXVII (1974).
24. B. A. Holderness, 'The English Land Market in the 18th Century: The Case of Lincolnshire', *Econ. Hist. Rev.*, 2nd series, XXVII (1974), p. 558 and *passim*.
25. J. V. Beckett, 'English Landownership in the Later 17th and 18th Centuries: The Debate and the Problems', *Econ. Hist. Rev.*, 2nd series, XXX (1977).
26. E. Kerridge, *The Agricultural Revolution* (1967); *Agrarian Problems in the 16th Century and After* (1969); *The Farmers of Old England* (1973); J. Thirsk (ed.), *The Agrarian History of England and Wales*, IV, 1500–1640 (1967); G. E. Mingay, 'The Agricultural Revolution in English History:

A Reconsideration', *Agricultural History*, XXXVII (1963). For the latest synthesis of recent research, see: Mingay (ed.), *The Agricultural Revolution: Changes in Agriculture 1650–1880* (1977), pp. 1–68.

27. E. L. Jones (ed.), *Agriculture and Economic Growth in England 1650– 1815* (1967), 'Introduction'; 'English and European Agricultural Development 1650–1750' in R. M. Hartwell (ed.), *The Industrial Revolution* (1970), p. 66 and *passim*. See also the same author's collected essays: *Agriculture and the Industrial Revolution* (1974).

28. G. E. Mingay, *English Landed Society in the 18th Century*, pp. 15–16. The most comprehensive guide to research on landownership, estate management, and landed society since then is the same author's *The Gentry: The Rise and Fall of a Ruling Class* (1976).

29. R. A. C. Parker, *Coke of Norfolk: A Financial and Agricultural Study, 1707–1842* (1975).

30. R. A. Kelch, *Newcastle. A Duke Without Money: Thomas Pelham-Holles, 1693–1768* (1974). For further case-studies relating partly or wholly to this period, see: E. F. Gay, 'Sir Richard Temple: the Debt Settlement and Estate Litigation, 1653–75', *Huntingdon Library Quarterly*, VI (1943); J. Wake, *The Brudenells of Deene* (2nd ed. 1954); H. J. Habakkuk, 'Daniel Finch, 2nd Earl of Nottingham: His House and Estate' in J. H. Plumb (ed.), *Studies in Social History* (1955); A. M. Mimardière, 'The Finances of a Warwickshire Gentry Family 1693–1726', *University of Birmingham Historical Journal*, IX (1964); R. Meredith, 'A Derbyshire Family in the 17th Century: The Eyres of Hassop and their Forfeited Estates', *Recusant History*, VIII (1965); O. R. F. Davies, 'The Wealth and Influence of John Holles, Duke of Newcastle, 1694–1711', *Renaissance and Modern Studies*, IX (1965); C. Clay, 'The Misfortunes of William, Fourth Lord Petre (1638–1655)', *Recusant History*, XI (1971); T. J. Raybould, *The Economic Emergence of the Black Country: A Study of the Dudley Estate* (1972); L. Stone, *Family and Fortune* (1973); T. Beastall, *A North Country Estate: The Lumleys and Saundersons as Landowners, 1600–1900* (1975).

31. J. P. Cooper, 'Patterns of Inheritance and Settlement by Great Landowners from the 15th to the 18th Centuries' in J. Goody, J. Thirsk & E. P. Thompson (eds.), *Family and Inheritance: Rural Society in Western Europe 1200–1800* (1976).

32. L. Stone, *The Family, Sex and Marriage in England 1500–1800* (1977).

33. T. H. Hollingsworth, 'The Demography of the British Peerage', Supplement to *Population Studies*, XVIII (1964).

34. B. H. Slicher van Bath, *The Agrarian History of Western Europe A.D. 500–1850* (1963), pp. 206–220; J. D. Chambers & G. E. Mingay, *The Agricultural Revolution 1750–1880* (1966), pp. 11–12, 39–42, 109–12, 167, 205–6.

35. H. J. Habakkuk, 'Preface' to M. E. Finch, *The Wealth of Five Northamptonshire Families 1540–1640*, p. xix.

36. L. Stone, *The Crisis of the Aristocracy 1558–1641*, p. 4.

37. J. V. Beckett, 'English Landownership in the Later 17th and 18th Centuries: The Debate and the Problems', p. 581.

38. F. W. Pixley, *A History of the Baronetage* (1900), pp. 18–19; J. T. Cliffe, *The Yorkshire Gentry: From the Reformation to the Civil War* (1969), pp. 6–7; L. Stone, *Crisis of the Aristocracy*, pp. 82–5.

39. J. T. Cliffe, pp. 8 (quotation), 111; *CB* I, pp. 30, 43–4, 48–9, 55, 103; J. P. Cooper, 'The Fortune of Thomas Wentworth, Earl of Strafford', *Econ. Hist. Rev.*, 2nd series, XI (1958–9), p. 227.

40. J. T. Cliffe, p. 7; L. Stone, pp. 85–6; F. W. Pixley, pp. 24–6, 58, 111, 143–4, 146, 173.

41. *CB* I, pp. 114, 131, 147, 153–4, 183; II, pp. 26, 407, 430; J. T. Cliffe, pp. 123, 225, 279, 363, 382.

42. *CB* I, pp. 135, 154; II, pp. 36, 61; J. T. Cliffe, pp. 86–7, 90–1, 94.

43. *CB* II, pp. 51, 61, 397–8, 409; J. T. Cliffe, pp. 126, 155; PRO C 22/27/13; Q.F.V.F——, 'The Vernatti Family and Its Connections', *The Herald and Genealogist*, V (1870), pp. 146–7; *CSPD* 1631–43, *passim*.

44. L. Stone, p. 95; *CB* II, pp. 115, 117, 128, 136, 139–40, 149; J. T. Cliffe, pp. 334, 337; *DNB* XIX, pp. 55–6; W. L. F. Nuttall, 'The Yorkshire Commissioners Appointed for the Trial of King Charles I', *YAJ*, XLIII (1971).

45. *CB* II, pp. 161–2, 174–6, 185; J. T. Cliffe, pp. 334, 350. The best single guide to family allegiance in Yorkshire during the Civil War is J. W. Clay, 'The Gentry of Yorkshire at the Time of the Civil War', *YAJ*, XXIII (1914–15), pp. 350–91.

46. *CB* II, pp. 139–40, 156–7, 196, 212; III, p. 11; J. T. Cliffe, pp. 96–7; J. Hunter, *South Yorkshire* (1828–31), I, p. 169.

47. *CB* III, pp. 211–12, 264, 287–8, 298; IV, p. 18; J. T. Cliffe, p. 230; P. G. Holiday, 'Royalist Composition Fines and Land Sales in Yorkshire, 1645–65', Ph.D. thesis, Leeds University, 1966, pp. 177, 374, 380; J. W. Pennyman, *Records of the Family of Pennyman of Ormesby* (1904), pp. 5–6; Sir T. Lawson-Tancred, *The Tancreds of Brampton* (1921), pp. 25–7.

48. *CB* III, pp. 55–6, 98–9, 155, 191, 262–3; *CSPD* 1660–1, p. 435; J. T. Cliffe, p. 382; P. G. Holiday, pp. 12, 23, 52, 102, 104, 376; Clay, *Dugdale*, III, pp. 335–6; J. Hunter, I, pp. 58–9.

49. *CB* III, pp. 46, 49, 101, 132, 186, 225, 247, 254; J. T. Cliffe, pp. 336–7; P. G. Holiday, pp. 12, 113, 309, 329, 382–3; Clay, *Dugdale*, I, pp. 176–80, 233; H. Aveling, *The Catholic Recusants of the West Riding of Yorkshire 1558–1790* (1963), p. 233; H. B. McCall, *The Story of the Family of Wandesforde of Kirklington and Castlecomer* (1904), p. 87; H. E. Chetwynd-Stapylton, *The Stapletons of Yorkshire* (1897), pp. 168–9, 293–5; H. K. G. Plantagenet-Harrison, *The History of Yorkshire*, I, *Wapentake of Gilling West* (1879), p. 237.

50. *CB* III, pp. 87, 126, 142–3, 147, 149–50, 292; *CTB* (1660–7), pp. 84, 328, 379; J. T. Cliffe, pp. 19, 270–1, 278, 335, 340, 358–9, 377–8; J. Hunter, II, p. 136; W. Robertshaw, 'The Manor of Tong', *Bradford Antiquary*, new series, pt. xxxviii (1956), p. 123.

51. *CB* III, p. 46; IV, p. 21; J. T. Cliffe, pp. 56, 98–9, 158–9, 283, 382; J. Hunter, II, pp. 136, 377; H. Aveling, p. 259; See below, pp. 263–5.

52. L. Stone, p. 96 (quotation); J. T. Cliffe, p. 19; H. K. G. Plantagenet-Harrison, p. 504.
53. *CB* III, pp. 98–9, 132, 225; *CTB* (1660–7), pp. 84, 328, 379; Clay, *Dugdale*, I, pp. 93–4; II, p. 60; P. G. Holiday, p. 374; J. Hunter, I, pp. 55–9; H. K. G. Plantagenet-Harrison, p. 504; Sir J. D. Legard, *The Legards of Anlaby and Ganton* (1926), pp. 89–90.
54. *CB* IV, pp. 49–50, 108, 115, 160; V, p. 13; Foster I (Hawksworth); J. T. Cliffe, pp. 57–8, 125, 134–5, 137, 247, 371–2, 381; J. Hunter, II, pp. 454–5; S. Margerison, 'A Yorkshire Royalist Squire', *Bradford Antiquary*, I (1888), pp. 57–66; See below, pp. 263, 265–6, 292–3.
55. *CB* IV, p. 171; C. M. Lowther-Bouch, 'Lowther of Marske (Cleveland) and Holker', *CWAA* new series, XLIV (1944), pp. 110–11 (quotation) and *passim*.
56. *CB* V, p. 25; C. M. Lowther-Bouch, 'Lowther of Swillington from Its Origin until 1788', *CWAA* new series, XLII (1942).
57. R. G. Wilson, *Gentlemen Merchants: The Merchant Community in Leeds, 1700–1830* (1971), p. 66.
58. *CB* V, pp. 39–40, 95–6; R. G. Wilson, pp. 76–81, 244, 246 and *passim*.
59. *CB* V, pp. 186, 232; R. G. Wilson, p. 14; Sir J. D. Legard, pp. 191–2; G. Jackson, *Hull in the 18th Century* (1972), pp. 103, 113, 153, 247, 251, 264 and *passim*.
60. Sir A. R. Wagner, *English Genealogy* (2nd ed. 1972), p. 108.
61. *CB* IV, p. 171; V, pp. 68–9, 218; Clay, *Dugdale*, I, pp. 60–2; *DNB* XVII, pp. 49–51; R. Sedgwick, *The House of Commons 1715–54* (1970), II, pp. 228, 277–8, 388–9; Sir L. Namier & J. Brooke, *The House of Commons 1754–90* (1964), III, pp. 568–9 (quotation); W. D. B———, 'Turner Family of Kirkleatham, North Riding of Yorkshire', *The Topographer and Genealogist*, I (1846), pp. 505–9.
62. *CB* V, pp. 95–6, 239; J. Hunter, II, p. 377; G. Jackson, pp. 113–14; Foster III (Dodsworth of Thornton for Smith).
63. *CB* V, pp. 198, 201–2, 244; J. T. Cliffe, pp. 378–9; J. Hunter, II, p. 125; Clay, *Dugdale*, II, pp. 210–13; Sir L. Namier & J. Brooke, III, pp. 654–5; J. Wilkinson, *Worthies, Families and Celebrities of Barnsley and District* (1883), pp. 16–17, 110–12; J. H. Coghill, *The Family of Coghill, 1377–1879* (1879), pp. 17–29.
64. W. Harwood-Long, 'Regional Farming in 17th Century Yorkshire', *Ag. Hist. Rev.*, VIII (1960); A. Harris, 'The Agriculture of the East Riding of Yorkshire before the Parliamentary Enclosures', *YAJ*, XL (1959); W. Marshall, *A Review of the Reports to the Board of Agriculture from the Northern Department* (1808), pp. 341–511; E. Hughes, *North Country Life in the 18th Century*, I, pp. 113–14.
65. *CB* V, pp. 304–5; Foster III (Belasyse); C. V. Collier, *An Account of the Boynton Family* (1914), pp. 21, 74, 81; J. W. Walker (ed.), *Hackness Manuscripts and Accounts, YASRS*, XCV (1937), p. 15.
66. *CP* IV, p. 453; J. T. Cliffe, p. 383; J. P. Cooper, pp. 227, 245, 248; H. B. McCall, p. 99; J. Hunter, I, p. 145.
67. J. T. Cliffe, pp. 49–66.
68. J. T. Cliffe, pp. 30–31, 371–2 (quotation); A. Browning (ed.), *Memoirs*

of Sir John Reresby (1936), p. 44; J. Bossy, *The English Catholic Community 1570–1850* (1975), pp. 173–81.

69. J. T. Cliffe, p. 57.

70. DDEV/56/30, ff. 126–7.

71. J. T. Cliffe, p. 45; C. W. Chalkin, *The Provincial Towns of Georgian England* (1974), pp. 4, 13–14, 23, 25, 38–41, 51–53.

72. BR III; WWM D 298, 303, 330, 360; WBD/I – XII, *passim*; Foster II (Ramsden); J. T. Cliffe, pp. 38, 53, 97, 356; S. Margerison (ed.), *Memorandum Book of Sir Walter Calverley, Bart.*, Surtees Society, LXXVII (1883), pp. 47–8, 66, 120–21; T. Dyson, *History of Huddersfield and District* (1932), p. 122; G. G. Hopkinson, 'The Development of the South Yorkshire and North Derbyshire Coalfield, 1500–1775' in J. Benson & R. G. Neville (eds.), *Studies in the Yorkshire Coal Industry* (1976), pp. 4–10; D. G. Hey, *The Rural Metalworkers of the Sheffield Region* (1972), pp. 9–15; 'A Dual Economy in South Yorkshire', *Ag. Hist. Rev.*, XVII (1969); R. G. Wilson, p. 229.

73. G. G. Hopkinson, 'The Charcoal Iron Industry in the Sheffield Region 1500–1775', *THAS*, VIII (1963), pp. 125, 127–9; A. Browning (ed.), p. 453; H. C. Foxcroft, *The Life and Letters of Sir George Savile, 1st Marquis of Halifax* (1898), I, pp. 57–8; *CP* IX, p. 744.

74. C. M. Lowther-Bouch, 'Lowther of Swillington', pp. 72–3; S. Margerison (ed.), *Memorandum Book*, pp. 136–7; H. B. McCall, pp. 301–2.

75. J. T. Cliffe, pp. 58, 64–5.

76. See below, pp. 207–8.

77. Sir H. Cholmely, *The Memoirs of Sir Hugh Cholmely* (1870), p. 293; R. Sedgwick, II, p. 487; H. B. McCall, pp. 145–6, 161, 298, 301–2; E. Hughes, *North Country Life in the 18th Century*, I, pp. 67, 116, 161–95, 210; J. Straker, *Memoirs of Sir Walter Blackett, Bart.* (1819), p. xxiv and *passim*.

78. T. S. Willan, 'Yorkshire River Navigation 1600–1750', *Geography*, XXII (1937); *River Navigation in England 1600–1750* (1936), pp. 52–62; *The Early History of the Don Navigation* (1965), pp. 1–40; G. G. Hopkinson, 'The Development of the Inland Navigation in South Yorkshire and North Derbyshire 1697–1850', *THAS*, VII (1956); R. G. Wilson, pp. 138–9.

79. D. M. Joslin, 'London Private Bankers 1720–85', *Econ. Hist. Rev.*, 2nd series, VII (1954–5); R. Robson, *The Attorney in 18th Century England* (1959), pp. 68–118.

80. J. T. Cliffe, p. 31.

81. J. D. Chambers & G. E. Mingay, pp. 22, 26, 32; W. Harwood-Long, 'Regional Farming in 17th Century Yorkshire', *Ag. Hist. Rev.*, VIII (1960), p. 113; D. Defoe, *A Tour Through the Whole Island of Gt. Britain* (Everyman rev. ed. 1962), II, p. 199; O. Wilkinson, *The Agricultural Revolution in the East Riding of Yorkshire* (1964), pp. 13–14; E. Hughes, *North Country Life in the 18th Century*, I, p. 146; R. Trow-Smith, *A History of British Livestock Husbandry to 1700* (1957), p. 240; R.

Sedgwick, II, p. 566; G. E. Mingay, *English Landed Society in the 18th Century*, pp. 165–7.

82. J. T. Cliffe, pp. 282–94.

83. J. T. Cliffe, pp. 293, 296–326, 350.

84. The information in this paragraph has been culled from many of the family and local histories listed in the bibliography. The most important general sources are: J. T. Cliffe, pp. 336–62; P. G. Holiday, p. 279 and *passim*; J. W. Clay, 'The Gentry of Yorkshire at the Time of the Civil War', pp. 349–94.

85. C. A. Goodricke, *History of the Goodricke Family* (rev. ed. 1897), pp. 16–24; H. B. McCall, pp. 85–91.

86. Quoted in A. M. W. Stirling, *The Hothams* (1918), I, pp. 64–5.

87. D. Parsons (ed.), *The Diary of Sir Henry Slingsby of Scriven, Bart.* (1836), p. 121.

88. A. Browning (ed.), pp. 3–21 (quotation p. 6).

89. C. Hill, *Reformation to Industrial Revolution* (1967), pp. 99–116; R. Carroll, 'Yorkshire Parliamentary Boroughs in the 17th Century', *Northern History*, III (1968); A. Gooder, *The Parliamentary Representation of the County of York 1258–1832*, II, *YASRS*, XCVI (1937); J. H. Plumb, *The Growth of Political Stability in England 1675–1725* (1967), pp. xiii–65.

90. DDEV/68/248, iv.

91. A. Browning (ed.), p. 53.

92. *CB* II, p. 117; IV, p. 131; *CP* V, p. 265; Clay, *Dugdale*, III, pp. 335–6; C. A. Goodricke, pp. 25–30; J. H. Coghill, pp. 23–8; Sir H. Cholmely, pp. 243–96; C. M. Lowther-Bouch, 'Lowther of Swillington', p. 73.

93. J. Hunter, I, pp. 143–4; *DNB* XVII, pp. 845–53.

94. A. Browning (ed.), p. 174 and *passim*.

95. J. H. Plumb, p. 101 and Chapter IV *passim*. For various facets of the growth of offices see: R. Davis, 'The Rise of Protection in England 1689–1786', *Econ. Hist. Rev.*, 2nd series, XIX (1966); E. E. Hoon, *The Organisation of the English Customs System 1696–1786* (1938), pp. 119, 165, 290; D. B. Horn, *The British Diplomatic Service 1689–1789* (1961), pp. 12–14.

96. E. Hughes, *Studies in Administration and Finance, 1558–1825* (1934), p. 267.

97. *DNB* IV, p. 1102; XIV, pp. 1185–6, 1191, 1195; XVII, pp. 49–51, 663–4, 850; C. A. Goodricke, pp. 30–2.

98. See below, pp. 84–5.

99. *CB* II, p. 115; III, p. 143; R. Sedgwick, II, p. 453; A. Gooder, II, pp. 102–3.

100. *CB* I, p. 103; WBC/94. See below, p. 128.

101. *CB* I, p. 103; III, p. 150; *DNB* XIII, p. 707; XVII, pp. 47–9; Clay, *Dugdale*, II, pp. 433–7; C. A. Goodricke, pp. 32, 37; R. Sedgwick, II, pp. 388, 555, 566; Sir L. Namier & J. Brooke, II, pp. 509–10; R. G. Wilson, pp. 150–3.

102. J. Thirsk, 'Younger Sons in the 17th Century', *History*, LIV (1969);

'The European Debate on Customs of Inheritance 1500–1700' in J. Goody, J. Thirsk & E. P. Thompson (eds.), *Family and Inheritance: Rural Society in Western Europe 1200–1800* (1976).

103. *DNB* XI, pp. 1025–33; C. M. Lowther-Bouch, 'Lowther of Swillington', pp. 76–85; R. Sedgwick, II, pp. 210–13, 378, 525–5; Sir L. Namier & J. Brooke, III, pp. 38–9; N. Carlisle, *History of the Family of Bland* (1826), pp. 52–6; C. A. Goodricke, p. 33.

104. *DNB* XIV, p. 1196.

105. J. T. Cliffe, pp. 21–4; J. H. Plumb, p. xv; S. Margerison, *Memorandum Book, passim*.

106. G. E. Mingay, *English Landed Society in the 18th Century*, pp. 137–8.

107. G. E. Mingay, p. 145.

108. A. Everitt, *Change in the Provinces: the 17th Century* (1969), p. 50.

109. L. Stone, 'Marriage among the English Nobility in the 16th and 17th Centuries', *Comparative Studies in Society and History*, III (1960–1), p. 195; for further evidence of this see P. Styles, 'The Social Structure of Kineton Hundred in the Reign of Charles II', *Transactions of the Birmingham Archaeological Society*, LXXVIII (1960), p. 104.

110. A. Browning (ed.), pp. 79–80; S. Margerison, *Memorandum Book*, pp. 61, 64–5. The Sheriff's main functions were 'honorary and expensive' (B. Williams, *The Whig Supremacy, 1714–60* (rev. C. H. Stuart, 1962), p. 49).

111. G. Jackson, p. 302; R. G. Wilson, pp. 207, 231.

112. Sir J. D. Legard, pp. 38–9, 99; J. W. Pennyman, p. 6; G. Jackson, p. 302; *DNB* XVIII, pp. 663–4; *CB* III, pp. 225–6; E. Hughes, *North Country Life in the 18th Century*, I, pp. 287–8; J. S. Cockburn, 'The North Riding Justices, 1690–1750: A Study in Local Administration', *YAJ*, XLI (1965), pp. 482–3.

113. *CB* I, pp. 147, 175; II, p. 398; IV, pp. 21–2; V, p. 13; Clay, *Dugdale*, II, pp. 110–11, 232, 315; III, pp. 262–3; R. G. Wilson, p. 14; C. M. Lowther-Bouch, 'Lowther of Swillington', p. 67; 'Lowther of Marske', p. 100; J. T. Cliffe, p. 86; J. Hunter, I, p. 169; J. Foster, III (Milbanke); J. W. Walker (ed.), pp. 1–16; H. C. Foxcroft, pp. 20–1; H. B. McCall, p. 99; J. H. Coghill, p. 23.

114. J. T. Cliffe, pp. 210–30; H. Aveling, pp. 233, 235–6 and *passim*; J. P. Kenyon, *The Popish Plot* (1972), esp. Ch. 1; M. B. Rowlands, 'The Iron Age of Double Taxes', *Staffordshire Catholic History*, III (1963). See below, pp. 169, 184–5.

115. *CB* II, p. 190; III, p. 101; IV, p. 19; Clay, *Dugdale*, I, p. 233; II, p. 315; H. Aveling, pp. 234, 259, 261; F. S. Colman, *A History of the Parish of Barwick in Elmet*, *Thoresby Society*, XVII (1908), pp. 155–8.

116. D. Parsons (ed.), p. 24.

117. J. C. Cox, 'The Household Books of Sir Miles Stapleton, Bart., 1656–1705', *The Ancestor*, ii & iii (1902); H. Aveling, p. 255; *DNB* XVII, p. 50.

118. W. G. Hoskins, 'The Rebuilding of Rural England, 1570–1640' in *Provincial England* (1963), p. 136.

119. A. Browning (ed.), p. 385.
120. R. Sedgwick, II, p. 442.
121. R. Sedgwick, II, p. 184.
122. R. Sedgwick, II, p. 228; Sir L. Namier & J. Brooke, II, p. 622; on the general question of spiralling electoral costs post 1688 see J. H. Plumb, pp. 85, 97, 139, 141, 173–4.
123. D. Sutherland, *The Landowners* (1968), p. 9.
124. *CB* III, p. 143; *CP* VII, p. 513; IX, pp. 743–4; R. Sedgwick, II, pp. 51, 428–9.

CHAPTER II

1. Quoted in the soundest (but neglected) work on Sir John's later public career: B. N. Reckitt, *Charles I and Hull 1639–45* (1952), pp. 19, 21. For other contemporary opinions of the first baronet see: BL Egerton MS 2884, ff. 48–50.
2. PRO C 6/161/20; *CSPD* 1645–47, p. 237; *DNB* IX, pp. 1302–5; P. Saltmarshe, *History and Chartulary of the Hothams of Scorborough, 1100–1700* (1914), p. 144; J. T..Cliffe, *The Yorkshire Gentry: From the Reformation to the Civil War* (1969), pp. 79, 92, 110, 123, 248. See Appendix 3.
3. DDHO/1/76, 77; P. Saltmarshe, p. 144; B. N. Reckitt, *passim*; J. T. Cliffe, *passim*.
4. See Appendix 4.
5. See M. J. Hawkins (ed.), *Sales of Wards in Somerset, 1603–41*, Somerset Record Society, LXVII (1965), pp. xv–xxxi.
6. DDHO/1/46, 78, 79; 20/7; 33/1; 53/3. The best guide to Sir John's dispositions is in P. Saltmarshe, pp. 151–62. £700 of his gross annual rental had come from property in Howsham tenanted by courtesy of the Norcliffe family whose daughter, Catherine, Sir John had taken as his fourth wife in 1631. Francis, the sole surviving issue of the marriage, tenanted the property until he died, unmarried, in 1652 when it returned to the Norcliffes (DDHO/20/7; P. Saltmarshe, p. 156). For subsequent litigation concerning surviving daughters' portions see: PRO C 6/161/20; C 33/207, ff. 289, 891, 1321; 209, ff. 27, 253, 476, 838, 1220; 211, ff. 24, 140.
7. *DNB* IX, pp. 1299–1300. In 1665 Durand answered the Royal Society's questionnaire on agricultural practice in Hunsley and Bainton in the East Riding (DX/16/1). This and other similar reports form the basis of: R. Lennard, 'English Agriculture under Charles II', *Econ. Hist. Rev.*, IV (1932).
8. DDHO/14/5, 18; 70/33; 71/1, 2; *CSPD* 1655, p. 290.
9. DDHO/1/65; 17/9; BL Stowe MS 744, f. 40; *CSPD* 1652–3, p. 405; 1653–4, p. 503; P. Saltmarshe, p. 160; G. Poulson, *Beverlac* (1829), p. 394; J. Dennett (ed.), *Beverley Borough Records 1575–1821*, *YASRS*, LXXXIV (1932), pp. 103, 121–2.
10. A. Browning (ed.), *Memoirs of Sir John Reresby* (1936), pp. 46–7.
11. DDEV/68/248, ff. 73–5; DDHA/18/14.

12. DDBC/1/19b; J. Dennett, pp. 120, 122, 125, 132; R. Carroll, 'Yorkshire Parliamentary Boroughs in the Seventeenth Century', *Northern History*, III (1968), pp. 86–7.

13. *CSPD* 1668–9, pp. 194, 247, 334, 339, 598.

14. *CSPD* 1678, p. 154; *HMC* 12th Report, Appendix, pt. 9 (*Beaufort MSS*), p. 112; *Portland MSS*, VIII, p. 15; *Ormonde MSS*, V, pp. 111, 396; J. R. Jones, *The First Whigs* (1961), p. 12. The Duke of York reputedly reminded the second baronet on one occasion of the fate of his father and grandfather in 1645, to which Sir John replied that he could never think of the subject 'without recollecting at the same time the fate of your father which followed it so soon' (DDHO/17/9).

15. DDHO/1/66; 37/2; 40/1; 46/1; 71/5; 73/2; DDGE/6/27, 28; PRO C 5/36/42; *HMC Finch MSS*, I, pp. 251, 469.

16. DDHO/15/2; 17/9; 29/4; 48/11, 13–24; 71/5.

17. DDHO/17/10; *HMC* 11th Report, Appendix, pt. 2 (*House of Lords MSS 1678–88*), no. 275, p. 192; J. Dennett, pp. 103–4, 106, 108, 167, 170–2, 174.

18. *CSPD* 1683, pp. 173, 199, 219.

19. DDHO/13/1.

20. DDHO/13/1; 29/1–3; BL Additional MS 40133, f. 104.

21. DDHO/13/1; 29/4, 5; 71/1, 4, 5; 74/8, 9.

22. DDHO/17/9; 70/15; 71/7.

23. DDHO/13/2; 17/9; A. Browning, p. 525.

24. DDHO/15/2; 20/23; 29/4; 73/16, 19; J. Dennett, p. 108; A. M. W. Stirling, *The Hothams* (1918), I, pp. 111–12.

25. DDGR/34/6; Borthwick Institute of Historical Research, York Ecclesiastical Court Records, Consistory Court Book, 23 April 1691. Katherine had five children by a second marriage to John Moyser of Beverley (Clay, *Dugdale*, III, p. 89).

26. DDHO/13/3; 15/2; 20/23; 73/18.

27. DDHO/15/2; 29/4; 71/8–10, 12; 73/19; 74/13.

28. DDHO/13/3; 20/100; BL Additional MS 5843, f. 138; *DNB* IX, pp. 1298–9; B. Wilson, *The Sedbergh School Register 1546–1909* (1909), p. 133.

29. DDHO/53/9–11, 13, 15, 17; 59/10; 71/20; 73/17–19; 74/13, 18; P. Saltmarshe, p. 161.

30. DDHO/74/13.

31. DDHO/13/4; *CSPD* 1698, p. 34; 1699–1700, pp. 310, 399; 1700–2, p. 253; 1702–3, p. 395; *HMC Various Collections*, VIII, p. 84; 13th Report, Appendix, pt. 2 (*Portland MSS*), pp. 182, 207; 15th Report, Appendix, pt. 4 (*Portland MSS*), p. 304; J. Dennett, pp. 108, 184; A. M. W. Stirling, I, p. 129.

32. DDHO/13/4; DDBC/21/10; *CTB* 1718, II, pp. 218, 242; J. Dennett, pp. 108, 142, 193, 195; K. A. McMahon (ed.), *Beverley Corporation Minute Books 1707–1835*, *YASRS*, CXXII (1956), pp. 1–9; *HMC* 15th Report, Appendix, pt. 4 (*Portland MSS*), pp. 324, 575; K. A. McMahon, 'The Building of the Beverley Market Cross', *Transactions of the East Riding Georgian Society*, III (1952–3).

33. DDHO/13/4; 17/9; BL Stowe MS 748, f. 108; C. Dalton, *George I's Army 1714–27* (1910–12), pp. 172–3.
34. DDHO/15/4; *CTB* 1705–6, III, p. 750; 1717, XXXI, pt. 3, pp. 732–6.
35. DDHO/3/32; *CTB* 1714–15, II, p. 529; 1717, II, pp. 69–70, 181; 1718, II, pp. 128, 163; *CTP* 1720–8, p. 177; *HMC House of Lords MSS, X* (1712–14), pp. 48, 220–1, 470; *Various Collections*, VIII, p. 248; C. Dalton, pp. 172–3, 246.
36. DDHO/14/15; 15/3, 4, 6, 7; 17/9; 37/12–19; 47/1; 53/14.
37. DDHO/71/16, 49, 52.
38. DDHO/14/1A; 29/4, 5; 32/2; DDBM/32/1–2.
39. DDHO/13/4; 15/4; 17/10; 29/4; DDBC/16/67; 39/10–12; BDR Book AI, p. 24, no. 51; K. A. McMahon, *Beverley Corporation Minute Books*, pp. 4–5, 7–8; H. M. Colvin, *A Biographical Dictionary of English Architects, 1660–1840* (1954), pp. 119–20; K. A. McMahon, 'The Beverley House of the Hotham Family', *Transactions of the East Riding Georgian Society*, IV (1955–6); I. & E. Hall, *Historic Beverley* (1973), pp. 52–4.
40. DDHO/3/32; 13/4; 17/9; 71/15; 74/18.
41. DDHO/3/32; DDBC/22/E, f. 1; C. Dalton, p. 363; G. Poulson, p. 394.
42. DDHO/3/32. The 1723 election cost Sir Charles £700 (DDHO/15/16).
43. DDHO/3/32, 39, 40; 15/6, 16; DDBC/25/E/1; *HMC Various Collections*, VI, p. 15; G. Poulson, p. 395; G. R. Park, *The Parliamentary Representation of Yorkshire 1290–1886* (1886), p. 244; K. A. McMahon, *Acts of Parliament and Proclamations relating to the East Riding of Yorkshire and Kingston upon Hull, 1529–1800* (1961), p. 29, no. 80; *Beverley Corporation Minute Books*, pp. 12–14; 'The Building of the Beverley Market Cross', p. 87.
44. DDHO/15/6; DDBC/25/E/2–4; G. R. Park, p. 245; McMahon, *Beverley Corporation Minute Books*, p. 19.
45. DDHO/3/2; BL Additional MS 23780, f. 116. For Viscount Percival's vivid description of the episode see *HMC Egmont MSS*, I, pp. 100–1.
46. DDHO/17/9; *CTP* 1729–30, pp. 320, 386, 548, 599; C. Dalton, p. 363.
47. Unless stated otherwise, the rest of this section is based on contemporary rentals and estate accounts (DDHO/14/15; 15/6) and on Sir Charles's own general accounts (DDHO/15/16 – See Table 4).
48. DDHO/71/20–22; DDGE/6/51–60.
49. DDHO/3/32; 42/5, 8–9; 54/5; BDR Book AI, p. 24, no. 51; K. A. McMahon, 'The Beverley House', p. 46.
50. DDHO/17/9; N. Pevsner, *The Buildings of England: York and the East Riding* (1972), p. 349.
51. DDHO/74/21, 24.
52. DDHO/4/1; 17/9; BL Additional MS 38332, f. 135; *CTBP* 1739–41, p. 624; 1742–5, p. 472.
53. PRO C 33/379/642; 381/331; 399/281; 38/481, 526.
54. DDHO/20/26.
55. Unless stated otherwise, the rest of this section is based on contemporary estate accounts (DDHO/15/6, 7 – See Table 6).
56. DDHO/15/24; 20/26; 74/24.

57. DDHO/74/24.
58. DDHO/17/10; A. M. W. Stirling, I, p. 274.
59. DDHO/29/10; 39/3; 48/62, 158, 216.
60. DDHO/15/22–3.
61. Apparently the only rent increase was that which concerned part of the Beverley property. After £150 had been spent by the guardians on providing a new garden wall and warehouse, the rent was doubled.
62. DDHO/15/7.
63. DDHO/15/24; 23/17; 42/10; 59/15, 17.
64. DDHO/15/24; 74/21, 24; A. M. W. Stirling, I, pp. 258, 273.
65. DDHO/4/1; 15/10; 17/9; 71/31; A. M. W. Stirling, I, p. 275.
66. DDHO/15/7; 70/33; 71/26–8.
67. DDHO/17/9; A. M. W. Stirling, I, p. 308.
68. DDHO/13/5; 17/9, 13; PRO PROB 11/971/374; 11/1007; J. T. Ward, *East Yorkshire Landed Estates in the 19th Century* (1964), p. 27.
69. DDHO/13/3.

CHAPTER III

1. MS 70; 203, f. 34; L. Tolson, *History of the Church of St. John the Baptist, Kirkheaton, Yorkshire, and Annals of the Parish* (1929), pp. 116–19; 'Dodsworth's Yorkshire Notes : Wapentake of Agbrigg', *YATJ*, VIII (1884), pp. 501–6. See Appendix 5.
2. WBS/40; WBC/37, 40; J. T. Cliffe, pp. 126, 146; *CB* II, p. 51; P. Ahier, *The Legends and Traditions of Huddersfield and Its District* (1940–5), I, pp. 40–1; W. D. Macray (ed.), *Beaumont Papers* (1884), pp. 13–67.
3. PRO C 22/27/13; WBG/40; WBL/99/8; WBS/41–2. See Appendix 6.
4. PRO C 22/27/13; WBD/II/57; III/121–2, 127; X/88–9; XII/121; WBG/40; WBW/23; J. T. Cliffe, p. 141.
5. *CCC*, p. 950; *CCAM*, pp. 662, 907, 911; L. Tolson, p. 122; J. W. Clay (ed.), *Royalist Composition Papers* I, *YASRS*, XV (1893), pp. 147–9; P. H. Hardacre, *The Royalists during the Puritan Revolution* (1956), pp. 20–1, 29, 68.
6. WBA/3, 5–6, 8–10, 12, 15–18; *CCC*, pp. ix–x, 380, 950, 958, 2144; *CCAM*, pp. viii–ix, xiii, 662, 911; J. W. Clay (ed.), pp. 147–9.
7. WBD/I/125; II/58–79; III/139–43; IV/188–90, 193, 195, 197, 199, 201, 207, 275, 309; WBS/50–1, 72; WBW/34/1; C. A. Hulbert, *Annals of the Church and Parish of Almondbury, Yorkshire* (1882), p. 331.
8. WBD/I/130; III/144; WBL/116/23, 29, 32; WBS/56; WBW/32.
9. WBA/16–18, 20–1; WBD/I/137; IV/87, 211, 311; WBF/II/93; WBL/91; WBW/35/10, 36; L. Tolson, pp. 121, 126–8; C. A. Hulbert, pp. 167–8.
10. WBW/35, 36; T. Dyson, *History of Huddersfield and District* (1932), p. 281.
11. WBD/IV/213; WBG/14; WBS/59; WBW/36.
12. WBD/I/143–4, 146; VI/52a; IX/88; WBE/22; WBL/92b; 99/8; 114/1; WBS/60; WBW/42.
13. WBD/II/70, 81; IV/314; WBL/99/5. For an analysis of the occupational distribution of the tenantry, see above, p. 37.

14. WBD/III/240; IV/222, 240.
15. WBD/II/64; III/94; IV/208.
16. WBD/IV/232.
17. WBD/II/64; III/149, 178; IV/314.
18. WBD/II/109; III/202; VI/60; XII/31.
19. WBD/II/64; III/161, 178, 211; IV/212.
20. WBD/I/146; II/94; VI/51-2; X/44, 55-7; XII/26; WBM/5.
21. WBC/56, 58; *CSPD* 1676-7, p. 32; *HMC Various Collections*, II, p. 402.
22. WBW/42.
23. WBD/X/23; WBE/121; WBL/99/8; WBS/62.
24. DD 70, Bundle 111; WBD/III/185; WBL/99/8; WBM/8; T. Dyson, p. 279.
25. WBE/37.
26. WBC/72; WBL/99/8.
27. WBC/69, 78-81, 83; WBD/III/185; IV/230, 234; WBF/21; WBL/94; 95/1-4; 98; 99/2, 13, 14; 116/23, 24, 29, 32; WBW/35/10; DD 70, Bundle 49; PRO C 5/446/97; *CSPD* 1671, p. 23; *CTB* 1676-9, p. 307; L. Tolson, p. 128.
28. The following three paragraphs are based on PRO C 22/27/13; WBC/75; WBL/99/4, 6-8; 107/2; WBW/42.
29. WBL/99/12.
30. WBC/89; WBE/1/5; WBL/99/7, 11.
31. WBC/88, 91-100. For transcripts of Kaye's correspondence with Richard, see P. Roebuck, 'The Country Squirearchy and the Fight for Place in the Early 18th Century: A Case Study', *YAJ*, XLVI (1974), pp. 103-9. 'No contemporary material illustrates more vividly the negative side of the country member's prejudices than' Sir Arthur's 'few surviving letters' (G. Holmes, *British Politics in the Age of Anne* (1967), p. 123).
32. WBD/I/161; III/186, 190; WBE/37; WBF/10, 11, 13; WBL/106/1-3; 107/3, 10; L. Tolson, p. 128.
33. WBL/107/10.
34. WBD/III/191-2; IV/235; VI/58; WBE/31-2, 34-38; WBL/110.
35. WBC/111-12; WBF/12.
36. PRO C 6/345/38; WBC/111; WBL/107/13-17, 20, 22; WBW/49.
37. WBL/107/21.
38. Clay, *Dugdale*, III, p. 224; WBW/59, 61.
39. WBE/34-5; WBF/12-13; WBW/59, 61.
40. Miss Horton seems to have instituted the first regular system of accounting on the estate. The account books, which are the basic source for the rest of this chapter (see Tables 11-14), contain a number of subsidiary accounts of arrears, disbursements, and the demesne, all of which are subsumed in a general account. For Miss Horton's summary of her financial affairs as guardian see WBW/61.
41. In August 1733 Ann Horton purchased a cottage and tannery in Whitley for £60, which were subsequently let for £8 a year (WBD/IX/55-57).
42. Although a letter of 1735 (WBC/116) to Ann Horton was addressed to Whitley Hall, the servants there were discharged within two years of

Dame Susannah's death. There were no household expenses for the period 1731–8 except for a month during 1731–2 'when Miss Horton was there', and another short period in 1735–6. The measures which preceded Henry Beaumont's coming-of-age (food and drink were laid in, floors sanded, etc.) indicate that the Hall was empty before then.

43. Elmsall was responsible for making payments in the south of England, and was in the family's service as early as 1722 (WBE/30).

44. On 19 January 1731 £9,400 was owed; by 15 December 1738 this figure had been reduced to £1,650 (WBL/109; WBW/61).

45. WBD/II/108.

46. A further repayment of £288 in 1743 (WBF/II/107) no doubt came from the money spent by Henry himself. £1,000 of his father's debts remained unpaid at Henry's death (WBE/I/16).

47. WBD/I/167a, 169; WBS/65.

48. The accounts, which are again the major source, were twice reorganized: from 1743–4 the financial year began on 1 January instead of, as previously, at Michaelmas; and from 1752–3 there were no separate demesne accounts.

49. WBE/39–41.

50. The cost of this wood, which was presumably used in repair work, was demanded of the tenants.

51. WBS/70.

52. WBD/V/35; WBS/71, 74.

53. WBC/130; WBD/V/37, 48–9; WBF/II/128.

54. WBC/125, 127, 129, 131, 133–4, 136, 138, 140.

55. WBD/III/204; IV/244; IX/58; WBE/39–41, 117.

56. L. Tolson, p. 124.

57. WBH/56.

58. WBD/V/37, 48–9; WBF/II/128.

59. WBS/66, 68, 73; Borthwick Institute of Historical Research, York Ecclesiastical Records, Will of Richard Beaumont (6 August 1762) and Probate (November 1764).

60. WBC/123.

61. WBD/V/35; WBE/II/6; WBF/22; WBS/71, 74; DDSY/101/54; Tolson, p. 123.

CHAPTER IV

1. J. T. Cliffe, pp. 222, 368–9; H. Aveling, 'The Northern Book of Compositions, 1629–32', *CRS*, LIII (1960), pp. 434–5; H. Foley, *Records of the English Province of the Society of Jesus* (1877–83), III, series 6, pp. 205–7.

2. DDEV/59/8, 10, 29, 30.

3. *CB* II, p. 187; *CCC*, pp. 1323–4; DDEV/9/77; 44/132–3, 190; 50/40, 164, 203; 68/248, ff. 26–30, 33; H. Aveling, 'Catholics and Parliamentary Sequestrations', *Ampleforth Journal*, June 1959, p. 110; *RCHM, Newark on Trent: The Civil War Siegeworks* (1964), p. 95.

4. DDEV/50/34, 37–8, 116; 53/13–17, 66, 85, 94–5; 60/2–3; 69/12.

5. *CCC*, pp. 1323–4; DDEV/44/132; 50/206/8, 210–11, 235–6; 53/6;

68/248, ff. 30–9; *JHC* 7i (1651–9), pp. 153, 198/202; C. H. Firth & R. S. Rait, *Acts and Ordinances of the Interregnum, 1642–60* (1940), II, pp. 623–52; *DNB* XVII, pp. 419–22.

6. *CCC*, p. 1324; DDEV/3/65; 31/96; 50/43–4, 47–8, 51, 168–9; 55/39, 45; 68/248, ff. 34, 37, 48–9.

7. DDEV/9/69, 76; 50/228–34; 68/248, ff. 56–60, 66–9.

8. DDEV/50/33, 60; 51/29–30, 125; 53/95; 55/35; 56/431, 501; 57/21; 59/8, 9; 68/248, ff. 30, 38, 62.

9. DDEV/1/31; 3/73; 9/62; 12/36; 31/101; 39/57, 60–1; 50/225–7; 58/57, 129; 59/9, 12; 60/2–3; 62/4.

10. DDEV/1/34; 9/162; 20/2; 24/5–19; 50/239; 62/5; 68/128, 248, f. 51.

11. DDEV/68/248, ff. 63, 77; *CSPD* 1655, p. 595; J. S. Hansom, 'Catholic Registers of St. Mary's Domestic Chapel, Everingham Park, Yorkshire', *CRS*, VII (1909), p. 262; R. C. Wilton, 'A List of Guests at Everingham Park, Christmas, 1662', *CRS*, XXVII (1927), p. 263. The best guide to the operation of the recusancy laws throughout this period is J. A. Williams, *Catholic Recusancy in Wiltshire, 1660–1791*, *CRS*, Monograph Series, I (1968), Ch. 1.

12. DDEV/60/3; 68/126; 248, ff. iv–v, 71, 73–5; *CRS*, VI (1909), pp. 77, 256.

13. DDEV/1/36; 9/165; 56/464; 60/6; 65/3; 67, *passim*; 68/248, ff. vi, 72; 69/54; *CSPD* 1663–4, pp. 271, 276; J. S. Hansom, p. 262; H. Aveling, *Post-Reformation Catholicism in East Yorkshire 1558–1790* (1960), p. 55.

14. DDEV/1/26, 29–30, 34–5, 39–40; 51/94; 56/408, 446; 59/19; 62/5.

15. DDEV/31/128, 248, 261; 60/3.

16. DDEV/1/34; 17/15–17; 60/3.

17. DDEV/44/136–44, 191–2, 203–10; 55/63; 60/3, 48; 62/6.

18. DDEV/55/56; 60/8; 69/45, 48–9, 52, 54, 59, 61; R. C. Wilton, 'A Tale of Old Stonyhurst', *Stonyhurst Magazine*, October 1916.

19. DDEV/1/34; 9/83; 56/408; 58/11, 63–9, 129; 59/19; 60/3, 5, 8; 68/248, ff. iv–v.

20. DDEV/56/446; 59/9, 12, 19; 68/128.

21. DDEV/9/56; 31/97, 110, 112; 39/58; 50/54, 59, 67; 56/408, 443; 58/132.

22. DDEV/12/20, 24; 38/1–2; 56/408; 69/46–9.

23. DDEV/53/19–28; 56/408.

24. DDEV/51/170–1.

25. DDEV/9/93; 35/6–8; 50/77; 56/408, 462; 58, *passim*; 62/5.

26. DDEV/9/96; 56/464; 68/248, ff. 80–1; H. Foley, p. 699; R. C. Wilton, *CRS*, XXVII, pp. 263–4; *HMC House of Lords MSS*, 1678–88, pp. 232, 240; *CSPD* 1679–80, p. 341; 1683–4, pp. 181–2, 223; 1684–5, p. 150; *CTB* 1681–5, p. 1343; 1685–9, p. 170.

27. DDEV/9/96; 51/56–8; 56/465; 57/28; 58/115; *CTB* 1685–9, p. 152.

28. DDEV/9/97; 31/4; 51/59–61; 55/67; 56/467; 58/115; 68/248, ff. 84–6; *CSPD* 1686–7, pp. 67–8, 403; *CTB* 1685–9, p. 152; H. Aveling, *Post-Reformation Catholicism in East Yorkshire*, pp. 49, 53.

29. DDEV/51/62; 60/10; 68/248, ff. 90–2; *CSPD* 1690–2, p. 338.

30. DDEV/1/43; 9/99–101; 12/31; 50/69, 73–4, 141–2, 178; 51/62–3; 55/68; 58/41; DDHO/31/4.

31. DDEV/53/22–4, 30–3; 55/70; 58/142.
32. DDEV/55/71; 56/414, 468; 60/10; 66/13; 68/152; 248, ff. 94–5; *CSPD* 1696, pp. 78, 240.
33. DDEV/50/75–6.
34. DDEV/9/104; 68/123.
35. Sir Philip leased a house in Piccadilly and spent most of his time in London from 1698 onwards (DDEV/47/3–5; 56/414).
36. DDEV/12/34; 56/19, 470; DDHO/31/6.
37. DDEV/1/49; 51/66–71, 115–18, 120; 56/415; 60/11; P. Roebuck, 'An English Catholic on Tour in Europe, 1701–3', *Recusant History*, XI (1971), pp. 156–9.
38. DDEV/31/174–5, 177; 50/79–82; 51/34–5; 56/414; 58/101; 60/12–13.
39. DDEV/44/151; 50/83–9; 51/72–80; 53/31–2; 54/12–13; 55/76–8; 56/414; 50/12–13.
40. DDEV/56/52, 58, 61, 415; 57/30; 60/13; 68/248, f. 53; H. Aveling, p. 53; R. Arnold, *Northern Lights* (1959), p. 53.
41. DDEV/1/52; 53/36; 54/14; 56/415; 60/58; 67/24–5; *HMC Various Collections*, VIII, p. 93; R. Arnold, p. 58.
42. DDEV/26/29–30; 31/9, 139, 178–9; 39/77; 44/194; 54/14; 55/81, 83A; 56/64–5, 184–5, 415.
43. E. Hughes, *North Country Life in the 18th Century*, I, pp. xvi–xviii.
44. DDEV/50/90–3; 55/82; 56/62–82, 483; 60/14.
45. DDEV/56/481; 60/13, 52.
46. DDEV/26/31; 31/140, 180, 182; 44/192; 50/94–5; 56/415, 483; 60/13.
47. DDEV/56/61–2, 182–3, 193; 57/30; 60/14; 68/248, ff. 100–2; J. S. Hansom, pp. 262–3; R. C. Wilton, 'Dom John Bede Potts', *Downside Review*, July, 1916; 'Some Annals of Everingham', *Dublin Review*, October, 1917; E. E. Estcourt & J. O. Payne, *The English Catholic Nonjurors of 1715* (1885), pp. 160, 303, 314; M. B. Rowlands, 'Staffordshire Papists and the Levy of 1723', *Staffordshire Catholic History*, II (1962), pp. 33–8; B. Magee, *The English Recusants* (1938), p. 177.
48. DDEV/55/80; 60/13, 52, 55, 60, 84–5; 66/18; P. R. Chalmers, *History of Hunting, The Lonsdale Library*, XXIII (1936), pp. 342–3; R. C. Wilton, 'Early 18th Century Catholics in England', *Catholic Historical Review*, IV (1925), pp. 367–87; 'Letters of a Jesuit Father in the Reign of George I', *Dublin Review*, April, 1916.
49. DDEV/44/195; 50/200; 54/16; 56/30, 197, 340; 59/28–30; 60/84.
50. DDEV/60/84.
51. DDEV/56/15, 25–7; 30, ff. 113–14, 116–17, 137–8, 142–5, 149–50, 164–5. For transcripts of the lengthy correspondence between the two men, see P. Roebuck (ed.), *Constable of Everingham Estate Correspondence 1726–43, YASRS*, CXXXVI (1974).
52. DDEV/60/86, ff. 42–4, 51–2, 55, 62–3, 75–6, 92, 97–8, 160–1.
53. DDEV/56/30, ff. 113–14, 124–7, 147, 160–1; 60/84; 86, ff. 2–4, 18–19, 34–6, 78–9, 84–5, 88, 91–2, 115, 124.
54. DDEV/56/157–64; 60/12–13; 86, ff. 42–4, 51–2, 55, 62–3, 75–6, 92, 97–8, 160–1.

55. DDEV/56/30, ff. 116–17, 122–5, 128, 147–8, 158–9; 60/86, ff. 8–9, 37–9, 74–5, 79–80.
56. DDEV/56/30, ff. 117–19, 146, 165–6; 60/86, ff. 1–2, 4–5, 31–3, 95–7, 122–3.
57. DDEV/56/30, ff. 128–9, 146–7, 150–4, 158–9; 60/13; 86, ff. 8–9, 20–2, 27–8, 33, 37–46, 63–4, 68, 72, 76–7, 80–2, 90–1, 102–3, 117–19, 122–3.
58. DDEV/56/30, ff. 113–14, 139–42.
59. DDEV/31/183–4; 56/30, f. 146; 91–166, 484b; 58/118; 60/86, ff. 122–3.
60. DDEV/31/187–8; 53/37–41; 54/16–17, 33, 38, 40; 60/85; 68/43; *CTBP* 1742–5, pp. 755, 768, 775; H. Foley, I, p. 628.
61. DDEV/60/85.
62. DDEV/60/16; 68/2, 6, 13, 43.
63. DDEV/60/16; 68/48.
64. DDEV/60/16, 18.
65. DDEV/21/60, 62, 71–2; 58/177; 60/16, 18.
66. DDEV/31/192, 196–8; 56/37, 283, 342; R. B. Wragg, 'Everingham Park: Carr's Work Authenticated', *Transactions of the East Riding Georgian Society*, IV (1955–6), pp. 53–5.
67. DDEV/9/183, 186; 56/32, 37, 163, 166, 204; 60/20, 22.
68. DDEV/53/43–4; 55/92–3; 56/37, 342.
69. DDEV/59/33.
70. DDEV/62/19, 22, 25–7, 32, 35.

CHAPTER V

1. DDHO/29/1–3; 31/4, 6; DDEV/26/30; 50/91; 68/44, f..2; L. Tolson, p. 128.
2. WW Boxes 40, 43, 45–7, *passim*; Bag. Coll. 3187; *Harleian Society*, LXVI (1915), p. 33; S. C. Newton, 'A Calendar of the Bright Papers', Dip. Arch. Admin. thesis, London University, 1959, Introduction. See Appendices 9 & 10, and above, p. 37.
3. BR 51, 111; WW Box 45, II, 9–10, 12; III, 27–8, 33–5; Box 46, III, 26–7; M. F. S. Hervey (ed.), *Correspondence and Collections of Thomas Howard, Earl of Arundel* (1921), pp. 306–7.
4. WWM.D. 132, 134.
5. BL Additional MSS 18979, 21417–22, 21426, *passim*; W. J. J. Glassby, 'The Hallamshire Family of Bright', *The Sheffield Miscellany*, 1897, p. 6; J. Hunter, *Hallamshire: The History and Topography of the Parish of Sheffield* (rev. A. Gatty, 1869), pp. 418–19; *DNB* II, p. 1241; C. Firth & G. Davies, *The Regimental History of Cromwell's Army* (1940), II, p. 526; M. Ashley, *Cromwell's Generals* (1954), p. 28.
6. PRO C 3/435/36; BL Additional MS 36996, f. 101; S. C. Newton, Appendix IV; 'The Pipe Roll of a Cromwellian Sheriff of Yorkshire', *YAJ*, XLI (1963–6), pp. 108–16.
7. WW Box 46, VI, 54–5; *CCC*, pp. 2461–4, 2473–4, 2476; BL Additional MSS 21417, ff. 83, 238, 241; 21418, f. 86; *CSPD* 1651, p. 361; S. C. Newton, Introduction; T. Birch (ed.), *A Collection of the State Papers of John Thurloe Esquire* (1742), VI, p. 784.

8. BR 55, 111.
9. BR 52, 54–5; G. G. Hopkinson, 'The Development of the South York-shire and North Derbyshire Coalfield, 1500–1775' in J. Benson & R. G. Neville (eds.), *Studies in the Yorkshire Coal Industry* (1976), pp. 8–9.
10. BR 71, 73–4, 111, 182; WW Box 41, I, 16; II, 17; Box 44, loose 28; Box 46, IV, 34–6; WWM.D. 618–20, 623, 694–5; TN/F 17/15(9); *HMC Various Collections*, II, pp. 377–8.
11. BR 73, 102b, 111, 182, 185(b)v, 193, 209; WW Box 40, I, 18; III, 20; Box 42, V, 48–51, 53; VI, 54; Box 46, IV, 38–9; V, 40; Box 47, IV, 5; WWM.D. 515, 582–4, 587–9, 611–14, 681–4, 686–7, 721; Bag. Coll. 3192.
12. BR 53, 55(32), 56, 111.
13. BR 16, 111.
14. WWM.D. 140; *CB* III, p. 87; *CSPD* 1667–8, p. 151; S. C. Newton, Appendix IV.
15. BR 73.
16. BR 16, 74, 111, 182, 185(b)v, x; WWM.D. 516–19, 673–4, 697–700; CM 451–5, 461, 463–4, 467–8, 471–2, 610–11; WW Box 42, VI, 55–6; Box 43, IV, 43–5; Box 44, I, 1–6; II, 11–20, 26–7; Box 46, V, 47–8; Box 47, I, 12–14, 17–18, 21–9, 31–3.
17. BR 16, 111, 182, 209; WWM.D. 544–7, 550, 627, 634–9, 696; WW Box 40, III, 20(xxv), loose 21; Box 41, II, 18–21, 23; III, 4, 8–9; Box 47, I, 30; II, 15, loose 1.
18. BR 16, 111–12, 156–8, 185(b)x, 185(c)iii; WWM.D. 165; WW Box 44, I, 7–8; Box 46, V, 53; Box 47, II, 13, 16.
19. BR 55–6.
20. BR 182; WW Box 41, III, 1.
21. BR 16, 111.
22. BR 71, 182, 209; WWM.D. 182, 209, 544–7, 550, 615, 618, 626–7, 696, 734; WW Box 47, IV, 6.
23. WWM.D. 148, 152–3, 164; *HMC Astley MSS*, p. 51; 12th Report, Appendix, pt. 5 (*Rutland MSS*), II, p. 72; B. Boothroyd, *History of Pontefract* (1807), p. 295.
24. BR 16, 72, 111, 185(b)i, iii; B. Boothroyd, p. 294.
25. BR 16; WWM.D. 136–8, 141–7, 149–50, 152–5, 164–5, 185; WW Box 46, V, 41.
26. W. J. J. Glassby, p. 7.
27. WWM. Misc. I. Sir John bequeathed further legacies totalling £1,475. Moreover, he instructed his executors to invest the money due to him on bonds and mortgages (the greater part of his personal estate) 'if it can be got in ... for the advantage of' his three other grandchildren – George, Elizabeth, and Michael Liddell (BR 214(2); WWM.D. 165).
28. WWM.D. 156; BAX. 60818/12–15; *CSPD* 1690–1, p. 96.
29. Unless stated otherwise, the source for the legal dispute described below is PRO C 5/333/6.
30. BR 178.
31. PRO C 33/307, ff. 14, 481, 573; 309, ff. 198, 209, 497; 311, ff. 14, 176, 481, 573; BFM 1010–13, 1015, 1019–28, 1030–1, 1249–50, 1254.

32. BR 211.
33. BR 175, 178, 208; WWM. Misc. I; WW Box 47, loose 3.
34. BR 22; WW Box 46, VII, 56, 58–60; BAX. 60812/1–3; 60817.
35. BR 176; W. W. Bean, *The Parliamentary Representation of the Six North-ern Counties of England, 1603–1886* (1890), p. 966.
36. BR 173.
37. BR 22–3, 175; WW Box 41, II, 27; Box 43, IV, 51–2; Box 45, III, 39–40; Box 47, II, 18–19, loose 1; WWM.D. 251–6, 258, 269, 551–2, 556.
38. BR 22, 158–62; WW Box 41, II, 28–32; Box 46, VIII, 64; E. Hughes, *North Country Life in the 18th Century*, I, pp. 388–9.
39. WWM.D. 166–7, 186, 199; WW Box, loose 25.
40. BR 173, 175; BAX. 60812/4–5, 7; WW Box 46, VII, 57.
41. BR 148A, 173–5.
42. BR 98–9, 102c.
43. BR 138, 156–7, 173, 175; WWM. Misc. I; M 10; WW Box 42, VI, 57–8; Box 44, loose 29, 30; Box 46, VIII, 61–2.
44. BR 174–5.
45. WWM. Misc. I; WWM.D. 172.
46. WWM.D. 160, 184, 186; R 159–4–1.
47. BR 136; WWM.D. 186–7, 199–200; WWM.A. 748; WWM.R. 182c; R 159–4–1.
48. WWM.D. 160, 166–7, 170–1, 184.
49. WWM.D. 187.
50. BR 136–38, 173; WWM.D. 162, 199.
51. WWM.D. 188. Katherine Bright married Dr Clifton Wintringham of York (WWM.D. 189).
52. BR 148; WWM.D. 159, 186, 190–1, 1502, 1504A, 1505.
53. R 159–4–1; *HMC Various Collections*, VIII, pp. 174–5; W. H. G. Armytage, 'Charles Watson-Wentworth, 2nd Marquess of Rockingham, F.R.S. (1730–82): Some Aspects of His Scientific Interests', *Notes and Records of the Royal Society of London*, XII (1956); J. T. Ward, 'The Earls Fitzwilliam and the Wentworth Woodhouse Estate in the 19th Century', *Yorkshire Bulletin of Economic and Social Research*, XII (1960).
54. WWM.R. 182c; WWM.D. 160, 176–7, 1507; R 159–4–1.
55. WWM.D. 162, 187, 198, 1509–12; R 226 (63106–2).
56. WWM.A. 748; R 226 (63106–2); *CP* XI, pp. 60–2; J. T. Ward, p. 22.

CHAPTER VI

1. For discussion of this point see in particular H. J. Habakkuk, 'Marriage Settlements in the 18th Century'; G. E. Mingay, *English Landed Society in the 18th Century*, pp. 176–7; C. Clay, 'Marriage, Inheritance, and the Rise of Large Estates in England, 1660–1815', p. 510; J. V. Beckett, 'English Landownership in the Later 17th and 18th Centuries', pp. 575–6.
2. G. E. Mingay, 'The 18th Century Land Steward', p. 7; 'Estate Manage-ment in 18th Century Kent', *Ag. Hist. Rev.*, IV (1956), pp. 108–9; F. M. L. Thompson, *English Landed Society in the 19th Century*, pp. 152–4.
3. For fuller treatment of this development see P. Roebuck,

'Post-Restoration Landownership: The Impact of the Abolition of Wardship', *Journal of British Studies*, XVIII, no. 1 (Fall, 1978).

4. H. C. Foxcroft, *The Life and Letters of Sir George Savile, 1st Marquis of Halifax*, I, p. 22; J. P. Cooper, 'The Fortune of Thomas Wentworth, Earl of Strafford', pp. 245–8; J. Hunter, *South Yorkshire*, II, p. 87; H. E. Chetwynd-Stapylton, *The Stapletons of Yorkshire*, pp. 167–9; Clay, *Dugdale*, II, pp. 196–200; J. Foster, II (Wentworth of N. Elmsall).

5. J. W. Clay, 'The Gentry of Yorkshire at the Time of the Civil War', p. 349. See above, p. 44.

6. R. B. Dobson, 'Admissions to the Freedom of the City of York in the Later Middle Ages', *Econ. Hist. Rev.*, 2nd series, XXVI (1973), p. 1, note 2; J. W. Clay (ed.), *Abstracts of Yorkshire Wills temp. Commonwealth*, *YASRS*, IX (1890), p. 146; C. A. Goodricke, *History of the Goodricke Family*, Appendix p. 14; N. Carlisle, *History of the Family of Bland*, pp. 46–7; A. Browning (ed.), *Memoirs of Sir John Reresby*, p. 411.

7. Quoted in H. Aveling, *The Catholic Recusants of the West Riding of Yorkshire*, p. 255.

8. Quoted in J. T. Cliffe, *The Yorkshire Gentry: From the Reformation to the Civil War*, p. 125.

9. J. T. Cliffe, p. 382; C. J——, 'The Jacksons of South Yorkshire', *The Herald and Genealogist*, V (1870), pp. 270–2; J. Hunter, II, pp. 135–8; Clay, *Dugdale*, I, pp. 11–13; BL Additional MS 24121, f. 6.

10. J. T. Cliffe, pp. 126, 148, 155–6, 162–3, 187; A. Browning (ed.), *passim*; *CB* II, p. 174; Clay, *Dugdale*, I, pp. 330–2; J. Hunter, II, pp. 40–1.

11. J. T. Cliffe, pp. 109, 367; Clay, *Dugdale*, I, pp. 348–50; *CB* IV, pp. 21–3; J. Hunter, II, pp. 376–7; P. G. Holiday, 'Royalist Composition Fines and Land Sales in Yorkshire, 1645–65', pp. 324–5.

12. *CB* III, p. 46; Clay, *Dugdale*, II, pp. 408–9; G. H. Plantagenet-Harrison, *History of Yorkshire: Wapentake of Gilling West*, pp. 233–46; T. D. Whitaker, *A History of Richmondshire, in the North Riding of the County of York* (1823), I, pp. 307–8, 314–15.

13. *CB* IV, pp. 49–50; Clay, *Dugdale*, III, pp. 146–8; E. Hughes, *North Country Life in the 18th Century*, I, pp. 1–3.

14. *DNB* XIV, pp. 1185–6, 1196; *CB* II, p. 190; Clay, *Dugdale*, II, pp. 48–50.

15. *CB* II, pp. 196–7; Clay, *Dugdale*, II, pp. 196–200; N. Carlisle, pp. 44–68; Sir L. Namier & J. Brooke, *The House of Commons 1754–90*, II, pp. 98–9; A. M. W. Stirling, *Annals of a Yorkshire House* (1911), pp. 162–3.

16. J. Hunter, II, pp. 320–7; *DNB* XIII, pp. 684–7, 706–10; R. Sedgwick, *The House of Commons 1715–54*, II, pp. 554–7; Sir L. Namier & J. Brooke, III, pp. 661–2; *CP* II, pp. 441–3.

17. *CB* V, pp. 68–9; *DNB* XVII, pp. 39–40, 49–51; Clay, *Dugdale*, I, pp. 287–8; G. H. Plantagenet-Harrison, pp. 327, 404–15, 453.

18. J. Bossy, *The English Catholic Community 1570–1850*, p. 150.

19. Quoted in J. Hunter, I, p. 143.

20. Quoted in Sir T. Lawson-Tancred, *The Tancreds of Brampton*, p. 31.

21. Clay, *Dugdale*, I, pp. 70–2; J. Foster, III (Osborne).

22. Sir A. Wagner, *English Genealogy* (2nd ed. 1972), p. 103.

23. P. Saltmarshe, *History and Chartulary of the Hothams of Scorborough, 1100–1700*, p. 190.
24. L. A. Clarkson, *The Pre-Industrial Economy in England 1500–1750* (1971), p. 213; T. H. Hollingsworth, 'The Demography of the British Peerage', p. 71 and *passim*.
25. F. W. Pixley, *A History of the Baronetage*, p. 26.
26. *CB* III, pp. 191–3, 298–9; V, pp. 68–9. The five baronets who, though granted special remainders, were succeeded by sons were Sir Philibert Vernatti, Sir Arthur Pilkington, Sir Henry Slingsby, Sir Francis Wood and Sir Richard van den Bempdé-Johnstone (*CB* II, pp. 397–8, 409, 430; V, pp. 244, 304–5).
27. Creations: *CB* II, p. 149; III, pp. 98–9, 174–5, 211–12; V, p. 25. Re-creations: *CB* IV, pp. 158–9; V, pp. 83–5, 132–3, 200, 212.
28. The following baronetage families were raised to the peerage: Belasyse, Wentworth of Wentworth Woodhouse, Savile of Thornhill, Osborne, Dawnay, Gower, Wandesford, Smithson, Savile of Methley, Wortley, Robinson of Newby, Robinson of Rokeby (*CB* I, pp. 30–1, 43–4, 48–51, 55, 147–8, 153–4; II, p. 176; III, pp. 98–9, 101–2, 254; IV, pp. 158–9; V, pp. 68–9). Although the demography of the baronetage has yet to be thoroughly investigated, R. J. Beevor noted fifty years ago that only 295 baronetcies (out of a grand total of 1,226 baronetcies of England and Gt. Britain granted between 1611 and 1800) had survived; the percentage of survivals was greater among the older than among the newer creations ('Distinction and Extinction', *The Genealogists' Magazine*, IV (1928), pp. 60–2).
29. *CB* V, pp. 186, 238–40.
30. *CB* II, pp. 61, 139–40, 186–7, 397–8; III, pp. 155–6; IV, pp. 115, 131.
31. *CB* I, p. 44; II, pp. 36, 72, 117–18, 174; III, pp. 46–8, 150; J. Foster, III (Constable of Flamborough); *DNB* XIII, pp. 89–90; J. T. Cliffe, pp. 123, 353; P. G. Holiday, p. 380.
32. *CB* II, pp. 26, 162; Clay, *Dugdale*, I, pp. 168–9, 239–40, 345–6; II, pp. 53–5; C. V. Collier, *An Account of the Boynton Family*, p. 74.
33. *CB* II, p. 197; *CP* II, pp. 442–3; Clay, *Dugdale*, II, pp. 180–1, 435–7.
34. J. Hunter, II, pp. 318–20; Clay, *Dugdale*, II, pp. 255–8.
35. *CB* III, p. 254; *CP* I, pp. 166–7; Clay, *Dugdale*, II, p. 60.
36. Clay, *Dugdale*, I, p. 233.
37. *CB* III, p. 299; IV, p. 75; Clay, *Dugdale*, II, p. 315; III, p. 16; J. W. Clay (ed.), *Abstracts of Yorkshire Wills*, p. 84; C.B. N——, 'Fairfaxiana', *The Herald and Genealogist*, VIII (1874), pp. 225–6.
38. *CB* II, pp. 409–11; *CP* VIII, pp. 684–5; Clay, *Dugdale*, I, pp. 55–8, 335–8; II, pp. 148–51; III, pp. 17–19.
39. Clay, *Dugdale*, I, pp. 176–80, 410–21; *CB* II, p. 149; V, pp. 83–5.
40. *CB* I, pp. 30–1, 175; J. Foster, III (Kaye); *CP* XI, pp. 58–61; XII, pt. 1, pp. 327–31; Clay, *Dugdale*, I, pp. 76–8; T. Dyson, *History of Huddersfield and District*, pp. 262, 274–6; J. J. Cartwright (ed.), *The Wentworth Papers 1705–39* (1883), pp. 6–7.
41. J. Foster, III (Belasyse); R. Sedgwick, II, p. 51.

42. *CB* II, pp. 115–16, 174–5; III, pp. 132–3; V, p. 212; Clay, *Dugdale*, I, pp. 92–4; II, pp. 351–2; III, pp. 123–7; J. Hunter, II, p. 215.

43. A. Browning (ed.), pp. 8a 3; J. W. Pennyman, *Records of the Family of Pennyman of Ormesby*, p. 5; J. Hunter, II, p. 125.

44. Sir J. D. Legard, *The Legards of Anlaby and Ganton*, pp. 10, 167.

45. S. Margerison (ed.), *Memorandum Book of Sir Walter Calverley*, *passim*; A. Browning (ed.), pp. 26, 43–4 and *passim*.

46. Sir J. D. Legard, p. 163; J. Hunter, I, p. 343; N. Carlisle, pp. 44–5, 52–6; J. W. Pennyman, pp. 31–3, 47.

47. *CB* III, p. 143; IV, pp. 49, 160; Clay, *Dugdale*, II, p. 352; J. Foster, III (Milbanke); C. V. Collier, p. 74; C. M. Lowther-Bouch, 'Lowther of Swillington', p. 68; Sir J. D. Legard, pp. 56, 165; F. S. Colman, *A History of the Parish of Barwick in Elmet*, p. 155.

48. *CB* III, p. 299; V, p. 13; Clay, *Dugdale*, II, pp. 130–1; J. Foster, III (Belasyse & Sykes); N. Carlisle, pp. 44–5; J. Kirk, J. H. Pollen & E. H. Burton (eds.), *Biographies of English Catholics in the 18th Century* (1909), p. 78; J. Straker, *Memoirs of the Public Life of Sir Walter Blackett*, pp. i–ii; J. Fairfax-Blakeborough, *Sykes of Sledmere* (1929), pp. 21, 33–5.

49. *CB* I, pp. 147–8; *CP* VI, pp. 36–8; XII, pt. 1, pp. 199–201; E. Richards, *The Leviathan of Wealth* (1973), pp. 5–13.

50. *CB* III, pp. 101–2; *CP* IX, pp. 743–4; R. Sedgwick, II, pp. 428–9.

51. C. Clay, 'Marriage, Inheritance, and the Rise of Large Estates', pp. 504–5; C. V. Collier, pp. 30–1; Clay, *Dugdale*, I, pp. 44–7; W. Robertshaw, 'The Manor of Tong', pp. 124–5; Sir L. Namier & J. Brooke, III, p. 61; C. M. Lowther-Bouch, 'Lowther of Marske', p. 116.

52. *CB* III, pp. 287–9; A. Gooder, 'Two Letters Relating to the Manor and Rectory of Birmingham, 1704–13', *University of Birmingham Historical Journal*, V (1957), pp. 191–9; J. W. Pennyman, pp. 9–10.

53. C. A. Goodricke, *History of the Goodricke Family*, pp. 37, Appendix 20–1.

54. C. M. Lowther-Bouch, 'Lowther of Marske', pp. 112–15; C. A. Goodricke, pp. 50–3.

55. J. Wilkinson, *Worthies, Families, and Celebrities of Barnsley and District*, pp. 135–6; J. Kirk, J. H. Pollen & E. H. Burton (eds.), p. 78.

56. Clay, *Dugdale*, III, p. 163; C. M. Lowther-Bouch, 'Lowther of Marske', p. 102; 'Lowther of Swillington', pp. 72–3; J. Hunter, I, p. 55; II, p. 215; J. W. Pennyman, pp. 5, 88; P. G. Holiday, pp. 94, 96, 115, 140, 219, 311–12, 374, 380; J. P. Cooper, 'The Fortune of Thomas Wentworth, Earl of Strafford', pp. 247–8.

57. *DNB* XIV, p. 1190; *CP* VII, p. 513; J. Hunter, I, pp. 143–5; R. Sedgwick, I, p. 607; J. Kirk, J. H. Pollen & E. H. Burton (eds.), p. 78; J. Wilkinson, pp. 135–6; P. Nunn, 'Aristocratic Estates and Employment in South Yorkshire 1700–1800' in S. Pollard & C. Holmes (eds.), *Essays in the Economic and Social History of South Yorkshire* (1976), pp. 29, 42.

58. G. E. Wentworth, 'History of the Wentworths of Woolley', *YAJ*, XII (1893), pp. 168, 177; T. D. Whitaker, I, p. 203; *CB* III, pp. 225–6; *DNB* XIII, p. 90; J. Hunter, I, p. 343; II, pp. 41, 394, 426; J. W.

Walker (ed.), *Hackness Manuscripts and Accounts*, p. 8; Sir J. D. Legard, p. 165; W. P. Baildon, *Baildon and the Baildons* (1912–27), I, p. 419; C. A. Goodricke, Appendix p. 23; J. Foster, I (Calverley); II (Pilkington); R. Sedgwick, I, p. 464; J. Straker, pp. vi, xxxiv; DDDA/4/30, 55; DAR.T.D. 101; Clay, *Dugdale*, III, p. 16; J. T. Ward, *East Yorkshire Landed Estates in the 19th Century*, pp. 48–9; J. Wilkinson, pp. 1–18; H. G. Plantagenet-Harrison, pp. 404–5.

59. J. Hunter, II, pp. 125, 377; *CB* V, p. 239; R. G. Wilson, *Gentlemen Merchants*, pp. 215, 222, 244; G. Poulson, *Holderness*, II, pp. 393, 410; G. Jackson, *Hull in the 18th Century*, pp. 112–14, 196, 228, 263–4.

60. *DNB* XIII, p. 90; DDDA/4/30, 55; DAR.T.D. 101; Clay, *Dugdale*, III, p. 16.

61. C. Clay, 'Marriage, Inheritance, and the Rise of Large Estates', pp. 515–18.

62. Quoted in J. T. Cliffe, p. 249 and Sir J. D. Legard, p. 55.

63. D. Parsons (ed.), *The Diary of Sir Henry Slingsby*, pp. 215, 217–18.

64. T. Fuller, *History of the Worthies of England*, (ed.) J. Nichols (1811), II, p. 523.

65. A. Browning (ed.), p. 401.

66. P. Nunn, pp. 30–1; D. G. Hey, 'The Parks at Tankersley and Wortley', *YAJ*, XLVII (1975); H. C. Darby (ed.), *A New Historical Geography of England* (1973), pp. 344–5.

67. DDHO/15/3, 4, 6; 37/12–19; 47/1; 53/4; DDEV/45/155; 50/185, 191; W. Marshall, *Review of Reports*, pp. 355, 357–8, 459, 511; J. T. Ward, p. 9.

68. H. C. Darby (ed.), pp. 323–4, 350, 475; J. C. Harvey, 'Common Field and Enclosure in the Lower Dearne Valley: A Case Study', *YAJ*, XLVI (1974); A. Harris, *The Rural Landscape of the East Riding of Yorkshire 1700–1850* (1961), pp. 1–60.

69. DDEV/60/15.

70. DDHO/13/5.

71. G. G. Hopkinson, 'The Development of the South Yorkshire and North Derbyshire Coalfield, 1500–1775'; 'The Charcoal Iron Industry in the Sheffield Region, 1500–1775'; W. B. Trigg, 'The Halifax Coalfield – Parts I – II', *Transactions of the Halifax Antiquarian Society* 1930, pp. 120, 123, 128; D. Neave, 'The Search for Coal in the East Riding in the 18th Century', *YAJ*, XLV (1973); D. H. Holmes, *The Mining and Quarrying Industries in the Huddersfield District* (1967), p. 25; A. Raistrick & E. Allen, 'The South Yorkshire Ironmasters 1690–1750', *Econ. Hist. Rev.*, IX (1938–9).

72. WBC/91.

73. DDEV/58/141.

74. A. Browning (ed.), p. 230.

75. DDEV/68/43.

76. W. G. Hoskins, 'The Rebuilding of Rural England, 1570–1640', p. 136.

77. P. Nunn, pp. 34–41.

78. N. Pevsner, *The Buildings of England: Yorkshire, The West Riding* (2nd ed. 1967), pp. 117, 303–6, 384, 399–400; *Yorkshire, The North Riding*

(1966), pp. 128, 219, 262, 392; C. A. Goodricke, pp. 8, 32; H. E. Chetwynd-Stapylton, *The Stapletons of Yorkshire*, p. 299; P. Nunn, p. 34 (quotation).

79. N. Pevsner, *The West Riding*, pp. 44–7, 141–3, 199, 375–6, 382–3, 546–8; *The North Riding*, pp. 42, 106–18, 202; *York and the East Riding*, p. 185; R. G. Wilson, p. 222; C. A. Goodricke, p. 87; P. Nunn, pp. 34–5 (quotation).

80. N. Pevsner, *The West Riding*, pp. 135, 138–9, 145–7; W. Robertshaw, 'The Manor of Tong', p. 125; S. Margerison (ed.), pp. 112, 129; T. Dyson, p. 157.

81. DDHA/14/26; N. Pevsner, *York and the East Riding*, pp. 36, 343–7; *The West Riding*, pp. 47, 380–2, 539–45, 559; *The North Riding*, pp. 276–7, 309–10; P. Nunn, p. 36.

82. N. Pevsner, *The North Riding*, pp. 90–1, 263–6, 354; *The West Riding*, pp. 106–7, 171, 255, 285, 292, 379, 622; *York and the East Riding*, pp. 194–5, 206–10; J. Hunter, II, p. 377; H. Speight, 'Hawkesworth Hall and Its Associations', *Bradford Antiquary*, new series, II (1905), p. 290.

83. J. Fairfax-Blakeborough, pp. 22, 23 (quotation).

84. N. Pevsner, *The West Riding*, pp. 147, 291, 382; *The North Riding*, pp. 218–21, 265, 277; *York and the East Riding*, pp. 40, 319, 348–9; H. M. Colvin, p. 122; J. Fairfax-Blakeborough, p. 23. See also York Georgian Society, *The Works in Architecture of John Carr* (1973).

85. N. Pevsner, *The West Riding*, pp. 153, 178, 256–7, 621; *The North Riding*, pp. 124–5, 364–5; *York and the East Riding*, pp. 318–19, 334; D. Stroud, *Capability Brown* (1975), pp. 173–4.

86. For further, recent evidence of this, see: B. A. Holderness, 'Credit in English Rural Society before the 19th Century, with special reference to the period 1650–1720', *Ag. Hist. Rev.*, XXIV (1976), p. 103.

87. For further elaboration of these points, see particularly: F. M. L. Thompson, 'Landownership and Economic Growth in England in the 18th Century' in E. L. Jones & S. J. Woolf (eds.), *Agrarian Change and Economic Development* (1969), pp. 56–60; H. Perkin, *The Origins of Modern English Society 1780–1880* (1969), Chaps. 1–3; J. H. Plumb, *The Commercialisation of Leisure in 18th-Century England* (1973).

APPENDIX I

The Yorkshire Baronetage:
Chronology of Creations 1611–1800

Belasye of Newburgh	29 June	1611
Constable of Flamborough	29 June	1611
Savile of Methley	29 June	1611
Savile of Thornhill	29 June	1611
Wentworth of Wentworth Woodhouse	29 June	1611
Wortley of Wortley	29 June	1611
Wyvill of Constable Burton	25 November	1611
Boynton of Barmston	15 May	1618
Bamburgh of Howsham	1 December	1619
Foulis of Ingleby Manor	6 February	1620
Gower of Stittenham	2 June	1620
Osborne of Kiveton	13 July	1620
Chaloner of Guisborough	20 July	1620
Hewett of Headley Hall	11 October	1621
Hotham of Scorborough	4 January	1622
Griffith of Burton Agnes	7 June	1627
Pennyman of Marske	6 May	1628
Beaumont of Whitley	15 August	1628
Slingsby of Scriven	22 October	1628
Vavasour of Hazlewood	24 October	1628
Twistleton of Barlby	2 April	1629
Vernatti of Carlton	7 June	1634
Gascoigne of Barnbow	8 June	1635
Pilkington of Stanley	29 June	1635
Slingsby of Scriven	2 March	1638
Strickland of Boynton	30 July	1641
Mauleverer of Allerton Mauleverer	4 August	1641
Cholmely of Whitby	10 August	1641
Sprignell of Copmanthorpe	14 August	1641
Goodrick of Ribston	14 August	1641
Armitage of Kirklees	15 December	1641
Kaye of Woodsome	4 February	1642
St. Quintin of Harpham	8 March	1642
Reresby of Thribergh	16 May	1642
Ingleby of Ripley	17 May	1642
Dawnay of Cowick	19 May	1642
Payler of Thoraldby	28 June	1642

Valkenberg of Middleing	20 July	1642
Constable of Everingham	20 July	1642
Hungate of Saxton	15 August	1642
Rudston of Hayton	29 August	1642
Bland of Kippax Park	30 August	1642
Vavasour of Copmanthorpe	17 July	1643
Forster of Stokesley	18 September	1649
Swale of Swale Hall	21 June	1660
Stapleton of Myton	22 June	1660
Hildyard of Patrington	25 June	1660
Bright of Badsworth	16 July	1660
Robinson of Newby	30 July	1660
Smithson of Stanwick	2 August	1660
Lewis of Ledston	15 October	1660
Winn of Nostell	3 December	1660
Frankland of Thirkleby	24 December	1660
Legard of Ganton	29 December	1660
Marwood of Little Busby	31 December	1660
Jackson of Hickleton	31 December	1660
Rokeby of Skiers	29 January	1661
Cayley of Brompton	26 April	1661
Cooke of Wheatley	10 May	1661
Copley of Sprotborough	17 June	1661
Milbanke of Halnaby	7 August	1661
Stapleton of Carlton	20 March	1662
Savile of Copley	24 July	1662
Wandesford of Kirklington	5 August	1662
Graham of Norton Conyers	17 November	1662
Tancred of Boroughbridge	17 November	1662
Pennyman of Ormesby	22 February	1664
Tempest of Tong	25 May	1664
Wentworth of Bretton	27 September	1664
Lawson of Brough	6 July	1665
Burdett of Birthwaite	25 July	1665
Chaytor of Croft	28 June	1671
Brookes of York	13 June	1676
Hawksworth of Hawksworth	6 December	1678
Beckwith of Aldborough	15 April	1681
Wytham of Goldsborough	13 December	1683
Ramsden of Byram	30 November	1689
Wentworth of North Elmsall	28 July	1692
Lowther of Marske	15 June	1697
Calverley of Calverley	11 December	1711

Lowther of Swillington	6 January	1715
Milner of Nun Appleton	26 February	1717
Robinson of Rokeby	10 March	1731
Ibbetson of Denton	12 May	1748
Etherington of Hull	22 November	1775
Wombwell of Wombwell	26 August	1778
Coghill of Coghill Hall	31 August	1778
Turner of Kirkleatham	8 May	1782
Sykes of Sledmere	28 March	1783
Wood of Barnsley	22 January	1784
Smith of Newland Park	22 January	1784
Rycroft of Calton	22 January	1784
Van-den-Bempdé-Johnstone of Hackness Hall	6 July	1795

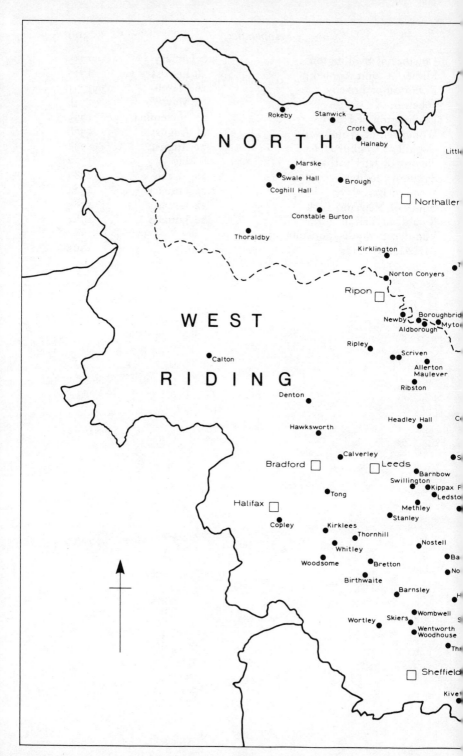

NORTH

Rokeby
Stanwick
Croft
Halnaby
Little

Marske
Swale Hall
Coghill Hall
Brough

Northaller

Constable Burton

Thoraldby

Kirklington

Norton Conyers

Ripon

WEST

Boroughbri
Newby
Myto
Aldborough

Ripley
Scriven
Allerton
Maulever
Ribston

RIDING

Calton

Denton

Headley Hall

Hawksworth

Calverley

Bradford
Leeds
Barnbow
Swillington
Kippax
Kippax F
Ledsto

Tong

Methley
Stanley

Halifax

Copley
Kirklees
Thornhill
Nostell

Whitley

Woodsome
Bretton
Ba

No

Birthwaite

Barnsley
H

Wortley
Skiers
Wombwell
S

Wentworth
Woodhouse
Th

Sheffield

Kive

37°

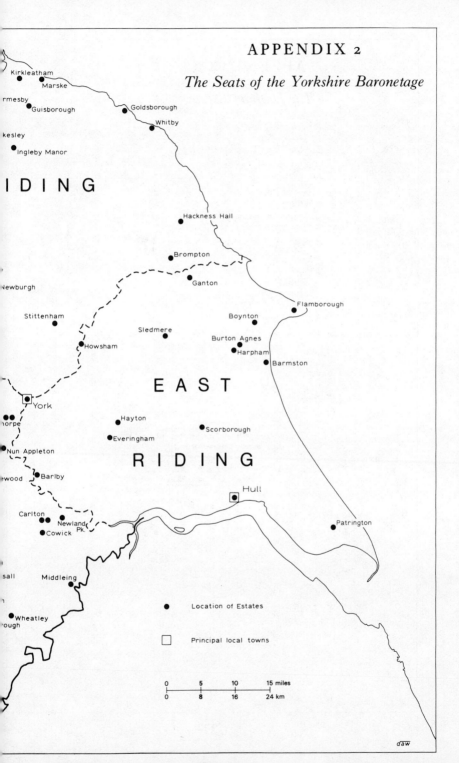

APPENDIX 2

The Seats of the Yorkshire Baronetage

Kirkleatham

Marske

rmesby

Guisborough

Goldsborough

Whitby

kesley

Ingleby Manor

IDING

Hackness Hall

Brompton

Newburgh

Ganton

Flamborough

Stittenham

Boynton

Sledmere

Burton Agnes

Howsham

Harpham

Barmston

EAST

York

horpe

Hayton

Scorborough

Nun Appleton

Everingham

wood

Barlby

RIDING

Hull

Carlton

Newland Pk.

Patrington

Cowick

sall

Middleing

●   Location of Estates

h

Wheatley

☐   Principal local towns

ough

0	5	10	15 miles
0	8	16	24 km

daw

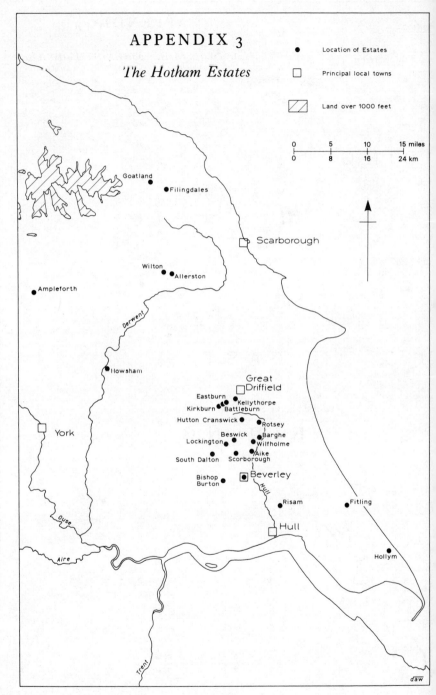

APPENDIX 3

The Hotham Estates

● Location of Estates

□ Principal local towns

▨ Land over 1000 feet

| 0 | 5 | 10 | 15 miles |
| 0 | 8 | 16 | 24 km |

Goatland

● Filingdales

□ Scarborough

Wilton

● Allerston

● Ampleforth

Derwent

● Howsham

York

Great
□ Driffield

Eastburn
Kirkburn ● ● Kellythorpe
● ● Battleburn
Hutton Cranswick ●
● Rotsey
Beswick ● ● Barghe
Lockington ● ● Wilfholme
● ● Aike
South Dalton ● Scorborough

Bishop ●
Burton □● Beverley

Ouse

Hull

● Risam

● Fitling

□ Hull

Aire

● Hollym

Trent

daw

372

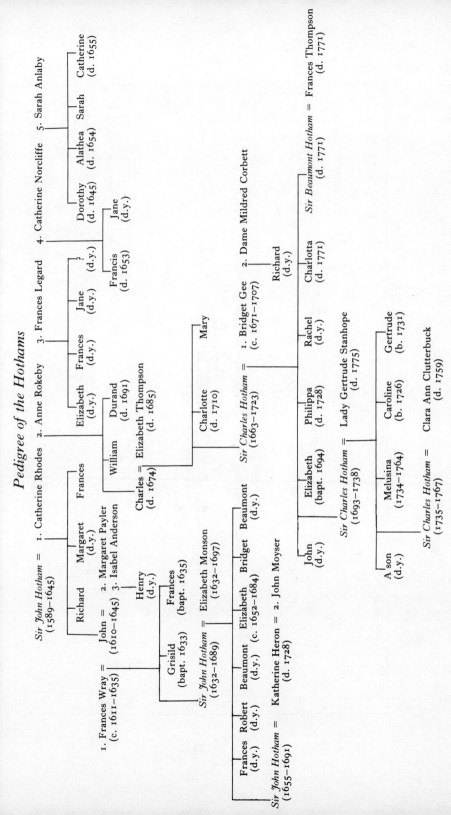

Pedigree of the Hothams

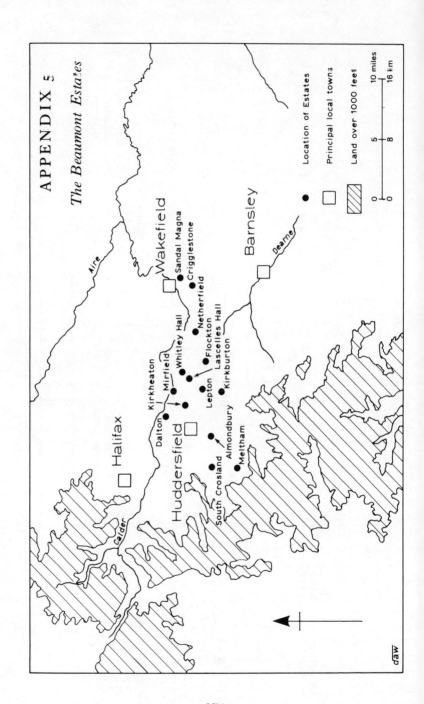

APPENDIX 5

The Beaumont Estates

Halifax

Wakefield

Barnsley

Huddersfield

Dalton
Kirkheaton
Mirfield
Whitley Hall
Netherfield
Flockton
Lepton
Lascelles Hall
Kirkburton
Almondbury
South Crosland
Meltham

Sandal Magna
Crigglestone

Aire
Calder
Dearne

Location of Estates
Principal local towns
Land over 1000 feet

10 miles
16 km
0
5
8

daw

374

APPENDIX 6

Pedigree of the Beaumonts

(d. 15/5?)

(bapt. 1605–1606)

(d. 1602?)

Grace (1572–c. 1610)   Margaret (d. 1611)

Sir Richard Beaumont (c. 1574–1631)

Adam (1631–1655) = Elizabeth Asshton

John (1635–1660)   William (1640–1683)   Thomas (1650–1661)   Anne (1633–1637)   Maria (d.y.)   Elizabeth (1634–1657)   Margaret (b. 1644)   Sarah (1646–1717)

Anne (b. 1655)

Richard Beaumont of Lascelles Hall (1638–1705) = Anne Ramsden (1638–1719)

Elizabeth (b. 1652)

Richard Beaumont (1654–1692) = Frances Lowther

Thomas (d.y.)   William (1673–1706)   Thomas (b. 1675)(d.y.)   Adam (b. 1680)   John (b. 1685)(d.y.)   A son (d.y.)   Elizabeth (b. 1669)(d.y.)   Anne (b. 1674)   Mary (b. 1678)   A daughter (b. 1681)

Richard Beaumont (1670–1723) = Susannah Horton (d. 1731)

Adam (d.y.)   Thomas (d.y.)   Frances (d.y.)   Mary (d.y.)

Richard Beaumont (1677–1704) = Katherine Stringer = 2. Thomas Fane, Earl of Westmorland (d. 1730) (d. 1736)

Anne (d.y.)   Susan (1708–1730)   Elizabeth (b. 1711)   Everilda (1712–1780)(d. 1772)   Mary (d. 1771)   Frances (1704–1735)   Charlotte (1722–1766)   Henrietta

Richard Beaumont (c. 1719–1764) = 1. Judith Ramsden   2. Elizabeth Holt

Henry Beaumont (c. 1716–1743)

Richard (d.y.)   Thomas (d.y.)   Anne (d.y.)   Susannah (d.y.)   Charlotte (d.y.)

Charles (d. 1774)   Thomas (d. 1782)   John (c. 1752–1831)

Richard Henry Beaumont (c. 1748–1810)

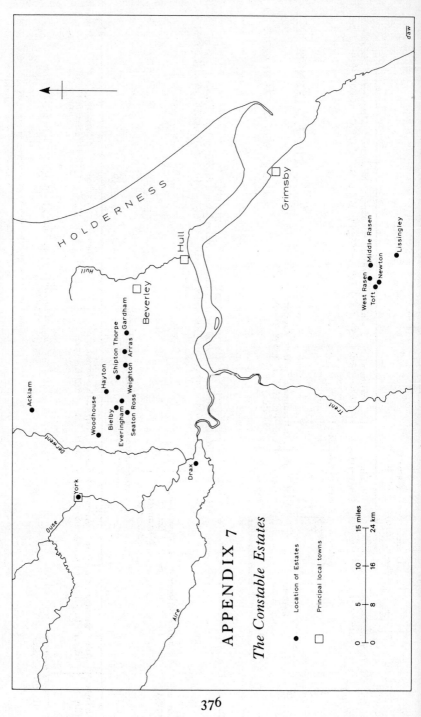

APPENDIX 7
The Constable Estates

Location of Estates ●
Principal local towns ☐

| 0 | 5 | 10 | 15 miles |
| 0 | 8 | 16 | 24 km |

HOLDERNESS

Grimsby

Hull

Beverley

West Rasen
Middle Rasen
Toft
Newton
Lissingley

Acklam

Woodhouse
Hayton
Bielby
Everingham
Seaton Ross
Weighton
Arras
Gardham
Shipton Thorpe

York

Drax

Derwent
Ouse
Aire
Hull
Trent

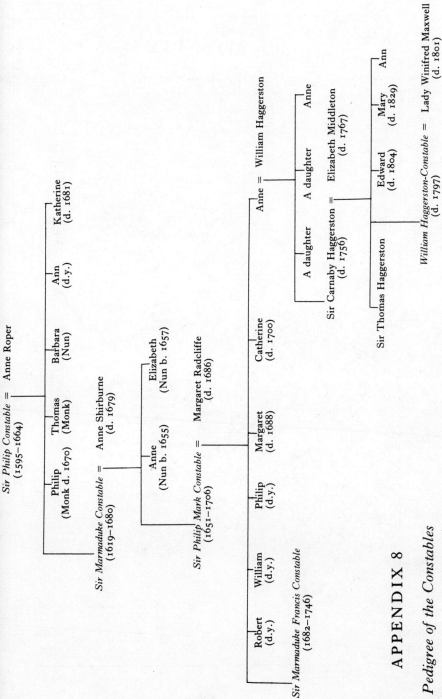

APPENDIX 8

Pedigree of the Constables

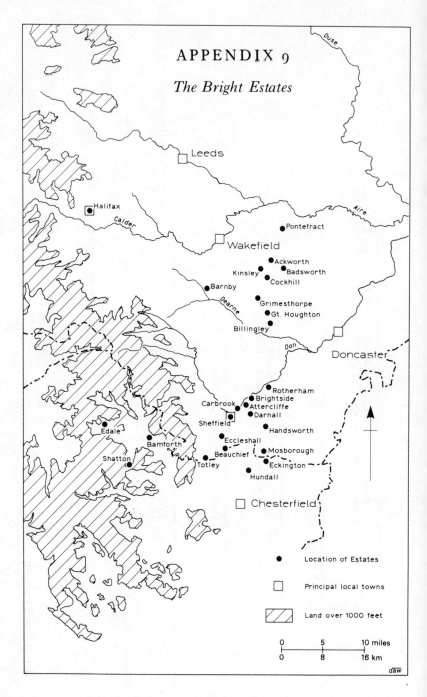

APPENDIX 9

The Bright Estates

Ouse

Leeds

Halifax
Calder

Pontefract

Wakefield

Ackworth
Kinsley
Badsworth
Cockhill
Barnby
Dearne

Grimesthorpe
Gt. Houghton

Billingley

Don

Doncaster

Rotherham
Brightside
Carbrook
Attercliffe
Darnall
Sheffield
Handsworth
Edale
Eccleshall
Bamforth
Mosborough
Beauchief
Shatton
Eckington
Totley
Hundall

Aire

Chesterfield

●   Location of Estates

▢   Principal local towns

▨   Land over 1000 feet

0	5	10 miles
0	8	16 km

daw

378

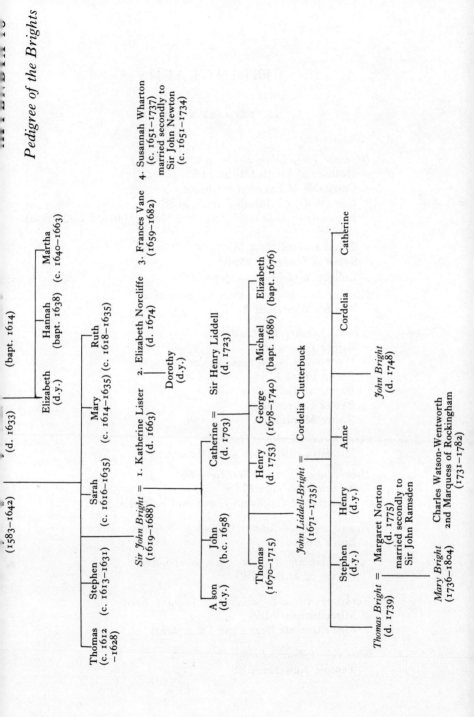

Pedigree of the Brights

BIBLIOGRAPHY

I. PRIMARY SOURCES

A. *Manuscripts*

Brynmor Jones Library, University of Hull
Hotham of South Dalton MSS
Constable of Everingham MSS
Gee (Watt) of Bishop Burton MSS
Langdale of Holme on Spalding Moor (Harford Collection) MSS
Macdonald of Sleat MSS
Sykes of Sledmere MSS
Collection of Miscellaneous MSS

Kirklees Metropolitan Library, Huddersfield
Whitley-Beaumont MSS

Central Library, Sheffield
Bright Papers
Wentworth Woodhouse Collection
Bacon Frank MSS
Bagshawe Collection
Baxter Collection
Crewe Muniments

Wentworth Woodhouse Hall
Miscellaneous Deeds and Documents

Humberside Record Office, Beverley
Beverley Borough MSS
Grimston of Grimston Garth and Kilnwick MSS

Registry of Deeds, Beverley
Entry Books

North Yorkshire Record Office, Northallerton
Darley of Aldby MSS

Yorkshire Archaeological Society Library, Leeds
Miscellaneous MSS
Miscellaneous Deeds and Documents

Sheepscar Library, Leeds
Temple Newsam MSS

Borthwick Institute of Historical Research, York
  Prerogative Court of York: Wills and Probates
                      Consistory Court Books

Public Record Office
  Court of Chancery: Proceedings
                Entry Books of Decrees and Orders
  Prerogative Court of Canterbury: Wills and Probates

British Library
  Additional MSS
  Stowe MSS
  Egerton MSS

B. *Printed*

Anonymous, *A Sketch of the Life and Character of Mr. Ratcliffe* (1746).
AVELING, H. (ed.), 'The Northern Book of Compositions 1629–32', *CRS*, LIII (1960).
BIRCH, T. (ed.), *A Collection of the State Papers of John Thurloe Esq.* (7 vols, 1742).
BROWNING, A. (ed.), *Memoirs of Sir John Reresby* (1936).
Calendar of State Papers, Domestic Series, 1640–1704 (69 vols, 1877–1924).
Calendar of the Proceedings of the Committee for the Advance of Money, 1642–56 (3 vols, 1888).
Calendar of the Proceedings of the Committee for Compounding, 1643–60 (5 vols, 1889–92).
Calendar of Treasury Books, 1660–1718 (64 vols, 1905–57).
Calendar of Treasury Papers, 1702–28 (4 vols, 1874–89).
Calendar of Treasury Books and Papers, 1729–45 (5 vols, 1897–1903).
CARTWRIGHT, J. J. (ed.), *The Wentworth Papers 1705–39* (1883).
CHOLMELY, Sir H., *The Memoirs of Sir Hugh Cholmely* (1787).
CLAY, J. W. (ed.), *Abstracts of Yorkshire Wills temp. Commonwealth*, *YASRS*, IX (1890).
—— *Yorkshire Royalist Composition Papers*, *YASRS*, XV, XVIII, XX (1893–96).
—— *Dugdale's Visitation of Yorkshire, with Additions* (3 vols, 1899–1917).
DEFOE, D., *A Tour Through the Whole Island of Gt. Britain* (2 vols, Everyman rev. ed. 1962).
DENNETT, J. (ed.), *Beverley Borough Records 1575–1821*, *YASRS*, LXXXIV (1932).

ELLIS, A. S. (ed.), 'Dodsworth's Yorkshire Notes: Wapentake of Agbrigg', *YATJ*, VIII (1884).

ESTCOURT, E. E. & PAYNE, J. O., *The English Catholic Nonjurors of 1715* (1885).

FIRTH, SIR C. & RAIT, R. S., *Acts and Ordinances of the Interregnum, 1642–60* (3 vols, 1911).

FOLEY, H. (ed.), *Records of the English Province of the Society of Jesus* (7 vols, 1877–83).

FORSTER, A. M. C. (ed.), *Selections from the Disbursements Book (1691–1709) of Sir Thomas Haggerston, Bart.*, Surtees Society CLXXX (1969).

FULLER, T., *History of the Worthies of England* (2 vols, ed. J. Nichols, 1811).

HAMILTON, Dom A. (ed.), *Chronicle of the English Augustinian Canonesses Regular of the Lateran, at St. Monica's in Louvain, 1548–1644* (2 vols, 1904).

HANSOM, J. S. (ed.), 'A List of Convicted Recusants in the Reign of King Charles II', *CRS*, VI (1909).

—— 'Catholic Registers of St. Mary's Domestic Chapel, Everingham Park, Yorkshire', *CRS*, VII (1909).

HERVEY, M. F. S. (ed.), *The Life, Correspondence and Collections of Thomas Howard, Earl of Arundel* (1921).

Historical Manuscripts Commission: *Reports* (various).

ILCHESTER, EARL of (ed.), *Lord Hervey and His Friends, 1726–38* (1950).

Journals of the House of Commons, 7i (1651–59).

MACRAY, W. D. (ed.), *Beaumont Papers* (1884).

McMAHON, K. A. (ed.), *Beverley Corporation Minute Books 1707–1835*, *YASRS*, CXXII (1956).

—— *Acts of Parliament and Proclamations Relating to the East Riding of Yorkshire and Kingston upon Hull, 1529–1800* (1961).

MARGERISON, S. (ed.), *Memorandum Book of Sir Walter Calverley, Bart.*, Surtees Society, LXXVII (1883).

MARSHALL, W., *A Review of the Reports to the Board of Agriculture from the Northern Department* (1808).

MORRIS, C. (ed.), *The Journeys of Celia Fiennes* (1947).

PARSONS, D. (ed.), *The Diary of Sir Henry Slingsby of Scriven, Bart.* (1836).

PENNYMAN, J. W. (ed.), *Records of the Family of Pennyman of Ormesby* (1904).

RAINE, J. (ed.), *Depositions from the Castle of York Relating to Offences Committed in the Northern Counties in the 17th Century*, Surtees Society, XL (1861).

ROEBUCK, P. (ed.), *Constable of Everingham Estate Correspondence 1726–43, YASRS,* CXXXVI (1974).

WAKE, J. & WEBSTER, D. C. (eds.), *The Letters of Daniel Eaton to the 3rd Earl of Cardigan, Northamptonshire Record Society,* XXIV (1971).

WALKER, J. W. (ed.), *Hackness Manuscripts and Accounts, YASRS,* XCV (1937).

WILSON, B. (ed.), *The Sedbergh School Register 1546–1909* (1909).

YOUNG, A., *A Six Months Tour Through the North of England* (4 vols, 1770).

II. SECONDARY SOURCES

A. *Yorkshire and Family Material*

AHIER, P., *The Legends and Traditions of Huddersfield and Its District* (2 vols, 1940–45).

ALLEN, T., *A New and Complete History of the County of York* (3 vols, 1828–31).

AMBLER, L., *The Old Halls and Manor Houses of Yorkshire* (1913).

ANONYMOUS, 'Sir Henry Frankland and the Frankland Family', *Herald and Genealogist,* VII (1873).

ARMYTAGE, W. H. G., 'Charles Watson Wentworth, 2nd Marquess of Rockingham, F.R.S. (1730–82): Some Aspects of his Scientific Interests', *Notes and Records of the Royal Society of London,* XII (1956).

AVELING, H., 'Catholics and Parliamentary Sequestrations', *Ampleforth Journal,* June 1959.

—— *Post-Reformation Catholicism in East Yorkshire 1558–1790, East Yorkshire Local History Society Pamphlets,* no. 11 (1960).

—— *The Catholic Rescusants of the West Riding of Yorkshire 1558–1790, Proceedings of the Leeds Philosophical and Literary Society,* X (1963).

BAILDON, W. P., *Baildon and the Baildons* (3 vols, 1912–27).

BERESFORD, M. W. & JONES, G. R. J. (eds.), *Leeds and Its Region* (1967).

BOOTHROYD, B., *History of Pontefract* (1807).

BROWNING, A., *Thomas Osborne, Earl of Danby and Duke of Leeds 1632–1712* (3 vols, 1951).

B——, W. D., 'Turner Family, of Kirkleatham, North Riding of Yorkshire', *The Topographer and Genealogist,* I (1846).

CARLISLE, N., *History of the Family of Bland* (1826).

CARROLL, R., 'Yorkshire Parliamentary Boroughs in the 17th Century', *Northern History,* III (1968).

CARTWRIGHT, J. J., *Chapters in the History of Yorkshire* (1872).

CHETWYND-STAPYLTON, H. E. C., *The Stapletons of Yorkshire* (1897).

CLAY, J. W., 'The Gentry of Yorkshire at the Time of the Civil War', *YAJ*, XXIII (1915).

CLIFFE, J. T., *The Yorkshire Gentry: From the Reformation to the Civil War* (1969).

COCKBURN, J. S., 'The North Riding Justices, 1690–1750: A Study in Local Administration', *YAJ*, XLI (1965).

COGHILL, J. H., *The Family of Coghill, 1377–1879* (1879).

—— *Slingsbys of Scriven Hall, 1135–1879* (1879).

COLLIER, C. V., *An Account of the Boynton Family* (1914).

COLMAN, F. S., *A History of the Parish of Barwick in Elmet, Thoresby Society*, XVII (1908).

COOPER, J. P., 'The Fortune of Thomas Wentworth, Earl of Strafford', *Econ. Hist. Rev.*, 2nd series, XI (1958–9).

COX, J. C., 'The Household Books of Sir Miles Stapleton Bart., 1656–1705', *The Ancestor*, II & III (1902).

DARBYSHIRE, H. S. & LUMB, G. D., *The History of Methley, Thoresby Society*, XXXV (1934).

DOBSON, R. B., 'Admissions to the Freedom of the City of York in the Later Middle Ages', *Econ. Hist. Rev.*, 2nd series, XXVI (1973).

DYSON, T., *History of Huddersfield and District* (1932).

FAIRFAX-BLAKEBOROUGH, J., *Sykes of Sledmere* (1929).

FLETCHER, J. S., *Yorkshiremen of the Restoration* (1921).

FORSTER, G. C. F., 'County Government in Yorkshire during the Interregnum', *Northern History*, XII (1977).

—— *The East Riding Justices of the Peace in the 17th Century, East Yorkshire Local History Society Pamphlets*, no. 30 (1973).

FOSTER, J., *Pedigrees of the County Families of Yorkshire* (4 vols, 1874–5).

FOXCROFT, H. C., *The Life and Letters of Sir George Savile, 1st Marquis of Halifax* (2 vols, 1898).

FRIEDMAN, T. F., 'Romanticism and Neo-Classicism for Parlington: The Tastes of Sir Thomas Gascoigne', *Leeds Arts Calendar*, LXVI (1970).

F——, Q. F. V., 'The Vernatti Family and Its Connections', *The Herald and Genealogist*, V (1870).

GLASSBY, W. J. J., 'The Hallamshire Family of Bright', *The Sheffield Miscellany* (1897).

GOODER, A., *The Parliamentary Representation of the County of York 1258–1832*, II, *YASRS*, XCVI (1937).

GOODRICKE, C. A., *History of the Goodricke Family* (1897).

—— *Ribston* (1902).

HAILSTONE, E. (ed.), *Portraits of Yorkshire Worthies* (2 vols, 1869).

HALL, I. & E., *Historic Beverley* (1973).

HALSBAND, R., *The Life of Lady Mary Wortley-Montague* (1956).

HARRIS, A., 'The Agriculture of the East Riding of Yorkshire before the Parliamentary Enclosures', *YAJ*, CLVII (1959).

—— *The Rural Landscape of the East Riding of Yorkshire 1700–1850* (1961).

—— *The Open Fields of East Yorkshire, East Yorkshire Local History Society Pamphlets*, no. 9 (1966).

HARVEY, J. C., 'Common Field and Enclosure in the Lower Dearne Valley: A Case Study', *YAJ*, XLVI (1974).

HARWOOD-LONG, W., 'Regional Farming in 17th Century Yorkshire', *Ag. Hist. Rev.*, VIII (1960).

HERRIES, LORD, 'The Constables of Flamborough', *Transactions of the East Riding Antiquarian Society*, VIII (1900).

HEY, D. G., 'A Dual Economy in South Yorkshire', *Ag. Hist. Rev.*, XVII (1969).

—— *The Rural Metalworkers of the Sheffield Region* (1972).

—— 'The Parks at Tankersley and Wortley', *YAJ*, XLVII (1975).

HOLIDAY, P. G., 'Royalist Composition Fines and Land Sales in Yorkshire, 1645–65', Ph.D. thesis, Leeds University, 1966.

—— 'Land Sales and Repurchases in Yorkshire after the Civil Wars, 1650–70', *Northern History*, V (1970).

HOLMES, D. H., *The Mining and Quarrying Industries in the Huddersfield District* (1967).

HOPKINSON, G. G., 'The Development of the Inland Navigation in South Yorkshire and North Derbyshire 1697–1850', *THAS*, VII (1956).

—— 'The Charcoal Iron Industry in the Sheffield Region, 1500–1775', *THAS*, VIII (1963).

—— 'The Development of the South Yorkshire and North Derbyshire Coalfield, 1500–1775' in J. Benson & R. G. Neville (eds.), *Studies in the Yorkshire Coal Industry* (1976).

HULBERT, C. A., *Annals of the Church and Parish of Almondbury, Yorkshire* (3 vols. 1882–85).

HUNTER, J., *South Yorkshire: The History and Topography of the Deanery of Doncaster* (2 vols, 1828–31).

—— *Hallamshire: The History and Topography of the Parish of Sheffield* (rev. A. Gatty, 1869).

INGRAM, M. E., *Leaves from a Family Tree* (1951).

JACKSON, G., *Hull in the 18th Century: A Study in Economic and Social History* (1972).

J——, C., 'The Jacksons of South Yorkshire', *The Herald and Genealogist*, V (1870).

LAWSON-TANCRED, Sir T., *The Tancreds of Brampton* (1921).

LEGARD, Sir J. D., *The Legards of Anlaby and Ganton* (1926),

LINTON, D. L. (ed.), *Sheffield and Its Region* (1956).

LOWTHER-BOUCII, C. M., 'Lowther of Swillington from Its Origin until 1788', *CWAA*, new series, XLII (1942).

—— 'Lowther of Marske (Cleveland) and Holker', *CWAA*, new series, XLIV (1944).

MARGERISON, S., 'A Yorkshire Royalist Squire', *The Bradford Antiquary*, I (1888).

—— 'The Furniture of a Squire's House', *The Bradford Antiquary*, I (1888).

MCCALL, H. B., *Story of the Family of Wandesforde of Kirklington and Castlecomer* (1904).

MCMAHON, K. A., 'The Building of the Beverley Market Cross', *Transactions of the East Riding Georgian Society*, III (1952-3).

—— 'The Beverley House of the Hotham Family', *Transactions of the East Riding Georgian Society*, IV (1955-6).

MILLER, N. J., *Winestead and Its Lord* (1932).

NEAVE, D., 'The Search for Coal in the East Riding in the 18th Century', *YAJ*, XLV (1973).

NEWTON, S. C., 'A Calendar of the Bright Papers', Dip. Arch. Admin. thesis, London University, 1959.

—— 'The Pipe Roll of a Cromwellian Sheriff of Yorkshire', *YAJ*, XLI (1963–66).

NUNN, P., 'Aristocratic Estates and Employment in South Yorkshire 1700–1800' in S. Pollard & C. Holmes (eds.), *Essays in the Economic and Social History of South Yorkshire* (1976).

NUTTALL, W. L. F., 'The Yorkshire Commissioners Appointed for the Trial of King Charles I', *YAJ*, XLIII (1971).

N——, C. B., 'Fairfaxiana', *The Herald and Genealogist*, VIII (1874).

OLIVER, G., *The History and Antiquities of the Town and Minster of Beverley* (1829).

PARK, G. R., *The Parliamentary Representation of Yorkshire 1290–1886* (1886).

PEVSNER, N., *The Buildings of England: Yorkshire, The North Riding* (1966).

—— *The Buildings of England: Yorkshire, The West Riding* (2nd ed. 1967).

—— *The Buildings of England: Yorkshire, York and the East Riding* (1972).

PLANTAGENET-HARRISON, G. H., *The History of Yorkshire: Wapentake of Gilling West* (1885).

POULSON, G., *Beverlac* (2 vols, 1829).

—— *The History and Antiquities of the Seigneury of Holderness* (2 vols, 1840).

RAISTRICK, A. & ALLEN, E., 'The South Yorkshire Ironmasters 1690–1750', *Econ. Hist. Rev.*, IX (1938–9).

RECKITT, B. N., *Charles I and Hull 1639–45* (1952).

ROBERTSHAW, W., 'The Manor of Tong', *The Bradford Antiquary*, new series, XXXVIII (1956).

ROEBUCK, P., 'The Constables of Everingham. The Fortunes of a Catholic Royalist Family during the Civil War and Interregnum', *Recusant History*, IX (1967).

—— 'An English Catholic on Tour in Europe, 1701–3', *Recusant History*, XI (1971).

—— 'Absentee Landownership in the Late 17th and Early 18th Centuries: A Neglected Factory in English Agrarian History', *Ag. Hist. Rev.*, XXI (1973).

—— 'The Country Squirearchy and the Fight for Place in the Early 18th Century: A Case Study', *YAJ*, XLVI (1974).

—— 'Post-Restoration Landownership: The Impact of the Abolition of Wardship', *Journal of British Studies*, XVIII, no. 1 (Fall, 1978).

SALTMARSHE, P., *History and Chartulary of the Hothams of Scorborough 1100–1700* (1914).

SHEAHAN, J. J., *History of the Town and Port of Kingston upon Hull* (2nd ed. 1866).

SPEIGHT, H., 'Hawksworth Hall and Its Associations', *The Bradford Antiquary*, new series, II (1901–5).

STIRLING, A. M. W., *Annals of a Yorkshire House* (2 vols, 1911).

—— *The Hothams* (2 vols, 1918).

STRAKER, J., *Memoirs of the Public Life of Sir Walter Blackett* (1819).

SUTHERLAND, F. H., *Marmaduke, Lord Langdale* (1926).

TAYLOR, R. V., *Biographia Leodiensis* (1865).

TICKELL, J., *History of the Town and County of Kingston upon Hull* (1798).

TOLSON, L., *History of the Church of St. John the Baptist, Kirkheaton, Yorkshire, and Annals of the Parish* (1929).

TRIGG, W. B., 'The Halifax Coalfield – Parts I & II', *Transactions of the Halifax Antiquarian Society*, 1930.

Victoria County History. *A History of Yorkshire* (3 vols, 1907–13).

—— *A History of Yorkshire: North Riding* (2 vols, 1914–23).

—— *A History of Yorkshire: The City of York* (1961).

—— *A History of Yorkshire: East Riding*, I, *City of Kingston upon Hull* (1969).

WALKER, J. W., 'Medicine in 17th Century Yorkshire', *YAJ*, XXXVI (1944–47).

WARD, J. T., 'The Earls Fitzwilliam and the Wentworth Woodhouse Estate in the 19th Century', *Yorkshire Bulletin of Economic and Social Research*, XII (1960).

—— 'A 19th Century Yorkshire Estate: Ribston and the Dent Family', *YAJ*, XLI (1963).

    East Yorkshire Landed Estates in the 19th Century, East Yorkshire Local History Society Pamphlets, no. 23 (1967).

WATSON, J., *The History and Antiquities of the Parish of Halifax* (1775).

WENTWORTH, G. E., 'History of the Wentworths of Woolley', *YAJ*, XII (1893).

WHITAKER, T. D., *A History of Richmondshire, in the North Riding of the County of York* (2 vols, 1823).

—— *The History and Antiquities of the Deanery of Craven* (3rd ed., ed. A. W. Morant, 1878).

WILKINSON, J., *Worthies, Families and Celebrities of Barnsley and District* (1883).

WILKINSON, O., *The Agricultural Revolution in the East Riding of Yorkshire, East Yorkshire Local History Society Pamphlets*, no. 5 (1965).

WILLAN, T. S., 'Yorkshire River Navigation 1600–1750', *Geography*, XVII (1937).

—— *The Early History of the Don Navigation* (1965).

WILSON, R. G., *Gentlemen Merchants: The Merchant Community in Leeds, 1700–1830* (1971).

WILTON, R. C., 'Letters of a Jesuit Father in the Reign of George I', *Dublin Review*, CLVIII (1916).

—— 'A Tale of Old Stonyhurst', *Stonyhurst Magazine*, October 1916.

—— 'Some Annals of Everingham', *Downside Review*, July 1916; *Dublin Review*, CLXI (1917).

—— 'Early 18th Century Catholics in England', *Catholic Historical Review*, X (1924).

—— 'A List of Guests at Everingham Park, Christmas 1662', *CRS*, XXVII (1927).

WOOD, G. B., *Historic Homes of Yorkshire* (1957).

WRAGG, R. B., 'Everingham Park: Carr's Work Authenticated', *Transactions of the East Riding Georgian Society*, IV (1955–6).

York Georgian Society. *The Works in Architecture of John Carr* (1973).

B. General

ANDERSON, B. L., 'The Attorney and the Early Capital Market in Lancashire' in J. R. Harris (ed.), *Liverpool and Merseyside* (1969).

—— 'Provincial Aspects of the Financial Revolution of the 18th Century', *Business History*, XI (1969).

ARNOLD, R., *Northern Lights: The Story of Lord Derwentwater* (1959).

ASHLEY, M., *Cromwell's Generals* (1954).

BARNARD, E. A. B., *A 17th-Century Country Gentleman* (1944).

BATEMAN, J., *The Great Landowners of Gt. Britain and Ireland* (ed. D. Spring, 1971).

BAXTER, S. B., *The Development of the Treasury 1660–1702* (1957).

BEAN, W. W., *The Parliamentary Representation of the Six Northern Counties of England 1603–1886* (1890).

BEASTALL, T. W., *A North Country Estate: The Lumleys and Saundersons as Landowners, 1600–1900* (1975).

BECKETT, J. V., 'Local Custom and the "New Taxation" in the 17th and 18th Centuries: the Example of Cumberland', *Northern History*, XII (1976).

—— 'English Landownership in the Later 17th and 18th Centuries: The Debate and the Problems', *Econ. Hist. Rev.*, 2nd series, XXX (1977).

BEEVOR, R. J., 'Distinction and Extinction', *The Genealogists' Magazine*, IV (1928).

BELL, H. E., *An Introduction to the History and Records of the Court of Wards and Liveries* (1953).

BELOFF, M., 'Humphrey Shalcrosse and the Great Civil War', *English Historical Review*, LIV (1939).

BOSSY, J., *The English Catholic Community 1570–1850* (1975).

BRENNER, R., 'Agrarian Class Structure and Economic Development in Pre-Industrial Europe', *Past and Present*, no. 70 (1976).

BURKE, J. & J. B., *The Extinct and Dormant Baronetcies of England* (2nd ed. 1844).

CARR, A. D., 'Deeds of Title', *History*, L (1965).

CARSWELL, J. P., *The South Sea Bubble* (1960).

CHALKIN, C. W., *The Provincial Towns of Georgian England* (1974).

CHALMERS, P. R., *History of Hunting, The Lonsdale Library*, XXIII (1936).

CHAMBERS, J. D. & MINGAY, G. E., *The Agricultural Revolution 1750–1880* (1966).

CHESNEY, H. E., 'The Transference of Lands in England 1640–60', *TRHS*, 4th series, XV (1932).

CLARKSON, L. A., *The Pre-Industrial Economy in England 1500–1750* (1971).

CLAY, C., 'Marriage, Inheritance, and the Rise of Large Estates in England, 1660–1815', *Econ. Hist. Rev.*, 2nd series, XXI (1968).

—— 'The Misfortunes of William, Fourth Lord Petre (1638–55)', *Recusant History*, XI (1971).

—— 'The Price of Freehold Land in the Later 17th and 18th Centuries', *Econ. Hist. Rev.*, 2nd series, XXVII (1974).

COCKAYNE, G. E., *The Complete Baronetage 1611–1800* (6 vols, 1900–9).

COLEMAN, D. C., 'London Scrivenors and the Estate Market in the Later 17th Century', *Econ. Hist. Rev.*, 2nd series, IV (1951).

COLVIN, II. M., *A Biographical Dictionary of English Architects, 1660–1840* (1954).

COOPER, J. P., 'The Counting of Manors', *Econ. Hist. Rev.*, 2nd series, VIII (1955–6).

—— 'Patterns of Inheritance and Settlement by Great Landowners from the 15th to the 18th Centuries' in J. Goody, J. Thirsk & E. P. Thompson (eds.), *Family and Inheritance: Rural Society in Western Europe 1200–1800* (1976).

DALTON, C., *George I's Army 1714–27* (2 vols, 1910–12).

DARBY, H. C. (ed.), *A New Historical Geography of England* (1973).

DAVIES, M. G., 'Country Gentry and Payments to London, 1650–1714', *Econ. Hist. Rev.*, 2nd series, XXIV (1971).

—— 'Country Gentry and Falling Rents in the 1660s and 1670s', *Midland History*, IV (1977).

DAVIES, O. R. F., 'The Wealth and Influence of John Holles, Duke of Newcastle, 1694–1711', *Renaissance and Modern Studies*, IX (1965).

DAVIS, R., 'The Rise of Protection in England 1689–1786', *Econ. Hist. Rev.*, 2nd series, XIX (1966).

Dictionary of National Biography

DOWELL, S., *History of Taxation and Taxes in England from the Earliest Times to the Year 1885* (4 vols, 1888).

EMERSON, W. R., 'The Economic Development of the Estates of the Petre Family in Essex in the 16th and 17th Centuries', D.Phil. thesis, Oxford University, 1951.

ERNLE, LORD, *English Farming Past and Present* (6th ed., eds. G. E. Fussell & O. R. MacGregor, 1961).

EVERITT, A., *Change in the Provinces: The 17th Century* (1969).

FINCH, M. E., *The Wealth of Five Northamptonshire Families 1540–1640, Northamptonshire Record Society*, XIX (1954–5).

FIRTH, SIR C. & DAVIES, G., *The Regimental History of Cromwell's Army* (2 vols, 1940).

FUSSELL, G. E., 'Agriculture from the Restoration to Anne', *Econ. Hist. Rev.*, IX (1938–9).

GAY, E. F., 'Sir Richard Temple: The Debt Settlement and Estate Litigation, 1653–75', *Huntingdon Library Quarterly*, VI (1943).

GIBBS, V., DOUBLEDAY, H. A. *et. al.*, *The Complete Peerage* (14 vols, 1910–59).

GILLOW, J. A., *A Biographical Dictionary of English Catholics* (5 vols, 1895–1902).

GOODER, A., 'Two Letters Relating to the Manor and Rectory of

Birmingham, 1704–13', *University of Birmingham Historical Journal*, V (1957).

HABAKKUK, H. J., 'English Landownership 1680–1740', *Econ. Hist. Rev.*, X (1939–40).

—— 'Marriage Settlements in the 18th Century', *TRHS*, 4th series, XXXII (1950).

—— 'The Long-Term Rate of Interest and the Price of Land in the 17th Century', *Econ. Hist. Rev.*, 2nd series, V (1952–3).

—— 'The Economic Functions of English Landowners in the 17th and 18th Centuries', *Explorations in Entrepreneurial History*, VI (1953).

—— 'England' in A. Goodwin (ed.), *The European Nobility in the 18th Century* (1953).

—— 'Daniel Finch, 2nd Earl of Nottingham: His House and Estate' in J. H. Plumb (ed.), *Studies in Social History* (1955).

—— 'The English Land Market in the 18th Century' in J. S. Bromley & E. H. Kossmann (eds.), *Britain and the Netherlands* (1960).

—— 'Public Finance and the Sale of Confiscated Property during the Interregnum', *Econ. Hist. Rev.*, 2nd series, XV (1962–3).

—— '*La Disparition du Paysan Anglais*', *Annales*, XX (1965).

—— 'Landowners and the Civil War', *Econ. Hist. Rev.*, 2nd series, XVIII (1965).

—— 'The Parliamentary Army and the Crown Lands', *Welsh Historical Review*, III (1967).

HARDACRE, P. H., *The Royalists during the Puritan Revolution* (1956).

HARTE, N. B. (ed.), *The Study of Economic History* (1971).

HAWKINS, M. J. (ed.), *Sales of Wards in Somerset 1603–41*, Somerset Record Society, LXVII (1965).

—— 'Royal Wardship in the 17th Century', *The Genealogists' Magazine*, XVI (1969).

HILL, C., *Puritanism and Revolution* (1962).

—— *The Century of Revolution 1603–1714* (1964).

—— *Reformation to Industrial Revolution* (1967).

HOLDERNESS, B. A., 'The English Land Market in the 18th Century: The Case of Lincolnshire', *Econ. Hist. Rev.*, 2nd series, XXVII (1974).

—— 'Credit in English Rural Society before the 19th Century, with special reference to the period 1650–1720', *Ag. Hist. Rev.*, XXIV (1976).

HOLDSWORTH, Sir W., *A History of English Law* (16 vols, eds. A. L. Goodhart & H. G. Hanbury, 1933–66).

HOLLINGSWORTH, T. H., 'The Demography of the British Peerage', Supplement to *Population Studies*, XVIII (1964).

HOLMES, G., *British Politics in the Age of Anne* (1967).

HOON, E. E., *The Organisation of the English Customs System 1696–1786* (1938).

HORN, D. B., *The British Diplomatic Service 1689–1789* (1961).

HOSKINS, W. G., 'The Estates of the Caroline Gentry' in Hoskins & H. P. R. Finberg (eds.), *Devonshire Studies* (1952).

—— *Local History in England* (1959).

—— *Provincial England* (1963).

HOWELL, D. W., 'The Economy of the Landed Estates of Pembrokeshire 1680–1830', *Welsh Historical Review*, III (1967).

HUGHES, E., *Studies in Administration and Finance, 1558–1825* (1934).

—— 'The 18th-Century Estate Agent' in H. A. Cronne, T. W. Moody & D. B. Quinn (eds.), *Essays in British and Irish History* (1949).

—— *North Country Life in the 18th Century*, I, *The North-East, 1700–50* (1952).

—— *North Country Life in the 18th Century*, II, *Cumberland and Westmoreland, 1700–1830* (1965).

JESSUP, F. W., *Sir Roger Twysden 1597–1672* (1965).

JOHN, A. H., 'The Course of Agricultural Change 1660–1760' in L. S. Pressnell (ed.), *Studies in the Industrial Revolution* (1960).

JONES, E. L. (ed.), *Agriculture and Economic Growth in England, 1650–1815* (1967).

—— 'English and European Agricultural Development 1650–1750' in R. M. Hartwell (ed.), *The Industrial Revolution* (1970).

—— *Agriculture and the Industrial Revolution* (1974).

JONES, J. R., *The First Whigs: The Politics of the Exclusion Crisis 1678–83* (1961).

JOSLIN, D. M., 'London Private Bankers 1720–85', *Econ. Hist. Rev.*, 2nd series, VII (1954–5).

KELCH, R. A., *Newcastle. A Duke Without Money: Thomas Pelham-Holles, 1693–1768* (1974).

KENYON, J. P., *The Popish Plot* (1972).

KERRIDGE, E., *The Agricultural Revolution* (1967).

—— *Agrarian Problems in the 16th Century and After* (1969).

—— *The Farmers of Old England* (1973).

KIRK, J., POLLEN, J. H. & BURTON, E. H. (eds.), *Biographies of English Catholics in the 18th Century* (1909).

KLOTZ, E. L. & DAVIES, G., 'The Wealth of Royalist Peers and Baronets during the Puritan Revolution', *English Historical Review*, LVIII (1943).

LASLETT, P., 'The Gentry of Kent in 1640', *Historical Journal*, IX (1948).

LENNARD, R., 'English Agriculture under Charles II: The Evidence of the Royal Society's "Enquiries"', *Econ. Hist. Rev.*, IV (1932).

LLOYD, H. A., *The Gentry of South-West Wales 1540–1640* (1968).

MAGEE, B., *The English Recusants* (1938).

MEREDITH, R., 'A Derbyshire Family in the 17th Century: The Eyres of Hassop and their Forfeited Estates', *Recusant History*, VIII (1965).

MIMARDIÈRE, A. M., 'The Warwickshire Gentry 1660–1730', M.A. thesis, Birmingham University, 1963.

—— 'The Finances of a Warwickshire Gentry Family 1693–1726', *University of Birmingham Historical Journal*, IX (1964).

MINGAY, G. E., 'The Agricultural Depression 1730–50', *Econ. Hist. Rev.*, 2nd series, VIII (1955–6).

—— 'Estate Management in 18th-Century Kent', *Ag. Hist. Rev.*, IV (1956).

—— 'Thrumpton, A Nottinghamshire Estate in the 18th Century', *Transactions of the Thoroton Society*, LXI (1957).

—— 'The Large Estate in 18th-Century England' in *Contributions to the 1st International Conference of Economic History*, Stockholm, 1960.

—— 'The Size of Farms in the 18th Century', *Econ. Hist. Rev.*, 2nd series, XIV (1961–2).

—— 'The Agricultural Revolution in English History: A Reconsideration', *Agricultural History*, XXXVII (1963).

—— *English Landed Society in the 18th Century* (1963).

—— 'The Land Tax Assessments and the Small Landowner', *Econ. Hist. Rev.*, 2nd series, XVII (1964–5).

—— 'The 18th-Century Land Steward' in E. L. Jones & Mingay (eds.), *Land, Labour and Population in the Industrial Revolution* (1967).

—— *Enclosure and the Small Farmer in the Age of the Industrial Revolution* (1968).

—— *The Gentry: The Rise and Fall of a Ruling Class* (1976).

—— (ed.) *The Agricultural Revolution: Changes in Agriculture 1650–1880* (1977).

MORGAN, E. V. & THOMAS, W. A., *The Stock Exchange: Its History and Functions* (1962).

NAMIER, Sir L. & BROOKE, J., *The House of Commons 1754–90* (3 vols, 1964).

PARKER, R. A. C., 'Direct Taxation on the Coke Estates in the 18th Century', *English Historical Review*, LXXI (1956).

—— *Coke of Norfolk: A Financial and Agricultural Study, 1707–1842* (1975).

PARRY, R. H. (ed.), *The English Civil War and After 1642–58* (1970).

PERKIN, H., *The Origins of Modern English Society 1780–1880* (1969).

PIXLEY, F. W., *A History of the Baronetage* (1900).

PLUMB, J. H., *Men and Places* (1966).
—— *The Growth of Political Stability in England 1675–1725* (1967).
—— *The Commercialization of Leisure in 18th-Century England* (1973).
RAYBOULD, T. J., *The Economic Emergence of the Black Country: A Study of the Dudley Estate* (1972).
Royal Commission on Historic Monuments. *Newark on Trent: The Civil War Siegeworks* (1964).
RICHARDS, E., *The Leviathan of Wealth* (1973).
RICHARDS, R. D., 'The Lottery in the History of English Government Finance', *Economic History*, III (1934).
ROBSON, R., *The Attorney in 18th-Century England* (1959).
ROWLANDS, M. B., 'Staffordshire Papists and the Levy of 1723', *Staffordshire Catholic History*, II (1962).
—— 'The Iron Age of Double Taxes', *Staffordshire Catholic History*, III (1963).
SCOTT-THOMSON, G., *The Russells in Bloomsbury 1669–1771* (1940).
—— *Letters of a Grandmother 1732–35* (1943).
—— *Life in a Noble Household 1641–1700* (paperback ed. 1965).
SEDGWICK, R., *The House of Commons 1715–54* (2 vols, 1970).
SIMMONS, J., 'The English County Historians', *THAS*, VIII (1963).
SIMPSON, A., *The Wealth of the Gentry 1540–1660* (1961).
SLICHER VAN BATH, B. H., *The Agrarian History of Western Europe A.D. 500–1850* (1963).
SPRING, D., *The Large Estate in 19th-Century England: Its Administration* (1963).
—— 'English Landed Society in the 18th and 19th Centuries', *Econ. Hist. Rev.*, 2nd series, XVII (1964–5).
STONE, L., 'Marriage among the English Nobility in the 16th and 17th Centuries', *Comparative Studies in Society and History*, III (1961).
—— *The Crisis of the Aristocracy 1558–1641* (1965).
—— 'Social Mobility in England, 1500–1700', *Past and Present*, no. 33 (1966).
—— 'Literacy and Education in England, 1640–1900', *Past and Present*, no. 42 (1969).
—— *The Causes of the English Revolution 1529–1642* (1972).
—— *Family and Fortune* (1973).
—— *The Family, Sex and Marriage in England 1500–1800* (1977).
STROUD, D., *Capability Brown* (rev. ed. 1975).
STYLES, P., 'The Social Structure of Kineton Hundred in the Reign of Charles II', *Transactions of the Birmingham Archaeological Society*, LXXVIII (1960).
SUTHERLAND, D., *The Landowners* (1968).

TATHAM, G. B., 'Sales of Episcopal Lands during the Civil Wars and Commonwealth', *English Historical Review*, XXIII (1908).

THIRSK, J., 'The Sales of Royalist Land during the Interregnum', *Econ. Hist. Rev.*, 2nd series, V (1952–3).

—— 'The Restoration Land Settlement', *Journal of Modern History*, XXVI (1954).

—— (ed.) *The Agrarian History of England and Wales*, IV, *1500–1640* (1967).

—— 'Younger Sons in the 17th Century', *History*, LIV (1969).

—— 'The European Debate on Customs of Inheritance 1500–1700' in J. Goody, J. Thirsk & E. P. Thompson (eds.), *Family and Inheritance: Rural Society in Western Europe 1200–1800* (1976).

—— *The Restoration* (1976).

THOMPSON, F. M. L., *English Landed Society in the 19th Century* (1963).

—— 'Land and Politics in England in the 19th Century', *TRHS*, 5th series, XV (1965).

—— 'The Social Distribution of Landed Property in England since the 16th Century', *Econ. Hist. Rev.*, 2nd series, XIX (1966).

—— 'Landownership and Economic Growth in England in the 18th Century', in E. L. Jones & S. J. Woolf (eds.), *Agrarian Change and Economic Development* (1969).

THOMSON, T. R., *A Catalogue of British Family Histories* (2nd ed. 1935).

THOROLD-ROGERS, J. E., *A History of Agriculture and Prices in England* (7 vols, 1866–1902).

TONGUE, C., 'A Troublesome Guardianship in the 18th Century', *Northamptonshire Past and Present*, IV (1966).

TROW-SMITH, R., *A History of British Livestock Husbandry* (2 vols, 1957–59).

WAGNER, Sir A., *English Genealogy* (2nd ed. 1972).

WAKE, J., *The Brudenells of Deene* (2nd ed. 1954).

WILLAN, T. S., *River Navigation in England 1600–1750* (1936).

WILLIAMS, B., *The Whig Supremacy, 1714–60* (rev. C. H. Stuart, 1962).

WILLIAMS, J. A., *Catholic Recusancy in Wiltshire, 1660–1791*, *CRS*, Monograph Series, I (1968).

WILSON, C., *England's Apprenticeship 1603–1763* (1967).

INDEX